Library of Congress Catalog Card Number 91-060227
ISBN 0-9621367-4-3

 100% Recycled

A Short History

BIG GAME
IN NORTH DAKOTA

By Joseph Knue

Published by the North Dakota Game and Fish Department
George A. Sinner, Governor
Lloyd A. Jones, Director
Bismarck, North Dakota

FOREWORD

Large mammalian herbivores evolved with the grasslands of what is now North Dakota. This book, **Big Game in North Dakota: A Short History**, offers a compendium of those big game species present when this land was first explored and subsequently settled; their struggle to adapt to constraints imposed on them by preemption of their habitats; their responses to efforts of a public fired by a conservation consciousness and a growing knowledge of their intrinsic requirements; and their actual or potential role in the future.

The early explorers found a land teeming with wildlife. Large ungulates included moose and white-tailed deer along the major rivers and streams and in the native forests of the north and east; elk state-wide, from the Red River in the east through the Badlands in the west; American pronghorn in all areas except native woodlands and the tall grass biome in the Red River Valley; mule deer in the rougher "breaks" mostly south and west of the Missouri River; bighorns in the rugged, more inaccessible portions of the Badlands; and bison—literally uncountable numbers—in all portions of what is now North Dakota.

Then pioneers and settlers appeared on the scene. The promise of free land and a new life started a trickle of immigrants which swelled to a flood, washing over section after section of native grassland. Suddenly, large grazing animals that had evolved here over thousands of years were swept toward extinction. Considered at best a nuisance, but most often a threat to the homesteaders, these animals were exploited for food, for their hides, and finally even for their bones to be used as fertilizer. Bison, moose, elk, and bighorn sheep were extirpated from the North Dakota landscape. White-tailed deer, mule deer, and American pronghorns retreated to refugia of their former ranges where they faced an unknown future.

The pendulum started to swing in favor of the big game herbivores when the harsh realities of the arid grassland environment exerted uncompromising pressures on these numerous but generally small landholders. Native vegetation reoccupied many tracts of land as they were abandoned. Slowly at first but with increasing momentum mule deer, white-tailed deer, and pronghorns repopulated portions of their former range and began to adapt to the changing scene. Simultaneously a new conservation consciousness took form and was heard: "There was room, yes, and a need to have this remaining native fauna and even more—perhaps even those ghosts of the past that the plow and the cow had so recently replaced."

Now, 100 years after statehood, North Dakota can proudly accept her due praise for the restoration and enhancement of all of the large mammalian herbivore species that were present when that first explorer made his appearance. That this has become a reality is a tremendous tribute to a multitude of unnamed North Dakotans whose foresight, encouragement, and insistence "fired the boilers" to get things started and those unnamed professionals whose expertise, enthusiasm, and dedication "piloted" this effort to the present time. Now it is you who will take the tiller and steer this ark through the uncharted waters of the future—Bon Voyage!

James V. McKenzie, Big Game Supervisor
North Dakota Game and Fish Department

CONTENTS

Maps and Charts

APPENDICES

1. Summary of Deer Rifle Seasons and Regulations, 1881-1989
2. Table One—Profile of Deer Rifle Seasons, 1931-1989
   Table Two—Profile of Deer Archery Seasons, 1984-1989
3. Summary of Changes in Pronghorn Seasons and Regulations, 1881-1989
4. Table One—Profile of Pronghorn Rifle Seasons, 1951-1989
   Table Two—Profile of Pronghorn Archery Seasons, 1985-1989
5. Mutual Agreement Between Theodore Roosevelt National Memorial Park and North Dakota Game and Fish Department
6. Bighorn Sheep Translocation Record in North Dakota
7. Profiles of North Dakota's Big Game Special Seasons
8. Boone and Crockett Official Scoring Systems
9. Comparison of Hunter Expenditures, 1986 Big Game Seasons
10. Locations and Descriptions of Wildlife Management Areas

ACKNOWLEDGEMENTS

I would like to acknowledge the contributions to this book by the following people: Jack Samuelson, Roger Johnson, H. Ted Upgren, Jr., Arlen Harmoning, and James McKenzie. Each of them has helped by supplying materials, review of the manuscript, and encouragement throughout the process. Much of the credit for the book must go to them; its faults and errors are my own.

Joseph Knue

INTRODUCTION

There are, it seems to me, two "forces"—if they might be called that—which have come together to make, to shape the history of big game animals in this region we now call North Dakota. The first of these is the force of environmental change. Changes in climate, in soils, in vegetation brought about by "events" like the ice age had a great deal to do with the different big game animals which have lived here. So have the changes to the environment brought about by human beings. The second great force in the history of big game in North Dakota is the animals' own biology. Changes to the environment affect big game animals according to the limits of their biology. Animals which have been biologically able to take advantage of changes to the environment have thrived; others, less fit for new circumstances, have disappeared. All of the history of big game here can be seen in these terms. Environmental changes have come together with biology to produce opportunities for some animals and limits for others.

This book divides the history of big game into two periods. The first part covers the immense period of time during which the forces of change and biology worked "blindly" to shape the history of big game animals, offering opportunities and imposing limits at random. These were huge climatic events like the ice age, and small, relatively sudden changes like plowing the prairies. The second part of this book covers the very short period of time—from 1940 to the present—during which human beings have tried to understand the limits and opportunities placed on big game by biology and use the knowledge to restore to North Dakota what had been so blindly lost.

We can phrase this another way. Part One of this book describes the conditions which allowed huge numbers of big game animals to thrive here, and why, when people, like some force of nature, exploited big game and changed the face of the landscape, big game nearly disappeared. Part Two is the history of game management in North Dakota, from its first, tentative steps in the 1940s, to the complex balance today between economic development and healthy wildlife populations. Inevitably, both Part One and Part Two must deal with the ways that people have thought about and valued big game.

A word or two about sources. In addition to biologists, Part One owes much to paleontologists and archaeologists. Paleontologists dig into the earth to reveal and interpret the fossil record. From them we learn of the shifts in climate and vegetation on which the great creatures of the past rose and fell. With their help we can, perhaps, trace the lineages of the great creatures of today. Likewise archaeologists, studying the discarded debris of human habitation, uncover the significance of big game to early people.

Part One comes also from the people who were there and who wrote down what they did and what they saw. In the early days of what we now call North Dakota, these were explorers like Lewis and Clark, traders like Alexander Henry, and naturalists like John J. Audubon. Much of what we know about big game populations, habits, habitats, and movements comes from these men. Other people—explorers, traders, hunters, and finally settlers—help to track the shifts in how people—native and non-native—have valued big game.

I have used journals extensively to round out a picture of North Dakota as it was in the days before settlement. Some—like Alexander Henry's—have had the benefit of extensive editing by literate hands. Others, especially the journals of Lewis and Clark, have come down to us as they were written, complete with colorful grammar and picturesque spelling. William Clark especially was not an educated man. But the journals are never so bad that we can't make our way through them.

Part Two comes mostly from records kept by the North Dakota Game and Fish Department. These are the Department's annual reports, articles and stories from fifty years of **North Dakota Outdoors**, and hundreds of Pittman-Robertson project reports. These trace not only the growing body of knowledge, over the last fifty years, of what North Dakota's big game populations need to keep growing and thriving, but also changes in the scope of game management as North Dakota itself has changed.

Part One was, in many ways, easier to write than Part Two. The natural history of North Dakota, and the early history of big game and people are fairly well understood. Part Two is much less straightforward. The progress of game management is not a straight line from understanding an animal's biology and habitat needs to a management plan. The path has instead many curves and detours, around the larger needs of people and over the hills and valleys of public opinion. The reasons for game management decisions are not always easy to see. But throughout I have tried to present not only what happened but some sense of why.

It is inevitable that some things have been left out. To include everything that has happened would have been impossible. Worse, if I had been able to include everything, we would have lost the forest in the trees. I have tried to discuss the most important events in the history of big game in North Dakota, and I have tried to show how one event grew out of others. If important events and significant work has been left out, I apologize. I had the highest intentions.

One of the troubles with writing history is that you can never get to the ends of it—either the start or the finish. You can only try to be faithful to the time in between. This work is dedicated to all of us who are in between—past, present, and those who will carry the history of big game into the future.

PART ONE

ND Game and Fish Department

CHAPTER ONE

LIFE ON THE GRASSLANDS

PREHISTORY

It is hard to decide where a history of big game in North Dakota should begin. Maybe it starts ninety–odd million years ago when the first recognizable grasses evolved. It is hard to think about North Dakota without thinking about grass.

But other events are just as important. For forty million years, mammals have dominated the earth. Does the story of big game begin with that? Or does it begin with the great geologic and climatic events which lifted mountains or sent colossal sheets of ice to grind the contours of North Dakota and to alter the course of its rivers?

The answer is, of course, that all of these events were necessary. The fact is that North Dakota was not always a grassland populated by buffalo and antelope. Buried under North Dakota's rolling surface, in successive layers of rock and history, there have been several North Dakotas. Explorers found evidence of these early periods where the movement of rivers had cut through the sediment of passing centuries:

> April 9, 1805—The Bluffs of the river which we passed today [contained] many horizontal stratas of carbonated wood, having every appearance of pit coal...the hills of the river are very broken, and many of them have the appearance of having been on fire at some former period... —*Meriwether Lewis*

> October 24, 1833—Several beaver hunters arrived today, among whom was the Cree Indian *Piah-Sukah-Ketutt*...He...affirmed that he had...found the entire skeleton of a colossal serpent. A part of a tooth which he brought proved that these bones belonged to a fossil mastodon... —*Maximilian, Prince of Wied*

The prairies and Great Plains of North America, of which North Dakota is a part, did not become grasslands until climatic and geologic changes which began some twenty to twenty-five million years ago began to favor grass over trees. Before that time, the climate of this part of the continent of North America was warm and moist, much like the climate that Florida enjoys today. Semi-tropical trees and vegetation covered the land, the remains of which Lewis and Clark noted as layers of lignite coal revealed in the bluffs of the Missouri River. Alligator-like reptiles lived as far north as the Dakotas. The great mammals of these early epochs were the mastodons whose teeth were examined by Maximilian in 1833, an

4

immense rhinoceros, and the sabre-toothed tiger.

Then, perhaps twenty million years ago, the climate began to cool. Geologic forces under the earth's crust pushed the Rocky Mountains higher, and moisture-bearing clouds dropped their rain on the western slopes. The drier, cooler climate east of the mountains began to favor grasses over sub-tropical trees and ferns. It is not a coincidence that during this same time period animals which had physical characteristics to match the growing abundance of grassland began also to increase in numbers. An example was the *Merychippus*, a predecessor of today's horses, the first of the horse family to have high-crowned teeth, adapted to chewing tough grasses instead of browsing on leaves.

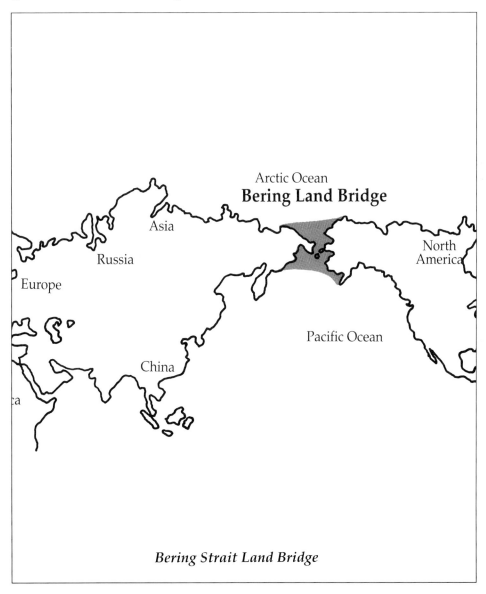

Bering Strait Land Bridge

5

About a million years ago another geologic event began its process of reshaping large parts of the northern hemisphere. The climate became increasingly cold, and large sheets of ice began to flow from the polar regions, carving new faces on continents as they went. The ice age did more than create lakes and dam the course of rivers on the North American continent. More than once the flowing glaciers locked up so much water that they lowered the level of the sea; and in a tiny corner of a frozen wasteland between what is now Alaska and Siberia, a bridge of land was exposed. Animals which evolved in the Old World of Europe and Asia—bison, for example, and bighorn sheep—crossed over into the New World of North America. Along with these grassland creatures came man.

During the ice age, the glaciers which flowed over the land were thousands of feet thick; and the last of the glaciers receded from what is now North Dakota only twelve thousand years ago. If a man lived a century, and such lives were stretched end-to-end, it would take ten thousand lifetimes to reach from the present into the origins of the ice age. But the image of a North American continent locked in ice for a million years is misleading. The ice age was not, in fact, one continuous frozen stretch of time. A period of intense cold and advancing continental ice sheets—lasting perhaps as long as the recorded history of man—would be followed by an equally long period in which the ice sheets would ebb. Century followed century in these interludes, and plants and animals formed entire new communities of existence on the reshaped continents. Then the advancing glaciers would again change the conditions of existence, and whole communities would disappear, found now only in the fossil record.

There were two recent periods of time during which the land bridge now covered by the waters of the Bering Strait was open. The first period was forty or fifty thousand years ago, and the second was between ten and thirty thousand years ago. Not only did animals (man included) cross from the Old World to the New, but species which evolved in the New World crossed over into the Old. Some of them, like camels and horses, became extinct here, but continued to flourish in Asia. During the long periods when vast areas of the North American continent were ice-free, these new species of animals migrated over much of the New World. When advancing ice isolated them, they were left to pursue their own evolutionary path, distinct from their ancestral stock.

The ice age was not an immense stretch of time when only the hardiest of species survived. Instead we should look at it as a time of enormous evolutionary upheaval. As one biologist put it, "It was an epoch characterized by severe climates, by the development of tundra ecosystems, by the mixing of faunas when land bridges rose and glacial refugia coalesced, by numerous extinctions, but especially by an unusual evolutionary turmoil among large mammals. It produced in a short time and in great diversity new types of creatures, usually giants of their

Bison skull found in twenty-five feet of water at Spiritwood Lake on August 14, 1960.

respective families…" (Geist, 1971, p. xi).

Bison came from these times. During the early period when the land bridge to Alaska was open, an early bison known as the steppe wisent crossed over into North America. At least five distinct bison—four in North America and another in Europe—can be traced back to the steppe wisent.

The steppe wisent migrated south and east into the center of the North American continent. Isolated there by returning ice, it evolved into a creature whose horns could measure nine feet across. This bison—*Bison latifrons*—and a smaller-horned descendant—*Bison antiquus*—were both extinct by the late stages of the ice age.

In the intervening thousands of years, another bison had been evolving on the other side of the Alaskan-Siberian land bridge. This creature—*Bison occidentalis*—crossed the land bridge and migrated into the Great Plains of North America sometime after his predecessors had become extinct. It is from this bison—*occidentalis*—that both the American bison and the European wisent can be traced.

So it was that the ice age encouraged the spread and diversity of species in the Northern Hemisphere. Sometime toward the middle of the ice age—

perhaps 400,000 years ago—one of the more successful creatures of the age made his appearance. This creature was *Homo sapiens*—man. Modern *Homo sapiens*—people who look the way we do today—have been around for 35,000 or more years. We have been able to adapt to or overcome the difficulties presented by shifts in climate, vegetation, and wildlife, and have remained relatively unchanged as a species.

Man crossed over the land bridge between Alaska and Siberia and spread out over the continent, following and hunting other Old World animals—bison, moose, deer, caribou, mountain sheep, and large cats. Evidence suggests that man might have been in North America for as long as 27,000 years. An archeological site called Old Crow Flats in the Yukon has been dated that old (Cassels, 1983, p. 13). Most archeologists, however, place man in North America around 12,000 years ago. For most of that time he has been essentially nomadic, essentially a hunter.

Since the passing of the ice age, the forces acting on the surface of the continent have been the patient ones of wind and water; the sudden eruptions of volcanos; and violent but relatively small-scale movements as the earth's crust slides along fault lines. The surface of North America looks much the same now as it has since the retreat of the glaciers thousands of years ago. It was during the ice age that the mountain ranges of the world reached their present height; and the glaciers themselves carved the contours of great land masses and changed the courses of such rivers as the Missouri. The ice age assisted the rearrangement of the wildlife and peoples of the world.

GRASSLANDS

In what is known, geologically, as the "Recent" period—the time after the ice age until the present—the prairies and Great Plains of North America have been grasslands. Grasslands are a kind of middle ground—a transition zone—between forests on the one hand and deserts on the other. What makes a grassland a grassland instead of a forest or a desert is the amount of rain or snow that falls.

To be accurate about it, it is the amount of moisture that the land receives divided by the amount of moisture that evaporates from it. When the land receives more moisture than evaporates from it, trees do well. When more moisture evaporates from the soil than falls on it, deserts are created. Grasslands exist when rainfall and evaporation are roughly the same. In North America, the grasslands receive—roughly—between 10 and 30 inches of rain each year. Regions which get below 10 inches tend to be deserts, and above 30, forests.

Rainfall is only one of the things that goes into determining whether or not a place is a forest or grassland or desert. There are things which affect the amount of rainfall that the land absorbs—things like soil type and slope. There are also things which change the rate at which the soil loses

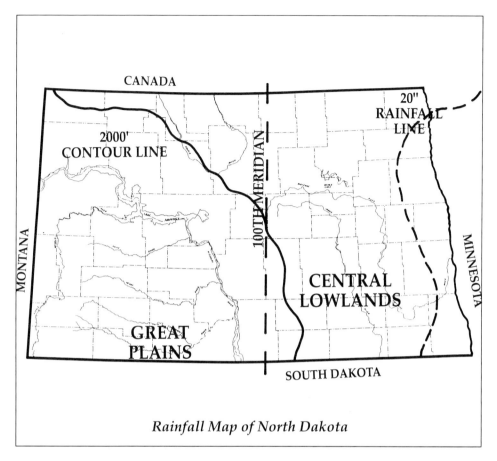

Rainfall Map of North Dakota

moisture—things like wind, and even the time of year when that moisture falls. But rainfall is the main one. In the grasslands of the United States, rainfall diminishes from the east to the west. At the eastern edge of the grasslands, at the verge of the forest, are the true prairies of the United States. The grasses here once stood as high as a man on horseback. As one moves westward rainfall declines at a rate of an inch per fifty miles; at the 98th meridian we cross over into what are properly known as plains—the midgrass prairies, and then farther west, the shortgrass prairies.

The climate of grasslands is often characterized by large seasonal swings in temperature. Grasslands are often windy. Windy places favor grasses because wind increases evaporation from the soil and from large flat surfaces like tree leaves; grasses grow lower to the ground, and their long thin blades retain scanty moisture. Fire, too, can favor grasses because grasses live to a large degree underground, out of harm's way, whereas a forest, once burned, will be a long time recovering. In a natural grassland, fire is likely to come far too often to permit the patient growth of trees.

Grasslands are among the most productive environments on earth. North American grasslands once supported immense herds of big game animals—the buffalo, antelope, and elk about which we will have so much more to say. The grasslands supported a huge diversity of wildlife—not only big game, but animals which depended on the herds for survival—wolves, coyotes, and man; birds—upland birds, waterfowl, and songbirds—for which the grasslands provided food and cover and places to rear their young; burrowing mammals like the prairie dogs and ground squirrels; raptors, reptiles, insects; altogether a huge tangle of life, all interrelated to the point where it seems impossible to sort one thing from another. The grassland soil itself is full of bacterial and microbial life. Grasslands are a very complex set of ecological relationships. It is important to understand them at least at the most basic level because the history of big game in North Dakota reflects the history of changes in those relationships.

The relationships begin with grass, rainfall, and the soil. The rainfall in a natural grassland—which is enough for grasses but not enough for trees—is also not enough to wash away the topsoil and nutrients. As long as the soil remains covered with grass, the leaves of the grass protect the soil from the impact of the rain; and the roots help keep the soil from being washed away. In this way grasses have adapted to protect their environment, to help it sustain itself. Grass cover can protect the soil from some of the sun's heat, reducing temperature fluctuations and keeping the surface loose and able to absorb moisture.

Grass has a relatively short life-cycle compared to trees. It grows quickly, dies, and decays, adding humus—organic matter—to the soil, improving its ability to retain moisture and sustain grass. This relatively quick turnover time for grasses also means that a greater portion of the grass plant can be used as food by plant-eating animals. This means that grasslands can support larger herds of animals than forests.

Look at it this way. Most of the plant material of trees is in the form of wood. Browsing plant-eaters like deer mostly use leaves, buds, and young shoots—not wood. Compared to grass, a huge proportion of the plant material in a tree is unusable. You can't sustain as many deer in an acre of forest as you can buffalo in an acre of tall grass. When shifts in climate began to favor grass over trees, all sorts of new opportunities for plant eaters were created as a result.

Some animals were more suited to take advantage of this situation than others. Taking advantage of the grassland took some special qualities or characteristics. Grasslands offer a vast food supply. But grasslands like the Great Plains are also subject to extremes of climate. They offer almost no place to get out of the wind and weather or to hide from predators. To be successful on the grassland, an animal had to be able to make use of the grassland's food supply, and it had to have some strategy for withstanding its dangers. Among the more obvious strategies is spending as little time in the open as possible—getting as much food as possible in the least amount of time, and then retiring to cover to hide or to escape the wind and the cold. Other useful characteristics would be to be bigger or faster than predators, or to be able to dig.

10

Animals which were successful on the grassland shared some or all of these characteristics. Buffalo, for example, and pronghorns are ruminants. They have a digestive system which gives them two advantages for living on the grasslands. First, it enables them to use plant material for food, and second, it allows them to eat a lot of food quickly, and then chew and digest it slowly in some more comfortable place. To accomplish this, they have a special chambered digestive system. Valerius Geist (1987, p. 314) explains:

> No mammal has enzymes capable of digesting [plant] cellulose; the ruminants culture microorganisms—bacteria and protozoa— to do it for them. These organisms grow within the rumen, an organ where fodder ferments by bacterial action. Fermentation produces fatty acids and other products which enter the animal's bloodstream directly from the rumen. Then the bacteria and residue from the fodder go into the stomach and gut, where the bacteria are digested to further supply the ruminant's protein, mineral, and vitamin requirements.

In order for microorganisms to work well on such food, it has to be ground to a fine consistency—the rechewing known as chewing the cud

Grazing bison.

11

that cows and all other ruminants do. It is this slow rechewing of food that is done at the animal's leisure.

There are other survival strategies. Both buffalo and pronghorns can run at surprising speeds for fair distances. Other creatures of the grasslands live most of their lives underground; an example is the pocket gopher, described by Meriwether Lewis: "I have observed in many parts of the plains and prairies, the work of an anamal of which I could never obtain a view...it never appears above the ground. the little hillocks which are thrown up by these anamals have much the appearance of ten or twelve pounds of loose earth poared out of a vessel on the surface of the plain" (Lewis, April 9, 1805). A large number of the mammals in North Dakota live, for some part of their lives, underground.

The opening of the grasslands created what biologists call "selective pressure" for certain kinds of characteristics in animals—rumination or speed, as we have seen, and others: hoofs in horses instead of toes, or the coloring of mule deer fawns, making them hard to see when bedded down in cover. Grazing exerted similar pressures on the grasses. One of the selected characteristics of grass is that the more a grass stem is cut—as, for example, by the teeth of a cow or buffalo—the more side shoots and new stems it produces. Thus—within limits—grazing can actually strengthen and build the range. Some biologists feel that grazing by buffalo herds was as great a force as rainfall in producing the shortgrass prairie of the arid west.

The community of life on the grassland—the animals, the plants, the insects, the reptiles—grew into equilibrium over a very long period of time. The sort of biological weeding out of unfit characteristics—and the encouragement of useful ones—takes many generations of a species, and in the case of long-lived and slow reproducing animals such as buffalo it can take centuries. Another aspect of time and the equilibrium of the grassland ecosystem is that so many things can happen to change the balance. Consider a prolonged period of drought. During such a time the characteristics of the grassland change. Tall grasses decline in favor of shorter ones. In shortgrass regions, the desert begins to invade. If the rains return, the balance will shift again. The extent of the world's grasslands has not yet recovered ground lost to ice during the last stage of the ice age. Equilibrium is a long-term concept, with many short-term fluctuations.

This brings to mind one other characteristic of North America's grassland that was especially important to animals like the buffalo and antelope. That was its sheer size. When things like prairie fire, or prolonged drought, or even their own trampling and grazing devastated huge expanses of their range, the buffalo merely wandered elsewhere, to fresh grass and abundant water. Time, then, would have the opportunity to work its magic, and the grassland would recover. When settlers cut the grassland with plows and divided it with fences, it would have a severe impact on the big game of the prairies.

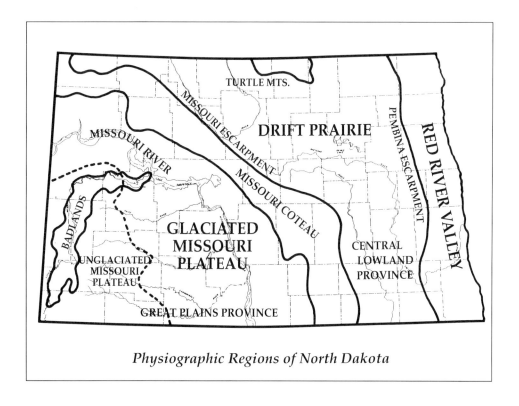

Physiographic Regions of North Dakota

NORTH DAKOTA GRASSLANDS

There is no mystery about why the land which we call North Dakota became a grassland. First of all, it has the right amount of rainfall. On the average, the western part of North Dakota receives more than ten inches of rain every year; in the east, although it rains more than it does in the west, it still is under the thirty or so inches of rain which would favor trees.

It is windy in North Dakota. North Dakota is in the middle of the continent of North America, away from mountains and away from the weather-moderating effects of oceans. Great masses of air move freely across North Dakota, moving temperatures up and down, making it cold in the winter, hot in the summer. Free moving cold air from one place mixes with warm air from another, making North Dakota windy most of the time.

Grasses are remarkably tolerant of all of this. It is not that trees won't grow in places like North Dakota—there were always trees in protected places with plenty of water—the river bottoms, for example. And people have managed to grow them around farmsteads and in towns. But to grow trees people have had to cultivate around them to keep the tough grasses from choking them out; and people have had to haul water to the trees when the rains failed. It seems safe to say that even the best efforts of people could not turn North Dakota into a forest.

13

North Dakota became a grassland; but it became different kinds of grasslands in different places, and in some places not a grassland at all. As the landscape of North Dakota marches east to west it rises in steps. The east is the lakebed topography of the Red River Valley. The somewhat higher and drier middle is the Drift Prairie, the rolling, stony topography left by the glaciers. And the west, which is higher and drier yet, is characterized and divided by the Missouri River. East of the Missouri is the Coteau, the Hills of the Missouri, and west is the Missouri Slope, which is rougher country, less glaciated, and contains the Badlands. As you would expect, as North Dakota rises and dries out east to west, soils and vegetation change, soils becoming lighter and grasses shorter. The places in North Dakota which are not properly grasslands at all are the forested regions of the Turtle Mountains, the Pembina Hills, and what is left of the riparian forests of the Red, James, Sheyenne, and Missouri River valleys.

Ecologists have a concept for which they use the word "niche." To describe an animal's niche is to describe the set of conditions within which it can live. Across the world, grasslands are similar environments, and they provide similar niches to animals. It should not surprise us that an animal in one of the world's grasslands would have a counterpart in another. The role played by the bison on the Great Plains is played by the kangaroo in Australia. It also should not surprise us that animals which evolved separately solved the problems of living on the grasslands in remarkably similar ways. The pronghorn and the antelope are very similar animals, but they evolved in different parts of the world.

Soil type, vegetation, and topography all have a role in defining these niches. As rainfall decreases east to west across North Dakota, slope increases, and soils lighten; shorter grasses begin to out-compete taller ones. The tallgrass areas once supported a greater density of buffalo than the western mid and shortgrass plains; in the barren and eroded Badlands there were bighorn sheep, but few buffalo. Animals have evolved, over time and many generations, physical and behavioral traits which allow them to live in specialized circumstances—which give them a better chance to succeed.

HISTORICAL BIG GAME IN NORTH DAKOTA

We have a fairly good idea of the wildlife here thanks to journals kept by early fur traders and explorers. Most of the animals they noted were big game species because that's what they depended upon for food.

East and north of North Dakota were the great fur forests which the first explorers, trappers, and traders came to exploit. Alexander Henry was one of these men, a fur trader for the North West Fur Company. Henry operated in the Red River Valley between 1800 and 1808, and in 1806 went from there to the Knife River villages of the Hidatsa and Mandans via the Assiniboine and Souris rivers. Other explorers—Lewis and Clark in particular, and some forty years later, John J. Audubon—made painstaking observations of wildlife as they journeyed up the Missouri.

When Alexander Henry first came to the Red River Valley he located his trading operations where the Park River enters the Red. From his Park River post he noted immense herds of buffalo and elk, which he called red deer, and other animals which are now rare in North Dakota:

> September 8, 1800—The entrance of this river is frequented by buffalo, red deer, moose, and bears; indeed it appears that the higher we go, the more numerous are red deer and bears. On the beach raccoon tracks are plentiful. Wolves are numerous and insolent.

Buffalo and elk appear to have been the most numerous in that area at that period of time; moose meat was apparently preferred to elk, and elk to buffalo: "For every moose [I gave the value of] six skins; for every red deer, five skins, to be paid for in whatever article of dry goods they might think proper to take…" (Henry, Autumn, 1799). "There was a cow herd at hand, but our hunters were killing plenty of red deer" (Henry, Nov. 21, 1800).

When Henry traveled east into what is now Minnesota, he remarked that "Red and fallow [white-tailed] deer were very numerous" (Oct. 28, 1800); but it was not until he had been in the Red River Valley for more than five years that he reported whitetails there: "The Indians saw three fallow deer and killed one—the first of the kind ever seen in this quarter" (March 31, 1806).

In July of 1806, just weeks prior to the return of the Lewis and Clark Expedition from the Pacific, Henry visited the Indian tribes along the Missouri. His route, northward through Canada and then south along the Souris River, took him out of moose country and into prairies covered with pronghorns. "Cabbrie [pronghorns] were in sight almost every moment, but so shy that we could not get a shot" (Henry, July 15, 1806). Although there were also large herds of buffalo and elk along with pronghorns (July 21, 1806—"I was present at the return of a hunting excursion…. They had killed as nearly as I could judge, about 500 animals—buffalo, red deer, and cabbrie"), the animals were not, perhaps, competing for the same range: "In this direction saw no buffalo, but numerous herds of cabbrie supplied that deficiency" (August 4, 1806).

Lewis and Clark noted similar changes in big game species as their expedition took them up the Missouri. In Missouri and Kansas, on their way up the Missouri in 1804, the expedition fed on whitetails and wild turkey; further north they encountered elk. While the expedition was in what is now South Dakota, William Clark killed what he described as the "Buck goat of this Countrey…he is more like the antilope or Gazelle of Africa than any other Species of Goat" (Sept. 14, 1804). Lewis and Clark were the first to describe the pronghorn in detail.

As the expedition proceeded north, it came upon another animal new to

15

them, "a curious kind of Deer of a Dark gray Colr. more so than common, hair long & fine, the ears large & long" (Sept. 17, 1804). This was the first description of the mule deer.

In what is now North Dakota Lewis and Clark found herds of antelope, elk, white-tailed deer, and buffalo; in the rough country of the west they found mule deer. One member of the expedition, Joseph Fields, who was sent up the Yellowstone to see if he could find any yellow stones, found bighorn sheep instead. White-tailed deer, so rare for Alexander Henry, were apparently quite plentiful along the Missouri.

Audubon followed Lewis and Clark up the Missouri after an interval of nearly forty years. In general, his account of the big game along the Missouri coincides with the journals of Lewis and Clark. Audubon entered the "buffalo country" at what is now South Dakota, seeing buffalo and antelope for the first time around the Niobrara River. He wrote, "[Buffalo] appear at this season more on the west side of the Missouri. The Elks, on the contrary, are found on the islands and low bottoms, well covered with timber; the common deer is found indifferently everywhere. All the antelopes we have seen were on the west side" (May 22, 1843). From the Niobrara north, all the way to Fort Union on the mouth of the Yellowstone, game seems to have been plentiful. Audubon was especially impressed with the numbers of elk in the vicinity of Fort Union: "These animals are abundant beyond belief hereabouts" (June 11, 1843).

Although we don't think of bears as big game in North Dakota today, both black bears and grizzlies once were plentiful. Alexander Henry's journal is the only extensive record of the distribution of bears in eastern North Dakota in those early days. Along the Red River he took many black bears, but few grizzlies. He wrote (Oct. 17, 1800), "Grizzly bears are not numerous along Red River…At Lac du Diable [Devils Lake]…they are very common—I am told as common as the black bear is here, and very malicious. Near that lake runs a principal branch of the Schian [Sheyenne], which is partially wooded. On the banks of this river I am informed they are also very numerous, and seldom molested by the hunters, it being the frontier of the Sioux, where none can hunt in safety…" In his eight years on the Red River, Henry's fur records show just under 1,000 black bears, but only 21 grizzlies (Reid and Gannon, 1928, p. 194).

There were more grizzlies in the western part of North Dakota, although it is hard to say how many. All of the visitors to the region, from Lewis and Clark in 1804 to Boller, who left in 1866, reported grizzlies. Lewis and Clark were especially concerned about them. Lewis wrote (June 28, 1805, near Great Falls), "The White bear have become so troublesome to us that I do not think it prudent to send one man alone on an errand of any kind, particularly where he has to pass through the brush…they come close arround our camp every night but have never yet ventured to attack us and our dog gives us timely notice of their visits, he keeps constantly padroling all night. I have made the men sleep with their arms by them as usual for fear of accidents."

16

Grizzly bear – from a painting by Karl Bodmer.

Lewis's and Clark's Corps of Discovery had considerable experience with grizzly bears, nearly all of it bad. Although no one was killed, several members of the expedition—including Lewis himself—had very close calls.

> June 2, 1805—The bear was very near catching Drewyer; it also pursued Charbono, who fired his gun in the air as he ran …
> —*Lewis*

> June 4, 1805—… near our camp we saw two white Bear, one of them was nearly catching Joseph Fields…the bear was so near that it struck his foot… —*Clark*

> June 14, 1805—… a large white…bear had…crept up on me within 20 steps before I discovered him;…I drew up my gun to shoot but at the same instant recollected that she was not loaded…It was an open level plain, not a bush within miles or a tree within 300 yards of me, the river bank was sloping and not more than three feet above the level of the water…. I ran about 80 yards and found he gained on me fast. I then ran into the water…about waste deep, & faced about and presented the point of my espontoon [a short pike or spear];…he suddenly wheeled about as if frightened, declined the combat,…and retreated…
> —*Lewis*

Even before this series of close encounters Lewis had written (May 11, 1805) "these bear being so hard to die reather intimidates us all, I must confess that I do not like the gentlemen and had reather fight 2 Indians than one bear." It is no wonder that the expedition was extremely cautious of them.

Things have changed since the time of the explorers. The numbers, species, and distribution of wildlife in North Dakota changed as the prairies themselves changed—with new economies on the prairies, mostly. The first economy—of the native tribes without any help from the white man—lasted for the longest time, perhaps as long as 12,000 years. At its earliest point this was a meager, nomadic existence for people who hunted and gathered. Later, native people learned to farm and to domesticate animals, giving them a measure of abundance. They gained some freedom from the need to follow the migrating herds, and perhaps gained the basis for trade with other groups.

It is hard to pinpoint when the sort of help the white man had to offer entered the prairie economy. Indian tribes on the upper Missouri had white trade goods long before the first white man visited them in 1738. It did not take very long for such goods—and whiskey—to become the focal point of the prairie economy, and as the tribes became more and more dependent, its downfall. For trade goods and whiskey, the tribes traded their livelihood—the big game of the prairies.

Market hunting became the next economy of the region, closely followed by the railroads and settlement. All of these changes to the prairies have had their effect on big game—the buffalo, deer, antelope, bighorn sheep, elk, and moose which were once native to North Dakota. We will look at each species in turn.

Sources

Journals of Early Explorers

Audubon, John James

Audubon, Maria R. 1986. Audubon and His Journals, With Zoological and Other Notes by Elliott Coues. 2 Vols. Dover Books, New York.

Henry, Alexander

Coues, Elliott, ed. 1965. New Light on the History of the Greater Northwest: The Manuscript Journals of Alexander Henry and David Thompson. 2 Vols. Ross and Haines, Inc., Minneapolis.

Reid, Russell and Clell G. Gannon. 1928. Natural History Notes on the Journals of Alexander Henry. North Dakota Historical Quarterly 2(3):168-201.

Lewis and Clark

Burroughs, Raymond Darwin. 1961. The Natural History of the Lewis and Clark Expedition. Michigan State University Press.

Cutright, Paul R. 1969. Lewis and Clark: Pioneering Naturalists. University of Nebraska Press.

Reid, Russell. 1988. Lewis and Clark in North Dakota. State Historical Society of North Dakota, Bismarck.

Thwaites, Reuben Gold, ed. 1905. Original Journals of the Lewis and Clark Expedition. 8 Vols. Dodd, Mead, and Co, New York.

Maximilian, Prince of Weid

Thomas, Davis and Karin Ronnefeldt. 1976. People of the First Man: Life Among the Plains Indians in Their Final Days of Glory. Dutton, New York.

Thwaites, Reuben Gold, ed. 1906. Early Western Travels, Vols 22-25. Arthur H. Clark Co, Cleveland.

Nicolette, Joseph N.

Bray, Edward C. and Martha Coleman Bray, eds. and trans. 1976. Joseph N. Nicolette on the Expeditions of 1838-39 with Journals, Letters and Notes on the Dakota Indians. Minnesota Historical Press, St. Paul.

Other Sources

Cassels, E. Steve. 1983. The Archaelogy of Colorado. Johnson Publishing Co., Boulder, Colorado.

Curry-Lindahl, Kai. 1981. Wildlife of the Prairies and Plains. Chanticleer Press. Henry N. Abrams, New York.

Geist, Valerius. 1971. Mountain Sheep: A Study in Behavior and Evolution. University of Chicago Press.

Geist, Valerius. 1987. Hoofed Mammals. pps. 313-320 of Wild Animals of North America. National Geographic Society, Washington, D.C.

Bison

CHAPTER TWO

THE LIVES
AND TIMES OF THE BUFFALO

Most Americans know what a buffalo looks like. Most of us have never actually seen one—or if we have seen buffalo we have not been close enough to measure our size against his, to feel his bulk and strength. Almost all of what we know of the buffalo is mythological. In our imaginations, the buffalo is what the prairies once were. The buffalo represents the past and the fate of Indian nations. The buffalo, by his belated rescue from extinction, symbolizes the notions and actions of the present.

There are many faces to this buffalo of our imaginations. In this chapter we will try to give them substance. We will look at the buffalo as a response to the environment of the grasslands; as the focus of the way of life of the tribes of the plains; and as a reflection of the peculiar relationship that yankee ingenuity has to the land which supports it.

THE WORLD OF THE BISON

"I had seen almost incredible numbers of buffalo in the fall, but nothing in comparison to the numbers I now beheld. The ground was covered at every point of the compass, as far as the eye could reach, and every animal was in motion." So reads the journal of Alexander Henry, January 14, 1801, perhaps the most famous impression of the herds that could appear on the North Dakota prairies. The bison, evolving from ice age ancestors, had become perfectly adapted to the grasslands of North America.

The primary range of the buffalo was from the Rocky Mountains in the west to the Mississippi River in the east; from the southern tip of Texas north into Saskatchewan and Manitoba. Although that seems an incredible span of distances, vegetation, and climates, buffalo had adapted to them; immense herds required the incredible vastness of the prairie. When the vastness was gone, the demise of the herds was inevitable.

Buffalo are by nature wanderers. They would have to be in order for herds of such immense size to exist. It took virtually no time for a buffalo herd to reduce lush grassland to trampled mud. Many of the early journal writers left reports of lands laid to waste by buffalo. Alexander Henry wrote (Sept., 1800), "The ravages of buffaloes at this place are astonishing to a person unaccustomed to these meadows. The beach, once a soft black mud into which a man would sink knee-deep, is now made as hard as pavement by the numerous herds going to drink. The willows are entirely

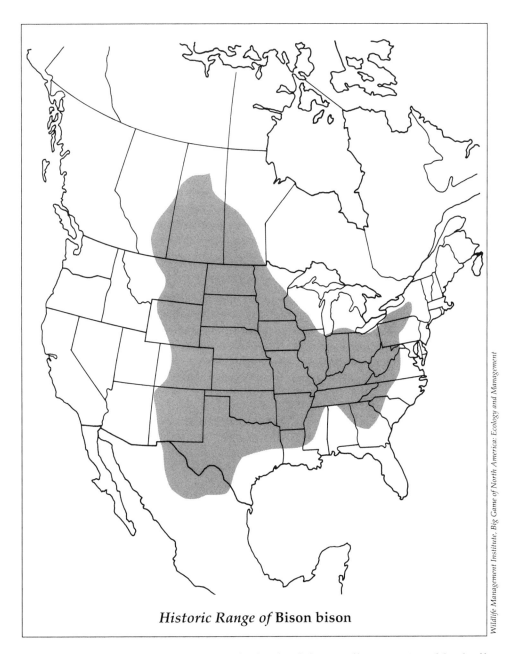

Historic Range of **Bison bison**

Wildlife Management Institute, Big Game of North America: Ecology and Management

trampled and torn to pieces; even the bark of the smaller trees is rubbed off in many places. The grass on the first bank of the river is entirely worn away…[T]he vast quantity of dung gives this place the appearance of a cattle yard." Years later, on his trip to the Missouri River, Henry wrote, "There must have been an astonishing number of buffalo in these parts during the summer, and, indeed, at all seasons. The grass is entirely destroyed, and the numerous ruts, both old and fresh, almost touch each other, and run in every direction" (July 24, 1806).

When the pasture in one place was used up, the buffalo moved on. There does not seem to have been any particular reason for their wanderings other than perhaps a dwindling supply of food and water. Buffalo are not fussy about what they eat. "Most favored are a few broad-leaved nongrassy herbs and many species of grasses: grama, buffalo, wheat, blue, blue-joint, June, dropseed, and windmill, as well as several fescues" (McHugh, 1972, p. 150). Thus the wanderings of the buffalo might be directed more by the amount of food available than by any particular species of grass. Rivers and streams did not intimidate them. Buffalo can swim; and when a buffalo herd, for whatever mysterious reason, decided to cross, not even a steamboat could turn them aside. Steamboat pilots learned that they may as well tie up as try to navigate a river clogged with buffalo.

Buffalo went where it pleased them to go. Their bones have been found in the mountains of Colorado as high as 12,000 feet—far above any likely source of food. Buffalo can survive the rigors of a northern prairie winter—the sort of weather which today is said to deter the riff-raff. They are well-insulated from the cold by fur and fat, and they can sweep aside

Ed Bry

the snow with their huge heads to tunnel their way to the grass. In his fine book on the buffalo, Tom McHugh describes some buffalo mired in deep snow: "When our light plane frightened a group of twenty-five in Hayden Valley, the animals blundered into a cornice twenty feet deep. Although they floundered—one buffalo even clambered across the back of a neighbor—they all finally managed to wade through" (McHugh, 1972, p. 244).

Buffalo are a tough bunch—although their hides may not be quite as thick as mythology has it. Their reputation for surviving blizzards— "When the storms challenge, the bison lowers its shaggy head, facing directly into the teeth of the wind" (Curry-Lindahl, 1981, p. 131)—may be more romance than fact. McHugh (1972, p. 243) remarks, "All the bison I've observed during storms have been facing in random directions." And he points to the experience of the fur trader Alexander Henry in 1776:

> ...a storm of wind and snow...continued all the night and part of the next day. Clouds of snow, raised by the wind, fell on the encampment...
>
> In the morning we were alarmed by the approach of a herd of oxen [buffalo], who came from the open ground to shelter themselves in the wood. Their numbers were so great, that we dreaded lest they should fairly trample down the camp.... The Indians killed several, when close upon their tents; but neither the fire of the Indians nor the noise of the dogs, could soon drive them away. Whatever were the terrors of the wood, they had no other escape from the terrors of the storm" (McHugh, 1972, p. 177).

Winter on the grassland could be a hazard to the buffalo, just as it could be to any creature caught out in the open. But spring was perhaps more destructive. The journals of traders and explorers are filled with descriptions of bloated buffalo corpses floating down the Red and the Missouri. Alexander Henry's account is again picturesque:

> April 1, 1800—The river clear of ice, but drowned buffalo continue to drift by entire herds.... It is really astonishing what vast numbers have perished; they formed one continuous line in the current for two days and nights.
>
> Apr. 18th—Rain; drowned buffalo still drifting down the river.
>
> Apr. 25th—Drowned buffalo drift down the river day and night.
>
> May 1st—The stench from the vast numbers of drowned buffalo along the river was intolerable.... I am informed that every spring it is the same.

Lewis and Clark did not make such a fuss over the number of dead buffalo, although they, as did Henry and others, found it remarkable that the Indians would make use of such animals:

> Mar. 30, 1805—I observed extrodanary dexterity of the Indians in jumping from one cake of ice to another for the purpose of Catching the buffalow as they float down.... —*Clark*

Even on the Missouri there were dead buffalo on the banks for a month following the thaw:

> Apr. 27, 1805—[F]or several days past we have observed a great number of buffaloe lying dead along the shore, some of them entire and others partly devoured by the wolves and bear. those anamals either drownded during the winter in attempting to pass the river on the ice...or by swiming acr[o]ss at present... —*Lewis*

The other great natural hazard to all grassland dwellers was fire. Even though fire is recognized as an important force in the regenerative process of grasslands, that is a long-term view. In the short-term, animals—especially those like buffalo, dwelling above ground, in the open—were often overtaken by fire as it was swept by the wind. From Henry's journal:

> Nov. 25, 1804—Plains burned in every direction and blind buffalo seen every moment wandering about. The poor beasts have all the hair singed off; even the skin in many places is shrivelled up and terribly burned, and their eyes are swollen and closed fast...In one spot we found a whole herd lying dead. The fire having passed only yesterday, these animals were still good and fresh, and many of them exceedingly fat...At sunset we arrived at the Indian camp, having made an extraordinary day's ride and seen an incredible number of dead and dying, blind, lame, singed, and roasted buffalo.

In spite of these disasters, millions of buffalo survived on the plains, which is a testament to their ability to compete successfully in that environment. In terms of his competitors, one of the buffalo's main advantages is his size. To the uninitiated—or to those who have seen buffalo from across an acre or so of National Park—buffalo may seem the equivalent of beef cattle. They are not. A buffalo bull is the largest land mammal in North America, weighing as much as a ton, and standing six feet tall at the shoulder. Few animals would attack a buffalo one-on-one; even those that attacked in groups the way wolves do picked out the weakest or oldest of the herd. Nor could another grazing animal take the choice pasture away from the buffalo.

To complement their size, buffalo travel together. Good eyesight would be a distinct advantage on the open prairie, but buffalo do not have it. They depend instead on hearing and smell and on their instinct for staying together. McHugh reports, "I have remained hidden in timber watching the herd. A single cow at the tail end of the group grazes over to a spot forty feet from my hiding place and discovers me. Turning, she walks purposefully through the herd of twenty-two animals; the others, who have not spotted me, respond immediately, and retreat with her for some distance until they are out of sight" (McHugh, 1972, p. 155). Alexander Henry, too, comments on this behavior:

> Nov. 7, 1799—It is surprising how sagacious those animals are. When in the least alarmed they will smell the track of even a single person in the grass, and run away in a contrary direction. I have seen large herds, walking very slowly to pasture, and feeding as they went, come to a place where some persons had passed on foot, when they would instantly stop, smell the ground, draw back a few paces, bellow, and tear up the earth with their horns. Sometimes the whole herd would range along the route, keeping up a terrible noise, until one of them was hardy enough to jump over, when they would all follow and run some distance.

The habit of following a leader en masse away from danger stood the buffalo in good stead for many thousands of years of living on the open plain. It is easy enough to see how a mass stampede could be a more effective defense against wolves than running in all directions. A would-be attacker stood a good chance of being trampled to death. A stampede is a maneuver for the open plain, where there is nothing for a solitary animal to hide behind; and an open plain is the only place which would support such a mass of foraging animals. Such a neat fitting together of habits and habitat is not accidental. But it will be interesting to see how, in later years, man was able to use the buffalo's natural defenses against them.

There is much we don't know about bison as they used to be. There is no way for us to know, for example, what the ratio of bulls to cows used to be, and no way to know what percentage of calves lived to become adults. We know from studying captive (but "unmanaged") herds today that although buffalo cows, after they are three years old, are capable of having a calf per year, actual production is far less than that. We also know that many calves do not survive their first year, and by the end of the third year perhaps 50 percent of the calves of a given year will have died (Meagher, 1978, p. 126). This low productivity may be a response to the limited range that buffalo have today—a regulatory mechanism. But it seems safe to say that under the best of circumstances, buffalo are a slow-reproducing species whose population would not show great fluctuations. They would remain very stable—but if disaster struck, they would not be able to recover very quickly.

Disaster did not strike the buffalo until after the arrival of white men and the changes they brought about. In the meantime—a fairly long meantime—the buffalo was the most important part of another way of life—the nomadic life of the Plains Indians.

Following the buffalo – from a drawing by George Catlin.

ND State Historical Society

INDIANS AND BUFFALO

Indians hunted all of the big game animals in North Dakota, and the buffalo became the most important to them. The nomadic way of life they practiced is of great antiquity. The first men to cross the Siberian-Alaskan land bridge crossed it to follow herds of mammoths and other big game. Archeological finds in the southwestern United States date the association of early people with bison—the now-extinct *antiquus* mentioned in Chapter

One—at perhaps 10,000 years. The evidence suggests that these early people "depend[ed] on herds of large animals for food, sinew (for sewing and for hafting weapons), hides (for clothing and shelter), and bones (for tools)..." (Cassels, 1983, p. 69).

The earliest plains dwellers wandered after the buffalo on foot. They were slow, slower than the buffalo, and they lived successfully on the prairie because they learned to use the evasive maneuvers of the buffalo—the tendency to follow the leader and to stampede—to their own advantage. Their hunting technique was simple and effective. When the nomads found a herd, they would try to get the buffalo running toward a cliff or cutbank. Once the lead buffalo headed over the bank, the entire herd would follow, smashing into one another at the bottom, easy prey for the Indian hunters. If a suitable cliff wasn't handy, the hunters made use of other features of the landscape—a box-end canyon, a bog, or, in winter, a frozen lakebed—to trap the animals. When there were no convenient hills or canyons, the hunters themselves formed the trap, surrounding the herd in an ever tightening "surround" of people.

Over many hundreds of years, Indian hunters refined their techniques. They learned to make better use of the landscape; and they used different methods of getting the buffalo to go the right direction. The following description is from Alexander Henry, in 1806.

> It is supposed that these people [the Assiniboins] are the most expert and dextrous nation of the plains in constructing pounds and in driving the buffalo into them. The pounds are of different dimensions, according to the number of tents in one camp. The common size is from 60 to 100 paces or yards in circumference and about five feet in height. Trees are cut down, laid upon one another, and interwoven with branches and green twigs.... This enclosure is commonly made between two hummocks...at the foot of rising ground. The entrance is about ten paces wide and always fronts the plains. On each side of this entrance commences a thick range of fascines [bundles of sticks tied together], the two ranges spreading asunder as they extend....
>
> Young men are usually sent out to collect and bring in the buffalo—a tedious task which requires great patience, for the herd must be started by slow degrees. This is done by setting fire to dung or grass. Three young men will bring in a herd of several hundred from a great distance. When the wind is aft it is most favorable, as they can then direct the buffalo with great ease. Having come in sight of the ranges, they generally drive the herd faster, until it begins to enter the ranges, where a swift footed person has been stationed with a buffalo robe over his head, to imitate that animal.... When he sees buffaloes approaching he moves slowly toward the pound until they appear to follow him, then he sets off at full speed, imitating a buffalo as well as he can, with the herd after him. The young men in the rear now discover

themselves, and drive the herd on with all possible speed. There is always a sentinel on some elevated spot to notify the camp when the buffalo appear; and this intelligence is no sooner given than every man, woman, and child runs to the ranges that lead to the pound to prevent the buffalo from taking a wrong direction...When the buffalo have been thus directed to the entrance of the pound, the Indian who leads them rushes into it and out of the other side, either by jumping over the enclosure or creeping through an opening left for that purpose. The buffalo tumble in pell mell at his heels, almost exhausted...

That is how the "impoundment" was supposed to work. The most hazardous job was the one of playing the decoy—the lead buffalo that the herd is supposed to follow. If the decoy fell down or could not get out of the enclosure soon enough, he had almost no chance of surviving.

In practice, the impoundment was not as precise as Henry's description makes it sound. Plenty of things could go wrong. Sometimes the follow-the-leader instincts of the buffalo saved them after leading them so close to destruction. If only one buffalo managed to get out of the trap—through a weak spot in the enclosure, or if one of the Indians out on the wings of the funnel leading to the entrance let a buffalo by him, or even, sometimes, through the opening left for the decoy—the rest of the herd followed, bringing the whole effort to nothing. Since opportunities for impounding buffalo were rare, failure often meant hunger. Or worse.

Such was the Indians' dependence on the buffalo for their livelihoods that they would go to considerable lengths to make sure that the hunt did not fail. Among the tribes there were various ceremonies to bring the buffalo and to guarantee the success of the hunt. Tom McHugh (1972, p. 58) describes the responsibilities of the *wathon* of the Omaha Tribe—the director of the hunt:

> During the four days leading up to the departure for the hunt, the *wathon* fasted. When the grand cavalcade set forth at last, he trailed behind, walking barefoot as further proof of his humility, beseeching the Spirit Father to grant him wisdom to lead his people well. In the days that followed, the *wathon* steered the tribe's march, selected overnight camping places, and dispatched some twenty runners to search for buffalo.

Thus the *wathon*, in addition to being spiritually acceptable to hunt the sacred buffalo, had some practical responsibilities; one of the most important was insuring, with strict police action, that no one, for whatever reason, could threaten the success of the hunt.

As time passed on the prairies, some tribes turned to agriculture to lessen their dependence on buffalo and the uncertainty of its wanderings. Among these were the Missouri River tribes—the Mandans, Hidatsas, and

Mandan dance for the coming of the buffalo – from a drawing by George Catlin.

Arikaras—who lived in permanent earth-lodge villages. Even though these tribes took up farming, it does not mean that they gave up hunting. Their lifestyle simply meant that they did not suffer from the lack of food and other essentials of life as often as the nomadic tribes.

That's one of the troubles with depending on an itinerant resource like buffalo. You have to be as mobile as the resource. Although the nomadic tribes were well-fed on the occasions when they caught up with a buffalo herd and managed to drive it over a cliff, there were other times when they had nothing. This would change later, when the plains tribes all had horses. But as late as 1738, when the first white trader—one Pierre Gaultier de Varennes, Sieur de La Verendrye—visited the Mandans, they still did not have horses, and were the most prosperous tribe in the region. They had enough food for themselves, and they had enough for trade. La Verendrye wrote, "They [the Mandans] are sharp traders, and clean the Assiniboin out of everything they have in the way of guns, powder, ball, kettles, axes, knives, and awls" (Reid, 1988, p. 71).

There were plenty of times in which both Indians and whites suffered from hunger. John Tanner, a white man captured and raised by Indians, wrote in his memoirs of hunger among the Ottawa Tribe in the late 1700s

31

and early 1800s. Others relate tribes reduced to eating their leather equipment when game was scarce.

In order to get through the lean times when game was scarce, the Indians invented pemmican. There were many different kinds of pemmican; one of the most common seems to have been made of dried and pounded buffalo meat mixed with dried chokecherries or berries. Pemmican was made up into bags made of buffalo rawhide and melted fat was poured into it, coating the mixture. The result was a nutritious food which would keep for years. But even pemmican—a pound of which might have the nutrition of five pounds of fresh meat—could not prevent hardship for horseless nomadic tribes. They could not carry enough of it.

European—and what was then "American"—tastes differed from those of the Indian tribes. People like John James Audubon were surprised at what the Indians considered delicacies. Some of these adventurers later learned not to let culture get in their way—Lewis Squires of the Audubon

John J. Audubon

Expedition is a case in point. Squires wrote this in Audubon's journal following a buffalo hunt:

> June 27, 1843—Owen McKenzie commenced eating the raw liver, and offered me a piece. What others can eat, I felt assured I could at least taste. I accordingly took it and ate quite a piece of it; to my utter astonishment, I found it not only palatable but very good…

Apparently Squires even came to relish this sort of food. Audubon wrote that on another buffalo hunt, "Mr. Culbertson broke open the head of 'my' bull, and ate part of the brains raw, and yet warm, and so did many of the others, even Squires."

Although Audubon himself occasionally tried these delicacies, he never learned to take them in stride:

> June 9, 1843—Whilst the butchers were at work, I was highly interested to see one of our Indians cutting out the milk-bag of the cow and eating it, quite fresh and raw, in pieces somewhat larger than a hen's egg. One of the stomachs was partially washed in a bucket of water, and an Indian swallowed a large portion of this…I had a piece well cleaned and tasted it; to my utter astonishment it was very good, but the idea was repulsive to me….

HORSES

Horses changed the way of life on the prairie. For the Indians, surrounding a buffalo herd with men on horses was far more effective than surrounding a herd with men on foot. It took fewer people to kill more buffalo in less time. The horsemen would attempt to enclose the herd in a tightening ring of horsemen, turning the lead buffalo back into the herd with arrows and lances. Tom McHugh (1972, p. 74-75) describes the chaotic scene:

> [C]aught in the tightening cordon, the herd, suddenly aware of its plight, would attempt to escape by probing for weak places in the line. Ricocheting from point to point as the ever-tightening circle of Indians drew in, the terrified animals were soon trapped within the pincers…Now the hunters galloped from animal to animal, loosing a barrage of arrows and lances. Buffalo by the score fell under the withering assault, littering the arena with carcasses that tripped pursued and pursuer alike…In time, almost all perished.

Indian hunting scene – from a painting by White Crow.

When a buffalo managed to escape the noose of the hunters, he would charge across the prairie with a hunter on his heels. Very likely it is such chases that led to the next step in buffalo hunting—buffalo running.

Running the buffalo was different than any other kind of buffalo hunting. For one thing, it takes a special view of life to go galloping across the prairie amidst a stampeding herd of buffalo. To such men life must be a precious thing; but a thing which must be risked to have flavor. You must have that view of life to live on the frontier. Audubon describes the buffalo running technique of the Mandans:

> August 11, 1843—Indians of different tribes hunt the Buffalo in different ways …[b]ut I will give you the manner pursued by the Mandans. Twenty to fifty men start, as the occasion suits, each provided with two horses, one of which is a pack-horse, the other fit for the chase. They have quivers with from twenty to fifty arrows, according to the wealth of the hunter. They ride the pack horse bareback, and travel on, til they see the game, when they leave the pack-horse, and leap on the hunter, and start at full speed and soon find themselves amid the Buffaloes, on the flanks of the herd, and on both sides. When within a few yards the arrow is sent, they shoot at a Buffalo somewhat ahead of them, and send the arrow in an oblique manner, so as to pass through the lights [lungs]. If the blood rushes out of the nose and mouth the animal is fatally wounded, and they shoot at it no more; if not, a second, and perhaps a third arrow is sent before this happens.

34

Audubon's account hardly gives us the excitement, the chaos, and the danger of the chase. For that we turn to Henry Boller (a trader in North Dakota in the 1850s), and an account of a rather amateurish chase by some white traders (Boller, Dec. 9, 1858):

> Wray had been left far to the rear, and was enabled to make a short cut, after the buffalo had been turned, and was now bearing down on them at his fastest pace. He rode straight for the head of the bull, who when he was near, lowered his head turned and charged! Quick as lightning Wray's pony wheeled short round and this avoided the shock, while at the same moment and with the same rapidity Wray exchanged his saddle for the prairie; it was the cleanest & most complete tumble I ever witnessed, nothing clumsy about; the horse ran off, leaving his rider sprawling and at the mercy of the enraged bull. Jeff shouted out "run like hell Wray!" but the advice was needless; Wray's feet, assisted by his hands making the snow fly in clouds. The rest of us moved by an impulse rushed on the bull, shouting; finding himself thus hotly pressed, the bull continued on, his movements quickened by a ball from Jeff's rifle…I looked back and saw Wray chasing his horse over the prairie.

White buffalo runners and some Indians preferred to use rifles to run buffalo. It took some skill to reload a rifle on a galloping horse. From McHugh (1972, p. 79):

> After the first shot of each run, the hunter stopped using wadding to hold in the charge. From then on he primed his rifle on the gallop only a few paces from the buffalo, tipping the powder horn hanging from his shoulder to pour a wildly guessed measure down the barrel. Then he spat a ball down the muzzle from the supply he carried in his mouth and rapped the butt on his thigh to settle the charge, counting on saliva to hold the ball until it was fired.

MÉTIS

Some of the most proficient—and most careless of their own well-being—of the buffalo runners were the métis—the mixed-blood descendents of Indians and French trappers. Although the métis made some half-hearted motions in the direction of agriculture—growing potatoes, tobacco, and a few vegetables in the Red River Valley—what they lived for was a twice-a-year buffalo hunt. As Elwyn Robinson (1966, p. 68) describes it:

> The hunt came to be a mania, the focal point of their [the métis] lives. They rode out on two hunts each year, a summer hunt

35

> beginning in the middle of June after the crops were planted and a fall hunt starting in October. The summer hunt was for provisions—pemmican, dried meat, and grease—and leather for moccasins and tipis. The fall hunt, too, was for provisions (the buffalo were fatter then), but also for buffalo robes…. Sometimes the métis divided into two parties; sometimes all would go out to the plains together.

The métis' hunts came to be very large. They used the wooden-wheeled carts now known as red river carts—by 1820 as many as 500 carts—and set out onto the prairie in search of a herd. Robinson continues:

> When a herd was found, the hunters, as many as four hundred men, formed a long line on their horses and, riding abreast, advanced slowly toward it in order to get as close as possible before the buffalo became frightened. When the buffalo fled, the hunters galloped into the herd, shooting them down at close range. They picked out the cows (tenderer meat), their horses unguided, following the twists and turns of the quarry. The hunter rode at full speed with a mouth full of balls….
>
> The average hunter could kill three or four buffalo in a half-hour chase; those with the fastest horses might get ten or twelve…. The galloping men, the rapid firing on every side, badger holes and uneven ground, the maddened buffalo, the dust and noise and confusion—all made the hunt dangerous. Frequently accidents killed or maimed a hunter.

The hunts of the plains tribes can't really be compared to those of the métis—the métis' hunts were more of an assault on the herd than a hunt, and they used only a small portion of the kill for themselves. The tribes heartily disliked the métis.

HORSES AND CULTURE

The buffalo was the Indians' storehouse of the necessities of life, and for that the Indians felt he deserved a profound respect. That made hunting the buffalo a doubly tricky business, for it is hard to show respect for what you are about to kill.

Buffalo running helped provide an honorable solution to a difficult problem. Only a truly worthy hunter could ride full tilt amid the charging herd, killing buffalo without being killed himself. The man who killed many buffalo in this manner was a remarkable man—wealthy in worldly goods, and rich in the respect of other people.

So it was that the best horseman became a powerful individual, and a man with no horses could not become anything. A man with no horses could not provide for his family; he had no means to carry goods and food

The best horsemen were powerful men – from a painting by Karl Bodmer.

when the camp moved from place to place; without help from men with horses, he could not even keep up with the camp. Mounted men could stay with the herds and men afoot went hungry.

The ability to acquire horses very soon became valuable to the nomadic tribes. Since people who had to follow wandering herds could not pause long enough to raise their own horses, they either had to trade for them or steal them. Stealing was more popular. Trading was hard—people who had no horses to begin with had nothing to trade for horses, and people who have wealth are unlikely to give the have-nots the means to take that wealth away. Besides, horse-stealing had many of the same honorable possibilities as running the buffalo. It was a risky business to steal a horse from under the nose of the owner; much depended on the skill and stealth of the individual; and the rewards of a successful raid were many. Joseph Nicollet, traveling across North Dakota in 1839, describes his party's vigilance against the loss of their horses:

> July 28, 1839—We can defend our lives, but it is very difficult to defend the horses…
>
> The Indians of the plains are so enterprising, so ingenious in ways unknown to the whites, that no matter the amount of

vigilance exercised, it is almost impossible to escape their attacks....

The Indians who need horses, as do all the Indians of the plains, will follow one caravan for weeks until they succeed. In this enterprise they will employ the same ruses and artifices they use in war. The theft of a horse counts as a coup. As it is a little easier to attain glory this way than by lifting a scalp, young Indians, motivated also by need, eagerly seek out this opportunity.

To hide themselves from travelers on the plains, they cover themselves with skins from the heads of prairie wolves or antelopes. They come in from all sides, while keeping their distances so that they can see all the movements of those they follow...At other times, the Indian crouched in the grass will put in front of his eyes one of the thousands of buffalo skulls that lie about the prairie, and will observe you at his leisure without giving you the idea that the head you observed this very morning conceals an enemy.

The horse and the cultural changes it brought about were the peak of the nomadic way of life on the plains, just as the Mandans were the most wealthy and powerful of the era before the horse. Horses gave the Plains Indians wealth and power; such freedom from hunger and want meant leisure to pursue other cultural values. Some of these were the honors acquired through raiding and warfare. There is no telling how long the way of life might have gone on. But the invading white civilization had other ideas about what the grasslands and its products might be used for.

THE WHITE MAN AND THE BUFFALO

The idea that there was any kind of spiritual connection between themselves and the buffalo—indeed, between themselves and any part of the world which supported them—was missing from the white estimation of the world. That is a pretty significant concept not to have. As a result it took more than a century after they arrived in the New World for the white culture to figure out that soil and water and rainfall and buffalo were all connected. It took a long time to learn that when one part of the environment was changed, the other parts were affected. By the time the white culture learned these lessons, it was already trying to restore some endangered wildlife species, knowing that it seemed important, but with only the vaguest notion why.

The early explorers and traders acknowledged the buffalo as the most abundant source of food on the grassland. During the winter of 1804–1805, Lewis and Clark questioned the Missouri tribes closely about the country to the west. It is estimated (Cutright, 1969, p. 110) that it took a full grown buffalo—or its equivalent of four deer or an elk and a deer—to feed the

"A KILLING of COWS & SPIKES.

expedition for a day. When the Mandans told Lewis and Clark that when they entered the mountains they would leave the buffalo behind, the expedition stocked up on buffalo meat. "Shannon, for instance, in just two or three days jerked 600 pounds, and Drouillard 800. Other men 'tried up' buffalo grease (that is, converted fat to tallow); Charbonneau alone produced enough to fill three kegs" (Cutright, 1969, p. 165).

Alexander Henry, in the Red River Valley, relied on pemmican to get him through lean times in the winter. "I made up my pemmican into bags of 90 pounds each—50 pounds of beef and 40 pounds of grease" (Henry, April 10, 1801). Henry apparently did not use any berries or chokecherries in his recipe—without them, pemmican would keep longer.

But that was as far as respect for the buffalo went. White men held no ceremonies to give thanks for the abundance of the buffalo. Such things were held in contempt; Indians were thought to have "most strange ideas of surrounding nature" (Maximilian, in Thomas and Ronnefeldt, 1976, p. 246). By the time that John James Audubon went up the Missouri in 1843, the waste of the buffalo, even on the remote northern prairies, sickened him:

> What a terrible destruction of life, as it were for nothing…One can hardly conceive…the immense numbers that are murdered almost daily on these boundless wastes called prairies…. But this cannot last; even now there is a perceptible difference in the size of the herds, and before many years the Buffalo, like the Great Auk, will have disappeared; surely this should not be permitted. (Audubon, July 21, Aug. 5, 1843)

But it was permitted, even encouraged. Tales of buffalo hunting attracted sportsmen from the east and from Europe—true sportsmen like

39

Parker Gillmore and John Palliser, both of whom wrote down their adventures on the prairies. There were others who were not so sporting. The most infamous of these may have been Sir George Gore, who went about the prairies with an entourage of servants, and wagons loaded with guns, wine, books, and a brass bedstead for him to sleep in. Gore's excesses were amazing even to those accustomed to slaughtering buffalo for their hides and tongues. From Henry Boller (Letter, May 20, 1858):

> I forgot to mention…that Sir George Gore the "Irish Butcher" is still about. He is, it is understood, selling off his guns, some of which cost him $500 in Hingland. He takes his meals in his private room, and like a bat makes his appearance about evening. He has a stable on Bloody Island, where he keeps 5 or 6 horses, 40 dogs, and 6 men. He contemplates a fishing expedition to the lakes this summer, and I sincerely hope he will soon return to "Hingland" and that no more Butchers will desecrate our western hunting grounds. Why this "Sportsman" (?) had a barber to shave him every morning in his tent, and another man to rub and wash him down every morning after rising!"

As a sidenote, washing appears to have been a noteworthy event to most frontiersmen. Even Maximilian, a German prince who visited the Mandans in 1833 and 1834, was said to have worn "the greasiest pair of trousers that ever encased princely legs."

Gore was not the only butcher to venture onto the plains. The publicity that such people received only brought more people out. "Buffalo hunting became the rage, its reputation swelled by the tales of returning eastern dudes, who had trooped to the plains in hordes to find out if reports of the celebrated herds were true. The railroads began to plug low-priced buffalo-hunting excursions across the Kansas prairies with exhibitions of live buffalo and advertisements headlining the numbers of animals shot on previous junkets" (McHugh, 1972, p. 249).

The period of time between 1840 and 1880—the period of the great slaughter of the bison—has been written about so much that it does not bear repeating here. It does bear repeating that people seemed to think that it could go on forever. In his story of buffalo hunter George Newton (**Tales from Buffalo Land**), Usher Burdick wrote (1939, p. 16-17):

> In 1882-1883 a great calamity came over the business of the buffalo hunter. Great preparations were made by the supply dealers along the Big Dry, the Little Dry and Frazer Creek to have a large supply of ammunition and food in readiness for the hunters. Mr. Newton estimated that…a thousand hunters were on hand to meet the great herds of buffalo as they would make their return from Canada, according to their custom. In the spring of 1882-1883…the buffalo were seen to drift gradually north in the direction of Canada and the supply dealers and the

hunters had every reason to believe that in the fall business would begin, but a very strange situation developed. No herds of buffalo ever came back from Canada in the fall of 1882-1883. The buffalo had disappeared like magic; traders removed their goods, closed their books, and left the country; hunters deserted the chase and after recovering from the shock incident to the magic disappearance of the buffalo, they wandered into other pursuits.

The reign of the buffalo on the prairie was over. All that was left of it were the bones which littered the prairie, providing cash to the settlers in between the time when the sod was being broken and the farms really began to produce.

SOME OTHER THEORIES

It is generally agreed that hide hunters exterminated the buffalo herds. But other possibilities have been presented. In 1983, Rudolph W. Koucky published an article which argued that while it might be possible to support an argument for the southern herds of buffalo being slaughtered, the same could not be said for the northern herds.

Dr. Koucky asserts that there were some 4,000,000 buffalo in the northern herds as late as 1880. Furthermore, he states that by 1883 these herds were almost gone, and that there is no way to account for this by looking at the records for hides shipped during that time. "Between 1881 and the spring of 1883, the entire herd of about 4,000,000 buffalo and their estimated 500,000 offspring disappeared almost completely. During this period a recorded total of 320,000 hides was shipped from the northern buffalo

Wagons full of bones at Devils Lake in 1885.

41

country. The three-year total was less than the anticipated propagation of the herd for one single year" (Koucky, 1983, p. 25).

Dr. Koucky proposes that cattle-borne disease is a more plausible explanation than extermination by hunters. He notes—as did George Newton above—that the disappearance of the buffalo was first seen in Montana; it coincides precisely with the arrival of Texas cattle into the Tongue River Valley. Dr. Koucky points to evidence that there was contact between the free-ranging cattle and the buffalo. "The mingling of cattle known to harbor the so-called tick fever with the buffalo exactly at the time and in the place where the disappearance of the buffalo first appeared is strong presumptive evidence that the buffalo were devastated by disease" (Koucky, 1983, p. 28).

Most people still lean toward the hide-hunter theory. Whichever is the truth, the buffalo did die, and their bones littered the northern prairies.

> In 1884, bone pickers began to bring their wares to Dickinson and Sully Springs, receiving from eight to ten dollars a ton. Freighters, hauling supplies from Dickinson to the Black Hills, increased their profits by picking up bones on the return trip. In 1886 piles of buffalo bones were stacked on every Northern Pacific platform from Jamestown westward, and the next year, when the Great Northern was ready to receive freight shipments at Minot, bones were the chief item. For months at Minot more than a hundred wagons a day unloaded bones along the track (Robinson, 1966, p. 186).

SAVED FROM EXTINCTION

In January of 1889, William Hornaday took a census of buffalo in the United States. Of free-ranging buffalo "he could account for no more than eighty-five. Elsewhere on the continent, he listed 200 under lax federal protection in Yellowstone National Park, some 550 in the vicinity of Great Slave Lake, and 256 scattered in various zoos or private herds" (McHugh 1972, p. 294). These were what was left of herds which once numbered thirty to sixty million.

In 1905, Hornaday was elected president of a newly-formed organization called the American Bison Society. The purpose of the society was to rescue the bison from imminent extinction. But in spite of extravagant efforts on the part of one Ernest Harold Baynes (see McHugh for an account of them), the Society had a difficult time arousing public enthusiasm for buffalo. During the next four years, the Society managed to convince Congress and private individuals to fund the purchase of a total of 49 buffalo to be stocked onto two ranges.

The Society did not, however, give up. Its members continued to work for increased areas set aside for buffalo, and more buffalo with which to

Dr. William T. Hornaday

stock them. "By 1915, the members of the American Bison Society could reflect happily on the accomplishments of their first ten years. During this decade they had overseen a general population increase of about 270 percent. Buffalo were now established in the new Wichita, Niobrara, Wind Cave, and Custer preserves, and even Yellowstone Park's 'wild herd'...had doubled its ranks" (McHugh, 1972, p. 304). By 1930, the rescue of the buffalo from extinction seemed assured.

The people charged with caring for these captive buffalo herds managed them as carefully as anyone ever managed cattle. "Herding, rotation of pastures, castration of bull calves, separation of calves for weaning, round-ups, haying, and winter feeding were part of the operation at various times" (Meagher, 1978, p. 131). In private herds and in some preserves, these practices are still carried out. But the national parks are treated as "natural areas" and buffalo in the parks are allowed to take their chances with predators, with the weather, with the vegetation, and with all the other hazards they faced throughout their long history. Though they will never again blacken the prairies, they are at least holding their own.

Sources

Journals of Early Explorers

Audubon, John James

Audubon, Maria R. 1986. Audubon and His Journals, With Zoological and Other Notes by Elliott Coues. 2 Vols. Dover Books, New York.

Henry, Alexander

Coues, Elliott, ed. 1965. New Light on the History of the Greater Northwest: The Manuscript Journals of Alexander Henry and David Thompson. 2 Vols. Ross and Haines, Inc., Minneapolis.

Reid, Russell and Clell G. Gannon. 1928. Natural History Notes on the Journals of Alexander Henry. North Dakota Historical Quarterly 2(3):168-201.

Lewis and Clark

Burroughs, Raymond Darwin. 1961. The Natural History of the Lewis and Clark Expedition. Michigan State University Press.

Cutright, Paul R. 1969. Lewis and Clark: Pioneering Naturalists. University of Nebraska Press.

Reid, Russell. 1988. Lewis and Clark in North Dakota. State Historical Society of North Dakota, Bismarck.

Thwaites, Reuben Gold, ed. 1905. Original Journals of the Lewis and Clark Expedition. 8 Vols. Dodd, Mead, and Co, New York.

Maximilian, Prince of Weid

Thomas, Davis and Karin Ronnefeldt. 1976. People of the First Man: Life Among the Plains Indians in Their Final Days of Glory. Dutton, New York.

Thwaites, Reuben Gold, ed. 1906. Early Western Travels, Vols 22-25. Arthur H. Clark Co, Cleveland.

Nicolette, Joseph N.

Bray, Edward C. and Martha Coleman Bray, eds. and trans. 1976. Joseph N. Nicolette on the Expeditions of 1838-39 with Journals, Letters and Notes on the Dakota Indians. Minnesota Historical Press, St. Paul.

Other Sources

Boller, Henry. 1966. The Letters of Henry Boller: Upper Missouri Fur Trader. ed. by R. H. Matteson. North Dakota History 33(2):106-219.

Boller, Henry. 1966. Journal of a Trip to and Residence in, the Indian Country, Commenced Saturday, May 22, 1858. North Dakota History 33(3):260-315.

Burdick, Usher L. 1939. Tales From Buffalo Land: The Story of George "W" Newton (Old Time Buffalo Hunter of Dakota and Montana). Wirth Bros., Baltimore.

Cassels, E. Steve. 1983. The Archaelogy of Colorado. Johnson Publishing Co., Boulder, Colorado.

Curry-Lindahl, Kai. 1981. Wildlife of the Prairies and Plains. Chanticleer Press, Henry N. Abrams, New York.

Koucky, Rudolph W. 1983. The Buffalo Disaster of 1882. North Dakota History 50(1):23-30.

McHugh, Tom. 1972. The Time of the Buffalo. University of Nebraska Press.

Meagher, Margaret M. 1978. Bison. pps. 123-133 of Big Game of North America: Ecology and Management. Wildlife Management Institute. Stackpole Books, Harrisburg, PA.

Robinson, Elwyn. 1966. History of North Dakota. University of Nebraska Press.

Pronghorn antelope

CHAPTER THREE

PRONGHORNS

In the year 1540, Francisco Vasquez de Coronado set out from New Spain—Mexico—and worked his way north into what is now Arizona and New Mexico. Coronado was looking for the "seven cities of Cibola" and for Quivera, places legendary for fabulous wealth in gold. His king, Charles V, Holy Roman Emperor and King of Spain, needed the treasure of the New World to finance his struggles to keep his far-flung dominions together.

Coronado found adobe pueblos in place of the seven cities; a teepee village of Wichita Indians where Quivera was reputed to be; and, in between, vast distances full of "hunch-backed cattle" and "goats." These animals were less interesting than gold, and did not serve the purposes of the king, who was preoccupied with the threat of war with France and a religious revolt started by Martin Luther. Coronado returned to New Spain; and credit for the first descriptions of antelope accurate enough for technical use went to Meriwether Lewis and William Clark.

> September 14, 1804—in my walk I Killed a Buck Goat of this Countrey, about the hight of a Grown deer. its body Shorter the Horns which is not very hard and forks 2/3 up one prong Short the other round and Sharp arched, and is imediately above its eyes the color is a light gray with black behind its ears down its neck, and its face white round its neck. its Sides and its rump round its tail which is short and white: verry actively made, has only a pair of hoofs to each foot. his brains on the back of his head, his Norstrals large, his eyes like a sheep he is more like the Antilope or Gazella of Africa than any other species of Goat.
>
> —*Clark*

> September 17, 1804—We found the Antelope extreemly shye and watchfull insomuch that we had been unable to get a shot at them; when at rest they generally seelect the most elivated point in the neighbourhood, and as they are watchfull and extreemly quick of sight and their sense of smelling very accute it is almost impossible to approach them within gun-shot...they will frequently discover and flee from you at the distance of three miles. I had this day an opportunity of witnessing the agility and superior fleetness of this animal which was to me really astonishing...I got within about 200 paces of them when they smelt me and fled; I gained the top of the eminence on which they stood, as soon as possible from whence I had an extensive view of the country the antilopes which had disappeared in a steep

reveene now appeared at a distance of about three miles…so soon had these antilopes gained the distance at which they had again appeared…I doubted at ferst that they were the same that I had just surprised, but my doubts soon vanished when I beheld the rapidity of their flight along the ridge before me…I think I can safely venture the assertion that the speed of this anamel is equal if not superior to that of the finest blooded courser. —*Lewis*

Craig Bihrle

Watchful pronghorn.

GRASSLAND NATIVE

Lewis's and Clark's descriptions go straight to the heart of how pronghorns survive on the grassland. Pronghorns live on the open grasslands, and depend on their superior speed and eyesight to protect them from danger. Long distance eyesight is an advantage only in open areas, and so, as Lewis noted, the animals "seelect the most elivated point in the neighbourhood." Pronghorns are indeed "actively made." They have long, slim legs and muscular rumps and shoulders. They have "a pair of hoofs to each foot"—two well-padded, pointed toes, well-suited to running on the hard prairie ground. His "Norstrals large," his lungs and heart huge, the pronghorn is abundantly equipped for speed, and when he is alarmed he can outrun any creature in "the neighbourhood."

Pronghorns are neither antelopes nor goats, even though their technical family name—Antilocapridae—combines the Latin words for antelope and goat. Most early journalists decided that pronghorns were most properly called goats, and used the Spanish word *cabre*—although, as Clark noted in his journal, "None of those goats has any beard." Lewis preferred to call them antelopes.

But pronghorns shed their horns, which is something no true antelope does. No one, however, knew in 1804 whether pronghorns did or didn't shed their horns; naturalists were still puzzling over it forty years later when Audubon wrote:

> June 19, 1843—I am quite amazed at the differences of opinion respecting the shedding—or not shedding—of the horns of the Antelope; and this must be looked into with the greatest severity, for if these animals do shed their horns, they are no longer Antelopes.

Audubon suspected the truth—that pronghorns do shed their horns— but like a good scientist, was cautious:

> July 24, 1843—I have been drawing the head of one of these beautiful female Antelopes; but their horns puzzle me, and all of us; they seem to me as if they were new horns, soft and short; time, however, will prove whether they shed them or not.

The pronghorn is, in fact, all alone in the world. It has no close relatives. The pronghorn evolved in the New World—it did not cross over the Alaskan-Siberian land bridge—and so it has no Old World relatives. All of its New World relatives have become extinct. Pronghorns are the only living mammal with hollow branched horns which are shed every year.

Coronado and other Spanish explorers saw antelope as far south as central Mexico; pronghorns ranged west to southern California and Baja, and north into the Canadian Great Plains. Alexander Henry wrote constantly of elk, moose, bear, and buffalo during his years in the Red River Valley, but only once mentions antelope: October 15, 1801—"An Indian brought me a large cabbrie, which had four inches of fat on the rump." But when he moved west, into the plains, "Cabbrie were in sight almost every moment, but so shy that we could not get a shot" (July 15, 1806).

Thus pronghorns once roamed over all of the Great Plains and into the deserts of the southwest. Pronghorns like it best in the open prairie where vegetation averages only 15 inches in height and is composed of a good

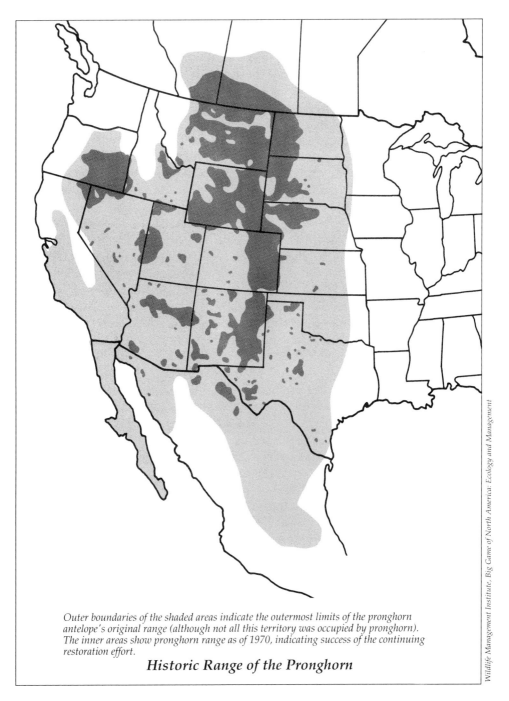

Outer boundaries of the shaded areas indicate the outermost limits of the pronghorn antelope's original range (although not all this territory was occupied by pronghorn). The inner areas show pronghorn range as of 1970, indicating success of the continuing restoration effort.

Historic Range of the Pronghorn

Wildlife Management Institute, Big Game of North America: Ecology and Management

variety of plants. They avoid the woods and the tall grass. "These animals appear...scattered over the plains which they seem invariably to prefer to the woodlands. if they happen accidentally in the woodlands and are allarmed they run immediately to the plains, seeming to plaise a just confidence in their superior fleetness..." (Lewis, July 25, 1805).

51

Pronghorns are well-designed for their native open grassland. On the northern plains, when the days grow short and the wind turns cold, the pronghorn's hair grows longer. The hairs themselves are hollow, which helps to insulate the animals from the cold. In the long hot summers of the plains, a pronghorn can make the hair on its body stand up to let the wind blow through to keep it cool.

Pronghorns eat grass, sagebrush, and other plants native to the prairies. They are not like buffalo; in winter they cannot sweep the snow aside to work their way down to the grass. When the snow gets too deep, pronghorns are forced to move to where the wind has blown the ground clear, or to places where there is less snow. It is the depth of the snow rather than temperature which forces pronghorns to move.

Indians and explorers took note of such seasonal movements. On October 17, 1804, William Clark wrote, "Great numbers of Goats are flocking down to the S. Side of the river, on their way to the Black Mountains where they winter. Those animals return in the Spring in the Same way & scatter in different directions." On April 9, 1805—the following spring—Lewis wrote, "Three miles above the mouth of this creek we passed a hunting camp of Minitres [Hidatsas] who…were waiting the return of the Antelope which usually pass the Missouri at this season of the year from the Black hills on the South side to the open plains on the north side of the river…" Most early journalists attributed such movements to true migrations; Clark, however, did note that on December 12, 1804, with the temperature at 38 below zero, there were "Great numbers of those animals [pronghorns]…near our fort (so that they do not all return to rock mountain…)."

Estimates of the pre-settlement pronghorn population rival those of the buffalo—perhaps as many as forty million animals. But we should note the conditions under which they lived. It was an open country, with no mountains pronghorns could not scale, no rivers they could not swim, and no fences they could not cross. There was the abundance and variety of plants which is typical of native prairie, but which is not typical of farms and towns. Pronghorns are tough animals, well-equipped for survival, but only under certain conditions. And conditions changed.

ANTELOPE HUNTING

Although pronghorns were not the storehouse of useful things that the buffalo were, they provided the Indians with food and clothing. The major trick for the Indians—for anyone, for that matter—was to catch them. Audubon wrote, "Nothing can be possibly keener than the senses of hearing and sight, as well as of smell, in the Antelope. Not one was ever known to jump up close to a hunter; and the very motion of the grasses, as these are wafted by the wind, will keep them awake and on the alert" (June 6, 1843). Audubon was very impressed with the pronghorn antelope.

52

ND State Historical Society

William Clark

The favorite method of catching antelope by the Missouri River tribes was to build a pound or pen and drive the the animals into it. Meriwether Lewis described the procedure:

> April 15, 1805—I saw the remains of several camps of the Assiniboins; near one of which, in a small revene, there was a park which they had formed of timber and brush, for the purpose of taking the cabrie or Antelope. it was constructed in the following manner. a strong pound was first made of timbers, on one side of which there was a small apparture, sufficiently large to admit an Antelope; from each side of this apparture a curtain was extended to a considerable distance, widening as they receded from the pound.

The antelope were then driven into the enclosure and, according to Audubon, "despatched with clubs."

There were other methods for taking antelope. One of the most effective was to take them while they were in the water. In order to get where they wanted to go, antelope frequently had to swim across streams and rivers. They did not seem to hesitate to swim, but they were not very good at it, and a man could easily overtake them. As William Clark wrote:

> October 16, 1804—Capt. Lewis & the Indian Chief walked on Shore, soon after I discovered great numbers of goats in the river and Indians on the Shore on each Side, as I approached...I discovered boys in the water Killing the goats with Sticks and halling them to Shore. Those on the banks Shot them with arrows and as they approached the Shore would turn them back. of this Gangue of Goats I counted 58 of which they had killed on the Shore, one of our hunters out with Capt. Lewis killed three Goats.

Antelope are the fastest mammals on the prairie, but they are sprinters rather than long-distance runners. Wolves learned to overcome the speed of the pronghorn with teamwork. "[W]e have frequently seen the wolves in pursuit of the Antelope in the plains; they appear to decoy a single one from the flock and then pursue it, alternately releiving each other untill they take it" (Lewis, April 29, 1805). The Indians took a page from the wolves' notebook in trying to run the antelope down with horses:

> August 14, 1805—This animal is so extreemly fleet and dureable that a single horse has no possible chance to over take them or run them down. The Indians are therefore obliged to have recorse to a strategem—when they discover a herd of Antelope they separate and scatter themselves to the distance of five or six miles in different directions arround them—generally selecting some commanding eminence for a stand; some one or two now pursue the herd at full speed over the hills and vallies, gullies and the sides of precipices that are tremendous to view. Thus after running them five or six or seven miles the fresh horses that were waiting head them and drive them back persuing as far or perhaps further quite to the other extreem of the hunters who now in turn pursue on their fresh horses thus worrying the poor animal down and finally killing them with their arrows...I was very much entertained with a view of this Indian chase; it was after a herd of about 10 antelope, and about 20 hunters. It lasted about 2 hours and considerable part of the chase was in view from my tent. About 1 p.m. the hunters returned–had not killed a single Antelope. My hunters returned soon after and had been equally unsuccessful... —*Lewis*

White explorers, trappers, and traders seemed to think of the antelope as an oddity to look at and a challenge to shoot. Audubon could only describe the pronghorn in terms of other animals: July 27, 1843—"The snorting of the Antelope is more like a whistling, sneezing sound, than like the long, clear snorting of our common Deer, and it is also very frequently repeated, say every few minutes, when in sight of an object of which the animal does not yet know the nature; for the moment it is assured of danger it bounds three or four times like a sheep, and then either trots off or gallops like a horse."

Antelope hunting in the West.

To shoot pronghorns, white explorers, too, had "recorse to a strategem." They soon learned that antelopes are curious animals who will investigate what puzzles them. Audubon, though he was more than sixty years old, did not stand on dignity when it came to trying to shoot antelope:

> July 21, 1843—We returned to the camp and saw a Wolf cross our path, and an Antelope looking at us. We determined to stop and try to bring him to us; I lay on my back and threw my legs up, kicking first one and then the other foot, and sure enough, the Antelope walked towards us, slowly and carefully, however. In about twenty minutes he had come two or three hundred yards; he was a superb male, and I looked at him for some minutes; when about sixty yards off I could see his eyes, and being loaded with buck-shot pulled the trigger without rising from my awkward position. Off he went; Harris fired, but he only ran faster for some hundred yards, when he turned, looked at us again, and was off.

Parker Gillmore, a sportsman who, in 1874 published his adventures in pursuit of game on the prairies, gave his thoughts on the subject of antelope hunting:

> ...From their wonderful fleetness and extreme watchfulness, horses and hounds are useless in their pursuit. Frequently, however, they are brought within range of the sportsman by waving a colored handkerchief or other unknown object.... I can imagine no weapon better suited for killing this game than the new express rifle. In no description of field-sports that I know of will the skill of the stalker be better tried than in the pursuit of this handsome indigenous game...(p. 130).

ANTELOPE AND THE SETTLERS

There was never a concerted effort to hunt antelope the way there was for buffalo. None of the early writers saw the destruction of the immense herds of antelope as a necessary prelude to the settlement of the country. Audubon foresaw the end of the buffalo as early as 1843, but no one foresaw an end for the antelope. Yet by the turn of the century, antelope were—like the buffalo—facing extinction.

The fate of the antelope in what is now North Dakota is typical of what happened everywhere. Before 1870 there were almost no settlers in North Dakota, and antelope ranged throughout the state, except for parts of the Red River Valley, and wooded places such as the Turtle Mountains. Settlement began to fill in the country in the 1870s as the Indians were forced onto reservations and the railroads advanced east to west. In the late 1870s and early 1880s, farming operations spread out of the Red River Valley west as bonanza farmers demonstrated the fertility of the soil and the government made land cheap. Vernon Bailey, interviewing settlers for his **Biological Survey of North Dakota** in 1926, learned that in the Devils Lake area, antelope "were numerous...up to 1872 and common to 1876," but only "a few remained into the eighties." Antelope persisted longer in the northwest: "In 1887 the animals were reported as still common in the Mouse River country" (Bailey, 1926, p.29).

Morris Johnson, interviewing old-timers in the 1960s for his **Feathers From the Prairie**, heard much the same story—of antelope being pushed west in front of settlement:

> Charles Wenz, born in New Rockford in 1888: There have never been any [antelope] around while I've lived here.

> H.B. Spiller, Cavalier: I remember seeing a bunch of antelope on the prairie in Dickey County when I was 12-13 years old [1887-88]. They were wild and we could not get too close to them.

56

Everett Hyatt, who had lived at Ludden since 1898: We've never seen any around here in our time, but there were supposedly a lot here earlier.

Fred Petrie, Linton: I can remember when I was four years old in 1895 seeing antelope northeast of Linton about 10 miles. There were seven in the bunch. In 1887 the old timers said a herd of 35 antelope passed through the Winchester area.

Ben Baenen, Jamestown: The last ones I ever saw in this area were sometime after 1894.

Ludwig Lesmeister, who came to Harvey in 1895: I would estimate that by 1908-09 they were extinct in this area.

Arthur Anderson, Belfield: Antelope were thick on our homestead between 1884-1890 and our family lived on antelope the year around...As near as I can remember the big population decline had started by 1900 or before.

George Harvey, Williston: When I was here in 1894 or 95 I saw three local hunters with 25 or 30 antelope they'd killed and stacked on a bobsled. They had been killed north of here someplace, but not too far away. The antelope were killed off by the late 1890s.

By the time people were moving onto the shorter-grass prairies—the good antelope range—buffalo were just about done as a major pioneer food source. Antelope, hard as they were to hunt, filled the gap. Without the wildlife of the grassland, many people would have starved. But since they saw wildlife as something which would tide them over until their farms and livestock operations became productive and profitable, few settlers looked ahead.

Overhunting was only one of several aspects of settlement which changed conditions of life for antelope. Two farm and ranch tools—the plow and the fence—may have done much more damage. The plow uprooted the native prairie and put in its place nice rows of plants which the antelope had never learned to eat; and fences—fences are worse yet. Antelope are made for wide-open spaces, made for traveling long distances when food supplies are short as they are in hard winters; antelope are long-sighted and fast running. But they will seldom jump fences, and so their natural defenses were of no value in this new situation. Antelope became far more vulnerable to hunters and predators; competition between antelope and domestic livestock became serious; antelope range shrank until the only places for antelope were places which were of no great value to people—and which would support only greatly reduced numbers of antelope.

Early North Dakota antelope hunters, probably before 1900.

In 1880, there were 4,000 farms in North Dakota, totalling a little more than a million acres. By 1920, there were 78,000 farms, totalling thirty-six and a quarter million acres. In 1925, E. W. Nelson wrote his famous report on the status of antelope in North Dakota: "Antelope have almost disappeared from North Dakota. The remaining herds now number only five and aggregate only 225 animals. Their future appears to be extremely doubtful...."

The situation across the entire range of the pronghorn was equally dismal. E. W. Nelson (1925) estimated the total North American antelope population to be 26,700 animals. People had been aware of the dwindling populations for some years. As early as 1894 the North Dakota Game and Fish Commissioner had written, "We have but a few of the following animals in our State: fawns, elks, moose, buffalo, mountain sheep, caribou, and antelopes, and as they are valuable animals, and much desired for food purposes, it is evidently wise to protect them for a series of years" (ND Game and Fish Comm., 1894, p. 5). People knew about the problem, but they didn't know what could be done about it. In the same 1894 report, the Game and Fish Commissioner wrote, "On assuming the duties of this office I made these discoveries: An almost universal belief amongst the people that...anyone was at liberty to remove fish from our waters in any manner that might suit his convenience, and to kill game birds and animals at any season of the year, and to ship them to any point within and without the State, at any time and in any quantity as might be convenient or desirable" (p. 9).

A day's sport in Dakota.

Saving the pronghorn from extinction would be an uphill battle, to say the least. At the time, concerned people had no tools to work with. Game and Fish officers had a little enforcement power and a lot of hope. Most of their hope was put into refuges. The 1923-24 report of the North Dakota State Game and Fish Commission stated, "We have approximately 200 head (of antelope) roaming in chosen localities, usually in small bands. If we want to keep them for posterity a determined effort must be made in the next few years to provide large reserves for them" (p. 11). But it was a dimming hope. In their very next report, the Commission reported, "Our antelope are not increasing as they should...The problem of providing absolute protection for them is very difficult and practically impossible" (p. 20).

And so it would remain for another 25 years. The story of the recovery of the pronghorn antelope will be carried on in Part II—the era of Game Management.

Sources

Journals of Early Explorers

Audubon, John James

   Audubon, Maria R. 1986. Audubon and His Journals, With Zoological and Other Notes by Elliott Coues. 2 Vols. Dover Books, New York.

Henry, Alexander

   Coues, Elliott, ed. 1965. New Light on the History of the Greater Northwest: The Manuscript Journals of Alexander Henry and David Thompson. 2 Vols. Ross and Haines, Inc., Minneapolis.

   Reid, Russell and Clell G. Gannon. 1928. Natural History Notes on the Journals of Alexander Henry. North Dakota Historical Quarterly 2(3):168-201.

Lewis and Clark

   Burroughs, Raymond Darwin. 1961. The Natural History of the Lewis and Clark Expedition. Michigan State University Press.

   Cutright, Paul R. 1969. Lewis and Clark: Pioneering Naturalists. University of Nebraska Press.

   Reid, Russell. 1988. Lewis and Clark in North Dakota. State Historical Society of North Dakota, Bismarck.

   Thwaites, Reuben Gold, ed. 1905. Original Journals of the Lewis and Clark Expedition. 8 Vols. Dodd, Mead, and Co, New York.

Maximilian, Prince of Weid

   Thomas, Davis and Karin Ronnefeldt. 1976. People of the First Man: Life Among the Plains Indians in Their Final Days of Glory. Dutton, New York.

   Thwaites, Reuben Gold, ed. 1906. Early Western Travels, Vols 22-25. Arthur H. Clark Co, Cleveland.

Nicolette, Joseph N.

   Bray, Edward C. and Martha Coleman Bray, eds. and trans. 1976. Joseph N. Nicolette on the Expeditions of 1838-39 with Journals, Letters and Notes on the Dakota Indians. Minnesota Historical Press, St. Paul.

Other Sources

Bailey, Vernon. 1926. A Biological Survey of North Dakota. North American Fauna No. 49. U.S. Bureau of Biological Survey.

Gillmore, Parker. 1874. Prairie and Forest: A Description of the Game of North America with Personal Adventures in Their Pursuit. Harper and Bros., New York.

Johnson, Morris D. 1962. Old Timer's Statements. North Dakota Game and Fish Department, Bismarck.

Nelson, E. W. 1925. The Status of the Pronghorn Antelope, 1922-25. U.S. Dept. of Agric. Bulletin No. 1364.

North Dakota Game and Fish Commission. 1894. 1st Biennial Report of the State Game and Fish Commission. North Dakota Game and Fish Department, Bismarck.

North Dakota Game and Fish Commission. 1924. Eighth Biennial Report of the State Game and Fish Commission. North Dakota Game and Fish Department, Bismarck.

Ovis canadensis auduboni

CHAPTER FOUR

THE AUDUBON BIGHORN

Once upon a time there were eight races of bighorn sheep. Now there are only seven: *Ovis canadensis canadensis*, the Rocky Mountain bighorn; *O. canadensis californiana*, the California bighorn; and five races of desert bighorns, which are *O. c. nelsoni*, *O. c. mexicana*, *O. c. texiana*, *O. c. cremnobates*, and *O. c. weemsi*. The race of bighorns which is extinct is the one that lived in the Badlands of North Dakota and South Dakota—*O. c. auduboni*, the Audubon bighorn.

Vernon Bailey, in **A Biological Survey of North Dakota** (1926) describes the Audubon bighorn as possibly the largest of the bighorn sheep, as big or bigger than the Rocky Mountain bighorn. Its development, like that of bison and other giants of the earth, owes much to the ice age. Bighorns "appear to be the offspring of the Rupicaprini, the goat antelopes...[a group of] short-horned, light-skulled, generally hairy bovids of small size" (Geist, 1971, p. 1); during Pleistocene times—the ice age—they were pushed by monstrous glacial forces in the direction of the big horned, thick skulled, generally hairy bovids we have now.

When the pre-ice age climate grew cooler and drier, and grasslands invaded the forest, a vast new food supply became available. Such mammals as could take advantage grew huge on the abundance. When the climate got cooler yet, and ice began to spread over the food supply, the large mammals were better equipped to survive. "A large animal has proportionately less skin surface in relation to body volume than does a small animal. In cold climates this makes large size an advantage for retaining body heat." And "when two members of a species compete for food, the larger one can usually find more to eat" (Geist, 1987, p. 313).

During the Pleistocene, climates cooled and then warmed, and glaciers flowed and ebbed like an immeasurably slow tide. During warmer, ice-free interludes, large and hardy ice age mammals surged into the newly exposed food supply, and grew even larger. Advancing ice would consolidate the gains of the mammals which could survive the new harshness in the climate and cope successfully with new scarcity in the food supply. The others were driven to extinction.

As well as large bodies, these ice age mammals grew large horns and antlers. There are plenty of examples besides the wild sheep. The early North American bison, *Bison latifrons*, (see Chapter One) had horns measuring nine feet tip to tip. The so-called Irish Elk (*Megacerous*), and even today's North American elk owes his antlers to that Pleistocene extravagance. It was, apparently, first a matter of food: when the ice retreated, there was more food than these animals were used to.

64

GEOLOGIC TIME SCALE

ERA	PERIOD		EPOCH	APPROXIMATE TIME BOUNDARIES	LIFE FORMS ORIGINATING
CENOZOIC	QUATERNARY		RECENT		MAN
			PLEISTOCENE	2,500,000 YRS.	
	TERTIARY		PLIOCENE	12,000,000	
			MIOCENE	26,000,000	
			OLIGOCENE	38,000,000	
			EOCENE	54,000,000	
			PALEOCENE	65,000,000	
MESOZOIC	CRETACEOUS			136,000,000	PRIMATES — FLOWERING PLANTS
	JURASSIC			195,000,000	DINOSAURS — BIRDS
	TRIASSIC			225,000,000	MAMMALS
PALEOZOIC	PERMIAN			280,000,000	
	CARBON-IFEROUS	PENNSYLVANIAN		320,000,000	REPTILES
		MISSISSIPPIAN		345,000,000	
	DEVONIAN			395,000,000	AMPHIBIANS
	SILURIAN			430,000,000	VASCULAR LAND PLANTS
	ORDOVICIAN			500,000,000	
	CAMBRIAN			570,000,000	FISH — CHORDATES
PRECAMBRIAN				(700,000,000) (1,500,000,000) (3,500,000,000) 4,650,000,000 + (FORMATION OF THE EARTH)	INVERTEBRATES EUCARYOTIC CELLS PROCARYOTIC CELLS

Funk and Wagnalls New Encyclopedia, 1986

Nutritional needs being answered, the excess was put into such luxuries as larger horns. Bigger horns were an advantage—as weapons, say, the largest-horned male being best able to defend himself and best able to reproduce himself by driving poorly equipped rivals away from females. Then the horns exerted evolutionary pressures of their own, selecting for skull structures and so on which reflected how the horns were used.

Thus mountain sheep are a true ice age animal—large-bodied, large-horned, and well-adapted to cold and dry climates. The ebb of ice sheets opened large continuous expanses of new habitat, allowing mountain sheep to spread across an arc of mountain ranges through Europe, Asia, and North America; the flow of glaciers separated groups of sheep for immense periods of time, leaving them to evolve in similar but separate patterns. It is thought that mountain sheep crossed over the Siberian-Alaskan land bridge sometime late in the ice age—although it is hard to tell with any certainty from the fossil record. Mountain sheep live in rocky, mountainous habitat which was ground away at by successive continental ice sheets, and the fossil record is scanty. Once on the North American side, however, it appears that sheep were divided into two groups and pursued two separate evolutionary paths–the thinhorn sheep—*Ovis dalli*—in the north, and the bighorns—*Ovis canadensis*—in the south.

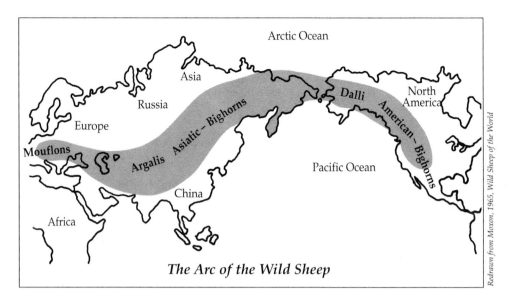

The labels on the map read: Arctic Ocean, Asia, Russia, Europe, Dalli, North America, Mouflons, Argalis, Asiatic~Bighorns, American~Bighorns, China, Pacific Ocean, Africa

The Arc of the Wild Sheep

THE BIGHORN AND HIS HABITAT

Even though the races of sheep are different, adapted to a wonderful range of temperatures and elevations, bighorn sheep share a few basic habitat requirements. They live in rough, steep, and slippery terrain where few other large mammals—particularly meat eating ones—can follow, and where open stands of grass and shrubs are nearby to provide food. Like buffalo and antelope, bighorns are ruminants (see Chapter One). But they are able to make use of different foods than either buffalo or antelope, and so they do not directly compete:

> Mountain sheep are some of the most specialized grazers, for they can live on hard, abrasive, dry plants. The grasses and herbs they pluck are often covered with dust and grit in the absence of snow. To counteract wear, sheep, like most grazers, evolved very long and broad molar teeth which are pushed out throughout life…Sheep also have a larger rumen than deer of equal size, which indicates that the tough grasses and dry plants are subject to a relatively longer period of digestion by bacteria than the softer browse plants on which deer feed…By being able to live on dry, dusty plants, sheep can exploit a reserve of poor forage and thrive where many other herbivores cannot (Geist, 1971, p. 11).

Much has been made of the hoof structure of bighorn sheep. Bighorn sheep have two-toed hoofs which are sharply edged and which are concave on the bottom, and sheep are remarkably sure-footed on the steep and slippery terrain where they choose to live. Bighorns also have remarkable jumping abilities, and when they are alarmed, they head for the rocks, jumping to places where few if any large animals can follow.

66

Bighorns are never far from such escape routes. Indeed, studies of their heart rates show that the farther they are from escape cover, the more stress they appear to suffer.

Bighorns' ability to eat tough dry forage and their ability to clamber around on steep and slippery surfaces are physical adaptations to their environment. Bighorns have also evolved social behavior which, like that of the buffalo, once allowed them to survive, but now, in a changed environment, might work against them. The following are examples of adaptive behavior, and are by no means an attempt to describe all there is to know about sheep behavior.

Bighorn sheep are social animals. They stay in groups and they occupy the same ranges year to year. To see these things as strategies for survival, we again have to go back to the retreat of the glacial ice sheets.

Thousands of years ago, the retreating glaciers left behind huge expanses of habitat which were favorable to bighorn sheep. Sheep which lived at the edges of these ice sheets followed the retreat. These new grasslands stimulated the increased horn size and body size we have already talked about. But it was not a situation which could go on forever. There came a time—some 10,000 years ago, when the last glacier had melted—when the range was no longer expanding and the available range was filled to capacity with bighorn sheep. Under these new conditions there was no advantage to being able to colonize new areas. In response to new conditions, sheep evolved new patterns of behavior, among them, staying in groups, and occupying the same home ranges year after year. Geist (1971, p. 126) explains:

> In this situation, no juvenile going out on its own could possibly discover new habitat. He can only find habitat...already exploited by the population...[or] miles of unsuitable terrain where he could be easily lost or killed. Dispersing juveniles have nothing to gain and everything to lose. Therefore, selection would be against dispersing juveniles and in favor of those that stick with older sheep and follow them...

It might be pointed out here that such group behavior is an advantage when sheep live in stable habitat for a long period of time. As we shall see in Part II of this book, it is not an advantage when you are trying to transplant sheep into new habitat.

Sheep live in social groups because it was advantageous to do so. As might be expected, this pattern of behavior has led to others. For example: to live in such groups, conflicts between sheep somehow have to be limited—a tall order when you consider the equipment carried by bighorn rams. In fact, however, most social ranking among bighorn rams is accomplished without head-to-head battles. Bighorn rams seem to be able to associate horn size to combat potential, and serious fighting takes place between rams of equal rank—that is to say, of equal horn size. "Male

Bighorns – a typical group in typical surroundings.

Ed Bry

dominance and breeding success run parallel with horn size, and rams use their horns not only as weapons or shields but also as rank symbols. A ram can thus tell a stranger's dominance rank from the size of his horns. These rank symbols allow rams to live in a predictable social surrounding and permit sheep to live in an open society. The largest-horned ram in a band automatically becomes the leader of the band since small rams follow him" (Geist, 1971, p. 131).

In their own way, bighorns were as successful in rough terrain as buffalo and antelope were on the open plain. Like the buffalo and antelope they are physically well-designed and socially well-adapted for the situations in which they live. Bighorn sheep have been around for a very long time, and their numbers remained stable until large numbers of people penetrated their habitat. And even then, only one race of bighorns has been driven to extinction, that being, of course, the Audubon bighorn.

O. C. AUDUBONI—THE AUDUBON BIGHORN

Joseph Fields, a member of the Lewis and Clark Expedition, is given credit for being the first white man to see a living Audubon bighorn sheep.

> April 26, 1805—Joseph Fields discovered a large creek falling into the Yellowstone River on the S.E. side 8 miles up near which he saw a big horned animal, he found in the Prarie the horn of one of those animals which was large and appeared to have laid several years. —Clark

One of the primary aims of the Lewis and Clark Expedition was to record and describe all of the new plants and animals they encountered in this unexplored region—which explains why they are given credit for so many "discoveries." The duties of chief naturalist fell to Meriwether Lewis, in whose abilities President Thomas Jefferson had great faith. Jefferson described Lewis as "guarded, by exact observation of the vegetables and animals of his country, against losing time in the description of objects already possessed; honest, disinterested, liberal, of sound understanding, and a fidelity to truth so scrupulous that whatever he should report would be as certain as if seen by ourselves..." (Cutright, 1969, p. 17). Lewis seems to have justified such praise. Even though he could not name many of the animals he saw, his descriptions were accurate enough to allow later scientists to make the identification.

But Lewis was more than the impersonal recording machine that Thomas Jefferson described. Lewis was an adventurer, and the thought of each new sight gave him a thrill of anticipation. As the expedition left the Mandan villages in the spring of 1805 Lewis wrote (April 7, 1805):

69

This little fleet altho' not quite so rispectable as those of Columbus or Capt. Cook, were still viewed by us with as much pleasure as those deservedly famed adventurers ever beheld theirs; and I dare say with quite as much anxiety for their safety and preservation. we were now about to penetrate a country at least two thousand miles in width, on which the foot of civilized man had never trodden; the good or evil it had in store for us was for experiment yet to determine...the picture which now presented itself to me was a most pleasing one. entertaining as I do, the most confident hope of succeeding in a voyage which had formed a darling project of mine for the last ten years, I could but esteem this moment of my departure as among the most happy of my life.

Meriwether Lewis

ND State Historical Society

Lewis and Clark expected to find a bighorned animal on the upper Missouri. In October of 1804, they had learned from M. Jean Valle', a Frenchman living at the mouth of the Cheyenne River, that 300 miles above they would find a "kind of anamale with circular horns, this anamale is nearly the size of a Small Elk" (Clark, Oct. 1, 1804). They had a further description from the Missouri River tribes during the winter of 1804-05: "We procured two horns of the animale the french Call the rock Mountain Sheep those horns are not of the largest kind The Mandans Indians Call this sheep *Ar-Sar-ta* it is about the Size of a large Deer, or Small Elk, its Horns Come out and wind around the head like the horn of a Ram and the tecture not unlike it much larger and thicker, perticelarly that part with which they butt..." (Clark, Dec. 22. 1804).

Though Joseph Fields finally saw the live animal on the Yellowstone, Lewis and Clark were not able to shoot a bighorn while they were still in North Dakota. The animals were "so shy [they] could not get a shoot at them" (Lewis). Lewis gave a lengthy description of the Rocky Mountain bighorn, great numbers of which the expedition saw—and marveled at— in what is now Montana:

> May 25, 1805—The head and horns are remarkably large compared with the other part of the anamal.... [T]he head nostrils and division of the upper lip are precisely in form like the sheep. there legs resemble the sheep more than any other anamal with which I am acquainted tho' they are more delicately formed...the hoof is black and large in proportion, is divided, very open and roundly pointed at the toe, like the sheep, is much hollowed and sharp on the under edge like the Scotch goat.... The horns are largest at their base, and occupy the crown of the head almost entirely. they are compressed, bent backwards and lunated; the surface swelling into wavey rings which incircleing the horn continue to succeed each other from the base to the extremity and becoming less elivated and more distant as they recede from the head. the head for about two thirds of it's length is filled with a porus bone which is united with the frontal bone...[T]hey feed on grass but principally on the arromatic herbs which grow on the clifts at inaccessable hights which they usually frequent. the places they generally scelect to lodg is the cranies or crevices of the rocks in the faces of inaccessable precepices, where the wolf nor bear can reach them and where indeed man himself would in many instances find a similar deficiency; yet those anamals bound from rock to rock and stand apparently in the most careless manner on the sides of precepices of many hundreds of feet. they are very shye and are quick of both sent and sight.

Lewis's enthusiasm for his task gave his descriptions more scope than Clark's. Clark's reports seem bare: "On the side of the Hill near the place we dined [we] saw a gangue of...bighorn Animals I shot at them running and missed." Lewis brings more of his senses into use: "the flesh of this animal is extremely delicate, tender and well flavoured; they are now in fine order. Their flesh both in colour and flavour much resembles mutton though it is not so strong as our mutton." Even though he had no formal education in the natural sciences—or as an author—Lewis's journal is a remarkably complete picture of the expedition.

Bighorns along the Missouri – from a painting by Karl Bodmer.

One of the best-trained men to write about the bighorn in the early days was, of course, John James Audubon. Audubon had read about the country he was visiting, Lewis's and Clark's journals included; and he was ready to test earlier reports with his own eyes:

> June 29, 1843—Provost told me (and he is a respectable man) that during the breeding season of the Mountain Ram, the battering of the horns is often heard as far as a mile away, and that at such times they are approached with comparative ease; and there is no doubt that it is during such encounters that the horns are broken and twisted as I have seen them, and not by leaping from high places and falling on their horns, as poetical travellers have asserted.

Audubon brought considerable skepticism with him to the Upper Missouri. He was suspicious of most of what he had read, especially the work of George Catlin. "We have seen much remarkably handsome scenery, but nothing at all comparing with Catlin's descriptions; his book must, after all, be altogether a humbug" (June 11, 1843). Audubon had an equally low opinion of the hunters he hired to bring him bighorns for his collection. "I fear that all my former opinions…are likely to be realized; and I expect now that we shall have to make a regular turn-out ourselves, to kill both Grizzly Bears and Bighorns" (July 29, 1843). But Audubon was very impressed with the bighorn sheep which later bore his name:

> August 13, 1843—No one who has not seen these places [the Badlands] can form any idea of the resorts of the Rocky Mountain Rams, or the difficulty of approaching them, putting aside their extreme wildness and their marvellous activity. They form paths around these broken-headed cones (that are from three to fifteen hundred feet high) and run round them at full speed on a track that, to the hunter, does not appear to be more than a few inches wide, but which is, in fact, from a foot to eighteen inches in width. In some places there are piles of earth from eight to ten feet high, or even more, the tops of which form platforms of a hard and shelly rocky substance, where the bighorn is often seen looking on the hunter far below and standing immovable, as if a statue. No one can imagine how they reach these places, and that too, with their young, even when the latter are quite small. Hunters say that the young are usually born in such places, the mothers going there to save the helpless little one from the Wolves, which, after men, seem to be their greatest destroyers…Oftentimes when a Bighorn is seen on a hill-top, the hunter has to ramble about for three or four miles before he can aproach within gunshot of the game, and if the Bighorn ever sees his enemy, pursuit is useless.

When Audubon and his party did "make a regular turn-out" themselves to hunt bighorns, they had just as poor luck as the previous hunters. On August 9, 1843, Audubon wrote, "Squires, Provost, and La Fleur went off this morning…for Bighorns with orders not to return without some of these wild animals." On August 11, he wrote, "Squires returned this afternoon alone, having left Provost and La Fleur behind." And on August 12, "Provost returned with La Fleur this afternoon, had nothing." By that time Audubon knew the frustrations of hunting bighorns because he had tried it himself:

> August 13, 1843—The hunter sometimes, after toiling for an hour or two up the side of one of these hills, trying to reach the top in hopes that when there he will have for a short distance at least, either a level place or good path to walk on, finds to his disappointment that he has secured a point…scarcely large

enough to stand on…. I was thus deceived time and again, while in search of Bighorns. If the hill does not terminate in a point it is connected with another hill by a ridge so narrow that nothing but a Bighorn can walk on it. This is the country that the Mountain Ram inhabits, and if, from this imperfect description, any information can be derived, I shall be more than repaid for the trouble I have had in these tiresome hills…From the character of the lands where these animals are found, their own shyness, watchfulness, and agility, it is readily seen what the hunter must endure, and what difficulties he must undergo to [get] near these "Wild Goats." It is one constant time of toil, anxiety, fatigue, and danger. Such the country! Such the animal! Such the hunting!

The Indians of the region apparently had some luck hunting the bighorn because they made good use of his hide and horns. Meriwether Lewis wrote (May 25, 1805), "The horn is of a light brown colour; when dressed it is almost white extreemly transparent and very elastic…I have no doubt but it would make eligant and useful hair combs, and might answer as many valuable purposes to civilized man as it does to the savages, who form their water-cups, spoons and platters of it." Bighorns were by no means as useful to the Indians as other animals, no doubt because they were so difficult to hunt. The most unexpected use made of the horns was a bow constructed by laminating pieces of horn together: "[T]he bows of the bighorn are formed of small peices laid flat and cemented with gleue and rolled with sinews, after which they are covered on the back with sinews and glew, and highly ornamented as they are much prized" (Lewis, Aug. 23, 1805). According to a note by Audubon, such bows were valued more highly than a gun: July 6, 1843—"Boucherville came to me, and told me that…a rascally Indian had stolen his gun and Bighorn bow; the gun he said he could easily replace, but the loss of the bow he regretted exceedingly."

Bighorn meat was a delicacy prized by all early explorers and trappers. We have noted Lewis's remarks about its delicate flavor; David Thompson, who dined on Rocky Mountain bighorn meat first in November of 1800, found it to be "exceedingly sweet and tender and moderately fat" (Wishart, 1978, p. 161). Audubon does not mention eating bighorn meat, which is surprising because he—although fussy about his food—at least tasted what others seemed to relish. Audubon thought, for example, that antelope was "dry and usually tough." When offered a dog to eat, Audubon "with great care and some repugnance…put a very small piece in my mouth; but no sooner had the taste touched my palate than I changed my dislike to liking, and found this victim of the canine order most excellent" (July 12, 1843). On his return journey from the Missouri he wrote, "I cannot eat beef after being fed on Buffaloes" (Sept. 28, 1843). It seems that if Audubon had eaten bighorn, he would have had something to say about it.

THE END OF A LINE

By the time that big-time hunters and sportsmen like John Palliser, Parker Gillmore, and Theodore Roosevelt came to hunt the wild sheep of the Badlands, not nearly so many of them were left to hunt. Gillmore came in the early 1870s and Roosevelt in the 1880s; the time between abundance and scarcity was not very long at all. The date of the last known kill of Audubon bighorns in North Dakota has been reported as 1905 by Bailey (1926); as "around 1903" by Arthur Anderson (Johnson, 1962); and "approximately 1907-08" by Chris Rasmussen (Johnson, 1962). It is generally agreed that the last Audubon bighorn anywhere was gone by 1910.

No one seems to have ever tried to estimate the numbers of Audubon bighorns at the time of their peak abundance. Considering the size of their range, there could never have been very many. Almost all of the written accounts are from the North Dakota Badlands. Although Lewis and Clark had heard descriptions of bighorns and had seen shirts made of bighorn leather and utensils made of horn among the Mandans in 1804-05 (Clark bought a pair of horns from the Indians in December of 1804), no one from the expedition saw a live sheep until they reached the mouth of the Yellowstone the following spring. Both Maximilian in 1833 and Audubon in 1843 first reported bighorns above the mouth of the Little Knife River, near where New Town is today. William Clark records seeing a "large gangue of ewes & yearlins & fawns…of the big horn" in the area of the Yellowstone on his return trip in 1806. Audubon reports seeing bighorns mostly in groups of twos and threes. A group of twenty was remarkable, and his desire to collect eight or ten bighorn rams was still unrealized when he left Fort Union in August, 1843.

It is from sketchy reports like these that biologists have estimated the probable Audubon bighorn range. The heart of the range appears to have been the badlands country west of the Missouri, particularly the river breaks and buttes along the Little Missouri River. Audubon bighorns were common in the Black Hills of South Dakota, and, according to Harold Cook (1931), extended into northwestern Nebraska where he found a skull and horns. According to Buechner (1960, p. 13), the "[e]asternmost extensions of the [Audubon] range terminated approximately at the badlands of the Little Missouri River in western North Dakota, the badlands and Pine Ridge east of the Black Hills of South Dakota, [and] extreme northwestern Nebraska." Although a population of sheep once occupied the breaks of the North Platte River, the race of the sheep is "of questionable designation" (Buechner, 1960, p. 21). A map of the estimated range of the Audubon bighorn is on page 76.

At one time it was apparently accepted that Audubon bighorns were common on the open prairie and were driven to badlands terrain by

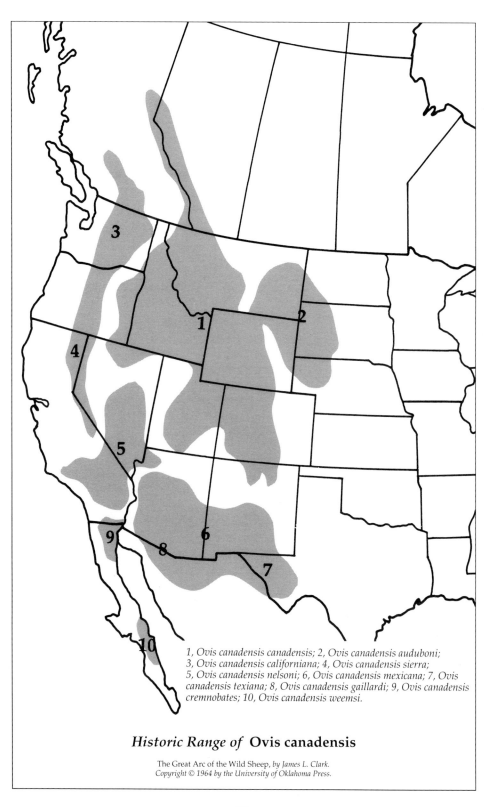

1, *Ovis canadensis canadensis*; 2, *Ovis canadensis auduboni*; 3, *Ovis canadensis californiana*; 4, *Ovis canadensis sierra*; 5, *Ovis canadensis nelsoni*; 6, *Ovis canadensis mexicana*; 7, *Ovis canadensis texiana*; 8, *Ovis canadensis gaillardi*; 9, *Ovis canadensis cremnobates*; 10, *Ovis canadensis weemsi*.

Historic Range of **Ovis canadensis**

The Great Arc of the Wild Sheep, *by James L. Clark.*
Copyright © 1964 by the University of Oklahoma Press.

hunters and settlers. People often say the same about elk. Although there were elk on the prairie when Lewis and Clark came to North Dakota, bighorns were never found far from the rough country so picturesquely described by Audubon. Nor, for that matter, were elk "driven" into the mountains. For elk history, look ahead to the next chapter.

The rapid plunge in bighorn populations in all ranges, and the extinction of the Audubon bighorn has been blamed on overhunting, on disease brought by domestic livestock, and on competition for the range by other grazers—mostly domestic sheep and cattle. It is not surprising that the Audubon bighorn race has disappeared. They were, as best can be determined, the fewest in number of all races of bighorns; they were, perhaps, the most specialized in terms of habitat; and their range was probably the most accessible to hunters and the most favorable for ranching.

But to really understand what happened to the Audubon bighorn sheep you have to remember what was going on in their primary range during the years between 1870 and 1890. In 1871, 1872, and 1873, survey parties for the Northern Pacific Railway were marking out the rail line in western North Dakota and eastern Montana. In 1874, George Custer returned from an expedition to the Black Hills with news of gold. In 1876, Custer met his end at the Little Big Horn, which brought more soldiers to the region. By 1879 the Northern Pacific was pushing west from Bismarck, and the army

Northern Pacific cattle train, late 1800s.

built a post at the crossing of the Little Missouri River—just about where Medora is today. In the early 1880s cattlemen began pushing longhorn cattle up from Texas to start large-scale ranching along the Little Missouri River.

That is a lot of activity for a place that is, after all, not very big. The railroad brought meat hunters, and reports of the good hunting brought sportsmen. A man named Frank Moore, once the post trader at the infantry post on the Little Missouri, opened the Pyramid Park Hotel for hunting parties, and attracted such notables as Howard Eaton and Theodore Roosevelt.

Probably of greater impact—or perhaps the final nail in the coffin—for the Audubon bighorn was the cattle and sheep industry. Men like Roosevelt and Eaton, men who had come to the Badlands first to hunt, returned to ranch. By 1884 there may have been 150,000 thousand head of cattle and sheep along the Little Missouri River (Robinson, 1966, p. 188).

With all of the new activity, some of the sheep's centuries-old survival techniques worked against them. An example: in bighorn society, the largest-horned rams are also the most dominant rams. They are the rams best equipped to perpetuate the species. But since they also make the best trophies, in the days of uncontrolled hunting, the best were the first to go.

Another example. Sheep occupy traditional ranges year after year, young sheep learning from older ones. When competition for the range came in the form of thousands of domestic cattle and sheep, bighorns had no adaptive mechanism to search out new range. Even though large-scale cattle ranching in the Badlands was wiped out by overgrazing and bitter winters in 1885 and 1886, sheep did not fill out the suddenly vacated range.

Disease may also have been a factor in the extinction of the Audubon bighorn. There is evidence that diseases from domestic sheep, particularly scabies, transferred to wild sheep during this period. Wild sheep, of course, had no resistance to the disease. No one knows, however, how large a factor this may have been in the extermination of the Audubon bighorn.

By the 1890s there were only a few bighorns left in the Badlands. Chris Rasmussen, an old-timer interviewed by Morris Johnson in 1960, felt that by that time people were leaving the bighorns alone. "The few mountain sheep still left in the 90s generally weren't hunted." Elizabeth Roberts, who became North Dakota's first female game warden in the 1920s, said (Johnson, 1962) "My husband, Frank Roberts...shot...a ewe in 1896 15 miles south of Medora on the east side of the Little Missouri River. The ewe had a baby and I took it to raise. I raised the little female on a bottle until it was about six months old and then sold it for $50.00 to Schenley Park, Pittsburg, Pennsylvania. The Park had a male mountain sheep and wanted the female to complete the pair.... I heard afterwards the female was killed by the male...."

Vernon Bailey (1926) reported that the last Audubon bighorn in North

Dakota was an old ram killed in around 1905 on Magpie Creek near Grassy Butte. Although the story of the Audubon bighorn came to an end there, a new chapter for bighorns in North Dakota started to be written very near this same spot some fifty years later. The record of the bighorn restoration in North Dakota will be continued in Part II.

Audubon Bighorns taken near Fairfield, ND, 1894.

Osborn Studio, Dickinson, ND and ND Game and Fish Department

Sources

Journals of Early Explorers

Audubon, John James

Audubon, Maria R. 1986. Audubon and His Journals, With Zoological and Other Notes by Elliott Coues. 2 Vols. Dover Books, New York.

Henry, Alexander

Coues, Elliott, ed. 1965. New Light on the History of the Greater Northwest: The Manuscript Journals of Alexander Henry and David Thompson. 2 Vols. Ross and Haines, Inc., Minneapolis.

Reid, Russell and Clell G. Gannon. 1928. Natural History Notes on the Journals of Alexander Henry. North Dakota Historical Quarterly 2(3):168-201.

Lewis and Clark

Burroughs, Raymond Darwin. 1961. The Natural History of the Lewis and Clark Expedition. Michigan State University Press.

Cutright, Paul R. 1969. Lewis and Clark: Pioneering Naturalists. University of Nebraska Press.

Reid, Russell. 1988. Lewis and Clark in North Dakota. State Historical Society of North Dakota, Bismarck.

Thwaites, Reuben Gold, ed. 1905. Original Journals of the Lewis and Clark Expedition. 8 Vols. Dodd, Mead, and Co, New York.

Maximilian, Prince of Weid

Thomas, Davis and Karin Ronnefeldt. 1976. People of the First Man: Life Among the Plains Indians in Their Final Days of Glory. Dutton, New York.

Thwaites, Reuben Gold, ed. 1906. Early Western Travels, Vols 22-25. Arthur H. Clark Co, Cleveland.

Nicolette, Joseph N.

Bray, Edward C. and Martha Coleman Bray, eds. and trans. 1976. Joseph N. Nicolette on the Expeditions of 1838-39 with Journals, Letters and Notes on the Dakota Indians. Minnesota Historical Press, St. Paul.

Other Sources

Bailey, Vernon. 1926. A Biological Survey of North Dakota. North American Fauna No. 49. U.S. Bureau of Biological Survey.

Buechner, Helmut K. 1960. The Bighorn Sheep in the United States, Its Past, Present and Future. Wildlife Monograph No. 4. The Wildlife Society, Washington, D.C.

Cook, Harold. 1931. A Mountain Sheep Record for Nebraska. J. Mammal. 12(2):170-171.

Geist, Valerius. 1971. Mountain Sheep: A Study in Behavior and Evolution. University of Chicago Press.

Johnson, Morris D. 1962. Old Timer's Statements. North Dakota Game and Fish Department, Bismarck.

Robinson, Elwyn. 1966. History of North Dakota. University of Nebraska Press.

Wishart, William. 1978. Bighorn Sheep. pps. 161-171 of Big Game of North America: Ecology and Management. Wildlife Management Institute. Stackpole Books, Harrisburg, PA.

White-tailed deer

CHAPTER FIVE

THE DEER FAMILY

WHAT MAKES A DEER A DEER

The science of identifying plants and animals and classifying them into related groups is called taxonomy. Taxonomy, with all its Latin and Greek terminologies—genus, species, and so on—may seem confusing, but the basis for it is not very complicated. Taxonomists put plants and animals into groups based on characteristics which they share. For example, there is a group—a large group—of life forms which are identified collectively as the "animal kingdom." These life forms share characteristics which distinguish them from another general group of life forms which are the "plant kingdom."

Creatures within the animal kingdom are, of course, very different from each other. But by examining all of these different animals, and looking for characteristics that animals have in common, scientists have identified a number of ways that these different animals can be grouped together. The groupings begin with very specific groups which contain only one animal—white-tailed deer, for example. Groupings then become more and more general, to include other related animals. In our example, whitetails are grouped first with other whitetails; then with other deer; and, as groupings become more general, with other animals which are not deer, but are related to them by means of characteristics they have in common. The basis for any grouping is always characteristics that the animals have in common.

Scientists have given the groups names. The most basic grouping is the species level—in our example, whitetails. Related species of animals are grouped into genera (genera is the plural of the word genus). Following through our example, whitetails and mule deer are different species of the same genus. Related genera are grouped into families. The family to which whitetails and mule deer belong also contains moose and elk. Related families are grouped into orders; orders are grouped into classes; and classes are grouped into phyla (phyla is the plural of the Greek word phylum). These groupings are sometimes made more specific with sub-headings—sub-species, sub-order, and so on.

The deer family—whose technical name is Cervidae—is represented in North Dakota by white-tailed deer, mule deer, moose, and elk. All of these animals share characteristics which identify them as cervids. The foremost characteristic is their headgear—their antlers. Members of the deer family have antlers, which are made entirely of bone and which are shed every year. This distinguishes them from another family—Bovidae—which

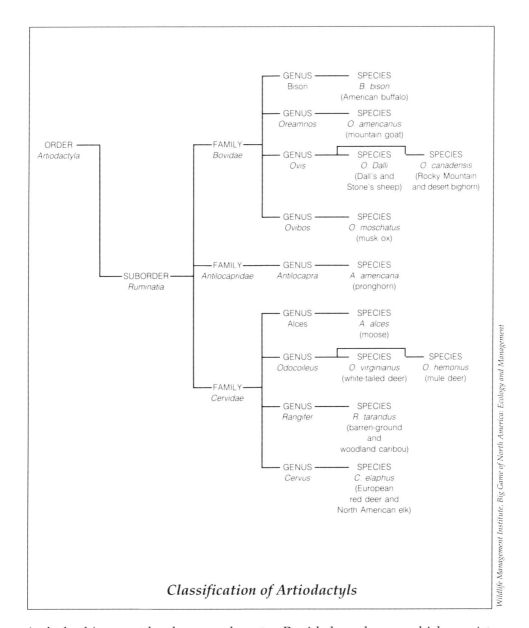

ORDER
Artiodactyla

SUBORDER
Ruminatia

FAMILY
Bovidae

GENUS
Bison

SPECIES
B. bison
(American buffalo)

GENUS
Oreamnos

SPECIES
O. americanus
(mountain goat)

GENUS
Ovis

SPECIES
O. Dalli
(Dall's and
Stone's sheep)

SPECIES
O. canadensis
(Rocky Mountain
and desert bighorn)

GENUS
Ovibos

SPECIES
O. moschatus
(musk ox)

FAMILY
Antilocapridae

GENUS
Antilocapra

SPECIES
A. americana
(pronghorn)

GENUS
Alces

SPECIES
A. alces
(moose)

GENUS
Odocoileus

SPECIES
O. virginianus
(white-tailed deer)

SPECIES
O. hemonius
(mule deer)

FAMILY
Cervidae

GENUS
Rangifer

SPECIES
R. tarandus
(barren-ground
and
woodland caribou)

GENUS
Cervus

SPECIES
C. elaphus
(European
red deer and
North American elk)

Wildlife Management Institute, Big Game of North America: Ecology and Management

Classification of Artiodactyls

includes bison, cattle, sheep, and goats. Bovids have horns, which consist of a bony core and an outer sheath and are never shed. Pronghorns are identified as being in a third family—Antilocapridae—because they have horns but they shed them yearly as if their horns were antlers.

Although these three families of animals are different in some ways, they are quite alike in others. They are all included in the sub-order Ruminantia. Chapter One has a discussion of a ruminant's chambered stomach into which it can stuff large quantities of relatively unchewed forage for later rechewing and final swallowing. Cervids, bovids, and antilocaprids are also members of the order Artiodactyla. This means that

White-tailed Deer
Approx. 3"

Pronghorn Antelope
Approx. 2½"

Mule Deer
Approx. 3¼"

Bighorn Sheep
Approx. 3"

Elk
Approx. 4½"

Moose
Approx. 7"

Bison
Approx. 5½"

Tracks of Artiodactyls

they are all ungulates—hoofed mammals—with an even number of "toes". There is also an order of ungulates which has an odd number of "toes"—perissodactyls—which includes horses (one toe) and rhinoceroses (three toes).

Artiodactyls, perissodactyls, and other orders are included in the class Mammalia—that is to say, they are all mammals. Mammals, along with reptiles, amphibians, aves (birds), and others are included in the phylum Chordata, which is essentially characterized by having a backbone.

All of this may seem confusing. But in many ways it is a very orderly way of understanding an animal's biology. A deer is not a deer because of any one aspect of its biology—antlers, let's say. A deer is a deer because of all sorts of characteristics, many of which it shares with other animals. All of these characteristics are important. In one way or another, these characteristics have allowed an animal to succeed. An example is an artiodactyl's two-toed hoof which gives it speed and sure-footedness in a variety of terrains.

These same characteristics can be looked at as limits. A deer is always a deer, and it can't become something else when conditions change. The history of deer in North Dakota—in fact, the history of big game altogether—runs along the path between success and limitation. We have already seen how various strategies for success became limitations for buffalo and pronghorns. But deer are not buffalo or pronghorns.

THE DEER FAMILY IN NORTH AMERICA

Members of the deer family, like other hoofed mammals in North America, were pushed around by the ebb and flow of glaciers during the ice age. They were pushed both in a geographic sense, and in an evolutionary sense. The recession of ice sheets opened new areas for animals to colonize; the advance of ice isolated populations for huge periods of time, allowing them to pursue independent evolutionary paths.

The movements of various genera of deer from the Old World to the New World and back are obscure. It appears that the evolutionary development of whitetails, mule deer, and moose took place mostly in the New World; the ancestry of what we here call an elk seems to have been in Eurasia—the Old World. The groupings are guided by such things as the way the hoofs are formed—New World deer have "a relatively primitive foot equipped with well-developed dewclaws and elastic hoofs, ideal for soft ground and for climbing," and Old World deer have hoofs "better suited for hard ground" (Geist, 1987a, p. 324). The exchange of Old World deer into the New World—represented by only one genus, *Cervus* (our elk)—and vice-versa was across the Bering Strait land bridge. By the time of their movements across the land bridge, they were quite recognizable, having already developed the characteristic hoofs and the antlers which are shed yearly.

Deer in general have shown—by their distribution across huge geographical areas and climates—to be a highly successful family. We have mentioned some of the adaptive equipment that they share—being ruminants, having antlers, and having hoofs with two "toes." They share other characteristics as well, particularly their teeth—that is to say, their molars—which are low-crowned, more useful for browsing than are the high-crowned molars of grazers like pronghorns and bison. Another characteristic—one which deer share with most other ruminants, in fact—are fused metacarpal and metatarsal bones, "structures analogous to human palm and instep bones" which "form the shock resistant 'cannon bone' of the lower leg" (Geist, 1987a, p. 324).

Sparring bucks occasionally lock antlers. It is usually fatal to both animals.

One assumes that since deer share these characteristics, and since deer are successful animals, these characteristics represent a formula for success. The question is, how? How are these characteristics—this equipment—a formula for success? Take antlers, for example. They are made of bone, and they are often quite large. Why shed them? Regrowing them each year would seem to be an extravagant waste of an animal's food resources. "Strange indeed was the course of evolution that developed the 'disposable' head ornaments of the Cervidae, especially when 'permanent' ones, like the bovids', might have served the same functions...[I]t seems almost too energy-expensive for the individuals to have endured, despite the fact that antlers grow...during the vegetative season when foods are usually plentiful" (Baker, 1984, p. 5). Biologists speculate that the answer lies in the fact that without antlers, male deer look like females. "Bucks busy sparring, fighting, and courting during the rutting season have little time to forage. After the rut they are exhausted, weakened, and vulnerable. Antlers make them stand out from the females; therefore, it's likely that predators would quickly learn that such standouts can be easy prey. Thus bucks have evolved the trait of shedding bone growth in order to look just like one of the crowd" (Geist, 1987a, p. 317).

Molar teeth we have talked a little about—as an adaptation to browse plants, a food source separate from that of the grazers like the bison. Early forms of deer also had long, tusk-like canine teeth. Today, like most ruminants, most deer have neither upper incisor teeth nor canines. An exception is the elk which has retained the upper canines—the noteworthy "bugler" teeth. Whatever selective pressure there may have been for tusks millions of years ago, it is gone now; today it is sufficient that deer be able to bite off the young shoots of trees and shrubs. The important teeth are the molars that grind up this relatively tough food.

Earlier, in the chapter on bighorns, we saw the adaptive value of the two-toed hoof in terms of getting around on a variety of terrains. The hoof of the bighorn is specialized to its mountainous habitat. Deer hoofs are less specialized. The differences between, for example, elk hoofs and moose hoofs have more to do with evolutionary origins millions of years ago than the habitats in which they might be found today. Elk are "Old World" deer, and their hoof structure is the same as their European relative, the red deer; moose are "New World" deer, and their hoofs resemble those of whitetails and mule deer, which also developed in the New World.

Although it might not be possible to trace every aspect of the "design" of an animal to its adaptive function, much of the way that animals are made and much of their behavior can be examined in terms of how it has helped animals survive in their environment. In that regard, each deer is unique.

WHITETAILS

You often hear that white-tailed deer are woodland animals, or are "associated with woodlands." The historic range of whitetails in North Dakota was, indeed, the forested regions connected with the bottomlands of the river systems. But to link up whitetails with forests and leave it at that is a little misleading.

First of all, whitetails are the most adaptable of all deer in North America. They have shown themselves to be able to adjust to different kinds of situations. We will discuss that more in Part II of this book. But what is most misleading about the association of white-tailed deer with forests is that whitetails thrive not in the forest, but along its edges.

Good whitetail habitat can be described as places where there is a good variety of low-growing woody plants, which are still tall and dense enough to provide good cover. Because of the lack of undergrowth, climax forest isn't the best whitetail habitat. The forests associated with rivers are perfect—long, but not particularly wide stretches of forest, with a lot of "edge." Later in the history of this region, with the influx of settlers, changes to the river bottom forest habitat would have great effect on the population of whitetails in North Dakota.

Whitetail fawn in hiding.

A whitetail fawn is born in late May or June, sometimes by itself, and sometimes, when conditions are good, as one of twins or even triplets. Its first months are spent mostly hiding in dense undergrowth, its spotted coat blending well with the dappling effect of sunlight through leaves. As the fawn grows older and stronger it begins to move with its mother, until by fall a fawn and its mother are always together.

A whitetail fawn grows quickly during the first seven months of its life—the time before its first winter. By fall its coat begins to change, exchanging its spots for its adult coloring, and growing the hollow-haired winter coat which will insulate it from the coming cold. As the seasons change, the fawn—whether it is male or female—will follow its mother as she is pushed by deepening snow to winter habitat where they are protected and where food is accessible. There they will stay until spring, joined by other deer.

Come spring, the yearling deer returns to the home range of its birth. After this year's fawning the yearling, if it is a female, will rejoin her mother and her fawns of the year, forming a typical family group—an adult doe, female yearling, and fawns of the year. If the yearling is a male, he will not rejoin his mother. He might move to a nearby range; he might wander to nearby ranges and then return to his original range, or he may never leave the range of his birth. But whatever he chooses as a yearling will, unless he is driven out, become his permanent range.

The breeding season—the rut—for whitetails begins in the fall. The breeding age for both bucks and does is usually 1½ years, although on very high quality range, does younger than a year sometimes breed and bear fawns. A bred doe will then begin her own family group, raising her fawns and showing them the seasonal ranges. A yearling buck, still small and subordinate, will begin to test himself against larger and more dominant males.

ND Game and Fish Department

Whitetails browsing in good cover.

91

The quality of the range has much to do with the growth and behavior of white-tailed deer. The ability of a doe to produce healthy fawns is a function of nutrition—in the case of whitetails, very likely a function of the condition and the variety of plants which are available to them. The size of the home range will change, depending on how far deer must travel to get food. Antler size and shape are affected by nutrition. During the rut, whitetail bucks spend very little time eating, and can lose 15 to 30 percent of their body weight. If they have not been well-fed before the breeding season, they will have a hard time surviving the winter.

A good variety of plants is necessary for nutrition, and it is necessary to provide whitetails with cover. Fawns hide in good cover; all deer need it to escape their natural enemies and to protect them from severe weather. It is something of a catch-22 that well-nourished deer do not need cover as much as under-nourished deer—but if their range is too poor to provide them food, it is unlikely to provide good cover either.

White-Tailed Deer in North Dakota

When explorers first came to North Dakota, they used a variety of names to describe different members of the deer family. The whitetail was often called a "fallow deer"—that is, a pale brown or yellow deer, distinguished from the "red deer," which is the European relative of our elk. Thus, Alexander Henry, on a trip into what is now Minnesota, wrote "Red deer were very numerous, and for the first time we saw numerous tracks and roads of the fallow deer...which we soon perceived jumping in all directions" (Oct. 28, 1800). This becomes a little confusing, first because of the European fallow deer, which did not exist in North America at that time. Lewis and Clark then used the term "fallow deer" to distinguish the subspecies of whitetail in the upper Missouri country from the "common deer" of the lower Missouri. Thus, on Sept. 17, 1804, near Chamberlain, South Dakota, Clark wrote, "8 fallow deer, 5 common and 3 buffalow killed today." And whitetails were also often called "long-tailed deer," and later, to distinguish them from mule deer, "Virginia deer." It's no wonder that taxonomists prefer scientific names when they discuss the identities of deer.

Whitetails then, as now, preferred the dense cover provided by trees and undergrowth along the banks of rivers. As the Lewis and Clark Expedition made its way north and west along the Missouri to the Cannonball River, the Arikaras assured them that there were "no black tail Deer as high up as this place;" Clark wrote, "those we find are of the fallow Deer kind" (Oct. 18, 1804). From the Cannonball north to their winter encampment at Fort Mandan, Lewis and Clark found "The Timber confined to the bottoms as useal [and] much larger than below" (Clark, Oct. 20, 1804). Whitetails from this "large timber" would provide them with a major portion of their food that winter.

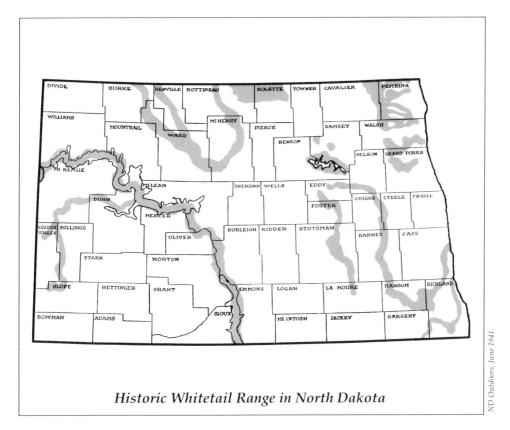

Historic Whitetail Range in North Dakota

There are relatively few descriptions of the habits of whitetails in the early journals—at least compared to descriptions of other game. Lewis's and Clark's journals note the game killed: "our hunters killed 10 deer & a goat." Audubon's notes, too, are scanty: May 19, 1843—"We saw a deer of the common kind swimming across the stream." Sept. 4. 1843—"The buck was brought in; it is of the same kind as at Fort Union, having a longer tail, we think, than the kind found East."

Their commonness explains why no one wrote much about white-tailed deer. Thomas Jefferson instructed Lewis and Clark to notice "the animals of the country generally, & especially those not known in the U.S." (Burroughs, 1961, p. 292). The explorers gave their attention to new and unusual animals. It would have taken unusual foresight for them to have thought that their journals of exploration would one day describe something long past.

Whitetails were a dependable source of food for explorers and Indians alike. Between May 14 and June 29, 1804, hunters for Lewis and Clark killed 70 deer, which provided the bulk of their food. As they proceeded north into the "buffalo country," they turned to these larger animals—one buffalo being the equivalent in food of four deer (see Chapter Two)—but during the long winter months deer once again became the staple. Whitetails did not wander away in search of food.

February 4, 1805—This morning fair tho' cold the thermometer stood at 18 below Naught, wind from N.W. Capt Clark set out with a hunting party...our stock of meat which we had procured in the Months of November and December is now nearly exhausted...no buffaloe have made their appearance in our neighborhood for some weeks...Shields killed two deer this evening... —*Lewis*

February 12, 1805—A little after dark this evening Capt Clark arrived with the hunting party since they set out they have killed forty Deer, three buffalo bulls, & sixteen Elk, most of them were so meager that they were unfit for uce, particularly the Buffalo and male Elk... —*Lewis*

Even in summer, travelers felt that they could depend on deer when there was no other game. Audubon wrote (July 15, 1843), "We had nothing for our breakfast except some vile coffee, and about three quarters of a sea-biscuit, which was soon settled among us...Provost had seen two Deer, but had had no shot, so of course we were in a quandary..." The following day, Audubon's party shot a wolf and were preparing to "dine upon its flesh;" Audubon, however, was not so inclined. He took the wolf's liver down to the river and caught 18 catfish, upon which they then made a meal. Though the meal "consisted wholly of fish," they "were all fairly satisfied."

We can get a good idea of typical whitetail habitat by where these adventurers went to hunt them. The following is from Henry Boller, written in his journal, November 25, 1858.

Clear & pleasant. Started long before day light, so as to be on the ground by sunrise, at which time the deer are feeding. Passed along the road to the point, having the moonlight directly on my path, the frozen snow crunching beneath my rapid tread. Arriving on the ground, I sat on a log, and waited for it to become light enough to follow tracts. After a while, an indistinct cloudy-looking mass showed itself to be timber, and as the dawn brightened, the trunks of trees, and the underbrush became strongly visible. Trailing my rifle, I hunted around until I came to a deer path, which I followed up; continuing on thus for some time, and seeing nothing, came out by "the lake," a favorite feeding place for deer. By aid of my glass, I discovered 3, two does & 1 buck, about 300 yards off. The wind was favorable, and I crept carefully on my hands & knees thro' the snow—one of the does had fed apart from the rest, and turning, scented me-The game was roused now sure, my rifle cracked, but the ball missed, and bounding high over the underbrush, fled to the woods, where they halted. I made a long, but unsuccessful detour to get near them, and as the sun was now up, I shouldered my rifle and set out for the Fort, picking up, however, a very handsome horn, (buck) to make rifle chargers with.

Henry Boller.

Audubon, too, went to the woods with the expectation of finding deer. On July 7, 1843, he wrote, "[On] the prairie I shot a Meadow Lark, but lost it, as we had unfortunately not taken Bragg (Harris's dog). We saw a patch of wood called in these regions a 'point;' we walked towards it for the purpose of shooting a deer....No deer there, however, and we made for the fort..."

Almost all of the reports of abundant white-tailed deer come from the trappers, explorers, and traders along the Missouri. Alexander Henry, who ran his trading posts in the Red River Valley and the Pembina Hills between 1800 and 1808, lists very few "fallow deer" even seen, much less killed. On March 31, 1806—having already been in the region for six years—Henry wrote, "The Indians saw three fallow deer, and killed one— the first of the kind ever seen in this quarter."

Whitetails were, perhaps, important to the Indians in the same way that they were important to the explorers. Both preferred to hunt buffalo. Deer provided meat, primarily in late fall and winter when buffalo were scarce, and the Indians used deer leather when buffalo leather was too stiff and heavy. Most clothing was made from the skins of deer and antelope; and with typical thriftiness, the Indians made use of the rest of the animal for tools, toys, and other necessities of life. In areas where there were no buffalo, whitetails replaced them, providing bowstrings from sinew, awls and needles and hoes from bone, pendants and rattles and jewelry from hoofs and hair. "Aside from the hide, the anatomical part of a whitetail carcass that was of the greatest utility to Indians was antler. Indians throughout the east and southeast used antler to make arrowheads, spear points and harpoon points...Antler was used for needles, flaking tools, clubs, combs, cutting tools, household utensils, and...as hair ornaments" (McCabe et. al., 1984, p. 33).

Before the Plains Indians could move out onto the grassland and fully exploit the buffalo, they had to have horses (see Chapter Two). Before they got horses, tribes like the Cheyenne lived near forested regions and along rivers; during these times, whitetails played a larger role in their lives. "Many of the...Indians of the Plains were familiar with and, to some extent, dependent on whitetails long before they focused subsistence activities on bison. For example, the Sioux word for white-tailed deer is 'tahca' or 'tahinca,' meaning 'the true meat, the real meat'" (McCabe et. al., 1984, p. 30). Whitetails had, apparently, been very highly regarded in Sioux culture.

Horses would not have been much use to Indians for hunting whitetails, even if they had had them. Most deer hunting was done on an individual basis, a lone hunter trying to provide food and other necessities for his family. Any large-scale harvest of white-tailed deer was a community effort, rather like the buffalo or antelope drives described in earlier chapters, usually taking place in the fall or winter, when deer were prime and concentrated. "One of the most widespread and successful hunting methods was the fire drive, and for this procedure the dormancy of vegetation was of critical importance in both spring and autumn. Spring fire drives were generally the safest...but autumn fire drives were the most productive (again, because of deer concentrations in that season)" (McCabe et. al., 1984, p. 39).

On the northern plains, where horses made it possible for the culture to center around the buffalo, Indians who hunted deer usually stalked them on foot through the woods. The method was like the one described by Henry Boller earlier—deer were tracked or trailed to mineral licks, feeding sites, or bedding places. Apparently Indians also used calls to lure deer in: "Assiniboine Indians of the Dakotas used a deer call made from a hollowed-out piece of thick bark: 'A piece of very thin gristle or membrane, pressed and dried, was cut to fit over the entire top.... A band of sinew was wrapped around the middle to hold the top parts together and allowed to dry. The device was placed halfway in the mouth...and with both hands cupped over it, was blown twice for each call'" (Kennedy, 1961, in McCabe et. al., 1984, p. 53). Many Indian hunters continued to use the bow and arrow for deer even after they had guns; whether this is a reflection on the quality of their guns, their confidence in using a particular weapon, or some other reason is a matter for speculation. It would seem that if you were hunting for your livelihood, you would use the surest method you had available. It has been noted (McCabe et. al., 1984, p. 54 and elsewhere) that a good bowman could put half-a-dozen arrows in the air during the time a rifleman could fire and load. No doubt breech loaders and repeaters would have ended the use of the bow and arrow.

Early white explorers adopted some of the Indian methods of hunting deer. Audubon mentions some of his party making deer calls: June 22, 1843—"Provost made a whistle to imitate the noise made by the fawns at this season, which is used to great advantage to decoy the female Deer." And June 27, 1843—"Provost has been making whistles to call the deer."

Other traders tried other methods to hunt deer—to the amusement of both whites and Indians. One method was first tried out on wolves. Henry Boller wrote:

> November 22, 1858—One of the men has invented, and is using with the most sanguine hopes of success a new kind of trap. It is very simple in its construction, being nothing more than a large fish-hook, tied to a line, and baited with meat.... We all wait to see how it succeeds with great interest.

> November 23—During the night the men visited their traps, and got two large wolves; also a small Indian dog on the patent hook.

> November 24—"the-man-that-is-fishing-for-wolves" has bad luck so far.

> December 7—"The-man-that-is-fishing-for-wolves" has caught nothing on his hook, or in his traps, & has now taken them up into the timber to catch deer!! He baits with hay and corn. We have plenty of quiet fun with this fellow, putting him up to all sorts of foolish & rediculous things, and he swallows everything.

It is said that in the north and southeastern United States the Indians had a large hand in the destruction of white-tailed deer populations, trading deerskins for white trade goods. That was not the case on the northern prairies. To quote Vernon Bailey, in his 1926 **Biological Survey of North Dakota** (p. 37), "the disappearance of these deer from the greater part of North Dakota was coincident with the settlement of the country."

What Bailey appears to say is that as people moved in, the deer moved out. But North Dakota was a place which was largely a grassland, without very much classic whitetail habitat. When settlers moved in, they broke up the grassland, creating a whole new succession of plants. It was also a time when a settler could get 160 acres of free land if he would plant ten acres of it into trees. On the face of it, it would seem as if settlement might give a boost to whitetails in North Dakota.

Bonanza farming.

But it didn't work that way. It might have given whitetails a boost if people moving into the state had been concerned about the deer. But the general attitude seems to have been that civilization and wildlife were incompatible. And since wildlife would eventually (and inevitably) disappear, there was no point in conservation. The following is from the **Rousseau County** (Minnesota) **Times**, April 10, 1896 (in McCabe et. al., 1984, p. 68). "Great country this for game in and out of season. We have venison...any time we take the trouble to have it brought in. Nothing like enjoying the good things on the frontier while they last and before civilization makes the game scarce."

In 1890, North Dakota had fewer than three people per square mile, but the deer were mostly gone already. Interviews conducted by Vernon Bailey for his **Survey** showed that after 1880, there were few deer to be found east of Valley City. When Bailey himself made a trip to what was then the Dakota Territory, he "found no trace of white-tails in the Red River Valley, which was then well-occupied by settlers, but they were still abundant along the Missouri River bottoms and were reported in the Pembina Hills and Turtle Mountains" (Bailey, 1926, p. 37-38).

By 1915, whitetails were so scarce in North Dakota that they could be counted in small bunches across the state. "Four or five" wintered in 1912 near Tolna; two were "killed at Bald Creek in 1912;" there were "a few deer in the Turtle Mountains, probably an overflow, however, from the well-stocked game preserve just across the line in Manitoba;" three were in Crosby, "seen during a heavy snowstorm at a farmhouse north of town." Their "last stronghold" was still the Missouri bottoms where, "in 1919, the deer were holding their own or were slightly on the increase, and it was thought would rapidly multiply and restock the timbered bottoms if they could be adequately protected" (Bailey, p. 38-39).

Morris Johnson, interviewing long-time North Dakota residents for his 1964 book **Feathers From the Prairie**, heard the same story as Bailey. After the turn of the century, whitetails were hard to find in North Dakota.

> Charles Stewart, Emmons County: There were evidently a lot of deer around in the 1880s and 1890s from what my dad said. He said that they could hunt them at that time and the [Missouri River] bottoms had lots of deer then. In the early 1900s they were really scarce.

> Harvey McConnell, Kenmare: There must have been more around the Kenmare area in the early 1880s than in the early 1900s. I can remember talking with Joe Overholt, former rider for the government mail route from Fort Berthold to Portal, North Dakota, in the early 1880s. He rode this route many times on horseback and he told me that deer—all whitetails—were thicker than flies in the coulees outside Des Lacs Lake during those years.

> John Bert Johnstone, Hansboro: There were none as far as I know in the Red River Valley in the 1890s. An old time Norwegian told me that he had killed deer west of Northwood in 1876. But they were gone in this area just a few years later.

> Arthur Anderson, Belfield: Deer were so scarce in the year 1902 we'd hunt all day and not see a deer. In fact, if you saw a fresh track in the snow it would be quite a thing.

Regulations passed by the Territorial Legislature in 1881 had made it "unlawful to leave any part or parts of buffalo, elk, deer, antelope, or mountain sheep" lying on the prairie. In 1891, new legislation made it illegal to kill buffalo, elk, deer, antelope, or mountain sheep between the first day of January and the first day of September. These regulations were not especially effective in maintaining deer populations. In the recommendations made by the North Dakota State Game and Fish Commission in its **First Biennial Report** in 1894 (p. 5), the Commissioner wrote that there were "but a few" deer left in the state, and that it might be a good idea to protect them. An October, 1894 **Field and Stream** article was quoted (p. 10) as saying that "the game of North Dakota is gradually but surely passing away under the murderous and increasing assaults yearly made by local and non-resident, legal and illegal shooters."

In 1899, the state legislature first placed a bag limit—eight animals—on big game in North Dakota. In 1901, the bag limit on deer was reduced to five, and deer season was limited to November 10 to December 10. In 1909, the North Dakota State Legislature took what it hoped would be a positive step in organizing and enforcing the game laws of the state. The legislature created a five member Game and Fish Board of Control—the first permanent agency for game and fish functions.

In 1911, the Board of Control made its first biennial report to the legislature. The report read (p. 31) that "if North Dakota is to preserve to future generations the members of the deer family that now remain within its territory, there must be prompt action on the part of the state and co-operation in the fullest sense on the part of the individual." The report went on to say (p. 31):

> The deer in this state are threatened with extinction at an early date unless something is done to remedy conditions rapidly growing worse. When the region west of the Missouri was sparsely settled there was a chance to permit a short season and still not greatly disturb Nature's balance, but with the rapid settlement of that region the problem is becoming more difficult. In the light of present conditions we are forced to the conclusion that the time is at hand when it would be expedient to close the season on deer for a term of years, and at the same time endeavor to add protective measures that will tend to the multiplication of the species or, if provision is made for refuges and game preserves to foster a more rapid increase of these animals, then to limit the killing of deer to two antlered deer in any one season.

The biennial report for 1911-12 repeated (p. 9) the urgency of the need for a closed deer season. "It seems to be an unanimous opinion of the sportsmen through the state that a closed deer season of at least three years

Deer hunt near Fort Clark in 1902-03.

should be declared, for the protection of these animals. They are becoming much less numerous each season and with the number of hunters that now congregate for the deer season, it is only a matter of a few years when they likely will be exterminated."

The 1915 legislature closed the deer season until 1920. The 1919 legislature extended the restriction until 1921. In 1923, after two years of "bucks only" seasons, the legislature closed the deer season again until 1931. In 1929 the North Dakota game and fish agency had been reorganized again, taking on the form it still has today. The **First Annual Report of the Game and Fish Commissioner** in 1930 read (p. 47):

> Due to protection, the Deer have increased in great numbers, to the extent that we are receiving complaints that during the summer months they are doing considerable damage to corn and alfalfa fields in the bottoms along the Missouri River, and from information received from reliable sources, we believe that the Deer have increased to such an extent during the closed season, that the object of the closed season has been realized.... This Department believes, that under the present conditions, the best interests of the Deer hunters of this State will be served by having an open season on Deer, and thus give everybody an opportunity, even if it is for only a short time, to satisfy their craving for a Deer hunt.

Game managers today express a certain amount of skepticism regarding the value of closed seasons in managing deer populations. But—at least in local areas—deer populations had increased to the point where, in 1931, a five day open season was held to hunt bucks only. Whether or not the closed season had accomplished its objective, deer numbers were still far under the numbers we are used to today. Regulations had become, as the years went by, more and more restrictive without increasing deer populations over much of the state. Interviews (Johnson, 1962) with old-timers again make this clear.

> Otto Kretschmar, Venturia: Only...since 1940 have we started having any deer in this area.

> C. J. Ness, Cando: There weren't many deer in this area [Bisbee] in the period 1912-1920. There are more deer now [1962] than at any time since I've lived here.

> Charles Stewart, Emmons County: In the early 1900s they were really scarce. We never really got them—none to amount to anything—until the late 1940s.

The big turnaround for whitetails in North Dakota did not really start until the 1940s. That story will be continued in Part II of this book.

101

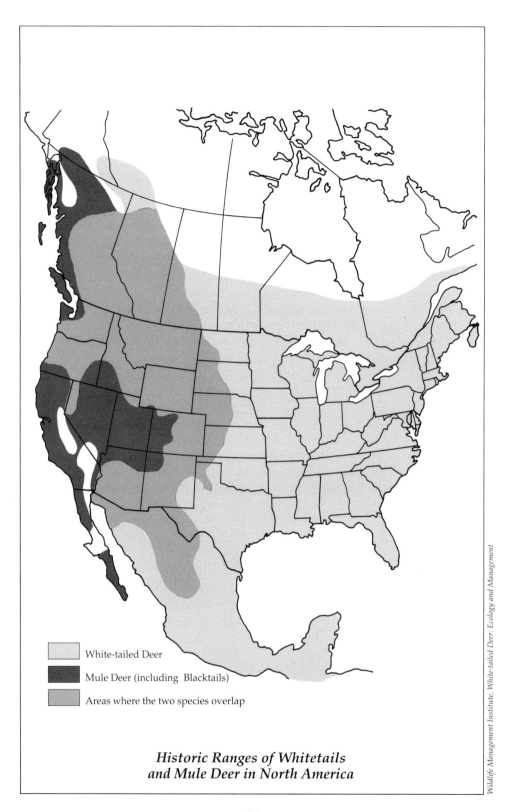

White-tailed Deer

Mule Deer (including Blacktails)

Areas where the two species overlap

**Historic Ranges of Whitetails
and Mule Deer in North America**

Wildlife Management Institute, White-tailed Deer: Ecology and Management

MULE DEER

To make generalizations about the differences between good whitetail habitat and good mule deer habitat is probably not a good idea. Both species of deer can adapt themselves to new sets of circumstances. Whitetail habitat and mule deer habitat overlap over much of the western United States. In the places where both species live, whitetails occupy the lower, flatter, more forested areas—in North Dakota that would be the wooded areas along river bottoms—and mule deer live in higher, rougher, more open terrain. As we are going to see from the journals of Lewis and Clark, mule deer once occupied a larger range than they do today—whitetails are apparently pushing them westward.

At the present time, the eastern edge of habitat overlap coincides roughly with the eastern boundary of the Great Plains. All sorts of things happen along that same boundary line. It is a precipitation boundary—east of the line is the tall grass prairie which gets twenty inches or more of rainfall each year, and west of the line is the mid and short grass prairie. Elevations and slopes change there too—the Great Plains are higher and steeper than the tall grass prairies to the east. Vegetation has adapted to these different conditions.

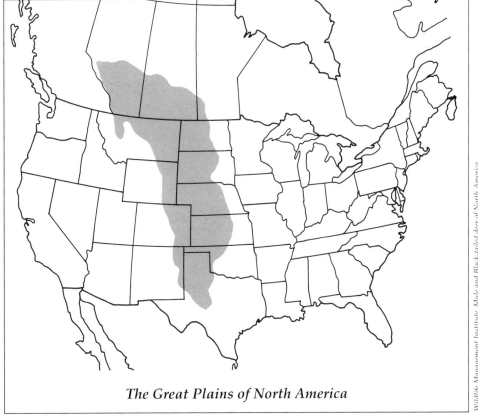

The Great Plains of North America

Wildlife Management Institute, Mule and Black-tailed deer of North America

The Great Plains are mostly a rolling grassland which is interspersed with shrubs and trees which grow in places where there is more moisture. East to west across the plains in North Dakota, elevations increase and slopes are steeper, creating places where rainfall can run off and collect. Low lying draws between hills have buffalo berry and choke cherry growing in them; where there is even more moisture, green ash and bur oak take hold. North-facing slopes, where moisture evaporates slowly, are covered with juniper and even some pine. These areas—the shrubby and woody draws and the juniper stands—are as important to mule deer as the woodlands are to whitetails. In them they find cover and food.

Many of the differences between the way mule deer and white-tailed deer behave can be seen as adaptations to habitat—presumably because of some advantage gained by behaving that way. Mule deer have, for example, the peculiar way of moving known as "stotting"—stiff-legged bounding uphill and across rough terrain. Most biologists see this particular way of moving as an escape tactic—by stotting, mule deer are able to change direction instantly and can put rocks and other obstacles between themselves and their pursuers. Obviously, it would be of little value in timber or on level, open ground. But it works in the rough and open habitat mule deer choose to live in.

In a chapter called "Adaptive Strategies in Mule Deer," (see Geist, 1981), Valerius Geist contrasts the ways that mule deer and whitetails move to protect themselves. From it we can see a little bit of how habitat has affected each of these animals. A whitetail that senses danger is first going to get into tall cover and freeze. If hiding doesn't work, or if a whitetail is surprised, he will explode out of cover and go as fast as he can to put distance between himself and whatever is after him. He will follow established trails, which has the advantages of keeping unexpected obstacles to a minimum and perhaps crossing the scent of other deer, giving the pursuer something else to think about. Then the deer will hide again and watch to see what will happen next.

By comparison, Geist tells us, mule deer "are showy, noisy, and smelly...When in groups, fawns call frequently and loudly, and bucks horn noisily for minutes on end. In daylight, mule deer move readily into the open, where they are easily seen. They urinate copiously on their hocks and have large glands on their hind legs and between the digits of the hooves" (p. 172). Obviously mule deer do not depend on hiding. They have other survival strategies.

It appears that their main strategy is to avoid places where they know there are predators. Mulies depend on being able to spot danger from a distance—they like openness and they have big ears—but they do not get very far from rough country—steep slopes and cover. When they sense danger they will move away from it, often slowly, always looking around to keep track of what the danger is doing. If a predator gets too close, the deer can bound—stot—uphill and over rocks, staying a jump or more ahead.

Stotting mule deer.

The different responses of whitetails and mule deer to habitat also affect the temperament of these animals. "Bounding…permits the [mule] deer, with each jump, to depart in a totally unpredictable direction. But with the predator close at hand, the deer must not jump until the last possible moment. Otherwise, the pursuer can redirect itself. Such escape techniques call for coolness in timing—making for a calm, collected type." The habits of whitetails, exploding violently out of cover, and running at full speed "make for a nervous, fidgety species" (Geist, 1987a, p. 319).

The strategies which are an advantage to mule deer when it comes to wolves or mountain lions can be disadvantages when it comes to men. Men find mule deer behavior predictable. When Meriwether Lewis first saw mule deer in action he wrote (May 10, 1805), "they prefer the open grounds and are seldom found in woodlands or river bottoms; when they are met with in the woodlands or river bottoms and are pursued, they invariably run to the hills or open country as the Elk do. The contrary happens with the common deer." Elizabeth Roberts, a long-time resident of the Badlands of North Dakota, also noted that particular difference, and she judged its value: "The blacktail got shot off because they didn't have sense enough to stay under cover…We had whitetails all the time and they were smarter and never lost out." Chris Rasmussen of Medora simply— and bluntly—echoed the feelings of many deer hunters. "The mule deer are a lot easier to hunt than the whitetails" (Johnson, 1962).

105

ND Game and Fish Department

Mule deer ears.

MULE DEER IN NORTH DAKOTA

Vernon Bailey (in **A Biological Survey of North Dakota**, 1926, p. 41) gives Charles LeRaye the credit for the name "mule deer." Others, including Burroughs and Cutright, give credit to Meriwether Lewis. LeRaye's journal was written in 1802, and Lewis's in 1805; LaRaye's journals were published in 1812, and Lewis's and Clark's finally in 1814. It appears that Bailey is correct, although Lewis's description is more famous:

> May 10, 1805—The ear and tail of this anamel when compared with those of the common deer, so well comported with those of the mule when compared with the horse, that we have, by way of distinction, adopted the appellation of the mule deer, which I think much more appropriate.

When Lewis's and Clark's Corps of Discovery first saw mule deer they were in the vicinity of the mouth of the White River, near where Chamberlain, South Dakota is today. Clark's description (September 17, 1804) is equally famous:

Colter killed…a curious kind of Deer of a Dark gray colour—or more so than common, hair long and fine, the ears large and long, a Small recepticle under the eyes like the Elk, the taile about the length of the Common Deer, round (like a cow) a tuft of black hair about the end, this Species of Deer jumps like a goat or Sheep.

Audubon's first sighting was farther south and east—south of the present site of Sioux City, Iowa:

May 12, 1843—On going along the banks bordering a long and wide prairie, thick with willows and other small brush-wood, we saw four Black-tailed Deer immediately on the bank; they trotted away without appearing to be much alarmed; after a few hundred yards, the largest, probably males, raised themselves on their hind feet and pawed at each other, after the manner of stallions. They trotted off again, stopping often, but after awhile disappeared; we saw them again some hundreds of yards farther on, when, becoming suddenly alarmed, they bounded off until out of sight. They did not trot or run irregularly as our Virginian deer does….

The accounts of Lewis and Clark and Audubon indicate that the range of the mule deer was larger then than it is today. At least the range of mule deer does not extend as far east as the Nebraska-Iowa line today. According to other sources, particularly Bailey, mule deer "apparently occupied all of North Dakota before the country was settled by whites" (Bailey, 1926, p. 419). But then, as now, the primary place to find mule deer was in the roughest and highest ground—most typically, the Badlands. Lewis wrote (May 10, 1805), "we saw several deer of the Mule kind of immence size and also three of the Big-horned anamals, from the appearance of the mule deer and the big-horned anamels we believe ourselves fast approaching a hilly or mountainous country; we have rarely found the mule deer in any except rough country…" Apparently the preferred habitat of mule deer was so predictable that the expedition knew what sort of terrain to expect when they saw them.

Lewis and Clark saw relatively few mule deer in North Dakota. Reid and Gannon (1928) and Cutright (1969) both felt that mule deer numbers might have been higher than Lewis and Clark indicate. The expedition did not get very far from the floodplains of the Missouri—and of course the more typical mule deer habitat is upland. On the other hand, Audubon, forty years after Lewis and Clark, went to considerable trouble in what he called the "Mauvaises Terres" to collect bighorns and mule deer; at the end of half a year in the region, he was still offering good prices to hunters who would bring him good specimens of male or female "black-tailed deer." Mulies were not abundant even then.

Early journal writers did not spend much time writing about deer. Whitetails in North Dakota were much like whitetails in other parts of the country; mule deer were discussed in terms of the differences between them and white-tailed deer. Meriwether Lewis wrote his usual thorough description:

> May 10, 1805—There are several essential differences between the Mule deer and the common deer as well in form as in habits. They are fully a third larger in general.... The ears are particularly large, I measured those of a large buck which I found to be eleven inches long, and 3½ in width at the widest part...their horns also differ, these in the common deer consist of two main beams from which one or more points project, the beam gradually diminishing as the points proceed from it; with the mule deer the horns consist of two beams which at the distance of four or six inches from the head divide themselves each into two equal branches which again either divide into two other equal branches, or terminate in a smaller.... The most striking difference of all is the white rump and tale.

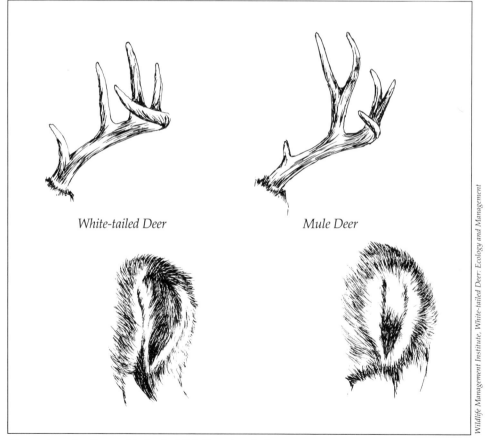

White-tailed Deer   Mule Deer

Wildlife Management Institute, White-tailed Deer: Ecology and Management

Comparison of antlers and tails of whitetails and mule deer.

Lewis goes on to give careful measurements of the lengths of the hair and tail. His observations were complete enough that Audubon and Maximilian, both trained naturalists (which Lewis was not), used his descriptions as a reference. Audubon wrote (June 27, 1843), "They ran a Long-tailed Deer, and describe its movements precisely as do Lewis and Clark. Between every three or four short leaps came the long leap of fully twenty-five feet, if not more."

If mule deer were relatively scarce in the first half of the nineteenth century, they became very scarce in the second half. "The decline of Plains deer followed extirpation of bison, which had disappeared from the northern Great Plains by 1883, and it closely paralleled the decline of pronghorn. The period 1880 to 1909 also marked settlement of the region" (Severson, 1981, p. 460-61). As was discussed in the chapter on bighorn sheep, the years 1880-1900 were a time of great activity and change in western North Dakota, particularly in the region along the Little Missouri River. Railroad-building reached the Badlands, and so did hunters—those hired by the railroad to feed its crews, market hunters who would use rail to ship meat to market, and sportsmen. By 1885 large-scale cattle operators were overgrazing the range. The winters of 1886 and 1887 were extremely severe, and thousands of cattle died on the depleted range. So did wildlife.

Richard Mackie (1987, p. 266) suggests that the downward trend for mule deer was reversed in the years following settlement, at least in the southwestern United States. "Widespread livestock grazing, logging, and burning led to more diverse range and forest vegetation and an abundance of palatable and nutritious deer food plants. Predatory animals were vigorously controlled, while possibly competitive animals such as elk, bighorn sheep, pronghorn antelope, and bison had become scarce or had disappeared. Also, hunting was restricted, and game law enforcement had become more effective."

Longhorned cattle in the Badlands.

109

But it did not happen that way in the North Dakota Badlands. Although after two tough winters in 1886 and 87 cattle ranching became a more cautious affair, and some of the other activities slowed down as well, mule deer populations did not rebound. Vernon Bailey (1926, p. 43) describes a bleak picture: "At the present time there may be a few mule deer in the most remote corners of the Badlands and an occasional wanderer from the

Wind erosion.

ND Game and Fish Department

110

Canadian side of the Turtle Mountains and Pembina Hills but, if not already extinct, this finest of all native species of the smaller deer will soon have vanished from the State. Its disappearance, while greatly to be regretted, is as inevitable as that of the elk and the buffalo."

A bleak picture indeed. The discussion of white-tailed deer earlier gave a brief look at the legislation in those early years designed to protect deer. None of the reports of the early game commissions acknowledged that mule deer and whitetails are different—most of the discussion, with references to the bottoms of the Missouri River, seems to be talking about whitetails. Certainly the open deer season in 1931 reflected a limited rebound in whitetail numbers, not mule deer.

The 1920s and 30s were very tough times for both people and wildlife in North Dakota. The drought which most people associate with the thirties started in North Dakota in the twenties. Crop yields were poor. People were having a hard time making ends meet.

By the 1920s, people had certain expectations of life. There were roads in North Dakota; there were schools, churches and libraries. Life was more comfortable—it was easier. Machines were taking over much of the work that had been done by hand.

Those are not things that people go back from. In response to hard times and poor crops, people tried to produce more by putting more land into production—maybe not the best land, but because of the new machinery, land which could be farmed. They cropped land more intensively than before, and grazed it harder.

In the 1930s that poor land blew away. It was a combination of circumstances. Even in good times, homesteads were small, probably too small to provide a good living except in the best of times. Remember that North Dakota, especially in the west, is a land of marginal rainfall, and it takes more land to produce the yields of places which have more rain. So the margin between success and failure has never been very wide. People tried to make up the difference by plowing unsuitable land and by putting too much livestock on too small a range for too long. Conservation farming—strip cropping, contour plowing, and so on—was unheard of in those days. The dry years of the twenties only increased the problem. And in the thirties it became a disaster.

Soil which is blowing around can't provide a livelihood for people or mule deer. The early 1930s were a low point for wildlife which had survived the earlier onslaughts of hide hunters and settlers. Competition from cattle outstripped any past competition from buffalo, bighorns, or pronghorns. Much habitat had been destroyed. And conditions for rebuilding populations were not very good.

In the 1940s, things began to look up for mule deer in North Dakota—for a variety of reasons, not the least of which was the fact that thousands of people left the state during the dustbowl years. But things have continued to improve, and that story will be continued in Part II.

111

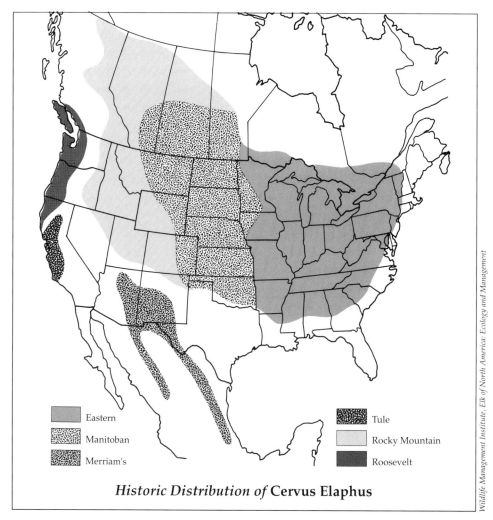

Wildlife Management Institute, Elk of North America: Ecology and Management

Eastern

Manitoban

Merriam's

Tule

Rocky Mountain

Roosevelt

Historic Distribution of **Cervus Elaphus**

ELK

In the days before European exploration and settlement, herds of elk lived on the northern prairies along with the buffalo and antelope. When Europeans came to the New World there were six distinct populations of elk living on the continent. There were, perhaps, ten million elk in these populations—making elk the third most numerous large mammal on the continent, next to bison and pronghorns. The European newcomers recognized our elk by his relatives in the Old World—the European red deer. "This beast most resembles the red deer, in colour, shape, and form of the horns, though it is a much larger animal, and of a stronger make; their horns are not palmated but round, a pair of which weighs upward of thirty pounds" (Catesby, 1754, in Bryant et. al., 1982, p. 4). If such writers had stayed with the name "red deer" they might have eliminated some later confusion about which animal they were talking about—"elk" in

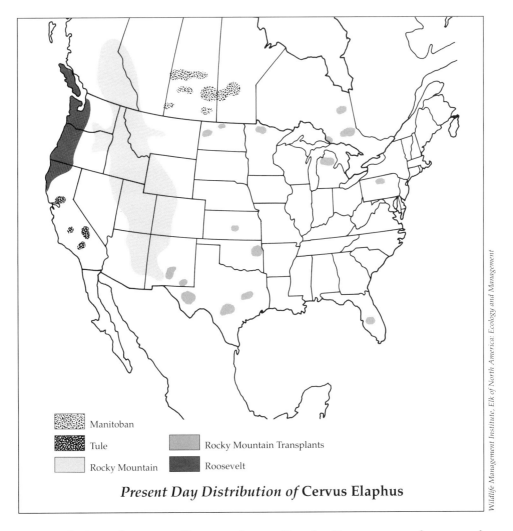

Manitoban

Tule

Rocky Mountain

Rocky Mountain Transplants

Roosevelt

Present Day Distribution of Cervus Elaphus

Wildlife Management Institute, Elk of North America: Ecology and Management

Europe being what we call moose here. But the European explorers and adventurers settled on the name elk, and elk they have remained, despite efforts to distinguish them with the Shawnee word *Wapiti*.

Elk are Old World deer. Most of their evolutionary history took place in the Old World of Europe and Asia. Whitetails, mule deer, and moose are New World deer—most of their evolutionary history took place in the New World. Elk as we know them have been isolated from their Old World relatives for only a short time. "Available evidence shows that recent elk in North America have been separated from recent Eurasian red deer for an exceedingly short period of geological time (about 10,000 years) (Bryant et. al., 1982, p. 12).

As a result of this (in geologic terms) relatively short time period, the North American elk and the European red deer have not grown very far apart. The two deer can interbreed and have fertile offspring. In addition, there has not been time for elk—especially the elk populations in different physiographic regions of North America—to become highly adapted to their various environments. It makes for an interesting problem in classification. Elk are of the order Artiodactyla and the family Cervidae (turn back to p. 85 for a chart of this classification); furthermore, both North American elk and European red deer are of the genus *Cervus*. Up to this point, taxonomists agree. But at the species and subspecies levels, there is some debate.

Are red deer and elk the same species? They can interbreed and produce fertile offspring—a generally accepted indicator that they are the same species. On the other hand, they have been geographically separated for 10,000 years and are quite different animals in appearance. When elk arrived on the North American continent, they found few competitors. The ice age had cleared the way. Such bounty pushed elk in the direction of big bodies and big horns. "The greater the availability of resources, the better developed are body tissues of low growth priority, leading to larger bodies and antlers, longer skulls, greater fat depots, fewer malformations, and a better immunity system" (Geist, 1982, p. 223). In the early part of this century, biologists granted separate species status to red deer and elk—they were both of the genus *Cervus*; red deer were *C. elaphus*, and North American elk were *C. canadensis*; the different North American elk were subspecies of *canadensis*—although there was some more debate as to how many actual subspecies there were. Today, largely because of their ability to interbreed and produce fertile offspring, elk and red deer are considered subspecies of *C. elaphus*. The thought is that the separation of species is complete when interbreeding becomes a disadvantage in terms of survival—as would be the case when infertile offspring are produced. Since that has not happened, red deer and elk are the same species.

Questions about the classification of animals—that is, how biologically and ecologically distinct one animal is from another—are important because to answer them we have to learn about the forces which cause species to evolve. Elk in the New World, at the time when Europeans first came, were being affected by one of the major forces of evolutionary change—geographic isolation. The land bridge which joined the New World with the Old had been closed for 10,000 years; and the changes brought about by the ice age to North America—ice barriers, the advances and retreats of forests and grasslands as climates changed—had distributed elk into six more or less distinct populations. These were Eastern elk, Manitoban elk, Merriam elk, Tule elk, Rocky Mountain elk, and Roosevelt elk; they were distributed over North America along lines of climate and vegetation. The maps on pages 112-113 illustrate clearly the boundaries of habitat and population.

Elk are described as "ecotone forms" (see Geist, 1982, p. 224)—which means that they are adapted to places where different vegetational types meet. They have the ability to live both in forests and in grasslands. The distribution and isolation of elk populations in North America, might, over time, have pushed these different elk populations—now considered to be subspecies of *C. elaphus*—in different directions, as grazers or browsers, as the case might have been. Presumably the different populations would have become more and more specialized in terms of habitat—become ecologically distinct—given sufficient time. Habitat would have perhaps changed the behavior of different populations. They might, thousands of years from now, have become different enough from each other—and from red deer—to be classified as different species of the genus *Cervus*. Settlement, and its large-scale destruction of elk populations, put an end to those developmental paths.

Of the six subspecies of elk to be found in North America before the Europeans came, two are extinct. These are Eastern elk and Merriam elk. The distribution of the remaining four subspecies has changed substantially. The maps on pages 112-113 show the distributions of the subspecies of elk and the changes to their distribution over time.

ELK IN NORTH DAKOTA

The subspecies of elk which originally inhabited the Great Plains was the Manitoban elk—*C. e. manitobensis*. Elk, as ice age creatures, well-suited to cold climates and able to eat a variety of foods, were ideal animals for the period of time following the retreat of the glaciers. As the climate warmed and dried, and grasslands replaced forests, elk were able to adjust. As the Great Plains evolved, so did a population of elk.

There is not very much information about actual numbers of Manitoban elk, or on the limits of their distribution. Records indicate that they ranged east to where the tall grass prairie abuts the eastern forest region, and west to the foot of the Rocky Mountains. Historically, the range of plains elk was limited more by the availability of cover from the wind than by the availability of food, especially in winter. The best protection was in riparian forest—the timber along the river banks. "As the Wisconsin glaciation receded, elk may have foraged in the same habitat as did the bison during the spring, summer, and autumn, but would have been forced into riparian communities by winter storms. The amount and distribution of riparian thermal cover would have dictated the carrying capacity of post-Wisconsin glacial stage elk ranges, and thus the elk's distribution in time and space" (Bryant et. al., 1982, p. 21).

Records show that there were plenty of elk in North Dakota in the early 1800s. They were an important game animal for the Indian tribes of the region, especially to those who were not nomadic or didn't have horses. John Tanner, a white man who was captured by Indians when he was a boy and who spent thirty years with Indians along the Red River, the Saskatchewan River, and the Assiniboin, wrote often of elk in his memoirs. Had it not been for elk, Tanner and his family might have starved. "It often happened that while we lived with *Waw-zhe-kwaw-maish-koon*, that we were suffering from hunger. Once, after a day and a night in which we had not tasted a mouthful, I went…to hunt, and we found a herd of elks. We killed two and wounded a third, which we pursued until night, when we overtook it…. all of which lasted us no more than two days" (Tanner, 1956, p. 89).

Alexander Henry, operating his Red River trading posts—and, incidentally, reporting some of the same events as Tanner, though from an opposing point of view—ate elk meat, and traded for elk skins. In the eight years he ran his posts, Henry's records show over 1100 elk skins— these are dressed skins traded for, and does not include the number of animals he and his men hunted and used for food or for other necessities of life on the frontier. Henry wrote often of the country and the animals they found:

> August 20, 1800 (on the Red River, near Winnipeg)—The S. side of the Assiniboine, particularly near the Forks, is a woody country, overgrown with poplars so thickly as scarcely to allow a man to pass on foot; this extends some miles W., when the wood is intersected by small meadows. This woody country continues S. up Red River to Riviere la Sale. On the E. side the land is low, overgrown with poplars and willows, frequently intersected by marshes, stagnant ponds, and small rivulets. Moose, red deer, and bears are numerous.

> Sept. 8, 1800—We went up [Park] River about a mile, when we fell in with two large harts [male elk]; we killed one and wounded the other, but did not go after him. Took off the skin and cut up the meat; the fat was four inches thick upon the rump….
>
> The entrance of this river is frequented by buffalo, red deer, moose, and bears; indeed it appears that the higher we go, the more numerous are red deer and bears. On the beach raccoon tracks are plentiful. Wolves are numerous and insolent.

In 1804, when Lewis and Clark were coming up the Missouri, Eastern elk had already been pressured hard along the Ohio and Mississippi rivers. On their ascent up the Missouri, Lewis and Clark first mention elk one month—and some 300 river miles—after they left behind the last white settlement on the river. "Deer not so plenty as usual, great deal of Elk sign" (Clark, July 5, 1804, near Independence, Missouri). Elk did not become plentiful until the expedition was on the threshold of the Great Plains. "Newman and Howard killed four fine Elk, we had the meat all jurked and the Skins Dried to cover the Perogue" (Clark, Sept. 2, 1804, above Yankton, South Dakota). During the winter of 1804 and 05, at Fort Mandan, Lewis and Clark frequently mention elk. "A little after dark this evening Capt Clark arrived with the hunting party since they set out they have killed forty Deer, three buffaloe bulls & sixteen Elk…" (Lewis, Feb. 12, 1805).

Elk-horn pyramid – from a painting by Karl Bodmer.

Besides being a preferred food for these adventurers—recall Henry's comment, Nov. 21, 1800, "There was a cow herd at hand, but our hunters were killing plenty of red deer"—elk were useful in other ways. Elk leather was the best for mocassins. Tanner wrote, "We returned to the woods to select some good elk and moose skins for mocassins. The skins of animals living in the open prairies are tender, and do not make good leather" (Tanner, 1956, p. 121). Sergeant Gass of the Lewis and Clark Expedition wrote that during the winter of 1805-06 they made 338 pairs of mocassins, "most of them…of the skins of elk" (Cutright, 1969, p. 257). Cutright (p. 257) notes that 12 pairs of mocassins could be made from an elk skin, but a deer hide was good for only five or six.

Elk tallow was used for candles: "This evening we exhausted the last of our candles, but fortunately had taken the precaution to bring with us moulds and wick, by means of which and some Elk's tallow in our possession we do not yet consider ourselves destitute of this necessary article" (Cutright, p. 256). Elk skins were used as blankets ("rained all the last night we covered ourselves as well as we could with Elk skins"—Clark); the hides were cut into strips and braided into ropes ("we have already prepared a large rope of Elk-skin and a windlass by means of which we have no doubt of being able to draw the boat on the bank provided we can free [it] from the ice"—Lewis). Lewis, in reserve against a time in which the expedition would have to abandon its wooden dugouts, had brought with him the frame of a portable "iron boat" which he planned to cover with skins. As the expedition approached Great Falls, Lewis began to get ready. "[T]he party killed several deer and some Elk...the Elk skins I now begin to reserve for making the leather boat at the falls" (Lewis, May 13, 1805). When the boat was finally assembled, Lewis found "that the Elk skins I had prepared for my boat were insufficient to compleat her, some of them having become dammaged by the weather and being frequently wet" (June 21, 1805). Lewis made up the insufficiency with singed buffalo hides. When it was complete, twenty-seven elk skins and four buffalo hides had been used. The seams where the skins were sewed were "paid" with a mixture of tallow, beeswax and charcoal. "Finally, on July 9th, she was launched and 'lay like a perfect cork on the water.' While loading the canoes for departure a violent wind sprang up forcing further delay. By evening when the storm had abated Lewis discovered that the charcoal mixture had separated from the skins and the 'iron' canoe was leaking badly.... Lewis' disappointment was doubly acute when he discovered that the section covered with buffalo hides did not leak" (Burroughs, 1961, p. 16-17). Elk skins had, at least in this case, been a poor choice. The expedition might have taken a lesson from the Indians' bullboats and used buffalo hides throughout.

Over on Red River, Alexander Henry had better luck with his elk hides. One of the more interesting uses he mentions is for storing bears' fat. "The raw fat will not keep many days, particularly when the weather is sultry, soon turning rancid; but when melted down and properly taken care of it will keep good and sweet at any season" (Henry, Sept. 17, 1800). Elk skins were, apparently, the first choice for storage containers. "My men were employed in cutting up and melting bears' fat, which we pour into red deer skins..." (Henry, Sept 17, 1800).

Both Indians and whites seem to have hunted elk at any season of the year. They made greater use of elk during the winter, however, for at least one obvious reason. Winter weather drove the animals to the protection of the woods, whereas the buffalo remained on the prairie. Elk do not manage in deep snow as well as buffalo. Tanner (1956, p. 88) describes one Indian hunting strategy, apparently most effective in winter:

> We found a herd of elks, and chasing them one day, overtook and killed four of them. When the Indians hunt elk in this manner, after starting the herd they follow them at such a gait as they think they can keep up for many hours. The elks being frightened outstrip them at first by many miles, but the Indians, following at a steady pace along the path, at length come in sight of them. They then make another effort, and are no more seen for an hour or two, but the intervals at which the Indians have them in sight, grow more and more frequent, and longer and longer, until they cease to lose sight of them at all. The elks are now so much fatigued that they can only move in a slow trot, at last they

can but walk, by which time the strength of the Indians is nearly exhausted. They are commonly able to come up and fire into the rear of the herd, but the discharge of a gun quickens the motions of the elk, and it is a very active and determined man that can in this way come near enough to do execution more than once or twice, unless the snow is pretty deep. The elk, in running, does not lift his feet well from the ground, so that, in deep snow, he is easily taken.

Alexander Henry describes a memorable elk hunt with a Chippewa hunter (Henry calls the Chippewa Tribe "Saulteurs") which took place on the White Earth River in 1799:

> We had not gone far from the house before we fell upon the fresh tracks of some red deer, and after discovered the herd in a thicket of willows and poplars; we both fired, and the deer disappeared in different directions. We pursued them, but to no purpose, as the country was unfavorable. We then returned to the spot where we had fired, as the Indian suspected we had wounded some of them. We searched to see if we could find any blood; on my part I could find tracks, but no blood. The Indian soon called out, and I went to him, but could see no blood, nor any sign that an animal had been wounded. However, he pointed out the track of a large buck among the many others and told me that from the manner in which this buck had started off he was certain the animal had been wounded. As the ground was beaten in every direction by animals, it was only after a tedious search that he found where the buck had struck off. But no blood was seen until, passing through a thicket of willows, he observed a drop upon a leaf, and next a little more. He then began to examine more strictly, to find out in what part of the body the animal had been wounded; and judging by the height and other signs, he told me that the wound must have been somewhere between the shoulder and neck. We advanced about a mile, but saw nothing of the deer, and no more blood. I was for giving up the chase; but he assured me that the wound was mortal, and that if the animal should lie down he could not rise again. We proceeded two miles further, when, coming upon a small open space, he told me that the animal was at no great distance, and very probably in this meadow. We accordingly advanced a few yards, and there we found the deer lying at the last gasp. The wound was exactly as I had been told. The sagacity of the Saulteurs is tracing strong wood animals is astonishing. I have frequently observed occurrences of this nature...(Henry, Aug. 9, 1808).

Presumably Indians who could indulge themselves in such painstaking and inefficient stalks as Henry describes were not in any great need of meat. For meat in quantity, the tribes depended on the buffalo; and when

119

hunting buffalo they used methods calculated for efficiency—surrounds, pounds, or, later, running them with horses. For descriptions of these methods, look back at the chapter on buffalo.

Elk hunting, either by whites or Indians, can in no way be compared to buffalo hunting. Although elk were useful to the Indians, providing meat, material for mocassins, and tools (Lewis wrote, August 23, 1805, "They renew the edge [of their flint knives] by flaking off the flint with the point of an Elk's horn...what wood they cut was done either with stone or Elk's horn—the latter they use always...to split their wood. They sometimes make bows of the Elk's horn...") the tribes depended on buffalo. Whitemen hunted elk heavily on the plains, but visible numbers of elk dwindled only after the buffalo were gone.

John James Audubon foresaw a time when the buffalo would be gone from the prairies—"before many years the Buffalo, like the Great Auk, will have disappeared" (Audubon, Aug. 5, 1843)—but of the elk he wrote, "the number of this fine species of Deer that are about us now is almost inconceivable," and "These animals are abundant beyond belief" (Audubon, June 9&11, 1843). That too would change. Joseph Henry Taylor, writing about the Painted Woods region near Washburn, North Dakota in the 1870s, wrote:

> Of the larger wild game about the Painted Woods and vicinity, next the buffalo and bear, the elk were the next to disappear, which owing to a kind of domestication or attachment to the points where they were born and raised, they usually remained in the one neighborhood until exterminated by the great influx of hunters that came in with, or followed the building of the Northern Pacific....
>
> The last elk killed in the immediate neighborhood of the Painted Woods proper was slaughtered in the summer of 1874. It was a large bull, and so noted and well marked had he become in warding off the bullets of the hunters that he was termed "Bull of the Woods." His haunts were in the neighborhood of what is known as Wash Out Lake, situated near the present village of Falconer (Taylor, 1904, p. 135-136).

The 1870s, as well as a time of great westward movement by the railroads and settlers, were also the time of the campaigns to wipe out the Indians who stood in the way. Parker Gillmore, one of the sportsmen-adventurers attracted to the praries by reports of game abundance wrote (Gillmore, 1874, p. 98-99):

> [Elk] habitat [once] commenced with the prairie country, say Illinois or Indiana. However, those States have long ceased to know them; for, like other large game, they have rapidly retired before the tide of emigration. The upper waters of the Missouri, the plains around the fork of the North and South Saskatchewan

are where, at the present day [1874] this mammoth stag will be found most abundant. The adventurer who would follow them to these fastnesses must be a brave, determined person, for it is the centre of the hunting-grounds of some of the most warlike and treacherous of all the Indian tribes; and of late years so many acts of retaliation—yes, and treachery—have been practiced by the white man upon the aborigines, that the aborigines are too apt to regard all pale-faces as their natural-born enemies. Thus to shoot Wapitti will probably entail shooting savages; for if you are not prepared to do so in self-defense, it is highly improbable that you will return to the land of your nativity to relate your knowledge of their habits, or the success you have had in their pursuit.

Although Gillmore—and others—have the elk herds "retiring before the tide" of settlement—that is to say, moving west—it is more likely that the elk which inhabited North Dakota were simply wiped out. The elk which inhabit the Rocky Mountains today are the subspecies which has always lived there; the elk of the Great Plains were Manitoban elk, which exist today only in small areas of Manitoba and Saskatchewan. Elk were largely gone in North Dakota in the 1880s. Theodore Roosevelt wrote, "They were very plentiful along this river [the Little Missouri] until 1881, but the last of the big bands were slaughtered or scattered about that time" (Roosevelt, quoted in Bailey, 1926, p. 34). Accordingly to Bailey, the last record of that time period of an elk being killed in the Turtle Mountains was in 1887. He found only one report of an elk being killed after 1900, that "near Plaza, in Mountrail County…but no one could tell where it had come from" (Bailey, 1926, p. 35).

From this kind of evidence it would seem that early North Dakota laws trying to protect elk in the state were mostly wishful thinking. In 1901, the legislature closed the season on elk as well as buffalo, moose, and mountain sheep, but later these species stopped being mentioned. The biennial report of the Game and Fish Board of Control for 1909-1910 admitted, "Our law makes no mention of elk or moose, presumably for the reason that normally we have none of these animals in the state…." But the report went on to say (p. 32) that:

> [D]uring the past two years several of these animals have wandered into the state from adjacent territory and have been killed. As matters now stand the Board is powerless to protect or punish in cases of this kind. It would be very desirable to have these animals come into the state and breed here. Their coming should be encouraged, and also in a spirit of co-operation we should throw the mantle of protection over the animals that our sister states are striving so hard to preserve.

Wishful thinking indeed. Reports of elk wandering into the state are scanty. The **10th Biennial Report of the Game and Fish Commission**

(1927-28) reported (p. 11) that "through the courtesy of the United States Department of Agriculture, three elks and three buffalo were secured" for a fenced tract of land in the Turtle Mountains owned and operated by the commission as a game reserve. By the end of 1930, the reserve, then known as the North Dakota Big Game Park contained "six Buffalo, four adults and two less than two years old; six Elk, five adults and one less than two years old; four adult White-tailed Deer" (**First Annual Report of the State Game and Fish Commissioner**, 1930, p. 26). The 1935 annual report stated that the Department was "planning on the propagation of deer and elk on a small scale. Those deer and elk will be trapped out of a park that the Department owns in the Turtle Mountains. The deer will be released in the Mouse River country and placed along the Missouri River. The elk will be transferred to the park out in the Badlands north of Medora. This propagation work will be carried on for the purpose of saving the deer from complete extermination, having an occasional open season, and the introduction of new blood."

In 1942, a service club called the Town Criers of Killdeer, North Dakota, took it upon themselves to try to reestablish a wild herd of elk in the state. The club got the animals from Wyoming with the intention of releasing them into the Badlands. While the Game and Fish Department congratulated the Town Criers on their enthusiasm in getting the project going, they expressed some doubts about its success:

> Officials of the department are not too optimistic about maintaining a large herd of elk in the state of North Dakota...As the herd increases the animals will roam throughout the western part of the state, and most of the land is privately owned. There will be farmers who will welcome the animals, and there will be others that won't want them competing with other livestock for a spot on the range (**ND Outdoors**, March, 1942).

Elk being released into the Killdeers, 1942.

Over time, the elk released by the Town Criers disappeared, and the release had to be judged a failure. Possible reasons for the failure will be discussed more completely in Part II of this book. When the elk were first brought to Killdeer in February of 1942, William J. Lowe, then Game and Fish Commissioner, cautioned enthusiastic sportsmen that "someday [they] may be able to shoot elk, but it is a long way in the future" (**Dickinson Press**, Feb. 20, 1942). Very likely he would have preferred to be wrong. An elk season was not held in North Dakota until 1983.

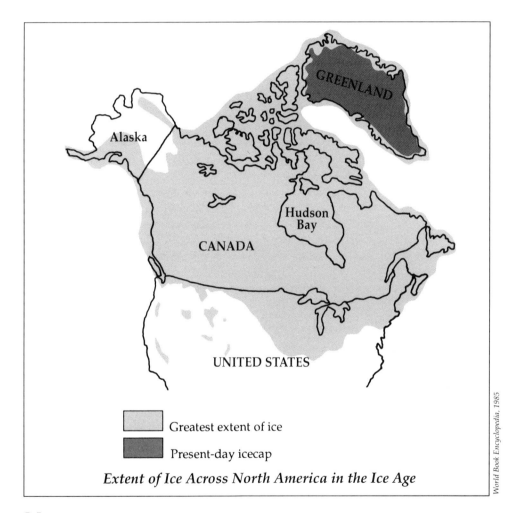

Greatest extent of ice

Present-day icecap

Extent of Ice Across North America in the Ice Age

World Book Encyclopedia, 1985

MOOSE

The mind's eye image of a moose—standing hock-deep in a woodlands lake placidly munching on water plants—doesn't fit with the mind's eye image of North Dakota. Yet there has been only a brief time—less than a century—since the end of the ice age when moose did not live within our borders.

Moose are the largest members of the deer family, and, like other deer, owe their recent history to the advance and retreat of glaciers. Primitive moose appeared as much as two and a half million years ago, but the evolutionary path to today's moose is impossible to follow. Today's moose is *Alces alces*—genus *Alces* and species *alces*. Its most probable ancestor is *Alces latifrons*—literally, "wide forehead"—which appeared in Alaska 200,000 years ago. *Latifrons* was a huge moose, weighing as much as 2,200 pounds with an antler spread of nine feet (see Geist, 1987b, p. 20). *Alces latifrons* and another of its descendents, *Alces scotti*, are extinct, leaving only one species of North American moose—*Alces alces*.

As with other big game species, the advance and retreat of glaciers gave moose a geographical and evolutionary push. During the last period of glaciation—known as the Wisconsin stage—ice covered a large portion of North America, including most of what is now North Dakota—see the map on page 123. Regions beyond the reach of the ice were covered with a coniferous forest like the forest in Ontario and Manitoba now. Such forests covered much of what became the Great Plains, and moose lived as far south as South Carolina. As the climate changed at the close of the Wisconsin stage, vegetation also changed. The northern forest followed the retreating ice north. In the Great Plains, warmer and drier conditions began to favor grasses over trees. In the more humid east, conifers were replaced by deciduous trees. Moose followed the coniferous forest north and retreated from the advancing grassland.

This doesn't mean what it seems to imply—that moose habitat is limited to the forests and the temperature ranges of the north and of the western mountains. In describing moose habitat, R. L. Peterson wrote, "The basis of a favorable habitat for moose is continual forest succession or regeneration. Moose populations apparently reach their maximum in the early stages of succession and decrease as the forest reaches maturity" (Peterson, 1955, p. 153). As the Wisconsin glacier retreated, a plant succession favorable to moose began, and moose moved into this newly-created habitat. To the south, moose continued to live marginally in places where climatic fluctuations made the tide of the grasslands ebb and flow.

Glacial ice has been gone for some 10,000 years—in some places less than that—and moose have spread over much of the northern half of the continent. At the time when European explorers came to North America there were four distinct subspecies of moose on the continent—the Alaskan moose (*Alces alces gigas*) in Alaska and the western Yukon Territory; Northwestern moose (*A. a. andersoni*) from the Yukon Territory southeast to the Great Lakes; Eastern moose (*A. a. americani*) in the northeastern United States and eastern Canada; and Shiras moose (*A. a. shirasi*) in the northern Rockies of the United States.

Moose are New World deer rather than Old World deer. They are more like white-tailed deer than they are like elk. Like whitetails, moose are browsers, feeding primarily on the young shoots and buds of deciduous

Craig Bihrle

trees and shrubs. As we have seen, moose are "pioneers"—they will move into places which provide them an abundance of this kind of food. Typically these are places where some event—like a forest fire or an avalanche or the advance and retreat of a glacier—has opened the way to new growth or regrowth. Moose are also adapted to cold climates, making habitat and climate the primary limits to moose range in North America. Albert Franzmann (1978, p. 79) wrote, "climates exceeding...82 degrees Fahrenheit for long periods without shade or access to lakes or rivers do not support moose." "[But] there is no evidence that extreme cold for short periods has adverse effects on moose if they can obtain shelter from wind."

Most of North Dakota is, of course, dry, open, windy, and often very hot or very cold—perfect for grasses but not very good for moose. Historically, North Dakota moose lived in the northeast corner of the state—where the northern forests edge into the Red River Valley—and in the Turtle Mountains. Vernon Bailey (1926, p. 32) described the Turtle Mountains as "a perfect moose paradise." "The country is ideal for them...combin[ing] dense forest, thickets, and a network of marshes and lakes, where the tule borders half hide the floating pads and golden globes of the cowlily..."

We can only guess at the numbers of moose in North Dakota in the period before settlement. Alexander Henry, who lived along the Red River and in the Pembina Hills between 1800 and 1808, writes of remarkable numbers of buffalo; other animals were, evidently, neither particularly abundant nor particularly rare.

> August 9, 1808, near the Pembina River—At the Long Reach we found more Indians to whom I gave some tobacco; they would have loaded us with moose and red deer meat...

> August 18, 1800—We saw several fresh tracks of moose, red deer, and bears; also some wolves and foxes.

One indication that moose may have been rarer than elk is the amount that Henry paid for them. Traders and trappers of Henry's day used beaver skins as the medium of exchange, and everything had its value in numbers of beaver skins.

> Autumn, 1799, Red River—For every moose [I gave the value of] six skins; for every red deer, five skins; to be paid for in whatever article of dry goods they might think proper to take, at the low price of four skins for a fathom of common blue strands or a blanket of 2-1/2 points, and other goods in proportion....

In places where moose were more abundant, they played a larger role in the native economy and in the new economy brought by Europeans. Randolph Peterson (1955, p. 20) wrote:

With the beginning of the seventeenth century the increased tempo of exploration brought about a great exploitation of the moose. More accurate, detailed, and complete accounts were made by the Jesuit missionaries in their Relations, in which they referred to moose as *l'elan* or *l'orignal*. From these accounts it is quite evident that moose provided one of the most important sources of food and clothing for the Indians and food for the missionaries of the St. Lawrence area, as well as for early travellers and residents across the northern coniferous forest belt. The missionaries refer frequently to hunger and starvation among the Indians and themselves because of failure to obtain moose. To the Indians, the moose had previously meant food, clothing, and materials for barter with other tribes or for fashioning various implements. The coming of the whiteman and fire-arms made moose meat and skins important articles of commerce which created an unprecedented exploitation of moose by both Indians and whites.

According to John Tanner, who spent thirty years with Indians in the moose country of Manitoba and Saskatchewan, Indians regarded moose as one of the most difficult big game animals to kill. In his **Narrative** (Tanner, 1956, p. 82-83) he related the following:

There is an opinion prevalent among the Indians, that the moose, among the methods of self-preservation with which he seems better acquainted than almost any other animal, has the power of remaining for a long time under water. Two men of the band of *Wa-ge-to-tah-gun,* whom I knew perfectly well, and considered very good and credible Indians, after a long day's absence on a hunt, came in, and stated that they had chased a moose into a small pond, that they had seen him in the middle of it, and disappear, and then, choosing positions, from which they could see every part of the circumference of the pond, smoked, and waited until near evening; during all which time, they could see no motion of the water, or any other indication of the position of the moose. At length, being discouraged, they had abandoned all hope of taking him, and returned home. Not long afterwards came a solitary hunter loaded with meat. He related that having followed the track of a moose for some distance, he had traced it to the pond before mentioned, but having also discovered the tracks of two men, made at the same time as those of the moose, he concluded they must have killed it. Nevertheless, approaching cautiously to the margin of the pond, he sat down to rest. Presently he saw the moose rise slowly in the center of the pond, which was not very deep, and wade towards the shore where he was sitting. When he came sufficiently near, he shot him in the water. The Indians consider moose shyer and more difficult to take than any other animal. He is more vigilant, and his senses more acute than those of the buffalo or caribou. He is fleeter than the elk, and more prudent and crafty than the antelope. In the most violent storm when the wind, and the thunder, and the falling timber are making the loudest and most incessant roar, if a man, either with his foot or his hand, breaks the smallest dry limb in the forest, the moose will hear it, and though he does not always run, he ceases eating, and rouses his attention to all sounds. If in the course of an hour, or thereabout, the man neither moves, nor makes the least noise, the animal may begin to feed again, but does not forget what he has heard, and is for many hours more vigilant than before.

Tanner's story makes a fine testimonial for the sport of moose hunting. But it is hard to see how the Indians could have depended on moose meat for food and moose hides for clothing. George Shiras, writing for **National Geographic Magazine** in 1912, had a less glowing opinion of them. "...no antlered animal of the earth is more obtuse and stolid than the moose, and no animal, when finally alarmed, is a greater victim of an increasing and progressive fear than this. At times it seems almost impossible to alarm them, and when this is accomplished, one wonders whether they ever recover from the shock" (Peterson, 1955, p. 101).

Whether or not moose were easy to hunt, their scarcity made them relatively unimportant to Indians in this region. Tanner wrote that "We...returned to the woods to select some good elk and moose skins for moccasins. The skins of animals living in the open prairies are tender, and do not make good leather" (Tanner, 1956, p. 121). Apparently, at least to some tribes, moose hide had special uses, but elk were more available.

In the early days of settlement, moose in North Dakota had been reduced to occasional strays from the populations to the north and east. The only attempt to put together records of moose during that period was Bailey's 1926 **Biological Survey of North Dakota**. In 1887, when Bailey himself was in Bottineau, North Dakota, there were still moose in the Turtle Mountains. But between then and 1926, reports of moose were few and far between. From Bailey (1926, p. 32):

> ...a moose [was] killed in 1898 by G. N. Brown at Rock Lake.... At Walhalla...one [was] killed...in 1889.
>
> In 1915, Remington Kellogg learned of a moose killed 3 miles south of Grafton, in 1900, and another on the Red River, 3 miles east of Grafton, in 1908. H. V. Williams reported one killed near Glasston in 1905, and another at Drayton, on the Red River, in 1906.
>
> W. B. Bell reported the capture of a cow moose in Sargent County in the fall of 1913. It was kept captive at the Ellendale Industrial School for a time, but later was sent to a public park in Minnesota. A bull and cow and two calves near Mayville, in Traill County, were also reported to Dr. Bell the same year, but the report was not fully verified.

That is not very many moose. When Morris Johnson was interviewing long-time North Dakota residents—people with close connections to wildlife—for **Feathers From the Prairie** in 1962, only one man mentioned moose at all. Patrick E. McMahon, who lived from 1909 to 1952 in Rugby, North Dakota, saw one moose in North Dakota in 1938. "This moose was running across a field of shocked grain, knocking over the shocks as he ran. The actual location was one-half mile east of Barton, North Dakota, and he was later sighted going right across Round Lake" (Johnson, 1962).

North Dakota Game and Fish documents have very few references to moose in the early days. When moose are mentioned at all, it is to say that there are no moose in North Dakota:

> **Biennial Report**, 1909-10: Our law makes no mention of elk or moose, presumably for the reason that normally we have none of these animals in the state....

> **Biennial Report**, 1923-24: Less than fifty years ago herds of Buffalo ranged the North Dakota prairies in great numbers, Elk were commonly found on suitable ranges, Moose could be found in the Turtle and Pembina Mountains.... The Buffalo, the Elk and the Moose have gone forever as a game to be hunted.

It is plain that almost no one in North Dakota thought that moose would ever return. The "official" attitude of the time was to keep a stiff upper lip about it. "In many cases the disappearance of the native game before the settlement of the country was wholly necessary and can be regretted only on the grounds that the methods employed were wasteful and the rate of depletion unnecessarily rapid." (**Annual Report of the Game and Fish Department**, 1948, p. 5). But it is doubtful that they did not regret the loss of the buffalo, elk, mountain sheep, antelope, and moose.

Moose have returned to North Dakota. They are inhabiting their historical range in the Pembina Hills and the Turtle Mountains, and they have turned up as far from their traditional habitat as Bismarck. The story of North Dakota moose and modern moose hunts will be continued in Part II of this book.

Sources

Journals of Early Explorers

Audubon, John James

Audubon, Maria R. 1986. Audubon and His Journals, With Zoological and Other Notes by Elliott Coues. 2 Vols. Dover Books, New York.

Henry, Alexander

Coues, Elliott, ed. 1965. New Light on the History of the Greater Northwest: The Manuscript Journals of Alexander Henry and David Thompson. 2 Vols. Ross and Haines, Inc., Minneapolis.

Reid, Russell and Clell G. Gannon. 1928. Natural History Notes on the Journals of Alexander Henry. North Dakota Historical Quarterly 2(3):168-201.

Lewis and Clark

Burroughs, Raymond Darwin. 1961. The Natural History of the Lewis and Clark Expedition. Michigan State University Press.

Cutright, Paul R. 1969. Lewis and Clark: Pioneering Naturalists. University of Nebraska Press.

Reid, Russell. 1988. Lewis and Clark in North Dakota. State Historical Society of North Dakota, Bismarck.

Thwaites, Reuben Gold, ed. 1905. Original Journals of the Lewis and Clark Expedition. 8 Vols. Dodd, Mead, and Co, New York.

Maximilian, Prince of Weid

Thomas, Davis and Karin Ronnefeldt. 1976. People of the First Man: Life Among the Plains Indians in Their Final Days of Glory. Dutton, New York.

Thwaites, Reuben Gold, ed. 1906. Early Western Travels, Vols 22-25. Arthur H. Clark Co, Cleveland.

Nicolette, Joseph N.

Bray, Edward C. and Martha Coleman Bray, eds. and trans. 1976. Joseph N. Nicolette on the Expeditions of 1838-39 with Journals, Letters and Notes on the Dakota Indians. Minnesota Historical Press, St. Paul.

Other Sources

Bailey, Vernon. 1926. A Biological Survey of North Dakota. North American Fauna No. 49. U.S. Bureau of Biological Survey.

Baker, Rollin H. 1984. Origin, Classification and Distribution. pps. 1-18 of White-tailed Deer: Ecology and Management. Wildlife Management Institute. Stackpole Books, Harrisburg, PA.

Boller, Henry. 1966. Journal of a Trip to, and Residence in, the Indian Country, Commenced Saturday, May 22, 1858. North Dakota History 33(3):260-315.

Bryant, Larry D. and Chris Maser. 1982. Classification and Distribution. pps. 1-60 of North American Elk: Ecology and Management. Wildlife Management Institute. Stackpole Books, Harrisburg, PA.

Franzmann, Albert W. 1978. Moose. pps. 67-82 of Big Game of North America: Ecology and Management. Wildlife Management Institute. Stackpole Books, Harrisburg, PA.

Geist, Valerius. 1981. Adaptive Strategies in Mule Deer. pps. 157-223 of Mule and Black-tailed Deer of North America. Wildlife Management Institute. University of Nebraska Press.

Geist, Valerius. 1982. Adaptive Behavioral Strategies. pps. 219-278 of North American Elk: Ecology and Management. Wildlife Management Institute. Stackpole Books, Harrisburg, PA.

Geist, Valerius. 1987a. Hoofed Mammals. pps. 313-320 of Wild Animals of North America. National Geographic Society, Washington D.C.

Geist, Valerius. 1987b. On the Evolution and Adaptation of Alces. Swedish Wildlife Research Suppl. 1, 1987: 11-23.

Gillmore. Parker. 1874. Prairie and Forest: A Description of the Game of North America with Personal Adventures in Their Pursuit. Harper and Bros., New York.

Johnson, Morris D. 1962. Old Timer's Statements. North Dakota Game and Fish Department, Bismarck.

Mackie, Richard J. 1987. Mule Deer. pps. 265-271 of Restoring America's Wildlife. U.S. Dept. of Interior Fish and Wildlife Service.

McCabe, Richard E. and Thomas R. McCabe. 1984. Of Slings and Arrows: An Historical Retrospection. pps. 19-72 of White-tailed Deer: Ecology and Management. Wildlife Management Institute. Stackpole Books, Harrisburg, PA.

North Dakota Game and Fish Board of Control. Biennial Reports of the North Dakota Game and Fish Board. North Dakota Game and Fish Department, Bismarck.

North Dakota Game and Fish Commission. Biennial Reports of the State Game and Fish Commission. North Dakota Game and Fish Department, Bismarck.

North Dakota Game and Fish Department. Annual Reports of the State Game and Fish Commissioner. North Dakota State Game and Fish Department, Bismarck.

Peterson, Randolph L. 1955. North American Moose. University of Toronto Press.

Severson, Kieth E. 1981. Plains Habitats. pps. 459-485 of Mule and Black-tailed Deer of North America. Wildlife Management Institute. Stackpole Books, Harrisburg, PA.

Tanner, John. 1956. A Narrative of the Captivity and Adventures of John Tanner During Thirty Years' Residence Among the Indians in the Interior of North America. Ross and Haines.

Taylor, Joseph Henry. 1904. Beavers—Their Ways and Other Sketches. Printed and published by the author. Washburn, North Dakota.

A Short History

BIG GAME
IN NORTH DAKOTA

COLOR PLATES

PRONGHORN ANTELOPE
BY ED BRY

BISON
BY TOM GIBSON

BIGHORN SHEEP
BY LYNN BENDER

MOOSE
BY CRAIG BIHRLE

MULE DEER
BY PAUL CHRISTIANSON

WHITE-TAILED DEER
BY LYNN BENDER

ELK
BY DAPHNE KINZLER

PART TWO

Ed Bry

A NEW BEGINNING

If you had to pick a year to mark the start of the turnaround for big game in North Dakota, 1939 might be a good choice. 1939 was a year for a new beginning in many ways. It marked, for example, the end of the worst economic ten years in North Dakota's short history. The people of the state were ready for a new beginning for themselves. In 1939 North Dakota also received its first money from the Federal Aid in Wildlife Restoration Act—the Pittman-Robertson Act, as it has come to be known. That represented a new beginning for wildlife in North Dakota.

In 1939, North Dakota was fifty years old. There was not very much to celebrate. The roster of big game animals was looking very short. Buffalo—once numbering in the millions—were gone. The last season on antelope had been in 1900. North Dakota's bighorn sheep were extinct, along with the Great Plains wolf. Grizzlies and black bears were long gone. Moose were gone. Elk were gone. The only huntable big game animals in North Dakota in 1939 were deer. And deer seasons were held very cautiously—every other year at best, and for a very limited number of hunters.

We should summarize what had happened. The wildlife story had followed a pattern laid down with the first Europeans in the New World. In North Dakota, it went like this: when the fur trappers and traders came to the northern prairies they saw a sea of grass. The grasses rose and fell like the swells of the ocean; and the horizon was unbroken by walls or fences or plows. Wildlife roamed the prairies like fish in the sea— belonging to no one and free for the taking. Land, of course, unlike the sea, can hold fenceposts—it can be claimed—so the first Europeans on the prairies claimed the land for their kings, and began to exploit the wildlife. The future of the region did not concern them very much. They did not think the region had a future. Henry Boller wrote as late as 1858, "I was struck while travelling with the barrenness and desolation of the country, no trees, the grass on the prairies parched and scanty, no limpid streams, only vast and numerous lakes of stagnant rain water, muddy and full of sedge & wild fowl, and highly flavored with buffalo urine. I don't think that this country will ever be fit for the use of civilized man, and must ever remain a wilderness" (Sept. 16, 1858).

But Boller and men like him were wrong. The grasslands turned out to have the richest agricultural soil of all, and a second generation of white thinking came to the prairies. To farmers, the buffalo, wolves, and bears were obstacles to settlement—bears and wolves because they were a threat to people and livestock, and buffalo in another, more subtle way. Buffalo

136

represented competition for the range. They were a nuisance for trains going across the prairie. Buffalo trampled over fencelines and property lines. But the main reason that buffalo were a threat to settlement was that they supported the culture of the native people. General Philip Sheridan praised the buffalo hunters: "They are destroying the Indians' commissary…. [F]or the sake of a lasting peace, let them kill, skin, and sell until the buffaloes are exterminated. Then your prairies can be covered with speckled cattle and the festive cowboy, who follows the hunter as a second forerunner of an advanced civilization" (McHugh, 1972, p. 285).

We will forego comment on that. Once the buffalo, bears, and wolves were gone, and the prairies were covered with cowboys, farmers, and speckled cattle, the big game animals that were left became valuable for food. The process of carving profitable, productive farms and livestock operations out of tough prairie sod took some time, and wild game made survival possible for those early pioneers. Early game laws in North Dakota—for example, making it illegal to leave any part of the carcass of big game animals lying on the prairie—were designed to restrict the waste of animals by market hunters, leaving more for the use of the settlers.

But many settlers themselves thought that the disappearance of big game was inevitable. Even though they depended on big game for food, settlers gave very little thought to conservation. The first North Dakota Game and Fish Commissioner wrote (NDGFD, 1894, p. 10), "On assuming the duties of this office I made these discoveries: An almost universal belief amongst the people that…anyone was at liberty to…kill game birds and animals at any season of the year…at any time and in any quantity as might be convenient or desirable. At least but very little regard was paid to the laws governing these matters…"

George Smith

Game meant survival to homesteaders.

137

Although wild game meant simple survival rather than wealth, the attitude of settlers was much the same as that of the trappers and hide hunters. The settlers were making conscious changes for a new way of life on the prairies. The ideas that buffalo and sod and soil fertility might be interconnected were many years away. Settlers made bold changes. Pioneering, after all, cannot be a cautious way of life.

The first wildlife conservationists were sportsmen. They were the very opposite of pioneers, content to see the frontier unplowed, unfenced, and full of game. Parker Gillmore, who came west to hunt around 1870, was typical: "The time may come—I do not wish to see it—when these broad acres will possess mills and factories, daily disgorging their inky smoke into the pure azure heavens, or their thousands of unwashed mortality over what is now a flower studded prairie" (Gillmore, 1874, p. 147). Men like Gillmore could be content because, more often than not, their fortunes were already made. They hunted because they enjoyed it, not because they needed to. They were likely to be wealthy, and had what we today would call leisure time. A future without sport would, for men like these, be an impoverished way of life.

As wealthy men often are, these sportsmen-conservationists were an influential and effective group. "Almost all of the early state and federal laws protecting wildlife were devised and promoted by local, state and national sportsmen's organizations. State wildlife agencies evolved similarly, a result of hunter demands that wildlife be protected and managed for use by future generations" (Williamson, 1986, p. 13). At a national level, prominent men—Theodore Roosevelt, William Hornaday, and John Lacey are familiar names—roused public interest in protecting wildlife, and worked for the passage of legislation. Hornaday's efforts on behalf of the buffalo were noted in Part I. As President, Theodore Roosevelt pushed for—among other things—the National Wildlife Refuge system. The Lacey Act, named for John Lacey, was the first federal wildlife law, making it a federal offense to ship illegally killed game across state lines. These are examples of efforts on the parts of many individual sportsmen and sportsmen's organizations to do something about the steady downward march of wildlife populations.

In North Dakota, new legislation was passed. In 1897, licenses to hunt were first required. The first game warden was appointed. In 1899, the first bag limits were placed on big game. In 1901, the season was closed on all big game except deer—very much a too little too late measure—marking the first time that game was protected by a closed season. In 1905, North Dakota got its first National Wildlife Refuge.

But for all of that, conservationists in North Dakota knew that they could accomplish nothing without a major change in attitude on the part of the citizens of the state. It was time for people to become sportsmen instead of pioneers. In 1894, the Game and Fish Commissioner had written that "as [big game animals] are...much desired for food purposes, it is evidently wise to protect them for a series of years." In 1910, we find this: "Aside from the pleasure of the sport with rod and gun, there is much benefit in the outdoor life, in the relaxation from the cares of a humdrum life, in the healthy exercise, pure air and wholesome food. It would be a calamity to the race if hunting and fishing were to be abolished or lost to mankind through the total disappearance of game and fish. For the sake of the future generations, as well as that we ourselves may enjoy the fruits of the earth, the wild creatures must be saved." A shift like that was an ambitious goal indeed.

For people new to this kind of persuasion, those early conservationists used some sophisticated techniques. They began what we would call today a media campaign to call attention to the need for conservation, to rally support, and to put offenders squarely in the public eye. In 1910, the Game and Fish Board of Control wrote (NDGFD, 1910, p. 7-8):

> A special debt of gratitude is due to the newspapers of the state for the very important part they have played in making the present game laws and the work of the Board...successful to the extent that it has been a success. The editors of North Dakota have done a great work...by giving freely of their space to the publication of the provisions of the law, by urging sportsmanlike restraint on the part of the people, and in giving wide publicity to the arrests of violators of the law and the penalties imposed for law breaking. We fully appreciate what we owe to such support...

However, by 1910, almost any effort to save big game in North Dakota was thought to be too little too late. No amount of legislation, no number of game refuges, and no recognition of the value of big game was going to revive the Audubon bighorn or make elk and moose reinhabit the state. Game birds got most of the attention. It seemed possible to protect them—and if necessary, to propagate them. To that end, Chinese pheasants and Hungarian partridges were brought into North Dakota. For deer, the best that could be hoped for was that with closed seasons and refuges they might rebound enough to have a hunt once in a while.

The sequence of events in North Dakota was, as we have said, a classic sequence for people and wildlife in this country. It was repeated over and over. At first wildlife seemed limitless—there was no way that the immense herds of buffalo and antelope could ever disappear. Then laws were passed—becoming increasingly restrictive as game populations continued to decline. Bounties on predators were set up. Eventually seasons had to be closed, and refuges were set aside where animals could live and reproduce away from people. When these too failed to bring back the game, new species were brought in to replace native ones—animals which, it was hoped, were more tolerant of people and their activities. North Dakota bypassed only one phase of that classic early sequence. The last phase has often been one in which adaptable species—whitetails usually—rebound beyond what anyone expects or even wants. John Schmidt illustrates the whole pattern (Schmidt, 1978, p. 269):

> Pennsylvania provides a good example. By 1900, white-tailed deer had been extirpated. In 1906, a stocking program was initiated and, in 1907, a buck-only law was passed giving deer populations protection from non-selective harvests. A lush food base from logged forests and overprotection caused a deer irruption. By 1925, deer exceeded the carrying capacity of their habitat. By 1935, the population was believed to be four times more than carrying capacity allowed. Ranges were overbrowsed, tree production was reduced, farm crop damage increased, and quality of the deer declined. The public continued to balk at the idea of more liberal hunting harvests. In the winter of 1935, an estimated 100,000 deer died from malnutrition or associated problems.

North Dakota has, so far, avoided a massive die-off of white-tailed deer. But, as we shall see in Chapter Seven, the combination of large herds and severe winter weather has caused its share of problems. But we are getting ahead of ourselves. In 1930 in North Dakota, the deer season had been closed since 1923; between 1931 and 1939, it was open only every other year, and the most licenses sold in any season was 3,114. There had been no great leap in deer numbers. And no one expected any.

THE DIRTY THIRTIES AND THE SECOND WORLD WAR

In fact, there is nothing in the history of the United States up to 1930 that would have led us to expect what has happened since. It is hard to think of anything today—any aspect of our lives—that does not owe something to events between 1930 and 1945. The Depression, the Dust Bowl, and the Second World War brought profound changes to our ideas about conservation, wildlife, and the outdoors, both directly and indirectly. We can only suggest a few of them.

For all of the efforts of game departments and conservationists in the early 1900s, it took the disaster of the Dust Bowl to change people's attitudes toward conservation. North Dakota was typical of the Dust Bowl states—perhaps even worse than typical. The twin plagues of the thirties—drought and depression—hit North Dakota in the twenties. Wheat and cattle prices had been poor, and rainfall minimal. Agricultural producers had plowed and grazed more land to make ends meet. Banks loaned too much money against too little on deposit. If rainfall and prices had recovered in the thirties, and if the nation's economy hadn't collapsed, North Dakota might have gotten away with it. But instead, the bottom fell out for North Dakota. Farmers lost their farms to the banks and the wind; then the banks failed. Thousands of people left the state.

Wind erosion.

Nationwide, hundreds of banks failed in the early 1930s. Hundreds of factories closed; more than 10 million workers were unemployed. Farm and house mortgages were foreclosed. And dust—the topsoil from millions of acres of mid-west farms—darkened the skies in Washington and New York. People did not know what to do.

We have just about forgotten the lessons of the Dust Bowl—if today's erosion problems are any indication. But the general panic of the thirties was the biggest boost conservation has ever had in this country. The disaster was so pervasive that only a comprehensive solution had a hope of working. In addition to new programs for soil and water conservation, Congress was willing to listen to ideas about conserving other resources— notably, the nation's wildlife. There was a group of men, organized and ready, who did know what to do (Williamson, 1987, p. 2):

> Fortunately for wildlife, the nation's "conservation elite" was prominent in the 1930's. That distinguished corps were sportsmen, but they were not the average. They were leaders of business, industry and science. Most were well-off financially. Early on, the group had included Theodore Roosevelt, George Bird Grinnell, Charles Sheldon, John Burnham and others. During the 1930's the likes of J. N. Darling, M. Hatley Dodge, Charles Horn, Carl Shoemaker, Aldo Leopold, Thomas Beck, Ira Gabrielson and Frederick Walcott were members of conservation's special forces. They were good at their work, but also, they arrived on the scene when the Federal Government was in a most innovative mood and devising programs to beat the Depression. Consequently, they took advantage of the situation and helped foster the most fruitful decade of wildlife conservation ever.

141

Another profound change on behalf of wildlife came indirectly, from an unexpected source. That was the Second World War. The conservation achievements of the thirties—which we shall get to in a minute—took a back seat to the war effort in the early forties. But the nation which existed following the war was far different than the one which floundered during the Dust Bowl. Having just won the war, it was a nation confident in its ability to get things done. Moreover, it had won the war by being able to out-produce its enemies. The technology which had won the war was the technology that would give each American a better life. A better life meant leisure—for everyone, not simply the wealthy. Leisure meant wildlife and the outdoors. After the war, America woke to a renewed fascination with—and concern for—wildlife.

"SCIENTIFIC" GAME MANAGEMENT

The leading conservationists of the late 1930s were a remarkable group of men. Aldo Leopold was, of course, the "father of modern game management." Carl Shoemaker was a lawyer and a newspaperman. In 1915 he became the head of the Oregon Fish and Game Commission. "Ding" Darling won a Pulitzer as a political cartoonist—and later became head of the U. S. Bureau of Biological Survey. Later still, he helped to found and became the first president of the National Wildlife Federation. These were men of considerable ability, wide-ranging interests, and great dedication. It all seems rather remarkable to us today, in these days of intense specialization.

All of these conservation-minded men were aware of how haphazard and ineffective past schemes to restore wildlife had been. They saw the need to put sound management principles into action—such as were laid out in Aldo Leopold's landmark book **Game Management**, published in 1933. And they set about creating the means to do it.

The vocabulary of game management is familiar to us today. It was at this time that words like "habitat," "carrying capacity," and "harvest" came into use. Leopold's theories acknowledged the relationship of wildlife populations to the environments in which they lived. Each wildlife species had particular habitat needs. "Leopold also recognized that each unit of habitat has a carrying capacity, an upper limit of animals of a given species that it can support in health and vigor throughout the year" (Poole and Trefethan, 1978, p. 341). Healthy wildlife populations were dependent on habitat. To increase—or, in many places, restore—wildlife populations, habitat needed to be increased or restored. Where wildlife populations exceeded the carrying capacity of the habitat, the surplus animals could be—indeed should be—"harvested" to protect the quality of the habitat and the health of the population. Game management was, to a very large degree, habitat management.

But much work needed to be done. The nutritional needs of most species were unknown. The links between habitat and reproduction, survival, and animal behavior were unknown. In many places, no one had ever analyzed the habitat itself—what vegetation there was to work with. There was very little reliable data to work from. One thing was very clear from the outset. The recreational hunter and the game manager were going to be very valuable to one another. Hunting was built into the concepts of carrying capacity and harvest. Just as hunters needed game managers to build and maintain wildlife populations, game managers needed hunters to control the size of the population. As time went on, hunting has also been a tool for managing the age and sex composition of game populations, and even the distribution of big game herds.

In 1930, no state game and fish agency was managing along these principles. Shoemaker and Darling and the rest of the "conservation elite" saw that some changes needed to be made. In most state agencies, politics played a larger role than science. Agencies needed people with better qualifications for the job. They also needed money. No state agency had the money to set up the long-term survey and research programs they needed. No state agency had the money to acquire or develop land for wildlife habitat. The money from license sales was neither large enough nor consistent enough to do what needed to be done. The question was, how?

PITTMAN-ROBERTSON

The "how" was provided by the Federal Aid in Wildlife Restoration Act—the Pittman-Robertson (P-R) Act, so-called in honor of its congressional sponsors. Pittman-Robertson has been called the most significant piece of wildlife legislation ever.

Pittman-Robertson was designed to provide that large and reliable funding source which would allow state agencies to do wildlife research, to find out what was going on with their wildlife populations, and to buy, develop, and manage habitat for wildlife. The act was passed by Congress in 1937, and by 1939, most states had passed their own legislation allowing them to take advantage of the program. North Dakota did so in 1939, which is why it is a significant year for big game.

Federal funding for P-R comes from an excise tax on arms, ammunition, and archery equipment. It is apportioned to the states, taking into account a state's area, and its total number of licensed hunters. States provide 25 percent of the funding for an approved P-R program, and 75 percent comes from federal assistance. When the program first began, three types of projects were approved for funding: "1. The purchase of land for wildlife-rehabilitation purposes. 2. The development of land to make it more suitable for wild mammals and birds... 3. Research projects set up on a definite basis and directed to the solution of problems that stand in the way of wildlife restoration" (Williamson, 1987, p. 12). Later, hunter-education programs were added to the list of approved projects.

In order for states to become eligible to receive funding, the P-R Act required state legislatures to pass laws, first to prevent hunting license fees from being spent on anything but administering the game and fish agency, and second, that game and fish personnel be trained and qualified for the work they were doing. The intent was to prevent money meant for wildlife from being siphoned off for other kinds of state projects, and to lessen the effects of political change on the programs of wildlife agencies.

In the 1930s, North Dakota was in the same position as most states. The Game and Fish Department had been reorganized in 1930 to the form it has today. To "manage" game, the Department had the power to issue general hunting licenses, deer licenses, trapping licenses, licenses for professional dog trainers, and licenses for taxidermists. The Department regulated the propagation and release of game birds. The Department had the power to enforce game laws through district and deputy wardens.

Prior to 1925, seasons and bag limits had been set by the legislature. In 1925, an act was passed which permitted the Governor to regulate seasons "to meet emergencies which could not be foreseen by the legislature."

The Game and Fish Department could establish game refuges and game

Pittman-Robertson projects.

farms. As of 1930, the Department had three game farms, although little was being done with them. A 70 acre tract of land near Bottineau was sold in 1931, and two others, near Mandan and Dawson, have now been converted to Wildlife Management Areas. As of 1930, the Department managed some 75,800 acres of land as wildlife refuges.

These, basically, were the tools the Game and Fish Department in North Dakota had to work with. It was not a lot. As we have said, most of the efforts were concentrated on birds. In 1930, seasons on deer had been closed since 1923. Seasons on antelope had been closed since 1900. There were no other big game animals except an occasional moose that might wander into the state from the Canadian side of the Turtle Mountains; these were usually poached before they could make it back to safety.

Between 1930 and 1939 there was little continuity in the direction of the newly formed Game and Fish Department. Five different men held the commissioner's office during those years. In April, 1939, William Lowe was appointed commissioner—he would stay in office for the next nine years—and the legislation necessary to take advantage of P-R funds was passed.

ND Game and Fish Department

Pittman-Robertson projects.

145

William Lowe, Commissioner, 1939-1948.

Like most state agencies, the North Dakota Game and Fish Department was not set up for these new kinds of projects. The Department needed new manpower to design and implement the programs. A new division—the "Federal Aid Division"—was set up within the Game and Fish Department to take advantage of the new opportunity, and the legislature appropriated funds to match the federal contribution. In 1939, North Dakota received $11,490 in federal apportionments. By way of comparison, in 1987, the Pittman-Robertson Act contributed $1,477,201 to North Dakota's wildlife programs.

The first P-R project for big game in North Dakota was an attempt to survey the numbers of white-tailed deer, mule deer, and antelope in the state. There had not been a comprehensive big game survey or "census" in the state since Vernon Bailey's in 1926. In 1940, the U.S. Fish and Wildlife Service had reported North Dakota's big game populations to be 13,324 white-tailed deer, 55 mule deer, and 18 each of elk, antelope, and buffalo (NDGFD, 1941, p. 17). Based on the amount of available habitat, Department people thought the estimate for whitetails was far too high. But they had no data to back up their feelings, either about the number of deer, or the amount of quality deer habitat.

By today's standards, this first management effort had modest ambitions. Part II of this History will document the considerable development of those ambitions as time went on. In 1940 there were only deer to consider as a huntable species; and during the 1941 season, hunters took only 2,890 animals. Today there are seasons on deer, antelope, elk, moose, and bighorn sheep; in 1987, over 75,000 deer licenses were issued. But even those numbers can't get at the scope of the change that has taken place. For the rest of the story, read on.

Sources

Boller, Henry. 1966. Journal of a Trip to, and Residence in, the Indian Country, Commenced Saturday, May 22d, 1858. North Dakota History 33(3):260-315.

Gillmore, Parker. 1874. Prairie and Forest: A Description of the Game of North America with Personal Adventures in Their Pursuit. Harper and Bros., New York.

McHugh, Tom. 1972. The Time of the Buffalo. University of Nebraska Press.

North Dakota Game and Fish Board. 1911. 1st Biennial Report of the North Dakota Game and Fish Board. North Dakota Game and Fish Department, Bismarck.

North Dakota Game and Fish Commission. 1894. 1st Biennial Report of the State Game and Fish Commissioner. North Dakota Game and Fish Department, Bismarck.

North Dakota Game and Fish Department. 1941. First Aerial Survey of North Dakota Big Game Completed. ND Outdoors 3(12):17-22.

Poole, Daniel A. and James B. Trefethon. 1978. The Maintenance of Wildlife Populations. pps. 339-349 of Wildlife in America. U.S. Dept of Interior, Fish and Wildlife Service and National Oceanic and Atmospheric Administration Council on Environmental Quality.

Schmidt, John L. 1978. Early Management: Intentional and Otherwise. pps. 257-270 of Big Game of North America: Ecology and Management. Wildlife Management Institute. Stackpole Books, Harrisburg, PA.

Williamson, Lonnie. 1986. The Hunter as a Conservationist. The Leader 7(2):13-14.

Williamson, Lonnie. 1987. Evolution of a Landmark Law. pps. 1-17 of Restoring America's Wildlife. U.S. Dept. of Interior Fish and Wildlife Service.

Mule deer

CHAPTER SEVEN

WHITETAILS AND MULE DEER

Of major and immediate importance to North Dakota was a survey or census of its big game. For not since the work of Vernon Bailey and his associates and contributors had any serious endeavor been made to determine the populations and ranges of its Virginia deer, mule deer, and antelope. The State's policies regarding this game, including the declaration of open seasons, had, of necessity, and for many years, been dependent upon data felt to be inadequate. The available information came for the most part from such sources as incidental personal observations of the game officials and local enforcement officers, from opinions of interested citizens, and even from the relative weights of petitions for or against certain policies, or for or against opening certain areas to hunting. Perhaps no one group realized the need for such a survey more than did the Game and Fish officials themselves. In view of these facts, it was with perhaps pardonable enthusiasm that preliminary plans for such a survey were considered early in January of this year.

North Dakota Game and Fish Department, 1941.

So began the era of "scientific" game management for big game in North Dakota. The year was 1941. There were whitetails in the trees along the river systems, and in the woods of the Turtle Mountains and Pembina Hills. Mule deer ranged in the higher and rougher country west of the Missouri. Scattered bands of pronghorns drifted across western rangelands. Whitetail numbers were apparently increasing, but no one knew how much or why. There was a lot to learn in North Dakota—a lot of ground to cover.

In the late 1930s and early 1940s, game departments all over the country were forming "federal aid divisions" to take advantage of Pittman-Robertson funds. The men in these divisions were biologists rather than politicians, and they set about inventing techniques to put the principles of game management into practice. These were pioneering times, when game departments were learning the most basic things about their wildlife populations, and making their first real efforts to manage them.

North Dakota was no exception. In this chapter we are going to look at the evolution of deer management in North Dakota, from its preliminaries in 1941 to its complexities today. Deer management evolved in North Dakota because it had to: large-scale land use changes gave white-tailed deer in North Dakota a new set of circumstances to live with. In particular, we shall look at water development along the Missouri, which eliminated much of what had been North Dakota's primary deer habitat, and some of the long range effects of that development on deer management. We'll look at how other events—the Soil Bank, for example—and the adaptability of white-tailed deer changed the ways that deer are managed in North Dakota. We are also going to talk about the Game and Fish Department—how the Department changed to respond to new management needs and public demands.

But all that is ahead of us. Things were just getting started in 1941. Such changes were in the future, and no one saw them coming. What North Dakota's new Federal Aid Division had on its mind in 1941 was putting the principles of scientific game management into action. That year there were two significant events for game management in North Dakota. In January, February, and March of 1941, the Game and Fish Department accomplished its first-ever aerial big game survey in the state. And in November of 1941, in cooperation with the U.S. Fish and Wildlife Service, the Department held an experimental hunt to reduce the deer population on the Lower Souris (now J. Clark Salyer) National Wildlife Refuge.

FIRST STEPS: THE AERIAL SURVEY

As the opening quotation suggests, a survey of the different big game populations was vital to the most basic decision a game department makes—setting the seasons. But the survey's usefulness was hardly limited to that. A good survey could tell you a good deal more than approximately how many animals you had. It could tell you, for example, where the population was, and how densely populated different areas of the state were. After a few years you would know if the population was rising or falling, and how fast. A good deer survey would tell you the relative number of bucks, does, and fawns in the population. Over time you would have a basic body of information on which to make management decisions.

Roy Bach

North Dakota needed a big game survey. They needed to start to build that basic body of data. But in 1941 no one had ever done a complete survey of big game in a place like North Dakota. The prospect was

151

somewhat intimidating. Roy Bach, one of the first biologists hired in North Dakota for the new Pittman-Robertson projects, and the man responsible for developing aerial census techniques, explains (NDGFD, 1941, p. 1):

> Several specific problems presented themselves from the start. North Dakota's weather with its snow, winds, and low temperatures, had to be reckoned with. The distribution of big game in the State was expected to be anything but homogeneous.... [I]f a complete and accurate picture of its big game was to be obtained, probably over 10,000 square miles of widely scattered territory would have to be surveyed. A personnel of two or three was to be available for this work, and the time element was to be made as short as possible.
>
> The more the problems involved were considered, the more difficult it became to imagine any standard system of census-taking that would result in a comprehensive survey that might be somewhat accurate without involving an extraordinary amount of time and money.

The "standard system of census-taking" that other states used at the time was called the "drive method." The drive method is a system "wherein a certain number of unit areas of any range are surrounded by workers and an attempt [is] made to count all the deer in each unit.... It may take from sixty to one hundred men to drive a section of land, and perhaps not more than two or three sections could be driven in a day" (NDGFD, 1944, p. 27). In January of 1941, the Game and Fish Department did a trial drive on an 800 acre big game park which they owned in the Turtle Mountains. At the time when they tried it, there was 18 inches of soft snow on the ground, and the men had to travel on snowshoes; many of the roads in the area were blocked by snowdrifts, and there was the constant threat of a blizzard. Drives did not seem a practical way to survey big game in North Dakota.

The things which weighed against this sort of ground survey in North Dakota—extreme weather, large distances to cover and few people to cover them—seemed to weigh in favor of using an airplane. But there were problems with that too. At that time, not much census type work had been done with airplanes. Those who had tried it had good results counting antelope and elk, but poor luck with whitetails. And what North Dakota needed most was a good count of whitetails.

In spite of the problems, the North Dakota Game and Fish Department decided to attempt an aerial survey. It was either try it or wait until there was more money and more manpower—something which might never happen. And we have to remember—these were pioneering times.

The first step was to find out what had gone wrong with other attempts to survey white-tailed deer by air. The Department wrote to several organizations which had tried to count deer from the air. It turned out that the biggest obstacle to counting deer in other states had been coniferous forests. Either the deer were bedded down in the cover of the trees, or, when the airplane flew over them, they ran to the cover of the trees. That would not be a problem in North Dakota. North Dakota's whitetails lived in the deciduous forests of the river drainages. So if an aerial survey was held after the leaves fell—and after a good snowfall—the deer should show up through the bare branches well enough to be counted. As it turned out, it was easier to see deer from the air than it was from the ground. The bare branches of the trees presented no obstacle at all.

North Dakota had other advantages too. Except for the Badlands, North Dakota is reasonably level—at least level enough to maintain a consistent altitude. And because the original land surveys in North Dakota had laid out the state in neat township and section squares—almost all roads and fencelines following the pattern—it's easy to keep track of distances and locations. Overall, North Dakota seemed tailor-made for an aerial count.

Roy Bach and Russell Stuart—who, from 1961 to 1979, would serve as Game and Fish Commissioner—worked out the details for that first big game survey. They planned carefully, to leave as little to trial and error as possible. The airplane, they thought, should have certain characteristics. It should be light, maneuverable, and not too fast. It should be a high-wing type, so that observers would have an un-obstructed view of the ground. Since it seemed that deer would show up best against a blanket of snow, the plane should be equipped for flying in North Dakota winter conditions. It should be able to fly in sub-zero temperatures, and it should have skis for landing on snow. The cabin should be heated.

Russell Stuart

The pilot should have certain qualifications. He should have considerable experience flying at low altitudes in adverse winter conditions, and he ought to be a good mechanic. In North Dakota in 1941, a pilot was largely on his own when it came to taking care of his airplane.

The observers, too, needed certain abilities. A tendency to airsickness, for example, would be a serious handicap. Good maps and an efficient form for recording the animals being counted seemed important—even though an airplane traveling at 80 miles per hour might be a slow airplane, it still covered a section of land in forty seconds.

But no matter how well things are anticipated, nothing is better than actual experience. Things which seemed like a good idea on the ground

153

turned out to be impractical in the air. For example, Bach and Stuart first tried to use binoculars to spot animals. But even at relatively low altitudes, small movements of the airplane made the field of vision swing wildly. Binoculars were just in the way. What finally worked out the best was to have one observer on each side of the airplane simply look out the window. With a little experience, observers had time to count not only deer, but grouse, foxes, and coyotes. It was even possible to distinguish deer tracks from sheep tracks. Seeing and counting deer was not a problem at all.

Two of the great "unknowns" of aerial surveying in 1941 were how much of the deer habitat you had to cover to get an accurate survey, and how you made sure that you covered it. From the beginning, Bach and Stuart knew that they couldn't count every deer in North Dakota. Exact numbers were not as important as population densities. If you think an area will support 10 deer, and you count 50, it doesn't matter if you are off by one or two. Although the aerial survey was often referred to as a "census," it was really a sample, small areas being used to represent larger ones. The question was, how much ground did you have to cover to get an accurate sample?

With a little experimenting, the census takers found that for most of the terrain in North Dakota, 25 percent coverage gave them accurate results. The number of deer they counted on a quarter section was representative of the whole section. If the pilot held the airplane at an altitude of 375 feet, an observer on each side of the plane could see a strip of ground an eighth of a mile wide. By holding to section lines as markers, one pass of the airplane over a section gave them the 25 percent coverage they were after. Two passes gave them 50 percent, and so on. The observers checked themselves by flying places where the number of deer were known.

> To date most of the white-tailed deer area in North Dakota has been surveyed on a basis of 25 per cent coverage. In some instances where the area is small and the concentration of animals is high, 50 per cent coverage has been used. In a few instances, 100 per cent coverage has been used. Total or 100 per cent coverage calls for extremely accurate flying on the part of the pilot, and for very careful observing on the part of the observers so that there is not a duplication on the count of the animals...
> (Saugstad, 1942, p. 350)

The first aerial survey of big game in North Dakota was completed in March of 1941. "The results of the...survey show[ed] that we had approximately 5,800 white-tailed deer, 900 mule deer and 580 antelope within the state. It also showed just where these animals were" (NDGFD, 1942, p. 28). The survey was interesting in other ways too. The observers took note of anything that they thought might be useful to them later—the activity of deer at different times of day, their reactions to the airplane, and, whenever practical, the ages and sexes within different groups of deer. In retrospect, this first flight confirmed at least one difference between mule deer and whitetails (see Chapter Five). Mule deer did not get as excited as whitetails. "[Even] when an attempt was made to photograph them and the plane was flown very near, [mule deer] rarely attempted to stampede or move much. Usually they gazed up at the odd vehicle and some of the bucks actually stood their ground and stamped" (NDGFD, 1941, p. 25). Mule deer were also harder to see, although this did not seem to affect the confidence of the observers in the accuracy of their results.

The Department put the information gathered from the survey to immediate use. In the fall of 1941, there was—by the standards of previous years—a very successful deer season. The Department sold over 5,000 deer licenses, and nearly 3,000 deer hunters took home a deer. It was not that North Dakota's Game and Fish Department had thrown the caution of previous years to the wind. Seasons in previous years had been extremely conservative because there was no reliable information on which to base decisions.

LOWER SOURIS HERD REDUCTION

The second major game management event of 1941 was a controlled hunt to reduce the deer herd on the Lower Souris Federal Refuge. "Unique in North Dakota's big game history was the opening of portions of the Lower Souris Federal Refuge to controlled deer hunting. For some time it had been felt that a deer population of between twelve hundred and fifteen hundred deer on (or in the vicinity of) the Lower Souris Refuge was too large a herd for this area to support. The Refuge Division of the Fish and

Wildlife Service was of the opinion that some four hundred deer could well be removed during the fall of 1941 without seriously depleting the breeding stock or seriously affecting the future of the herd" (Bach, 1941, p. 20).

Certainly, opening a refuge to hunting was unusual. But to the new Federal Aid Division of the Game and Fish Department it represented more than a deer hunt. Here was an unusual opportunity to gather information about North Dakota deer and deer hunters, and to test some game management techniques under very controlled conditions.

By 1941, two principles of game management had become well accepted nationwide. The first was that a major goal of game managers should be to maintain a sustainable yield of game animals for recreation purposes. The assumption was that "natural" controls on wildlife populations had ceased to exist long ago—the controls exerted by wolves and other predators, for example—and without them, animals like deer rapidly multiplied beyond the carrying capacity of their range. They would then eat themselves out of house and home, and the population would crash. To prevent wild swings in population, and to maintain the range, deer populations had to be controlled. The "sustainable yield" of animals represented the natural increase in populations which could be removed without harming the population—which, in fact, had to be removed or serious problems would result.

The second principle which had been accepted by game managers was that the major tool for controlling wildlife populations should be hunting. We will be talking about this some more later, but the major ideas are that on the one hand, licensed hunting provides game managers with significant control over what happens to wildlife populations, and on the other, hunting provides people with an increasingly necessary facet of their lives—outdoor recreation.

North Dakota's game managers wanted to test their ability to control a deer hunt to accomplish specific management objectives. They wanted to test, if they could, the reaction of North Dakota hunters to a deer hunt under very controlled conditions. They wanted to measure, if possible, the short and long term effects of the herd reduction on the remaining deer. And they wanted to collect as much data on the harvested animals as they could.

In order to keep track of the effects of the hunt on the deer population, the Lower Souris Refuge was censused by air just before the hunt, and it was censused again after the hunt. The long term effects would be measured by the yearly aerial survey. To control activity on the refuge, "the area was divided into three units numbered from one to three and set apart, more or less, geographically from each other.... Each unit had its checking station which was set up near some gate through which all hunters had to pass in order to enter or leave the refuge" (Bach, 1941, p. 20). A permit system was set up to control and keep track of the number of hunters in each unit. In addition, an air patrol flew over the area periodically to check the progress of the hunters, to locate crippled or dead animals, and, on occasion, to help hunters.

The controlled hunt succeeded beyond anyone's hopes. The hunt lasted four days, from November 22 to November 26. More than 750 hunters participated, taking 393 deer—very close to the management goal of 400. Contrary to expectations, hunters reacted very well to the controlled circumstances. "Hunter appreciation was practically unanimous…. [S]ome idea of hunter appreciation might be gleaned from the fact that all three checkers were compelled to graciously refuse more than one proffered cash tip…" (Bach, 1941, p. 22).

A great deal of information was collected at the checking stations—more than was expected. "In this connection, it should be pointed out that some fear had been expressed by the Regional Office [of the Fish and Wildlife Service] regarding the taking of too much data in the field. It was pointed out that hunters might be anxious to leave for home and would not like to cooperate with data collectors on their way out. Those in charge, however, proceeded on the assumption that the hunter might be glad to cooperate…. It is regretted now that an attempt was not made to take more data in the field, especially that of age determination by teeth examination" (Bach, 1941, p. 22). The men at the checking stations did collect information regarding the sex, weights, and condition of the animals, and, in some cases where an animal was killed close to a checking station, "very desirable information was obtained regarding the dressing losses of various sized specimens…as well as…making possible the taking of some data on blood loss" (Bach, 1941, p. 22).

The crew in the airplane learned a good deal as well. "[V]iewing such a hunting scene from a plane at an altitude of one hundred feet or so might be decidedly surprising to anyone who had not had the privilege…[T]he possibilities of such an air crew helping those on the ground are almost unlimited. Hunter groups can be directed where to stand and where to make drives. The exact number of deer within a prospective drive area can be ascertained…. It is quite impossible for a person on the ground to make such accurate observations" (Bach, 1941, p. 26). In at least one instance, the air crew was able, by dropping a note, to direct a hunter's attention to a large buck lying not far away. The crew learned a good deal about the abilities of hunters to spot game, and a whitetail's ability to hide. It was clear to all concerned that "the airplane, in the very near future, [would] be one of the most important adjuncts…to game management practices" (Bach, 1941, p. 26).

THE WAR YEARS

The Second World War put game management progress on hold. Manpower and money went to the war effort. The Game and Fish Department continued to fly its annual winter big game survey. The war put a few twists into the survey. "Three waivers to regular regulations made the work possible. These were: first, one allowing refueling in the field away from regular open and authorized airports; second, one allowing the pilot and ship seventy-two hour clearances from authorized open airports instead of the regular two-hour clearances; and third, one allowing the pilot to fly at altitudes below five hundred feet" (Bach, 1943, p. 1). Wartime caution made the census-takers extremely conscientious about notifying beforehand anyone who might be suspicious of a low-flying airplane—particularly when a flight might take them close to an international boundary or an important bridge. "[I]t would be quite awkward if one of these guards should take a shot at an innocent observer flying low over some bridge" (Bach, 1943, p. 5). Manpower was short. During the war years, the survey was accomplished with the pilot and only one observer—usually Roy Bach. But the survey itself and the techniques for accomplishing it became old-hat.

During the war, upland game got far more attention than big game. Pheasant populations were booming. In 1944 and 1945, hunters took nearly two and a half million birds each year, "in spite of the fact that a war was on, shotgun shells were scarce, gasoline was rationed, and many of the best hunters were in the armed forces" (Johnson and Knue, 1989, p. 133). The Game and Fish Department seemed relatively satisfied with the deer population and with having a deer season every other year. There may, in fact, have been some public opposition to having seasons as often as that. "In order that the deer population in the state will not compete with normal agricultural pursuits to a serious extent, it appears that the population should not be allowed to go much above 9,000 animals. Therefore it is necessary to have an open season every two years. The normal hunting pressure in North Dakota is just sufficient to take care of the harvestable surplus" (NDGFD, 1943, p. 7-8).

ND Game and Fish Department

158

The aerial survey itself got a few refinements. New areas along different river systems were added. 1944 was a mild, dry winter, which caused some unforeseen problems. Deer were scattered, and they were hard to see. Roy Bach wrote: "During the past year or so the writer has been of the opinion that the annual big game census should be run in North Dakota during the latter part of November and during the month of December...before the rigorous part of the winter sets in. He is not so sure at the present time...At the present time the writer would...put up with North Dakota's rigorous weather conditions...to obtain the ease and accuracy with which the census can be made while the deer are yarded" (Bach, 1944, p. 7-8). During these years the Department tried flying at various altitudes, only to find that experience in doing this kind of work was more important than altitude. "The writer has had additional experience this year in taking novices into the air for short periods...Without exception, these passengers not only failed to see deer and other game in clearly discernable locations, but even failed to see obvious landmarks when these were pointed out to them. All attested to the fact that they would want considerable practice before they would wish to attempt aerial observation work in an official way" (Bach, 1943, p. 3-4). In 1945, antelope were dropped from the winter survey. The feeling was that by January in a normal North Dakota winter, a large proportion of the antelope had moved out of the state. The mule deer herd had "increased very satisfactorily" since the first count in 1941. The whitetail herd was "increasing quite rapidly," but was still within the limits the Department thought reasonable at the time.

POST-WAR PROGRESS

When the Second World War was over, the scale of the job of deer management in North Dakota changed quickly and dramatically. In a very short time, the Game and Fish Department found that it had acquired new roles and new responsibilities—which, from today's perspective, have a very contemporary ring to them. Very soon after the war, the Department found that anticipating and responding to the needs of the public was a very large part of its responsibility. And the Department found itself in the position having to be the authority on how wildlife was affected by what people did. Two events in particular pushed the Department in these directions. The first was a shakeup of the Department's long-held assumptions about the state's white-tailed deer. The other event was the proposed diversion and development of the Missouri River. Let's begin with the deer herd.

In 1946, winter set in early and hard. "[W]inter weather had set in in earnest by Christmas and a considerable amount of snow had fallen throughout the state.... During February a considerable part of the rural population of North Dakota was snowbound. Travel to local towns in

159

Deer taken near Fort Ransom in 1943 – the first open season here in 20 years.

many instances was impossible and small planes were being used to deliver mail and groceries in isolated communities" (Bach, 1946, p. 1-2). Conditions were bad for most activities, but they should have been ideal for the annual deer survey. In conditions like these, deer should have been yarded up and easy to see. They should have been but they weren't. Roy Bach wrote (Bach, 1946, p. 2):

> It is quite apparent that some change in deer habits is taking place in this state. Four or five years ago one would normally expect to find the great bulk of the total deer herd in accepted winter ranges, i.e., in or close to available timber. Three years ago we began to note that regardless of snow conditions many of our white-tails failed to yard and many small groups were to be seen spending the winter out on the prairie somewhat far from timber. This tendency of movement to the prairies has seemingly increased…During the census covered by this report scarcely any yarding at all could be noted in any part of the state in spite of the winter. The writer has never seen more deer scattered so homogeneously through North Dakota. There were deer in practically every township of the state.

In earlier surveys, deer which were seen out on the prairie had been counted as "strays" and surveyors took a guess at their numbers. By 1946

160

it was clear that these deer were not strays. They were a significant part of the population and their range was not predictable with any information available at the time. "The animals in the sparsely populated areas we have called 'strays.' We try to estimate the number of these each year.... [T]he number of such deer has been increasing each year. On referring to the 1945 census we find that we have allowed 1,000 animals as 'strays.' Looking back...after this year's work, we might come to the conclusion that we did not allow a sufficient number.... One reason for thinking this is the fact that in the new areas covered this year for the first time and which were not too large in extent, over 500 deer were noted" (Bach, 1946, p. 5). The Department extended its deer count out into the Coteau region— places which "were not timbered areas in any sense of the word but are composed of rolling prairies dotted here and there with potholes and small lakes and subjected to limited agricultural land use" (Bach, 1946, p. 3). Bach noted, however, that "it would be uneconomical to census the entire state during any winter." Any estimate of "prairie" deer would be unreliable. But in 1947, the phenomenon of "prairie" deer was even more pronounced.

The 1947 annual deer survey revealed another noteworthy—if not alarming—situation. The deer herd was apparently increasing at an unprecedented rate. In 1946 the estimated deer population had been in the neighborhood of 6,000 animals. In 1947 (there was no deer season in 1946) the population was estimated at nearly 15,000. In the Department's estimation, that was far too many deer. A population of that size would quickly destroy its traditional range. Deer would begin to interfere with agriculture—if they were not doing so already. "[O]ur deer are learning to live closer to agriculture and are learning to utilize many of the agricultural fields for cover. Deer were noted last winter bedded down for the day in reed grass, sweet clover, stubble fields that had been combined and on prairie covered with snow and a supporting grass not over a foot high.

Deer on the prairie.

161

Farmers told us that deer graze with their cattle in pastures" (Bach, 1946, p. 3). Clearly, the Game and Fish Department needed to take charge of the situation. Russell Stuart wrote (Stuart, 1947, p. 4): "Figuring a normal increase…this spring and summer, it is very possible that North Dakota will be carrying 20,000 deer by this fall…. It is time that some thought be given to a management program for this species."

The phenomenon of "prairie" deer combined with surging deer numbers brought modern big game management to North Dakota. For the first time, the Game and Fish Department accepted the challenge of managing big game on a statewide scale. And, for the first time in a very long time, big game was a public issue.

Twenty thousand deer may not seem like very many deer today, but in 1947 the Game and Fish Department felt that 9,000 whitetails were about all that North Dakota could handle without serious conflicts between deer and agriculture. The Department had—as had game departments all over the country—some experience with such conflicts when pheasant populations boomed during the war. They did not want to repeat it with an animal as large and conspicuous as a deer.

The damage that too many deer might cause was one side of the public issue. At the other side of the issue were the reasons that game was being managed at all. Game was being managed in order to provide maximum recreation, which was, at that time, almost exclusively hunting. The Game and Fish Department's major reason for existence was to ensure that there would always be huntable populations of wildlife.

The job ahead of North Dakota's game managers in 1947 was first to trim the deer herd. In some sense, it was simply applying the techniques

Deer hunters near Oakes, 1948.

ND Game and Fish Department

used on the Lower Souris Refuge in 1941 on a statewide scale. The goal was the removal of the "harvestable surplus" of animals—the number of deer beyond what the range could sustain. In this case, it amounted to ten or twelve thousand animals. The Department wanted to achieve this management goal by means of the hunting season. With a management goal of removing 10,000 to 12,000 animals, and figuring a success rate of around fifty percent, the Department could put 20,000 hunters in the field. There was a tremendous opportunity for recreation in North Dakota. It was also a tremendous problem in terms of public relations.

The Department was reasonably sure that there were enough people interested in a deer hunt to reach their management goal. Each deer season since 1941 had seen a greatly increased number of hunters in the field. In 1945 the Arrowwood National Wildlife Refuge had been opened to bow hunters, and was again in 1947. But the scale of the proposed hunt in 1947 was a big leap. The problem facing the Department was this: how do you move from a deer harvest of 5,000 in 1945 to a harvest of what turned out to be 17,000 in 1947 and still convince the public that you are not wiping out the deer herd? How do you tell them that you are helping to maintain the deer herd? How do you convince them that you know what you're doing? It seems a tall order.

It led the Game and Fish Department straight into the business of public relations and education. The public had, of course always been there— Chapter Six summarizes its shifting ideas of the value of wildlife. But increased numbers of animals, increased interest in recreation, and increased potential for conflict between the needs of people and the needs of wildlife thrust big game management into the public eye. The public needed to know what the Department was doing and why. In the Department's annual report for 1948, Game and Fish Commissioner William J. Lowe wrote (p. 35-36):

> It has always been my contention that the more information we can give the general public about the conservation program and policies of the department the better it will be able to understand the problems to be solved.
>
> While it is not possible for the department to issue as many special bulletins and pamphlets relating to our wildlife resources as we would like to, we try through the medium of NORTH DAKOTA OUTDOORS to keep the people informed as to what is being done for the propagation and protection of North Dakota wildlife. We are also issuing a bi-weekly news release devoted to timely subjects and seasonal information....
>
> The Game and Fish Department recognizes the importance of individual expression of opinion and has provided a forum for such expression through the medium of the annual game conference. This conference is held in the late summer after sufficient survey and investigational work has been done to

determine as accurately as possible the fall population of game birds and animals. Representatives of all groups interested in wildlife management are invited to meet with the department personnel to review the results of the game surveys and to make recommendations as they see fit relative to bag limits and open seasons. These recommendations are given careful consideration in the final drafting of hunting regulations.

The department recognizes the importance of maintaining contact with all groups and individuals interested in wildlife management and regularly meets with the various chapters of the North Dakota Wildlife Federation, the Izaak Walton League of America, Farmers Organizations, 4-H groups, County Agricultural Extension Agents, Soil Conservation Representatives, Future Farmers of America and many others.

Nothing succeeds like success. When the Department called for what seemed like an disastrously large deer harvest in 1947, there was some public opposition. Despite the Department's public information efforts pointing to the limits of deer habitat in the state and the potential for problems, many people thought that the deer herd was simply being wiped out. As it turned out, however, the harvest was, perhaps, not large enough. In 1948, Russell Stuart wrote, "In spite of a large harvest during the 1947 season, the state is still carrying a fairly large deer herd even in areas where hunting pressure was greatest. The depth of snow and severity of the weather caused concentrations that created several problem areas in the state. More complaints were received from farmers reporting damage to farm crops than has ever before been received by the Game and Fish Department" (Stuart, 1948, p. 5). The predictions of the Department came true. And when the Department called for another season in 1948— remember that during this time, seasons were being held only every other year—public opinion was far more favorable.

The complexity of the Game and Fish Department's role in the contemporary world was beginning to emerge. In addition to managing hunters—setting seasons, setting bag limits, and enforcing the law—the Department was starting to respond to the demands of an increasingly interested and vocal public. The Department was emerging as the agency responsible for ensuring that the needs of wildlife were met. Once the Department acknowledged its responsibility to act on behalf of wildlife, there was no turning back. As we shall see, it was a role that provided great opportunities for controversy.

Missouri River Development

For all of us who think that concern about the effects of our activities on wildlife began in 1970, we point to this: in the Game and Fish

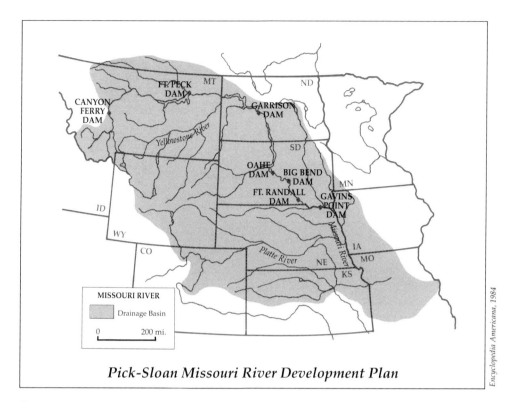

Pick-Sloan Missouri River Development Plan

Department's 1945 annual report (p. 29) the Federal Aid Division reported that it was investigating "the wildlife values, including cover types (plants) to be affected by the new Missouri development plans." In the late 1940s and early 1950s, nothing in North Dakota put the increasing value of wildlife and outdoor recreation more into focus than projects like the Garrison and Oahe dams.

Nearly everyone in North Dakota has a working familiarity with the history of the Garrison Dam and its reservoir, now called Lake Sakakawea. In brief, "Garrison Reservoir is a feature of a plan (Pick-Sloan) developed by the Army Corps of Engineers for the Missouri River below Fort Peck, Montana. The sites of five reservoirs—Gavins Point, Fort Randall, Big Bend, Oahe, and Garrison—are located on the river between Yankton, South Dakota and Trenton, North Dakota near the Montana state boundary. The primary purposes of this plan were flood control, power production, irrigation and navigation" (Enyeart, 1973). A map of the entire proposed development scheme for the Missouri Basin is shown above.

In its original plans and proposals, the Corps of Engineers made no provisions for wildlife. In 1945, the Department set about changing that. "Since no provision for fish and wildlife has been made, the North Dakota State Game and Fish Department, through the Federal Aid Division, initiated a preliminary survey to determine the possible effects of the Missouri Basin Development upon the wildlife of North Dakota" (Miller and Bach, 1945, p. 1). Considering the benefits that flood control, irrigation, and power generation might bring to North Dakota, to investigate the project for its possible negative effects on wildlife seems a pretty bold step. It points to considerable confidence on the part of North Dakota's game managers in the importance of wildlife to the people of North Dakota.

The Game and Fish Department gave the following conclusions and recommendations (Miller and Bach, 1945, p. 6):

> 1) Destroyed habitat, including timber, brush and grasslands, should be replaced in other favorable areas that will produce an equal amount of wildlife.
>
> 2) Water pools favorable to wildlife should be stabilized in all pools where it is practicable.
>
> 3) Suitable provision should be made for the protection of fish and for the stocking of appropriate species in favorable localities.
>
> 4) Consideration of wildlife values should be a required part of all new constructions and developments.
>
> 5) The State of North Dakota, through its Game and Fish Department, should be consulted during the planning and construction of developments within its borders.
>
> 6) The administration and management of wildlife resources in the newly developed areas should come under the jurisdiction of the State of North Dakota.

What's surprising about these conclusions is how clearly the Game and Fish Department seems to see its role. Even in 1946 it was quite clear that without some control over habitat conditions, the job of managing wildlife was impossible. And wildlife was important enough to be given the same consideration as other aspects of life in North Dakota.

The effects of the Garrison and Oahe dams on North Dakota's white-tailed deer herd cannot, even today, be underestimated. The land lost to the reservoirs represented a considerable percentage of North Dakota's best whitetail habitat. William Hanson wrote (Hanson, 1950, p. 6):

> About 100,000 acres of trees and timber are being lost on the Garrison Reservoir, all of which is wildlife cover and of use to many species. An unascertained number of acres will be lost below the dam due to changed land-use practices there.... There are about 600,000 wooded acres in the state...so at least 17% of the woods and brush of the state are being lost on this one reservoir....
> Perhaps the most disastrous effect of the reservoir will be on the deer herd. Between the Oahe and Garrison Reservoirs the

cover will be largely eliminated by a new and intensive agriculture in the bottoms where the danger of floods will soon be past. Already many land owners are bulldozing out the timber and brush on their land. As a result of these two dams the cover of the Missouri bottoms, plus a considerable amount on the tributaries, will be lost.

Mr. Hanson expected—as did everyone at the time—that the large scale destruction of habitat would mean the elimination of a large percentage of North Dakota's white-tailed deer herd. They knew full well that it would be impossible to recreate habitat to the extent that it was going to be lost. The Game and Fish Department encouraged hunters to use these areas heavily during the years just prior to inundation.

Even though the predicted permanent drop in deer numbers did not occur, we are still dealing with the loss of habitat brought about by the Oahe and Garrison dams. The dams have had a profound effect on the whitetail herd, and an equally profound effect on the way deer have to be managed in North Dakota. When deer and habitat in the Missouri River Basin were lost to the reservoirs, deer on the prairie—the "strays"— became, by process of elimination, much more significant. Although the size of this "prairie herd" was increasing, the Game and Fish Department had focused its management efforts on what they considered the "real" deer herd—the one that lived where it was supposed to, in the trees along the rivers. When the Missouri River deer were eliminated, the "prairie deer" got a bigger share of management attention. Prairie deer have had to be dealt with differently than deer in more typical circumstances.

In Chapter Five we discussed those typical circumstances. Traditionally, good whitetail habitats are places where there is a good variety of low-growing woody plants which are still tall and dense enough to provide good cover. River bottomlands provide this kind of habitat in abundance. In good habitat, when does are healthy and well fed, they bear twins or even triplets. Good habitat provides winter food and shelter from bad weather. In good habitat, fawn survival is high. Well-fed bucks, though they may lose weight during the rut, have a good chance to survive the winter.

The point is, deer are adapted to this woodland-edge habitat, and they are not, historically, adapted to grasslands. The critical time for whitetails on the prairie is winter, which can, of course, be extremely long and harsh. Woodlands provide dense woody cover and high quality food when the prairies are covered with drifted snow. Whitetails, caught out on the prairie when their food supply is covered with snow and with no protection from the wind, are at serious risk. A series of harsh winters could be disastrous.

We need to remember what was going on in North Dakota at the same time as these large-scale water projects were being built. Garrison Dam was closed in 1953 and Oahe seven years later, in 1960. Water, backing up from Garrison, did not reach what is called "full pool" until the mid sixties. As water backed up and covered the flood-plain habitat, the Game and Fish Department tried to direct hunting pressure into those areas to harvest the deer and to push them out of the areas which were going to be flooded. In 1956—just as the flooded areas were becoming significant—Congress passed the Soil Bank Act, which, over its life, took nearly 3,000,000 acres of land out of agricultural production in North Dakota. Winters during this period of time were mild. The stage was set for some changes for whitetails in North Dakota. With a food supply and a little cover supplied by Soil Bank lands—combined with mild winters—river bottom deer had a chance to adjust to being prairie deer. They spread out over the state, mostly in areas where land had been idled by the Soil Bank.

Deer management expanded to meet the new situation. In the 10 years between 1953 and 1963, the North Dakota Game and Fish Department studied the prairie deer herd and adopted new management techniques to deal with this new set of circumstances. The things that were known about deer in woodland habitats—what they ate, how they survived the winter—needed to be learned about deer in prairie habitats. Also, there was a lot more of North Dakota that the Department had to consider as deer habitat. It made for a different kind of management scheme.

Even though the total number of deer in North Dakota did not seem to increase appreciably, more of the deer were out of the river bottoms. It seemed pretty likely that deer would be getting into crops and hay supplies. Without the cover of the trees, there was a high risk of problems

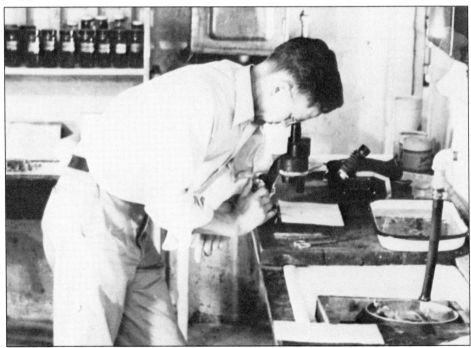

Biologist Bill McKean working on deer food habits study, 1953.

168

in a tough prairie winter. Even before the effects of the dams began to be felt, the Department started a food habits study to find out what these deer were eating. During the same time period, the Department started looking at deer which died of natural causes to see what the major causes were.

The first food habits study ran for five years, starting in 1947. "The long-time deer food project was designed to determine basic trends in the food habits of both white-tailed and mule deer.... Analysis of what deer consume was made by actual inspection of 711 deer stomachs.... Laboratory procedure consisted of washing, separating, estimating percentages, identification and recording of the stomach contents. This work showed the main content of our [deer's diet] to be buckbrush, juneberry, rose, weeds, willow, silverberry, chokecherry, flax, alfalfa, corn, and wheat. The most important single food of both species of deer was buckbrush..." (NDGFD, 1954, p. 16).

The study seemed to confirm what the Game and Fish researchers suspected. Whitetails were indeed making some use of crops and hay, but these were not the foods they would choose if other food was available. Regions which had the highest usage of crops were along the Sheyenne and James Rivers—places where little else was available. Grass hay especially did not make good deer food. Deer were found dead from malnutrition with their stomachs full of hay (McKean, 1954, p. 1). The highest chances of deer competing with agriculture were in places where land use for agriculture was the most intensive, and in winter.

The study of the natural causes of mortality in deer complemented the food study. Winter-killed deer died primarily from malnutrition. More deer died during harder winters—that is, years with more snow. More deer died in late winter, when snow depths were greatest. It was clear that during hard winters—winters with a lot of snow—browse plants like buckbrush would be covered. Where there was no other source of food, deer would turn to haystacks. When that happened, you could expect some losses.

It seemed a good idea, in the early fifties, to discourage deer from using hay for food. It was a good idea from the standpoint of the deer—hay didn't do them much good—and it was good from a public relations standpoint. The Department tried some commercial deer repellents and they tried a home brew made from lion scat and urine which they got from area zoos. The commercial repellents seemed to work but they were too expensive to use on any scale; interest in the homebrew seems to have dropped off fairly quickly, even though the stuff was cheap and available. Jim McKenzie, long-time big game biologist for the Department, cannot remember that the farmers who tried the formula ever came back for more.

When the deer herd was localized in the trees along the river bottomlands, there was a limited number of habitat types that deer managers had to deal with. As whitetails spread across the state, it became more complicated. In the early fifties, the state was divided into deer management areas or units, divided on the basis of topography or habitat

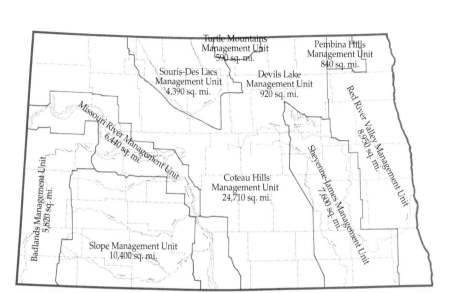

North Dakota = 70,660 square miles

Major White-tailed Deer Management Units

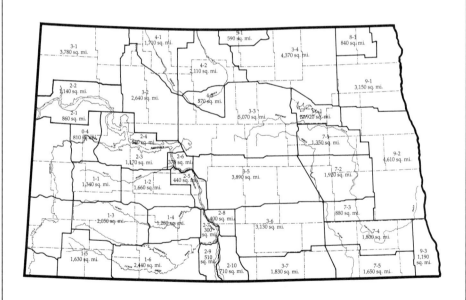

White-tailed Deer Management Sub-units

type. There were ten areas—the same major deer management units we have in North Dakota today—and each area would be handled as if it had a different deer herd. One unit was the Badlands Unit, another the Coteau, a third the Slope, and so on. The feeling was, when these management units were first set up, that differing habitat types imposed different limitations on deer living there. With deer living in different habitats all over the state, it did not make sense to manage on a statewide basis. What was good for the range in the Pembina Hills would not necessarily be good for the range in the slope country west of the Missouri. Unitized management might also help the Department keep track of its information if census data and harvest data referred to the same regions.

By 1959, the whitetail herd had spread itself around within the major management areas. There were deer in places where there never had been deer before—and where, considering the limits of traditional habitat, there shouldn't be deer. In those days—and in these days too—the primary tool that the Department had for managing deer was the ability to manipulate the harvest. By the same token, deer in all these new places were causing a lot of local excitement. More people wanted to hunt deer. The Department needed a better way to control the situation. It needed a way to direct hunters into the places where the herd needed to be trimmed. In 1959, the Department subdivided its ten large management units into 41 management sub-units, and went to the legislature and changed the way that deer licenses could be issued.

In years past, when a deer hunter bought a license in North Dakota he could hunt anywhere in the state that was open to deer hunting, and most years he could hunt any deer he wanted. The Department's ability to deal with local situations had been limited to opening and closing different areas to hunting, and to setting special seasons. An example of this was in 1957, when the Department held a special two and a half day season on whitetails in the Badlands and in the Turtle Mountains. Badlands whitetails were causing depredation problems, and the harvest during the regular season in the Badlands ran more to mule deer. In the Turtle Mountains, up to 20 percent of the deer herd was being lost each winter to malnutrition. The special season was directed at bringing these two populations in line with habitat conditions. With the increasing deer herd statewide, and the possibility of more of these local kinds of problems, the Department did not look forward to special seasons all over the state to deal with them. In 1959 the Department got a legislative change which allowed them to experiment with a unit-permit season in part of the state.

The unit-permit system gave the Department a much finer degree of control of the deer harvest than they had before. They could control the harvest by species—whitetail or mule deer—by the kind of permit they issued. And they could control the total harvest by the number of permits issued in a unit or sub-unit. The system was a powerful new management tool. The Department could put hunting pressure into places where the herd needed trimming, where depredation was a problem. To some extent, they could achieve a selective harvest.

It was a powerful tool for managing the hunt as well as the harvest. With the unit-permit system Department could set the maximum harvest in a unit. The season could be longer without increasing the harvest. The Department could extend the season with the idea of having fewer hunters in the area each day, and a more leisurely and careful hunt. For a couple of reasons, this was a desirable state of affairs.

A more leisurely hunt would be a safer hunt. But there was more to it than that. For some time, a split had been growing between hunters and landowners. The increased numbers of deer had greatly increased public enthusiasm for deer hunting. Instead of the two or three thousand deer licenses the Department sold in the 1930s, the Department was selling twenty or thirty thousand. New roads and good transportation made it possible for hunters to go to great lengths to hunt deer. Landowners who were used to having two or three hunters—the same ones year after year— were suddenly overrun with hunters. There was a growing problem with damage to property caused by careless hunters, and with game animals shot and left to rot. Farmers and ranchers were not very happy about having deer in their fields and haystacks, but they were not so sure that the answer was more hunters. There seemed to be a growing tendency for landowners to either post their land or to want to charge a fee for hunting. R. J. Christiansen wrote in **ND Outdoors** (Christiansen, 1959, p. 4):

> As the hunting improves, the hunting pressure in turn increases, and the problem of hunter-land-owner relations becomes more pronounced.
>
> With the concentration of population in the Eastern part of the country, the problem is old stuff...but the Dakotas...are just beginning to feel the squeeze.
>
> In my locality we were faced...with a group of land-owners having formed a block in some of the choicest hunting land, and charging a $25 fee to hunt on it. It is true that some of them have suffered property damage from careless hunters, so their attitude toward public hunting is partially justified.

This is the last thing the Department wanted or needed. No one needed to remind the Game and Fish Department that almost all the land in North Dakota is privately owned. Without the cooperation of landowners, there could be no such thing as game management, and very little recreation. For some years the Department had been working hard to cultivate a good relationship with landowners, mostly by means of regular visits from district game wardens. We will discuss this some more when we discuss the reorganization of the the Department to answer the needs of the rapidly changing times. By 1959, district wardens were working very hard to assure landowners that their concerns were being met; they were running classes on hunter safety and gun safety; and they were meeting

Warden Roger Kupper giving a class on gun safety.

ND Game and Fish Department

with sportsmen's clubs and other groups to talk about sportsman-landowner cooperation. A longer season, with its reduced numbers of hunters on any one day, and its hoped-for effect of a more leisurely and careful hunt, was an additional demonstration of the Department's commitment to good landowner-sportsman relations.

But the experiment with the unit-permit system in 1959 gave the Department another problem in public education and relations. In the 1959 season, the Department put hunting Unit II—the eastern third of the state that year—under the unit-permit system. The rest of the whitetail hunting units remained as usual. The season in Unit II was to last 9½ days, as opposed to 2½ days in other units. Both hunters and landowners resisted the change. Hunters felt that the new system infringed on their right to hunt in whatever part of the state they pleased. They were also concerned about finding new places to hunt when their old ones became restricted. Landowners had to be convinced that the permit system would ease the hunting pressure, and they had to be convinced that hunters were the solution to their deer depredation problems.

After the 1959 season, both sportsmen and landowners felt better about it. After the 1959 season, Commissioner I. G. Bue wrote, "The permit

173

system met with some opposition previous to the season, but after landowners and sportsmen had a chance to see it in operation, many were highly impressed and now favor this type of season.

"Many hunters reported that the permit system dispersed the hunting pressure. With the nine and one-half day season, hunters took their time in selecting a deer. There was no hurried shooting at the first object that moved…. Many landowners have reported the quietest season in years" (Bue, 1960). In 1959, nearly nine out of ten deer hunters got a deer in Unit II. The year before, only four out of ten hunters in that unit had been successful.

The longer season in Unit II was a safer hunt. "Not a single serious shooting accident was reported during the season. This more leisurely type of hunt may have reduced that sense of desperation which very likely caused some previous fatalities and crippling accidents" (McKenzie, 1960, p. 11).

The 1959 nine and a half day season was quite a success. It is a lot to ask of a season that it achieve your management goals, give you high hunter success, give you a high quality hunt, and help you achieve good landowner-sportsman relations.

We are, by now, a long way from the idea that the Garrison and Oahe dams forced the evolution of game management in North Dakota. But think back. Loss of habitat in the Missouri River bottomlands, by shifting management efforts to "prairie deer" instead of the "timber deer" of the bottoms, brought new management techniques. One of these was unitized management, and another was the permit system. Russell Stuart wrote (NDGFD, 1962, p. 6) that as the two reservoirs filled, the loss of habitat would "put more pressure on our prairie deer areas. Eventually it will

ND Game and Fish Department

174

mean that more of the state will have to be put on a permit basis."

Something else had also been established, almost without anyone noticing. Projects to "develop" the Missouri River have always had enormous popular support. Flood control, power generation, and especially irrigation, were long-cherished dreams for generations of North Dakotans. To stand in the way of such benefits because of the loss of habitat for 6,000 or so deer was sacrilege. Yet in September of 1952, even before the completion of Garrison Dam, Commissioner H. R. Morgan stood in front of the President's Water Commission and told them (Morgan, 1952, p. 6), "I appear before you in behalf of all of the wildlife within the Missouri River Basin; In behalf of an overall plan of development which will safeguard that wildlife but more especially in behalf of the wildlife of North Dakota which is about to be adversely influenced by water development which is now going forward..." The large-scale land use changes brought about by the projects, and the impossibility of mitigating the loss of wildlife habitat, forced the Game and Fish Department to make a stand on behalf of wildlife. Increasingly, the Department would see that the protection of wildlife values was its public responsibility. Proposed land use changes would have to take that into account.

Ed Bry

Mule Deer

Up to now in this discussion of the changes in deer management, we have left mule deer out, or acted as if they were the same as whitetails. In fact, for some years after the "era of scientific game management" began, mule deer played virtually no part in either the census or the deer season.

Starting in the winter of 1948-49, the Department began trying to get a better handle on mule deer. In 1949, William McKean, a Department biologist, wrote (McKean, 1949, p. 1):

> Federal aid reports of the past several years pertaining to deer have repeatedly mentioned the difficulty we are experiencing in obtaining mass data on mule deer populations by aerial census. The difficulty is simply inherent in the badlands terrain where these deer live. The observer is overwhelmed in his attempt to scan the multitude of slopes, draws, and ridges which are exposed to his view even during a straight-line flight. A second complication is the habit of mule deer of "freezing" in the juniper filled draws as the plane passes over. Unlike whitetails they seem not to bolt in fear into the open. We believe that many head are being missed. Consequently, our estimates of mule deer numbers have been based on generalizations more that we would like.

Since that report was written, the Department has experimented with other methods of getting a better count of mule deer numbers. Between 1948 and 1953, the Department enlisted the aid of ranchers in the Badlands in counting mule deer. "Ranchers were asked to cooperate with us by keeping a record of deer seen on their lands owned or leased during the...winter" (McKean, 1949, p. 1). The thought was that ranchers would have as good an idea as anyone of the deer numbers in their area, since they had to be out managing their stock. After several years the survey was dropped because it was too unreliable. McKean wrote (McKean, 1953, p 4):

> From the standpoint of producing reliable data, which can supplement our aerial censuses of big game elsewhere in the state, these rancher figures seem to need improvement. They do furnish an idea of the trend of events, but it was hoped that a deer per section figure might be developed which could be applied to the entire Badlands area. This has not proven to be possible...
> Still more important, however, are the rancher's attitudes toward this work. Some men are believed to be conscientious about this. Others are obviously not, judging by the reports submitted. In a survey of this type, it would take many reporters to equalize the effect of a few who are not sincere.... A few errors, if submitted by adjoining ranchers could be having a serious effect on the total result.

In 1954, the Department changed to something they thought would work better. "An experimental census method was initiated in 1954 whereby certain blocks of land representative of the Badlands were first censused by aerial counts and then spot checked on horseback to get a correction factor for the aerial observations" (Sjordal and Brazda, 1955, p. 2). "In this method, certain selected areas [were] censused by air at

176

Mule deer air/horseback survey 1954.

Pershing Carlson

daybreak, and then flushed as thoroughly as possible by horseback on the same day. While a correction factor between the aerial and horseback counts is one of the items it is hoped can be obtained, at present only the horseback count is used in estimating populations. These figures are then projected to cover relatively large areas of similar habitat" (NDGFD, 1955, p. 37). For the sake of the horsemen, this survey was run in the spring, after the snow had melted; for the sake of those in the airplane, it was run before the trees leafed out.

In 1954, only two of these "representative blocks of land" were counted; in 1955, the number was increased to seven. The number of what have come to be called mule deer study areas has gradually been increased, until today there are twenty-six of them. A map of the study areas follows on page 179. It took several more years—until 1959—to establish "a statistically reliable correction factor that can be applied to the aerial count to give an estimate of mule deer numbers" (McKenzie, 1960, p. 1). Once the Department felt that it had a good "correction factor," the horseback census was abandoned in favor of the cheaper and quicker airplane method.

Management practices for mule deer were not influenced by large-scale land use changes like Garrison Dam. New notions of game management were put into practice beginning in the fall of 1941, after the first big game survey. The season was opened on mule deer for the first time since 1922. But although the Department felt that North Dakota could—and should—

hold seasons on mule deer, it was cautious. In its 1944 annual report, the Department said (NDGFD, 1944, p. 20):

> The total herd size is...limited. And because hunters will negotiate the rough territory, if an open season is held and mule deer are not too wary, the herd may well stand a harvest only once each four or six years. The time period can easily be determined from population figures derived during the annual big game census. A permit system is suggested in order to manage the desired harvest.

At that time the yearly survey was recording under a thousand mule deer in the state. Game managers thought that the maximum number of mule deer that the state could sustain was on the order of 2,000 to 3,000. During the 1940s and 1950s deer seasons were held only every other year, except for 1947 and 1948, when consecutive seasons were held. In 1943, the season was closed on mule deer, even though it was open for whitetails. 1945, 1947, and 1950 were bucks-only seasons in the parts of the Badlands range open to deer hunting. In 1948, the season was closed in the mule deer range.

Mule deer gradually began to get more management attention because the herd was growing. By 1955, the population in the Badlands was estimated at 6,000 to 7,000 animals. Why mule deer were getting attention was obvious enough, but why the herd was increasing at this rate was not as clear. Mule deer populations had reached a low point in North Dakota in the 1920s. During the disastrous thirties, thousands of people left North Dakota, and suddenly mule deer had large portions of their Badlands range to themselves.

Considering the drought conditions of the thirties, however, it seems unlikely that mule deer had very much to take advantage of. Very likely, range conditions did not improve enough to help mule deer until the 1940s. In the forties, mule deer populations began to rise significantly, and they began to extend their range. It seems likely that improving range conditions and favorable weather had more effect on the mule deer herd than the Department's management efforts. "Management" during the late 1940s and early 1950s was really mostly protection—harvesting only a very conservative number of animals, and trying to build the herd with bucks-only seasons. To give hunters a little more recreation, a statewide bow season for deer had been held each open season since 1954, and mule deer made up a small percentage of that harvest.

By 1959, the mule deer herd had reached high enough densities to need more vigorous management techniques. In 1959, the Department went to the permit system for mule deer to get better control over the harvest. In 1960, the Department's annual report noted (NDGFD, 1960, p. 33), "A deer range study was initiated in the spring of 1960 in Billings County. The data, though limited, would suggest that portions of the Badlands deer herd range were being depleted at an alarming rate. This downward trend in the carrying capacity of this primary deer range had been the direct result of over-utilization by both deer and domestic livestock." Mule deer had reached the point where management efforts were directed at keeping the herd within the carrying capacity of the range and providing sustained surpluses for recreation.

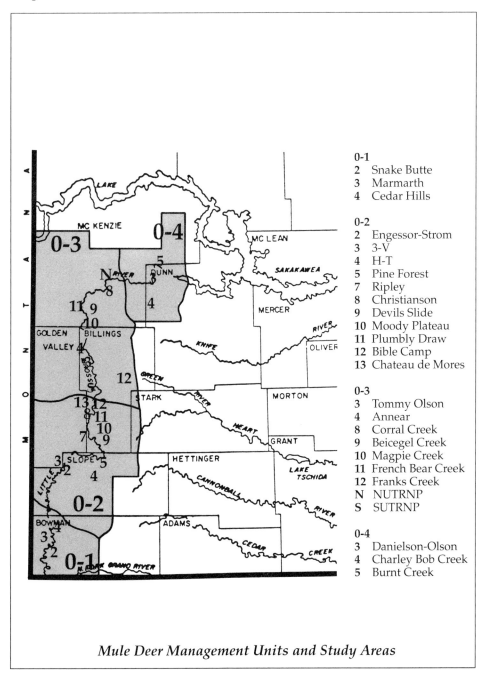

0-1	
2	Snake Butte
3	Marmarth
4	Cedar Hills

0-2	
2	Engessor-Strom
3	3-V
4	H-T
5	Pine Forest
7	Ripley
8	Christianson
9	Devils Slide
10	Moody Plateau
11	Plumbly Draw
12	Bible Camp
13	Chateau de Mores

0-3	
3	Tommy Olson
4	Annear
8	Corral Creek
9	Beicegel Creek
10	Magpie Creek
11	French Bear Creek
12	Franks Creek
N	NUTRNP
S	SUTRNP

0-4	
3	Danielson-Olson
4	Charley Bob Creek
5	Burnt Creek

Mule Deer Management Units and Study Areas

179

REORGANIZING THE GAME AND FISH DEPARTMENT

The Game and Fish Department had added a new division to its organization in 1939—the so-called "Federal Aid Division"—to handle the new Pittman-Robertson projects. Other than that, the 1948 Game and Fish Department was unchanged from the 1930 Department. What worked in 1930 quickly seemed inadequate in the 1940s, especially the 1940s after the war. In the annual report for 1948—the last report under his administration—Commissioner William J. Lowe set down a plan for reorganization (NDGFD, 1948, p. 34):

> In my opinion, the departmental functions should be organized under the direction of the commissioner and deputy commissioner into the following divisions:
>
> A division of game management under a competent superintendent under whose direction would come game refuges, surveys and investigations, public shooting, coordination and federal aid, restocking, food and cover planting, and fur resources. A division of fish management under whose direction would come lake and stream surveys and investigations, operation of fish hatcheries, dam construction and repair, and fish stocking. A division of law enforcement under the chief game warden under whose direction would be the various district wardens and special enforcement officers.... In addition there would be a division of publicity and education under the direction of competent personnel. This division would have direct charge of the departmental publication NORTH DAKOTA OUTDOORS, radio, educational pamphlets and books, slides and films, school programs, public relations and publicity releases.

ND Game and Fish Department

H.R. Morgan, Commissioner, 1948-1956

By the end of 1949, these changes were in effect. In addition to new complexities in the field of game management, the reorganization was a response to the new, larger scope of the Department's responsibility to the public. It shows up in the emphasis put on the new public relations division, and it shows up also in a rethinking of the enforcement division. H. R. Morgan, commissioner from 1948 to 1956, wrote (NDGFD, 1952, p. 7-8), "Today the North Dakota Game and Fish Department's warden has as his first job that of winning public support for the Department's program. He is schooled in Department policies and programs. He is expected to meet with you at your club meeting to explain these policies and programs, to meet with service clubs, youth groups and anyone else, particularly farmers. His second responsibility is that of bringing violators to justice." In practice, the Department depended on the warden force to keep tabs on how the public—particularly farmers—felt about game management programs, and as a sort of informal information network. For example, in 1955 and 1956, when the Department was looking for plots of land to establish as deer study areas, habitat biologists depended on the warden force to come up with combinations of likely study areas and cooperative landowners.

STUDIES AND STUDY TECHNIQUES

So far in this chapter we have looked at different management tools or techniques that came about as a result of land use changes like Garrison Dam and the Soil Bank. We have talked about how the Game and Fish Department tried to respond to a growing deer herd in a non-traditional range, armed with the principles of "scientific" game management and with a public education and public relations campaign. Except for a food habits study and a mortality factors study on "prairie" deer in the 1940s, we haven't talked much about research activities related to deer management.

In the 1940s, the phenomenon of prairie deer became important. In the late 1940s and early 1950s, the deer herd grew at a totally unexpected rate. In the late 1950s, significant deer habitat was being lost to flooding in the Missouri bottom lands. Department biologists had become very concerned that large numbers of prairie deer would cause problems with agricultural interests. And they were concerned about heavy deer losses in a hard winter. But these concerns were based on studies of deer in traditional habitat. Department biologists felt that they were working with inadequate information. They needed some studies which were specific to North Dakota. They needed to know about the relationship between deer and vegetation in these new prairie habitats.

It sounds easy to make such a study: you inventory the woody vegetation in an area, examine it to see if deer are using it—perhaps you watch a few deer in that regard as well, although it is very hard to tell, in a thicket of shrubby plants, which ones the deer are actually eating. You watch how deer move—where they are at certain times of day and night, and where they move if they are alarmed by something, usually yourself. At that point you know something about why deer are in that particular place. But you don't know that much, really. It's not that simple. You don't know, for example, if deer are in that place because they prefer to be there or if they are there simply because there is no other place. You don't know much about how many deer can be there, and you don't know what effect the deer are having on the vegetation. That would take observations over a fair period of time.

There are a great many other things that you don't know too. You don't know the effects of weather and the change of seasons on deer in your particular area—what times of year they move into the area and back out again. You don't know how far they move from the area. Weather is important, perhaps, in terms of intensity of use and in terms of the health of the plants. If agriculture is part of the picture, it becomes more complex. If, for example, cattle graze in the same area, it can affect how many deer can live there. Deer and cattle need not even compete directly. If cattle rub and trample the plants most important to deer, it limits the number of deer an area can carry.

The need for studies of white-tailed deer in prairie habitats was clear to the Game and Fish Department when the "prairie" deer herd—the "strays"—became significant. There were no guidelines to managing whitetails on the prairie. It was a new set of circumstances. In 1955, the Department entered into a cooperative agreement with the North Dakota Agricultural College (now NDSU) to use its graduate studies program to perform a study in the sandhills of southeastern North Dakota. The purpose of the study was to find out what woody vegetation might be available to deer in the area, to find out what deer were actually eating, and to investigate if there were any problems being caused by deer and cattle being in the same area. With its own personnel, the Department began similar studies in the Turtle Mountains and the Badlands.

The studies revealed a few things. The study in the sandhills country, for example, established that cattle did in fact limit the usefulness of an area for deer because cattle tended to trample brush and rub on trees,

Browsing mule deer.

breaking off the low growth which was the best deer food. Cattle did not use the area for food. The study suggested that if ranchers in the area used a slightly different pasture management system—that is, if cattle were fenced out of wooded areas which were of limited value to cattle but very important to deer—the areas would be far more productive for deer.

The potential value of such studies—browse studies—for managing deer seemed immense. In the early 1960s the Game and Fish Department extended its effort to "monitor and survey the condition and trend of shrub vegetation on big game range within the state" (Volesky, 1982, p. 1). Permanent browse study areas were established in different parts of the state, primarily in the Badlands and in the Coteau region east of the Missouri River—the places which, because of the flooding of the river bottoms, were becoming the prime deer range in North Dakota. There was much to be learned about what plants were in this new range and which of them were important to deer. Moreover, these areas had never had deer before. Deer themselves might be agents of change. Over time, changes in deer populations would be reflected in the browse plants. From changes in deer population and monitoring the effects on browse plants on study areas, researchers could get a rough notion of when the carrying capacity of the region had been reached. Used in combination with census information and harvest data, browse studies are important for management decisions—deciding the necessary harvest and setting the season.

Earlier in this chapter we discussed the time when the ten major deer management units were subdivided into 41 subunits. At that time we described the change in terms of fine-tuning the deer harvest to meet needs in small local areas. But there was more to it than that. The subdivision of the major management units in 1959 was also designed to improve the effectiveness of the annual winter deer survey, especially for the "prairie" deer who were spending the winter in the Slope and Coteau Hills Management Units (a map of the major management units and subunits is on page 170).

When the major management units were subdivided, Department personnel—wardens and other field people—were asked to locate areas within the new subunits where, over the years, deer seemed to congregate in January and February—the time when the annual survey was being run. The Department wanted to use these winter concentration areas as "population check areas." The reasoning was simple: in order to get a good idea of the trend in the deer population in a unit, you needed to be sure that you were seeing a significant percentage of the deer when you did your aerial count. Your work would be made a lot simpler if there was some area that you could depend on, year to year, to have the significant percentage of the population that you were looking for. An area of high winter deer concentration was made to order. It would have the significant percentage of the population the Department was looking for, and it came at a time when the deer could be counted relatively easily. Thus the winter concentration areas within the new management subunits became "population check areas."

During the winters of 1964-1965 and 1965-1966, the population check areas took on additional significance. The combination of winter and deer on the prairie had been an issue ever since Roy Bach and Russell Stuart found whitetails spending the winter on the prairie. But their fears had never been realized. There were some tough winters during the late 1940s, but at that time, traditional winter habitat was still there. During the 1950s, when winter habitat was being lost to water backing up from Garrison Dam and to agriculture, winters were mild. Several times in that period there wasn't enough snow in January and February to get a good aerial survey. The first real opportunity, if we can call it that, to see what these prairie deer were going to do in a severe winter came in 1964-1965 and 1965-1966.

The winters of 1964-65 and 1965-66 were long and there was a lot of snow in the prairie range of white-tailed deer. Of particular significance to this discussion was a blizzard which hit the state in early March of 1966, at the end of a fairly prolonged period of cold, snowy weather. It so happened that four population check areas had been censused just prior to that blizzard. It seemed an ideal opportunity to get some information about the effects of a severe storm on the prairie deer herd. The Department reported its findings (McKenzie, 1966, p. 2):

> General observations included the expected concentration of deer into the areas of better cover. Prior to the blizzard deer observations were most often of groups seldom larger than 6-8 animals. The post-storm observations showed concentrations as high as 35 deer in areas of more acceptable habitat or often on snow-free lands (open country) easily accessible from soil bank acres, marsh lands with good emergent vegetation or woody habitats.
>
> Individual deer were noted that were apparently suffering from the effects of the storm. Some deer appeared to be in a weakened condition.... [B]ut no dead deer were observed during the flights...It is obvious that storm mortality of whitetail deer was at a minimum during the March 2-4, 1966 blizzard...

This came as something of a surprise to biologists. The amount of food and cover in these areas of winter concentrations might be enough to get the animals through some of the easy winters of the 1950s, but no one thought that it was going to be sufficient for severe conditions. It was something well worth investigating.

In 1968, the Game and Fish Department took the first steps toward a long-term study of the relationship between white-tailed deer and these areas of winter concentration. "The observation that a particular (and often comparatively small) area may be vital or "key" to a local deer population has been advanced in recent years. However, the qualitative and quantitative evaluation of these somewhat unique portions of the total deer range has not been fully realized. This study is for this purpose" (McKenzie, 1971, Appendix, p. 1).

The population check area on the Dawson Game Management Area (now called the Dawson Wildlife Management Area) was chosen as the site for the study. Basic to the study was the idea that at some point during the winter deer began to concentrate in this area, and at some time in the spring they would begin to disperse and would move out to their summer range. By capturing and marking some of the deer in the area, researchers could follow their movements. Over a period of time, patterns of movement centered around the "key area" would emerge—seasonal movements, the range of movement, the effects of weather, and so on. Deer management could then be centered around these key areas, just as one time it had been centered around the habitat in the timbered land along the Missouri River.

Field work for the study began in 1970. The work was performed by graduate students from NDSU, under a cooperative agreement like the one in the 1950s. As with many projects, it sounds easier than it turned out to be. The first winter of the study was largely spent learning the best ways to catch and tag deer so that you could tell one deer from another and follow its movements. It was not a simple matter. To give an example: most of the deer were caught using walk-in traps made of steel tubing covered with netting. The deer were tagged by various means—ear tags, collars with different colors to distinguish individual deer, and so on. Occasionally a deer which had been caught, tagged, and released would be caught again. When that happened, the deer would manage to get his head through the netting around the trap, catch the ear tag in it, and tear the tag out. During that first year, two different deer were recaptured four times, by which time their ears were in bad shape. We might note too that the trapping was done in January, when the deer were concentrated in the "key area." It made trapping deer a more efficient business, but it was not particularly easy on the trappers.

As you might expect, some of the most significant results of the study were the things which were learned about how to study whitetails in this kind of environment—capturing them, tagging them for identification, and tracking them. Over the four years of the study, tagging deer with radio collars and tracking them both on the ground and in the air proved the most effective way of getting a clear picture of seasonal deer movements within and around the key area.

When biologists were thinking of using key wintering areas as the basis for deer management, they were apparently operating under certain assumptions. The first of these was that the key area was a key area because it provided deer with a winter food supply. Presumably then, deer populations would have to be kept within the carrying capacity of each key area. It may also have been in the backs of biologists' minds that if they knew how large an area each of these key areas served, and they

185

ND Game and Fish Department

ND Game and Fish Department

Above and right: Trapping, weighing, marking and releasing deer for study.

knew what the elements of food and cover were which made an area a key wintering area, they could achieve a better deer distribution by manipulating habitat.

Ecological situations are always more complex than you perhaps want them to be. Over the course of the study, the Dawson Game Management

ND Game and Fish Department

ND Game and Fish Department

Area proved indeed to be a key wintering area for a local white-tailed deer population. As temperatures fell and snow began to accumulate, whitetails began to concentrate in the Dawson GMA. As spring advanced, deer dispersed into the surrounding prairies and farms. "The Dawson State Game Management Area...does seem to definitely be a 'key area' within which at least a local population of deer will winter" (Aalgaard, 1972, p. ii). "It was shown that as temperatures warmed in spring, deer expanded their movements away from the Dawson State Game Management Area; but a drop in temperature or new snow would reverse their movements" (Harmoning, 1975, p. i). The extent of the movements of white-tailed deer which used the Dawson GMA as a key wintering area averaged between 20 and 30 miles. "Dispersal data suggests that deer who inhabit areas up to 25 miles away from their capture site during the spring and early summer will use the Dawson State Game Management Area as a wintering area" (Harmoning, 1973, p. iii).

ND Game and Fish Department

The idea, though, that whitetails concentrated on the Dawson GMA as winter deepened, and then dispersed randomly as spring growth provided other food sources proved to be too simplistic. First of all, deer did not seem to depend on woody browse in the Dawson GMA for winter food. Observations of deer during the period of the study made it clear that whitetails in the area were making more use of corn and alfalfa than they were browse plants. "Agricultural land supplied prairie-marsh white-tailed deer with a considerable quantity of their food supply through all the seasons of the year" (Aalgaard, 1973, p. 50). "It seems probable that whitetails in the study area possess a rumen microfloral population through the year to allow digestion of non-woody vegetation" (Aalgaard,

188

1973, p. 48). In fact, whitetails in the area seemed to be doing quite well on these non-traditional foods.

The relationship between the seasonal movements of deer and the Dawson GMA seemed much more complex. When deer dispersed in the spring, the distances they travelled and the habitat they selected were not random, but were related to social behavior and to adaptations for reproductive success.

Whitetails spend the winter in family groups. A doe will spend the winter with her fawns of previous springs. When spring comes again, and fawning time approaches, a pregnant doe will separate herself. The study of deer on the Dawson GMA (Harmoning, 1976) seemed to show that this break-up of the family group was the first push to disperse deer from their winter concentrations.

Juvenile deer tended to stay in a relatively confined area until either their habitat needs could no longer be met, or they were disturbed by something. Once disturbed, they would keep moving until they came to another place where all their needs were met, and they would stay until they used it up or were pushed out again. The distance they traveled depended more on the availability of habitat than on the "key area" of winter habitat.

For pregnant females, the pattern was different (Harmoning, 1976, p. 30):

> [T]he summer dispersion of fawning whitetails appears to be strongly influenced by cover type. For this group, permanent wetlands afford the only good cover free from human disturbance. The fawning deer of the Coteau population consistently utilized this type during the day while showing no particular consistency for any food type during the night period.
>
> The fawning does tend to be quite sedentary during the first part of the summer. During the latter part of August, when the fawns of the year begin to accompany them, they extend their area of use. Around mid-September to mid-October there appears to be some regrouping of females and their fawns with the previous year's female offspring and a slightly different pattern of dispersion develops.
>
> During the fall the dispersion seemed to be influenced primarily by agricultural land during both day and night.

From the studies of the Dawson GMA as a key wintering area for deer, it became apparent that agricultural practices in the surrounding area were as important to deer survival as anything they might find inside the GMA. Agricultural practices would have a great deal to do with the distances juvenile deer would travel in the spring; they would have a great deal to do with the cover that whitetail does would use for fawning. In winter, the tolerance of farmers would largely determine the food supply—and the "carrying capacity"—of the area.

SAVING THE DEER

This long tale of the evolution of deer management in North Dakota brings us, finally, to the winter of 1977-78. The winter of 1977-78 was the most recent reminder we have had of how long and miserable a winter can be here. That was the winter when North Dakotans got together in an effort to save the deer. In the story of the campaign to save the deer, we can see the interplay of many of the different considerations that go into the practice of deer management in North Dakota. We have already talked about most of them. One is the combination of winter and whitetails that live on the open prairie. Others are the science and the tools of game management. There is the biology of ruminants. There are the relationships between farmers and sportsmen, landowners and game managers. And there is another we haven't discussed very much, which is how public opinion shapes deer management.

The story goes something like this. Deer season opened on November 11 in 1977. It looked like it was going to be a very good season. Deer numbers were high over most of the state, except for a small area along the Little Missouri where disease had taken a heavy toll of whitetails the previous fall. The weather had been mild. There had been a wet snow in the middle of October. The summer had been dry. Crops were small, and hay was short. The wet snow was welcome.

On November 20, a heavy snowstorm all over the state pretty much closed the deer season. There were places where the deer harvest was down from what the Department hoped for, but there wasn't much that could be done about it.

A week or so after the November 20th snowstorm, another front moved in. The temperature was warm enough that North Dakota got two days of freezing rain instead of snow, and a wide swath from the southwest to the northeast was coated with an inch or more of ice. Things came to a standstill. In at least one small town in the path of the storm, no one could get up the hill out of town for more than two days. Conditions were especially tough on wildlife. Storms came one after another in the following weeks, until two feet of snow and ice covered most of the state.

By the middle of December, the Game and Fish Department was getting calls. "Come and get your deer. They're getting into my hay stacks," was the most common. Deer, their usual food sources covered with a layer of snow and ice they couldn't break through, were converging on stored hay, eating some, and tearing down the stacks. By the end of December, the calls were getting worse. Some landowners were getting ready to shoot the deer.

It was a tough situation. Hay supplies were short to begin with. In some areas, there was just about enough for livestock. In other places there may have been enough feed to go around, but deer destroyed more than they ate, and nobody could afford that. The sight of deer in the haystacks was made worse by the thought that it might not do those deer any good. A deer which lives on alfalfa all summer and fall might do well on alfalfa hay in winter. But a deer used to other foods can't digest it. It was a tough situation for both the landowners and for the deer.

The Game and Fish Department mobilized. Office people and field people were reassigned to assist the district wardens in answering complaints. They tried to scare the deer away from the haystacks by hazing them with airplanes and snowmobiles, with firecrackers, and with scareguns. It worked briefly, but as conditions got worse, the deer would hardly move away.

Winter, 1977-1978. Above: Deer in the haystacks. Below: Scaring deer.

191

Winter, 1977-78. Above: Trapping deer. Below: Trying to feed deer.

In the places where the problems were the worst, the Department tried trapping the deer and moving them to places where they might be able to find food. It was an expensive way to deal with the problem—someone later figured that it cost 125 dollars a deer to trap and move them. You can't spend that kind of money if the problem is very large. And this problem was getting huge.

By the end of December, Department officials knew they were going to have to come up with something else. Scare tactics weren't getting the job done. They didn't have the manpower or the money to either trap all the deer and move them or fence them out. And the deer in the real problem areas were getting weak. The strain was starting to show.

There were not many options left. The Department narrowed them down to two. Either they could try to feed the deer, propping them up with artificial food and keeping them off the haystacks; or they could devise special seasons in the areas where there were the most problems, letting hunters harvest them while they were still worth taking.

On December 30, 1977, at the request of the Game and Fish Department, the Governor of North Dakota proclaimed that a special deer season was to begin January 4, 1978, to reduce deer numbers in areas where deer depredation was a serious problem. The season was to be very strictly controlled, strictly to remove deer where they were causing problems.

There were both biological and financial reasons for the decision to have a season instead of trying to feed the deer. The Department did not have the financial resources to feed the deer in North Dakota even if they thought it was a good thing to do. And they did not think it was a good thing to do. The feeling was this: if deer were causing depredation problems it was a good indication that there were too many deer for the available habitat. If the situation was not controlled with the usual tools available to game managers—that is to say, with the annual deer season—then nature should be allowed to take its course. Artificial feeding, if it worked, would perpetuate a bad situation, and perhaps make it even worse. Moreover, it was pretty unlikely that it would work, because deer cannot adjust to new foods overnight. It was very possible that they would die in any event. A special season seemed both more practical in the short term, and more beneficial to the deer population in the long term.

The special deer season was never held. Public opinion was very much against it. In early January, the North Dakota Wildlife Federation passed a resolution to embark on a "Save the Deer" campaign, which would take public donations to buy food to feed the deer. By the 18th of January, newspapers, television stations and radio stations were getting the word out, telling people what the campaign was for and how they could help. Sportsmen's clubs and wildlife clubs were working with farmers and with others who had tried feeding programs to see what kinds of foods had been tried and where to get them. The Game and Fish Department had, of course, an extensive list of places where the feed should go—where deer were in the greatest trouble. The program was coordinated by the Game and Fish Department and the North Dakota Wildlife Federation. For the most part, district wardens handled the job of contacting landowners and helping them set up feeding stations. Donations came from all over the state, from individuals and organizations, and some even from Canada.

Winter did not let up that year. Another storm in February dumped 16 more inches of snow on some parts of the state. There were still snowdrifts in shelterbelts in May. When it was finally over, the Game and Fish Department tried to measure the effects of the winter and of the Save the Deer campaign. The Department wanted to know if the food had made a difference to the deer herd—had kept them from starving—and if feeding the deer had cut down on the problems of deer damaging livestock feed supplies.

The Department estimated that perhaps 10 percent of the deer herd was affected by the Save the Deer campaign. The Department surveyed both farmers and district wardens in the regions where depredation problems had been the worst and where feeding efforts had been concentrated. Both farmers and wardens felt that the feeding effort had helped. They felt that there had been more deer dying before the feeding effort than after it got started. They felt that the deer looked healthier after the feeding program got rolling. And they felt that the feeding effort had pulled the deer away from the haystacks and feed supplies where they had been a problem.

In the places where the feeding program was concentrated, it appears to have been successful. Deer got through a tough time, and it cut down on the damage they were doing to feed supplies. It was expensive—$27,000 were spent to feed 10 percent of the deer herd. And in the rest of the state, winter mortality on deer was not as high as expected, and reproduction in the spring was fairly good. No one would recommend deer feeding as a tool for large-scale deer management.

But it would be a mistake to minimize the long-range effects of the Save the Deer campaign on deer management in North Dakota. For example: as a result of the publicity surrounding the plight of the deer in 1977-1978, the public as a whole became more aware of the need for better deer habitat. In 1978, an initiated measure was approved by North Dakota voters to return the interest money from the North Dakota Game and Fish Fund to the Game and Fish Department to pay for wildlife habitat improvement on private land. One hundred thousand dollars of the fund was earmarked for depredation programs. This program may never have come about if it hadn't been for the damage caused by hungry deer and the effort to save them.

Something a little harder to measure are the effects of these hard winters on the relationships among landowners, sportsmen, and the Game and Fish Department. It may be that they came to understand each other a little better. The Department worked hard to come up with solutions to the problems landowners were having; on their part, landowners seemed more willing, afterwards, to allow sportsmen to hunt on their land— allowing the Department, thus, to exert some control over the deer

194

population before it got to be a problem for everyone.

The "Save the Deer" campaign of the winter of 1977-78 demonstrates a little bit of how deer management works in the real world. There is give and take among a host of different interests and points of view. Deer management has come considerable distance since the early 1940s when Roy Bach and Russell Stuart first set out to see if they could count the deer in North Dakota. The state has changed. In fact, today we fish in places where Bach and Stuart counted deer. There are more things to discuss about whitetails and mule deer in North Dakota. There will be, for example, some discussion about disease studies in Chapter Eleven. There is information about hunting seasons, regulations, harvest figures, and so on in the appendix.

Russell Stuart, Commissioner, 1961-1979

But the future direction of deer management in North Dakota seems clear. Deer populations today are as high as they have ever been, and deer provide more recreation than any other species in North Dakota. Although the deer population will always depend to some degree on the tolerance level of landowners in the state, it seems unlikely—if the Save the Deer campaign is any measure—that the public will allow the deer population to diminish. Deer management will have to take that into account.

Sources

Aalgaard, R. B. 1972. White-tailed Deer Movement Study. NDGFD Pittman-Robertson Division Project W-67-R-12, Phase C, Study C-IV, Report No. 179.

Aalgaard, R. B. 1973. Movements of the White-Tailed Deer *(Odocoileus virginianus)* in the Prairie-Marsh Deer Range of South-Central North Dakota (MS Thesis). NDGFD Pittman-Robertson Division Project W-67-R-12+13, Phase C, Report No. 179-A.

Bach, R. N. 1941. Some Notes Regarding the Deer of the Lower Souris Refuge and Vicinity. NDGFD Division of Federal Aid Project 7R, Report No. 26.

Bach, R. N. 1943. Aerial Survey of North Dakota's Big Game. NDGFD Division of Federal Aid Project 7R, Report No. 5.

Bach, R. N. 1944. 1944 Aerial Survey of North Dakota's Big Game. NDGFD Division of Federal Aid Project 7R, Report No. 6.

Bach, R. N. 1946. 1946 Aerial Survey of North Dakota's Big Game. NDGFD Division of Federal Aid Project 7R, Report No 8.

Bue, I G. 1960. A Look Back at 1959. ND Outdoors 22(7):2.

Christianson, R. J. 1954. No Hunting. ND Outdoors 22(4):4.

Enyeart, George W. 1973. Summary Report, Garrison and Snake Creek Reservoirs, 1955-1972: A Sixteen Year Resume of Research, Management, and Development Work Done on Garrison and Snake Creek Reservoirs. NDGFD Pittman-Robertson Division Projects W-23-D-27 and 67-R-12, Report No. A-954.

Hanson, W. R. 1950. A Plan for Habitat Restoration on Garrison Reservoir. NDGFD Division of Federal Aid Project 7R.

Harmoning, A. K. 1973. White-tailed Deer Movement Study. NDGFD Pittman-Robertson Division Project W-67-R-13, Phase C, Study C-IV, Report No. 185.

Harmoning, A. K. 1975. White-tailed Deer Movement Study. NDGFD Pittman-Robertson Division Project W-67-R-15, Phase C, Study C-IV, Report No. 199.

Harmoning, A. K. 1976. White-tailed Deer Dispersion and Habitat Utilization in Central North Dakota (MS Thesis). NDGFD Pittman-Robertson Division Project W-67-R-13, 14, and 15, Phase C, Report No. 199-A.

Johnson, Morris D. and Joseph Knue. 1989. Feathers From the Prairie. North Dakota Game and Fish Department, Bismarck.

McKean, W. T. 1949. A Survey of North Dakota Badlands Deer, Winter 1948-1949 by Rancher Cooperation. NDGFD Division of Federal Aid, Project 7R, Report No. 14.

McKean, W. T. 1953. Late-Winter Deer Counts by Badlands Ranchers, 1950-1951-1952. NDGFD Pittman-Robertson Division Project W-37-R-2, Report No 46.

McKean, W. T. 1954. Natural Mortality Factors Among White-tailed Deer in North Dakota 1947-1954. NDGFD Pittman-Robertson Division Projects W-7R-13 and W-37-R-1, Report No. 39.

McKenzie, J. V. 1960a. The 1959 Deer Season. ND Outdoors 22(7):11.

McKenzie, J. V. 1960b. Mule Deer Census. NDGFD Pittman-Robertson Division Project No. W-35-R-5, Report No. 78.

McKenzie, J. V. 1966. White-tailed Deer Census, 1965-1966. NDGFD Pittman-Robertson Division Project W-67-R-6, Report No. 127.

McKenzie, J. V. 1970. White-tailed Deer Movement Study (Literature Review and Work Plan). NDGFD Pittman-Robertson Division Project W-67-R-10, Phase C, Report No. 166.

Miller, W. L. and R. N. Bach. 1945. Preliminary Report of Physical and Biological Aspects of that Portion of the Missouri Basin to be Inundated in North Dakota. NDGFD Division of Federal Aid Project 7R.

Morgan, H. R. 1952. Garrison Dam and Wildlife Values! ND Outdoors 15(5):6-7+16.

North Dakota Game and Fish Department (NDGFD). 1941. Aerial Survey of North Dakota's Big Game. NDGFD Pittman-Robertson Wildlife Survey and Investigation Project Report No. 00.

NDGFD. 1942. Annual Report, December 1, 1940-June 30, 1942.

NDGFD. 1943. Annual Report, July 1, 1942-June 30, 1943.

NDGFD. 1944. Annual Report, July 1, 1943-June 30, 1944.

NDGFD. 1945. Annual Report, July 1, 1944-June 30, 1945.

NDGFD. 1948. Annual Report, July 1, 1947-June 30, 1948.

NDGFD. 1952. Annual Report, July 1, 1951-June 30, 1952.

NDGFD. 1955. Annual Report, July 1, 1954-June 30. 1955.

NDGFD. 1960. Annual Report, July 1, 1959-June 30, 1960.

NDGFD. 1962. Annual Report, July 1, 1961-June 30, 1962.

Saugstad, S. 1942. Aerial Census of Big Game in North Dakota. pps. 343-354 of Transactions of the Seventh North American Wildlife Conference. American Wildlife Institute.

Sjordal, J. E. and A. R. Brazda. 1955. Deer Census, Winter 1953-1954. NDGFD Pittman-Robertson Division Project W-37-R-5, Report No. 78.

Stuart, R. W. 1947. 1947 Aerial Survey of North Dakota's Big Game. NDGFD Division of Federal Aid Project 7R, Report No. 9.

I didn't need blinds, decoys or calls.
I just slipped into my old coveralls,
And with knife, wife and rifle with scope,
I took off to shoot a big antelope.

We arrived in our jeep at my unit to hunt,
But that rain and mud sure made hunting a stunt.
My windshield wipers weren't working so good,
So I laid the windshield down on the hood.

Then we bravely plowed forth down the rain-sodden track,
In search of the buck that I hoped to take back.
My wife was complaining that I'd ruined her dress.
(I had to admit we both looked a mess).

But what is a little discomfort I say,
A man can't hunt antelope just any old day.
Then off on a hill we saw a big bunch,
But they were mostly all mamas and kids having lunch.

Then we spotted what looked like the old patriarch,
And I drove like a madman, for this was my mark.
Then we slid in a wash-out and we really got stuck.
I just sat there and loudly cursed my bad luck.

I stepped from the jeep into the coldest of rains,
And was trying to put on those infernal old chains,
When my wife said, "Look, up there on the slope,"
And up there stood about twelve antelope.

I guess those characters had come back to see,
Just what in the world had happened to me.
Well, I grabbed up my rifle in spite of the rain,
And there was that big old grand-daddy again.

Well, I pulled up and fired my rifle until
Every last antelope ran over the hill.
Then I really blew up, I'm telling you.
My words turned the air and the sagebrush all blue.

Then my wife said, "You got it."
And I answered, "I did?"
She smirked, "It fell over,
When you flipped your lid."

I was still rather dubious, but I followed her gaze,
To the spot on the hillside nearly hidden by haze.
Yes, there lay an animal, an antelope I think.
So I galloped right over, as fast as a wink.

CHAPTER EIGHT

PRONGHORNS

It was a buck alright,
But I have a hunch
That we watched him earlier,
While he ate his lunch.

Oh well…I carefully cleaned him,
And snapped on my tag,
That's when the "missus,"
Really started to nag.

"…The poor little thing…
This rain and what mud…
And just look at your new jacket
All covered with blood…

"…I declare you're crazy,
And I'm soaking wet…
And put up the windshield,
How dumb can you get…"

So it went till at last
We turned in at our gate.
Her final word was,
"…And we get home so late."

I had suffered in silence,
But a thought brought me hope.
Next time I may get
That big antelope.

Trophy Hunting For Antelope,
Reprinted from **North Dakota Outdoors,** *January, 1960,*
Author known, but still cautious.

If you had asked one of North Dakota's game managers back in 1940 if he thought that anyone would be writing poems about hunting antelope here, he might have laughed. In 1940, hopes for such hunts were pretty dim. The February, 1940 issue of **North Dakota Outdoors** quoted a Bureau of Biological Survey (today's Fish and Wildlife Service) study which said that there were only 50 pronghorns in the state. Although that figure was almost certainly too low, the season on antelope had been closed since 1900, and no one expected it to be opened any time soon.

In the early 1940s, more attention was paid to deer, which were huntable. Antelope were counted when the annual deer survey was flown—the census takers estimated that there were 580 pronghorns in North Dakota in 1941 and 750 in 1942. Based on information from other states, North Dakota's game biologists came up with some goals for North Dakota: "The antelope range of North Dakota at the present time will approximate 5,500 square miles. At one time in North Dakota's early history, antelope ranged throughout most of the state, and it is a possibility that the present range, under careful management, may be greatly increased. It is entirely possible that an antelope herd of 6,000 to 10,000 animals may be carried in North Dakota" (NDGFD, 1944, p. 20-21). In light of today's populations, those are some pretty realistic population numbers. But they were largely based on situations in South Dakota and Wyoming. Actual plans for North Dakota's pronghorns were still fairly vague.

Moving pronghorns.

200

Plans remained vague until the late 1940s and early 1950s, but there were some changes. In 1943, the Federal Aid Division of the Game and Fish Department experimented with a summer antelope census, and in 1945, the change was made permanent. There were several reasons for it. It was assumed that North Dakota's antelope population was subject to rather large seasonal shifts. It had been established as long ago as Lewis and Clark that pronghorns were migratory—that is, that like migratory birds, herds of antelope would follow established routes and work their way south every fall, and return every spring. Recall (Chapter Three) the camp of Hidatsa Indians that Meriwether Lewis met in the spring of 1805, waiting along the banks of the Missouri for the return of the antelope. Observations in 1941 and 1942 seemed to indicate that antelope still followed the old pattern (Bach, 1945, p. 1):

> We have found during the past six years that we may expect a rather heavy migration of these animals [antelope] from the summer North Dakota range to areas west and south outside of North Dakota. As an example, during the latter part of February, 1945, only 15 antelope were seen during the time the deer census was being made in the western part of the state.
>
> It seems that the extent of this fall or winter migration depends largely upon such winter conditions as snowfall, temperature, ice conditions, availability of forage, etc. We have indeed experienced several seasons when scarcely any migration had occurred by February.
>
> It seems the best policy then that our annual antelope censuses...should be run sometime during the summer residence period.

Another reason for the change was to keep track of antelope reproduction. "[I]t was felt that the kids might be about right size during the latter part of July so that they might not be as well hidden in July as they might be earlier in the year and yet be of such size that they could readily be told from the older animals" (Bach, 1943, p. 1). The number of fawns per doe is important information for measuring the health of the herd. If, for example, for every 100 does there are 100 fawns that survive, it is a sign that nutrition is good, reproduction is excellent, and the herd is healthy and growing. But if there were only 20 or so fawns for 100 does, reproduction is way down or a lot of fawns are dying, and it's high time to be seeing where the problems are.

Although the Department saw large potential for the pronghorn herd, no one in 1948 seemed optimistic that the potential would be fulfilled. Pronghorns remained only in the southwest corner of the state—some 5,000 to 6,000 square miles—and land use changes and poaching in the area caused much concern (Stuart and McKean, 1948, p. 1):

It is increasingly apparent that changing ranch land use practices in the antelope areas are affecting the distribution of the antelope, if not the total numbers. Thousands of acres of virgin sod were broken up during the past two years and seeded to flax. This practice has decreased the usable antelope range...It became apparent that the antelope were occurring in larger and less numerous bunches.... Such a situation, if prolonged many years will mean range depletion on the few remaining spots, greater natural losses, more successful poaching and possibly a subsequent permanent elimination of the herd in North Dakota. We haven't far to go.

It may seem odd, then, to find active management for pronghorns begin three years later, in 1951, with a hunting season in exactly the area where antelope seemed most vulnerable. Less surprising is the effort, beginning in 1953, to trap antelope in places like Montana and transplant them into open areas of North Dakota. Yet the reasons for the hunting season and for the trap-transplant effort are closely related. To explain it, we have to take some of the things that we know about antelope, combine them with events in southwestern North Dakota, and reconstruct the situation.

Picture, if you will, the pronghorn range in southwestern North Dakota before settlement. The land was a continuous, rolling, shortgrass prairie. Although it was called a grassland, other plants mixed with the grasses and found suitable niches according to moisture, slope and soil. There were no mountains, forests, or gorges to restrict the free movement of either wind or antelope. There were far more antelope then, and when winter's snow began to close the northern ranges, they pushed south, into places where the vegetation grew higher, out of the snow. In the spring, there may have been an equal pressure to move north, away from winter's concentrations; to follow the emerging green plants; to scatter for fawning and to escape the attention of wolves.

Pronghorns in typical habitat.

Antelope had adapted to the open grasslands environment—its plants, climate, topography, and so on. As we saw in Chapter Three, all that came to an end with settlement. Plowed fields, cattle and sheep pastures, and fences formed barriers to the once free-moving antelope, cutting their range into pieces as small as a quarter-section. The things which made them successful on the open prairie were useless to them in the new situation. Unrestricted hunting, which lasted well into the twentieth century, decimated the pronghorn.

But when a long period of drought came to North Dakota in the 1920s and 1930s, many settlers abandoned their homesteads. Abandoned cropland grew up in sage and Russian thistle. When the rains came again in the 1940s, overgrazed rangeland came back. You would think that pronghorns would have recovered too.

But they didn't. Pronghorn populations in North Dakota in the 1940s remained very small—on the edge of elimination, as we have seen—and they stayed on the same range in the southwest corner of North Dakota, moving short distances into Montana and South Dakota. We know that when conditions are right, pronghorn populations can increase quickly. Adult pronghorn does most often have twin fawns, and if survival is good, the population can build very quickly. Something—or a combination of things—was limiting the pronghorn population.

First on the roster of possible limiting factors are food, water, and cover. Weak, malnourished animals in poor cover are vulnerable to the weather, to disease, and to the attacks of predators. Reproduction can be affected. Malnourished mothers have fewer, weaker young, and poor cover can increase the effects of weather or give predators better opportunities. Other things which can limit populations are land use practices—which affect food, water, and cover—and other causes of death—poaching, for example.

ND Game and Fish Department

Pronghorns take advantage of long-range vision.

As we have said, pronghorn populations can increase quickly if conditions are right. The right conditions start with food and water. For pronghorns, food has to be available, and it must be in the right combinations. It's hard to list an ideal antelope menu because they eat different things in different parts of the country. Using native shortgrass prairie as a guide, a good food situation for pronghorns would have a mix of grasses, forbs, and browse plants, which green up at different times and mature at different rates. A monocrop situation such as you might find in a wheatfield or even a tallgrass prairie is bad for pronghorns. Pronghorns avoid tall grass and other places with vegetation over 15-30 inches high—cornfields, for example—which would interfere with mobility and long-range vision. Water appears to be important. Antelope seem to prefer places where sources of open water are spaced no more than five miles apart.

Coyote with rabbit.

204

If food and water are there in the right proportions, you have to look elsewhere for potential limitations. Weather can have serious consequences for pronghorns. We are going to look at some examples shortly. In the early days, unregulated hunting and, later, poaching kept populations down.

Predators can be a limiting factor. In most places, coyotes are the most serious predator on antelope. And, although coyotes, working in tandem, can take adult antelope, their usual targets are fawns, especially newborns. It does not take very long before a pronghorn fawn can outrun a coyote. Studies (Vriend and Barrett, 1978) suggest that the number of fawns that survives the first three months of their lives is critical to the growth of the population. This makes for a wonderfully fertile field for controversy and argument. On the face of it, if you have fewer coyotes, you should have more surviving antelope fawns, and higher populations. Indeed, this is precisely the point of view you have to take if you were going to treat wildlife populations as if they were domestic livestock. Game managers try, however, to treat antelope and other wildlife populations as if they were part of an intact, operating, ecological system

From the perspective of ecological systems, there is a great deal of hazard in seeing things in terms of such direct relationships as fewer coyotes/more antelope. The worlds of both coyotes and antelope are much larger than that. Just because there are coyotes and antelope does not mean that coyotes are killing and eating antelope fawns.

There may be other things to consider. Coyotes have survived in spite of a very bad reputation, partly because they can do well on whatever prey is easiest for them to catch. If antelope and rabbits were both abundant, and rabbits were easier to catch, then coyotes would eat more rabbits than antelope. Abundance alone is not enough. Something has to be added to the mixture to make antelope a good target. Furthermore, coyotes don't really go looking for antelope or anything else. A coyote has a territory in which he lives most of his life. The size of the territory stays the same, year after year. The amount of his territory he visits may vary season to season, and the size of the territory may get smaller if coyote densities increase. But he doesn't usually leave his territory, even if there happens to be some antelope nearby. It is easy to see that if habitat for antelope was continuous for thousands of miles—as it was in pre-settlement days—and coyotes were scarce, then coyotes would not be much of a limiting factor on antelope reproduction. On the other hand, if coyote populations were fairly dense, and antelope movements within the territories of a lot of coyotes were restricted, the odds for coyote predation would go up.

Having gone through all of this, we're about ready to try and reconstruct what was happening in the 1940s and 1950s—why management efforts took the form of a hunting season and a trap-transplant program.

To be sure, no one at the time was measuring things like the mix of grasses, forbs, and browse plants to see if they were right for antelope. No one was looking at how much cover there was after heavy grazing and the

205

Pronghorns around abandoned farmstead.

drought of the past twenty years. But we know a few things. We know, for example, what happened to people.

In the dry years of the 1920s and in the drought years of the 1930s, a homestead size parcel of land in southwestern North Dakota was not nearly large enough to provide a livelihood. Thousands of homesteaders simply abandoned their land.

But the land could not all revert to native prairie. Large areas were good for pronghorns, but the good areas may have been separated by other areas that were not, or divided by abandoned fences. Antelope populations did not spread out and reoccupy their historic range. They remained in a fairly confined region in the southwest corner of the state.

Nor did populations grow within the region. Reports from the early 1940s indicate that coyote densities in the region were pretty high. What seems to have been going on is that there was a relatively captive antelope population living within fairly densely populated coyote territory. It seems to have been a fairly balanced situation—coyotes keeping the pronghorn population within the limits of the restricted habitat. As people started to break up land for crops again in the later forties, there was a tendency for antelope to be pushed together into clumps, making them even easier prey for coyotes, and causing the concern among game managers we saw earlier.

Starting in about 1949, that situation began to change. 1949 saw the introduction of 1080 coyote poison, and the number of coyotes dropped dramatically. It is no coincidence that when coyote populations dropped, complaints from landowners about antelope went up. Antelope populations were starting to rise; more land was being turned back into cropland. It was a combination which made it seem, at least in a few places, as if there were too many antelope. "Complicating the range

206

problem here is the fact that great acreages of sod and sagebrush have only recently been broken up and planted. The antelope relish the new flax, grain, and alfalfa in their diet, while it is available. It seems reasonable to report an estimate th[at] 90% of the antelope seen this summer were standing actually in some crop or were on native pasture within a mile of cropland" (McKean, 1949, p. 2). At the same time, of course, there were large areas of apparently good antelope range which were completely unoccupied.

Landowner complaints about the damage that antelope were causing brought about the first antelope season in 1951. The season was aimed at reducing antelope numbers in particular areas where there were problems, and when it came time to issue hunting permits, resident landowners were given preference over the general public. In 1953, the Game and Fish Department began a program to trap antelope and transplant them into the large areas of habitat that they had failed to occupy for themselves. The modern era of antelope management in North Dakota had begun.

Antelope trapping near Gardiner, Montana, 1954.

TRAPPING AND TRANSLOCATING THE WILD PRONGHORN

In Chapter Three, there is a description from Meriwether Lewis of a structure built by the Indian tribes along the Missouri to catch antelope. The structure most commonly used by game and fish departments when they want to catch a bunch of antelope uses materials which make it portable and has a few refinements which the Indians did not need, but it is recognizably the same structure as the one the Indians used. It is basically a corral with an opening in it and two fairly long wings spreading out from it to funnel the animals into the trap.

207

The Indians did not need to worry about what happened to the animals they trapped, and they did not need to handle live antelope. Game managers do, and so antelope trapping has gone through some refinement. Handling live, excited wild animals can be quite an experience. One trap used by game departments in the early days had a holding pen attached to the side of the main corral. One animal at a time was herded into the holding pen for tagging or whatever other purpose the trappers had in mind. The real fun began in the holding pen. Charles Cadieux and Art Brazda, working for the North Dakota Game and Fish Department in 1954, faced the job of tagging and getting a blood sample from 134 trapped antelope. Cadieux describes the experience (Cadieux, 1986, p. 90-91):

> Finally, we fooled one young buck. He jumped into the holding pen and we slammed the door shut before he could reverse his course. Art moved in for the catch.
> There was a huge cloud of dust, a blurred whirling of man and pronghorn, and then Art loomed out of the cloud of dust. He had the antelope in a bear hug, clutched around the middle, just behind the front legs, and he held the 100-pound animal off the ground. Blood streamed from Art's forehead.... We moved in and got the necessary blood sample and ear-tagged the buck, then lugged him to the waiting semi-trailer.
> The second antelope ripped Art's blue jeans all the way down one side. The third one caused more damage. Art was a tough man, but obviously he had little chance of enduring the capture of all 134 antelope. Putting two men in the holding pen helped a little, but only a little. When we had 13 antelope processed, Art's blue jeans were a series of rags hanging from his belt, and his longjohns were beginning to show the wear.

Most of the refinements to trapping wild animals have to do with the welfare of the animals and the trappers. Generally speaking, if you want to keep trapped wild animals from harming themselves, each other, or you, you need to keep them as calm as possible.

In a corral trap like the one described above, the sides are made of netting, and the antelope can see through them. The antelope think they can get through the netting or over it, and they can do themselves a lot of damage trying. It seems to calm them down to drop a curtain around the corral. Most game departments that use a corral trap rig it so that a rolled-up burlap curtain can be dropped all the way around the corral with one pull of a rope. Once the curtain is dropped, the antelope are left alone for a time to let them calm down and to cool off.

What happens now depends on the reasons for trapping the animals. If all you want to do is move them to a new release area, then the trick is to get the antelope into the truck as calmly as possible, settle them down, and move them. With antelope it works best to maneuver them up onto a loading chute which has solid sides and a top, and into a truck which is rigged to exclude light but which permits good ventilation. Darkness seems to keep the animals calm, but antelope don't do well in a truck when the temperature gets above 70 degrees. The other thing that game managers have learned to do is cut the tips off the horns of horned male antelope or blindfold them to keep them from goring other antelope. The motion of the trucks also seems to calm the animals.

Most of the time though, trapping antelope means handling the animals for tagging, for measuring, for giving them medicine, and so on. For that, another whole set of techniques comes into play. The main maneuvers are to separate the animals you want to work with from the main group of trapped animals, and then to restrain them for whatever period of time you need.

It can be, as we have seen, easier said than done. Various techniques for separating animals have been tried—one was the holding pen used in the 1950s. Most often today, trappers try to segregate small groups of antelope behind curtains, and then move in with workers—one or two to an antelope—to restrain and blindfold them, and do the tagging or whatever needs to be done. This mostly consists of getting the animal off its feet, at which point it stops struggling. If the trapper needs the animal immobilized for any length of time, he usually uses some kind of tranquilizing drug.

When it comes to live-trapping wild animals, each species causes different concerns. We will see some of the differences between techniques for antelope and those for bighorn sheep in the next chapter. One of the major considerations for pronghorns—besides the technique for trapping—is the season of the year. If pregnant antelope does are trapped too close to fawning, it causes problems. If antelope are trapped late in the winter, there are problems with hair loss. This can be quite serious for antelope because (see Chapter Three) their hair is an important part of how pronghorns stay warm and cool. Late in the winter—from January on— antelope hair seems to grow brittle. When the animals thrash around in a net they can lose patches of hair, making them much more susceptible to the effects of cold weather. Trapping in hot weather causes the opposite problem—the animals die from being overheated. The best time for trapping and translocating antelope is in the late fall and early winter, after the rut is over and all does are bred, but before the weather turns too cold and does become too heavy.

North Dakota trapped its first antelope in Montana in 1953. The project was done with Pittman-Robertson funds, and there were some specific constraints put on the Department with regard to the release sites (McKean, 1953a, p. 6-7):

> The requirements of the Fish and Wildlife Service concerning transplanting big game with Pittman-Robertson funds are rather exacting but fundamentally sound.... [E]vidence must be presented...that a substantial area of wild and undisturbed land

exists where the transplanting...is proposed. Evidence must be shown that a low predator population exists on the transplanting sites. This is designed to prevent loss of fawns especially during the first few years. Likewise, agreement must be given that no hunting of these transplanted animals will take place for at least five years after their introduction into new areas.

Antelope release, 1950s.

There were other considerations in North Dakota which were not answered by the Fish and Wildlife Service's guidelines. Pronghorn release sites in North Dakota were on private land. The Department's experiences with pronghorns in the southwest corner of the state made it careful about getting landowners' consent from large areas around potential release sites. Many landowners seemed to want antelope—there were many more requests for antelope than there were either antelope or good range for them—but the Department wanted to be sure that there would be no surprises. The Department warned landowners by letter of possible problems (Cadieux, 1954):

> This request is being turned over to big game biologists Wm. McKean and Art Brazda for possible future study. There are a few factors which I should point out to you, however, which may affect the possible stocking of pronghorns in those areas. First, the antelope is capable of causing heavy damage to crops, therefore we will not stock antelope on land which has a heavy proportion of farmed acres. The antelope must have grassland. In the plantings made previous to this time, we have contacted the farmers and landowners involved and made sure that an overwhelming majority of them favored the introduction of antelope before we considered the area as even a remote possibility. Have you thought of the landowner reaction in these areas?

In spite of the warnings, the possibility of antelope causing large-scale crop damage did not seem very high. In the fall of 1951, the Game and Fish Department collected antelope stomachs from hunters to analyze what the animals were eating. They expected to find—and did find—that antelope were making some use of flax and alfalfa. They also found that antelope turned to crops in places where traditional range was damaged. "[T]he antelope in western North Dakota depend heavily on browse and weeds for fall foods. They have not turned to the abundant wild grasses, but rather have preferred the newer, more succulent farm crops in lieu of loss of browse and weeds" (McKean, 1953b, p. 7). Observations of antelope during annual surveys seemed to point in the same direction: good range made for less crop damage. "A check of the type of land the antelope were using…was made in conjunction with the census…. In comparing with 1952 data, animals observed on cereal crops dropped off considerably. These data suggest that the above normal condition of pasture land in 1953 may have been instrumental in keeping crop usage down" (Brazda, 1954, p. 5). It appeared to the Game and Fish Department that if release sites were chosen carefully, there would be few problems between landowners and pronghorns.

The first antelope to be trapped and translocated in North Dakota were trapped near Helena, Montana, and were released in former antelope range east of the Missouri River in November of 1953. Sixty animals were released near Mercer, North Dakota, and 70 were released east of Ruso. In January, 1954, a group of 57 antelope were trapped near Gardiner, Montana, and were released northeast of Hebron, North Dakota. In 1955, antelope were again trapped in Montana. Seventy-four were released near Grassy Butte, 54 near Raleigh, and 43 near Marshall, North Dakota. In 1956, the Game and Fish Department trapped 49 antelope near New England, North Dakota, and released them into two different sites north of Stanley. By the early 1960s, pronghorns were well distributed throughout all the western counties in North Dakota. In 1964, pronghorn populations reached a modern day high of over 14,000 animals.

"KILLER WINTERS"

In Chapter Seven we talked about the effect of North Dakota's winters on whitetails. No one talks as much about winter's effect on pronghorns. But since 1964, winter has been far tougher on pronghorns than it has on any other big game animal. In the winter of 1964-65, the pronghorn population in North Dakota went from its modern day high of over 14,000 animals to an estimated 6,000—an almost 60 percent loss. In the winter of 1968-69, North Dakota lost nearly a quarter of its antelope. In 1977-1979, back-to-back winters cut the pronghorn population from an estimated 9,200 animals to 1,200—an 87 percent loss, which caused the season on antelope to be closed for the first time in a quarter of a century.

ND Game and Fish Department

Pronghorns spend the winter in the open.

Pronghorns do not get the attention that whitetails do. Nonetheless, the loss of that great a proportion of a wildlife population is extremely serious. It raises very serious questions. Why should an animal which is native to North Dakota, adapted to living on the open prairie, suffer such extreme losses? And, importantly for a game manager, what can be done about it? Does North Dakota have to accept the periodic devastation of the pronghorn herd, or can something be done to prevent these losses?

To get some answers to these questions, let's look at events during those tough winters. We have talked about the winter of 1977-78 in the previous chapter. The winter of 1964-65 also came early and stayed late. Temperatures were mostly below normal during that winter, but there were seven different times that the temperature went high enough to melt the surface of the snow cover. "[M]uch of the snow that fell on our pronghorn range stay[ed] on the ground for most of the entire…period. The reported snow depth…on November 27 was 6 inches and it was still 6 inches on March 30. It never dropped below 4 inches and it ranged up to 17 inches in depth. In fact, during 65 days of the winter, the average snow depth was 10 inches or more for this portion of North Dakota. Keep in mind that this snow had thawed and then froze into seven distinct crusts or strata. There was literally an impenetrable layer of ice over much of the pronghorn range in North Dakota" (McKenzie, 1970). The effect was much the same as in 1977 when a storm in early December coated parts of the state in an inch of ice.

212

Maybe a hundred years ago a winter like these would have pushed the antelope south and west to a different range. During these recent severe winters, antelope moved very little. Perhaps they were prevented by manmade changes—fences, highways, and blocks of unusable habitat. It is, as we have said before, often suggested that the large scale migrations of antelope observed by explorers like Lewis and Clark came to an end because of such barriers. During the winters of 1964-65 and 1977-79 it would have been hard for a herd of antelope to find better range within many hundreds of miles. Severe winter conditions covered the range south into the range in South Dakota, west into the range in Montana, and north into Saskatchewan and Alberta. All of these places recorded heavy pronghorn losses, especially during the winter of 1977-78.

The immediate cause of death for pronghorns during these winters was exposure and malnutrition. But an alliance of severe weather and certain aspects of pronghorn behavior is what got them into trouble. Early deep snow prevented even limited movement to better winter ranges. Pronghorns do not move into heavy cover during winter in any event. When they move it is into rougher country. Their survival strategy is to bunch up during winter, using each other to keep warm, but staying out in the open. Tight "rosettes" of antelope are often seen lying in relatively exposed areas during the winter. It takes a considerable amount of high quality, high energy food to maintain an antelope under these conditions. Antelope can cope with loose snow by pawing their way through it. But ice conditions during these tough winters took away even those opportunities.

Some unusual things happened. Alberta biologists found antelope simply staying in one place for days at a time. During a hard blow, the energy cost of moving was apparently too high, and the animals stayed put. In other instances, animals which bedded down during a blizzard were literally frozen to the ground by snow. When the storm was over, the animal, though still alive, could not break free of the crusted snow. In North Dakota in January of 1965, "eight animals were collected from a group of about 35 pronghorns marooned in a farm area and who were attempting to survive in or adjacent to a field of stunted corn. Several other animals were already dead in the field. The viscera of each animal was removed...and analyzed. Not surprisingly, paunch samples showed about 99% by volume was corn stalks, leaves, and some grain. Also, antelope hair was found in all paunches—this would not have been so surprising in itself had one sample not been 5% by volume antelope flesh" (McKenzie, 1970). In the winter of 1964-65, antelope which wintered in places where they had high value food that they were used to eating survived. Left to eat cornstalks or wheat straw, antelope died.

The winters that we have been talking about were unusual, even for places where the winters are normally harsh. In normal winters, the wind usually blows certain areas clear and leaves some vegetation that antelope can make use of above the snow. In the winters we've been talking about, ice and crusted snow kept that from happening. "All there was was a vast sea of white. There was virtually nothing sticking out of the snow in that country. I couldn't believe it. The antelope were not even in their traditional winter ranges...The snow was so deep in there they were up on the ridges, and the snow was so deep on those ridges there was nothing sticking out of there as far as vegetation went" (Gjersing, in Barrett, 1978).

In these conditions, the way the shortgrass prairie is today, the survival strategies of the pronghorn were useless to them. They couldn't move out of the snow, and there was no place for large numbers of antelope to herd together and wait out the winter. White-tailed deer, stuck in the same predicament in 1978, struck a sympathetic chord in the North Dakota public, and a massive effort to feed the deer was launched. There was no such large-scale effort to save the antelope, even though mortality for them was proportionately much higher. A community effort to feed antelope was made in Alberta, Canada, during the winter of 1977-78, and in southwest North Dakota in 1964-65, but the efforts did not seem to help. According to Alberta biologists (Barrett, 1978) it would have been hard for anyone coming upon the scene to tell the difference between fed and unfed antelope. The consensus about feeding antelope at the present time is that the effort will probably fail. Like deer, pronghorns are ruminants, and if they get started on a food early enough, they can culture the right microorganisms in their rumens to digest it. But, given their lifestyle, pronghorns need an extremely high energy food. So far, we haven't been able to give them anything that fills the need. And the economics of antelope are not like the economics of deer. We have been able to take the loss and to let populations rebuild.

That is not to say that nothing can or should be done to help pronghorns make it through a tough winter. It might be said that there are at least three prerequisites for getting pronghorns through the winter. First, the herd has to be in good condition going into the winter. Sick, old, and very young animals are the most at risk. North Dakota biologists feel (see McKenzie, 1970) that the heavy losses during the winter of 1964-65 may have helped the pronghorn herd get through the severe winter of 1968-69 because the remaining animals were the strongest. To a large degree, a healthy herd can be achieved by manipulating an annual harvest. Although the hunting season does not cull the weak and the old from the herd, it can keep the herd within the capacity of the habitat and can keep the male-to-female ratio at a good level for reproduction.

Second, antelope range has to be in good condition. It has to provide the animals with food and water. Antelope thrive in places where the vegetation is composed of 40-60 percent grasses, 10-30 percent forbs, and 5-20 percent browse. They need a variety of species within these groups (see Yoakum, 1978). Range management which decreases the vegetative composition and variety limits its usefulness to pronghorns. In winter, pronghorns move to rougher topography where they are dependent on shrubs, particularly sagebrush. Range practices which eliminate these from the range could be catastrophic for pronghorns.

Third, pronghorns have to be able to get to the range. Even though pronghorns have had to deal with fences for a hundred years, they still have not learned what to do about them. We have talked about this with regard to pronghorn populations in the late 1940s and early 1950s. Pronghorns are fully capable of jumping fences, but they rarely will. They prefer to go under fences when they have to deal with them. That being the case, it's easy to see how a fence could be a barrier to antelope. Net-wire fences almost always stop them. Barbed wire fences cause them problems. If the bottom strand is high enough and is smooth, pronghorns can usually manage it—until snow gets too deep. Pronghorn managers recommend that in places that are heavily traveled by antelope or seem to be on their route between summer and winter ranges, fences be constructed with lay-down panels or pass structures.

Pronghorns still have trouble with fences.

PRONGHORNS AND PEOPLE

Pronghorn populations have steadily rebuilt since the recent low point after the winter of 1979. Today in North Dakota, at the time of this writing, the antelope census projected a population of 7,882 animals. The age and sex composition of the herd was 45 bucks per 100 does, and 74 fawns per 100 does. Pronghorn densities are still highest in the pronghorn management units in the southwest corner of the state. The population appears to be in good shape.

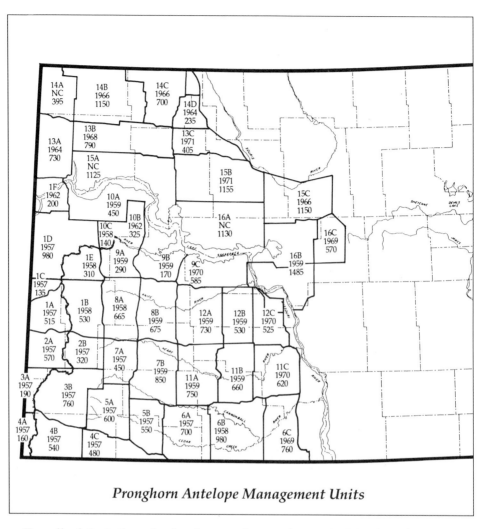

Pronghorn Antelope Management Units

For all of that, though, the future of pronghorns in North Dakota is not as secure as it might be. For the past decade, winters have been mild in North Dakota, but weather always poses a threat here. In the 1970s the land use trends were in the direction of more intensive use for agriculture and increased development of coal and oil resources, all of which had a negative effect on the quality of the range for antelope. The economics of the 80s reversed those trends, and the outlook for pronghorns brightened. North Dakota's game managers would prefer not to have to depend on a depressed agricultural economy to maintain a healthy pronghorn range.

The fortunes of the pronghorn in North Dakota depend on the shifting tides of agriculture and energy development. That implies that the antelope themselves have relatively little value to North Dakotans, at least compared with the value given to white-tailed deer. North Dakotans will campaign and raise money to "Save the Deer," but antelope are left to shift for themselves. Not that we should, necessarily, try to feed antelope or any other wildlife species. The "Save the Deer" campaign was an expression of the value placed on deer. During that campaign, both hunters and non-hunters got behind the effort. There is an active interest in antelope hunting—there are always more applicants than there are licenses—but otherwise, antelope are not often in the public mind.

It seems that numbers have a lot to do with the interest North Dakotans have in the fortunes of antelope. Antelope are not very dense anywhere in the state, but they are the most dense down in the southwest corner of the state in Bowman and Slope counties. In some of the pronghorn management units in those counties there are more pronghorns per square mile than there are people. What that adds up to is that very few people see antelope very often in North Dakota. It is not surprising that pronghorns are not much in the public mind.

ND Game and Fish Department

On the other hand, some of the people who do see antelope seem to see far too many of them. If an agricultural operator has both deer and antelope on his property, he is apt to tolerate the deer and want to be rid of the antelope. Pronghorn behavior is partly to blame for this. Deer spend daylight hours in heavy cover and move into a feeding and bedding area at night. They prefer taller cover. Pronghorns, on the other hand, stay out in the open. For them it is a survival strategy—they can see everything that is going on around them for quite a distance. They are rarely in cover taller than 15 inches unless they are passing through it on the way to somewhere else. Their habits make them far more visible than deer, and perhaps they give the impression that there are more of them than there are deer.

You almost need to see them from the air to understand the distribution of antelope herds. From the air you can see how antelope clusters are distributed close to small scattered patches of grassland. More and more these small grassland areas have been surrounded by cropland, turning them into islands. To think that pronghorns are there for the cropland which surrounds them is a mistaken impression. But it is easy to see how the impression is created.

The key to the future security of the pronghorn in North Dakota is habitat, just as it is the key for every wildlife species. We cannot "manage" the game of North Dakota without it. Without habitat, pronghorns will not go into the winter healthy, and they might not come out of the winter at all. But as we have seen, good habitat is more than food and water. To understand good habitat we—"we" being not only people responsible for game management but people who own the land that pronghorns live on—have to understand some of the life history and behavior of pronghorns. Creating that understanding is part of the job of game management. If it is done well, then perhaps this beautiful animal will continue to be part of North Dakota's big game.

Sources

Bach, R. N. 1945. 1945 Antelope Census of North Dakota. NDGFD Division of Federal Aid Project 7R, Report No. 17.

Barrett, M. W. (Chairman). 1978. The Impact of a Severe Winter on Northern Pronghorn Ranges. Proceedings of the Eighth Biennial Pronghorn Antelope Workshop, pps. 337-359.

Brazda, A. R. 1954. Results of the 1953 Antelope Census. NDGFD Pittman-Robertson Division Project W-37-R, Report No. 38.

Cadieux, C. L. 1954. Letter. North Dakota Game and Fish Department, Bismarck.

Cadieux, C. L. 1986. Pronghorn, America's Unique Antelope. Stackpole Books, Harrisburg, PA.

McKean, W. T. 1949. 1949 Antelope Census. NDGFD Division of Federal Aid Project 7R, Report No. 20.

McKean, W. T. 1953a. Operation Antelope Lift. ND Outdoors. 25(12):6-7.

McKean, W. T. 1953b. Fall Foods of North Dakota Antelope. NDGFD Pittman-Robertson Division Project W-37-R-1 Report No. 35.

McKenzie, J. V. 1970. Two "Killer Winters," 1964-65 and 1968-69 in North Dakota. Proc. Antelope States Workshop 4:36-40.

North Dakota Game and Fish Department. 1944. Annual Report, July 1, 1943-June 30, 1944.

Stuart, R. W. and W. T. McKean. 1948. North Dakota Antelope Census for 1947 and 1948. NDGFD Division of Federal Aid Project 7R, Report No. 19.

Vriend, H. G. and M. W. Barrett. 1978. Low Pronghorn Recruitment—Is It an Issue? Proceedings of the Eighth Biennial Pronghorn Workshop, pps. 360-377.

Yoakum, J. D. 1978. Pronghorn. pps. 103-121 of Big Game of North America: Ecology and Management. Wildlife Management Institute. Stackpole Books, Harrisburg PA.

California bighorn

CHAPTER NINE

THE CALIFORNIA BIGHORN

The Game and Fish Department has been seriously interested in re-introducing bighorn sheep into the badlands since the late 1940's; but until recently it had been unable to locate a source of bighorn stock, at least a source of stock of a suitable race.

In 1955 Dr. James Hatter, Chief Game Biologist of the British Columbia Game Commission, indicated that the British Columbia Department might be in a position to provide bighorn sheep for transplanting, providing the details of the proposed project met with the approval of that organization. Following Dr. Hatter's proposal, the British Columbia Commission was supplied with written and pictorial material describing the topographic, floral, faunal, and land use aspects of the badlands plus a history of bighorn sheep in that area.

*Having considered the various aspects of the proposed transplant, the British Columbia Game Commission indicated that it considered the proposal to be feasible and that sheep would probably be available in the fall of 1956. The race of sheep under consideration was the California bighorn (*Ovis canadensis californiana*). This subspecies was considered adaptable to the North Dakota badlands because, like the extinct Audubon bighorn, it inhabits the lower elevations of the mountain sheep range. In a sense it is a western counterpart of the Audubon bighorn which inhabited the lower elevations east of the Rocky Mountains.*

Ray Murdy, 1957.

The Federal Aid in Wildlife Restoration program—Pittman-Robertson—and the dream of bringing bighorns back to the Badlands was a marriage made in heaven. The bighorn project was nearly everything that a wildlife restoration project should be. It had benefits for people—giving North Dakota hunters a fine trophy animal and a very sporting hunt. There were benefits for the animal—bringing the California bighorn to the Badlands created a new herd, "scatter[ing] the population so that disease, adverse weather, or other disastrous factors could not wipe out the entire stock" (Moxon, 1965). In some small degree the project would even rectify the mistakes of our fathers, who drove the Audubon bighorn to extinction. The only thing that would have made the project better would have been to revive the Audubon bighorn itself.

Projects like the bighorn sheep restoration project are few and far between. Many—if not most—P-R projects make dull reading. Data—like census counts—are slowly accumulated, and biologists use various tools to

222

transform this body of facts into useful knowledge. A basic project, for example, is to take census, license, and harvest information and put it into the computer to chart population trends and harvest trends. Other data might give a profile of the typical North Dakota hunter—his or her age, the animal he or she would prefer to hunt, or even the most and least popular places to hunt. There is a great deal of mathematics, statistics, and computer modeling to the business of game management these days. A project which offers the benefits offered by the bighorn restoration is a rare project indeed.

Without Pittman-Robertson, the subject of restoring bighorns might never have come up. Before Pittman-Robertson, game department budgets were small, and they were spent very conservatively. After P-R, more things seemed possible. It's human nature: if you are a game department and you know that for every dollar you can commit to a project, you can add three federal dollars, you tend to have more ideas about things you want to do. Indeed, P-R was intended to encourage more ambitious projects. In Chapter Six we discussed the importance of Pittman-Robertson in providing state game and fish departments with a large and reliable funding source.

At this juncture, it might be a good idea to look at how Pittman-Robertson projects come to be—that is to say, how a project gets to be qualified for federal aid through the Pittman-Robertson Act. The availability of Pittman-Robertson funds encourages game and fish departments across the country to come up with imaginative ways to work with their wildlife populations. But that doesn't mean that any project, no matter how wild, will receive funding. There is an approval process. There needs to be some kind of assurance that projects are feasible, are being performed well and by qualified people, and that the project is valuable. We can demonstrate the process with the bighorn restoration project.

In most P-R projects there are two agencies involved: the state agency that is going to perform the project, and the U.S. Fish and Wildlife Service, (USFWS) which is the agency which approves or disapproves projects for federal aid funding. In the case of the bighorn project, there were three agencies, the third one being the British Columbia Game Commission (now the British Columbia Fish and Wildlife Branch). Fish and Wildlife Service involvement came very late in the game.

The North Dakota Game and Fish Department had the idea for restoring bighorns to the Badlands in the late 1940s, seven years before a proposal was submitted to the Fish and Wildlife Service. "Approximately seven years ago, an inquiry was sent to the Colorado Game and Fish Commission in reference to obtaining bighorn sheep to be planted in North Dakota. They agreed, but due to unfortunate circumstances, the project could not be carried out. Other states having sheep populations were contacted, but upon learning they had none to spare, the project was temporarily abandoned" (Brazda, 1956, p. 7). Interest in the project revived after 1954, when the state of Oregon, working in cooperation with the British Columbia Game Commission, transplanted 20 California bighorns from British Columbia to a holding pasture on Hart Mountain, Oregon. In 1955, the North Dakota Game and Fish Department approached the British Columbia Game Commission with a proposal for a similar effort in North Dakota.

B. C. was interested in the project. For the British Columbia Game Commission, a transplant like this one represented a means to protect the California bighorn from the fate of the Audubon bighorn. The more populations of sheep there were in widely scattered areas, the better protection there would be. The B. C. Commission was not interested in a project which did not have a very high chance of success. Before British Columbia would agree to the transplant, the Game Commission requested specific kinds of information about the area where the sheep would be released. Bighorns are adapted to certain kinds of topographical features and to certain kinds of vegetation—see Chapter Four—and the B. C. Commission was concerned that these minimum habitat requirements were going to be met. Some other considerations were land use practices in the area—farming and grazing—and other animal species. Of particular concern were animals which might compete with the sheep, and predators. The North Dakota Game and Fish Department supplied British Columbia with information on the proposed release area in the Badlands and a history of bighorn sheep in the area. Based on all of that, the North Dakota Game and Fish Department and the British Columbia Game Commission agreed—tentatively—to cooperate on a project to trap bighorn sheep in British Columbia and release them in North Dakota. The following conditions were to be met (Murdy, 1957):

1. All transportation costs would be borne by North Dakota,

2. All papers necessary for the clearance of the sheep across the international border would be procured by North Dakota officials,

3. A suitable large enclosure would be constructed at the point of liberation to hold the sheep for a period of one year for acclimatization, and to further assure that the sheep will remain together as a unit when once liberated,

4. North Dakota would send one man to British Columbia to assist in trapping the sheep,

5. If extra resident help should be needed in trapping the sheep the expense would be borne by North Dakota,

6. Any other expenses incurred in the trapping, holding, and transporting of the sheep would be borne by North Dakota.

Inspecting the Grassy Butte release site, 1956.

And there was one other condition for the transplant. British Columbia was primarily interested in protecting the California bighorn. To receive California bighorns from British Columbia, North Dakota agreed that no other race of wild sheep would be brought to the area.

The agreements had to be tentative because they had not yet been proposed to the Fish and Wildlife Service for Pittman-Robertson funding. In the spring of 1956, the North Dakota Game and Fish Department finally submitted the following letter to the Secretary of the Interior:

> Sir:
>
> The State of North Dakota by and through the State Game and Fish Commissioner constituting the State Game and Fish Department, and pursuant to the Federal Aid in Wildlife Restoration Act (50 Stat. 917) and to the Rules and Regulations of the Secretary of the Interior made and published thereunder, does hereby submit this statement describing a wildlife development project and requests authorized financing thereof. Said project is proposed as a means of promoting efficient management of wildlife resources, and will be executed under the provisions of said Act and said Rules and Regulations.

Biologist Bill Hickling at the sheep enclosure, 1956.

The proposal went on to request financing for two types of work: the construction of a 160 acre holding pasture and the trapping and transplanting of bighorn sheep. In August of 1956, Game and Fish Commissioner H. R. Morgan signed an agreement with the U. S. Forest Service allowing the Department to construct a sheep-proof fence around a quarter section of Forest Service land about 15 miles west of Grassy Butte, North Dakota—very near to the place where the last of North Dakota's Audubon bighorns was killed.

The Fish and Wildlife Service responded to the proposal with many of the same concerns as the B. C. Game Commission. "We would appreciate some discussion on the status and ownership of the [release site], use by livestock, condition of the range, and possible contact or intermingling of the sheep with domestic livestock.... There should also be some comment on your intent regarding predator control..." (USFWS, 1956).

The release site west of Grassy Butte, along Magpie Creek, had been chosen carefully. "In respect to topography, and vegetation, it is typical of the rougher badlands which because of their roughness have, for all practical purposes, received only grazing use and, for this and other reasons, have changed relatively little since the days of the Audubon bighorn. The area was one of the last strongholds of the indigenous race of bighorns, and it was in this drainage that the last known Audubon bighorn in North Dakota was shot in 1905. The area is almost entirely government land under the jurisdiction of the Forest Service.... The range is in good condition and very few, if any, domestic sheep are run in the badlands,

226

especially in the area concerned. The area is isolated with no through highways and a relatively few improved roads and trails leading only to ranch headquarters" (Murdy, 1957). Much of what we now know about bighorn sheep in general and California bighorns in particular had yet to be learned in 1956. But the feeling was that if the range had supported Audubon bighorns, and had remained relatively unchanged, it would supply the habitat requirements of the new race.

One other factor affecting the welfare of the sheep which was taken into account was the reactions of people living in the area of the release site. "Very few ranch headquarters are located in this roughest badlands country, and the ranchers who do live there favor the re-introduction of bighorns" (Murdy, 1957). The reaction of ranchers was, in fact, better than hoped for. After the release, local ranchers took it upon themselves to be "custodians" for the sheep, reporting to the Department that the sheep were doing fine.

On the strength of the Game and Fish Department's background work with the British Columbia Game Commission and the agreements with the Forest Service, the plan to transplant California bighorns into North Dakota got approval. Construction began on the enclosure in late August of 1956. Other details were worked out: "arrangements were made for a Canadian veterinarian to inspect the sheep at Williams Lake [British Columbia] and supply a certificate of health..." (Murdy, 1957); and on October 18, 1956, biologists Art Brazda and Bill Hickling, and two assistants, Balzar Vetter and Dennis Shearer, left Bismarck for British Columbia.

Not every Pittman-Robertson project goes through as much preparation as the bighorn project did. In most respects, it has been an unusual project. But the process is similar for all P-R projects. Even on-going projects like census work are subject to periodic review to see if the Department is getting the most it can for the money. Demands for funding are constantly growing, and the time may not be far off when game management budgets are stretched pretty thin.

TRAPPING THE WILD BIGHORN

The original 18 California bighorn sheep that were brought into North Dakota were trapped at Williams Lake, British Columbia on November 2, 1956. Williams Lake was chosen for two reasons. First, there were about 100 bighorns in the area. Second—and perhaps most important—the drop gate trap that had been built by the Oregon State Game Commission in 1954 was still on the site and still functional. "This trap was an oval enclosure constructed of woven wire, eight feet high, and about 80 by 150 yards in size. Openings on the two ends of the trap could be closed by gates which were suspended by ¾ inch rope. The gates operated by remote control. Blasting caps attached to the ropes could be fired by a blasting

Loading sheep at Williams Lake, 1956.

machine, severing the ropes and dropping the gates. The trap was located on Riske Creek on the Jack Moon Ranch about 27 miles west of Williams Lake" (Murdy, 1957).

The trapping process was a slow one, involving first getting the sheep used to the trap and to the bait. The trap was baited with raw cabbage and dairy feed, starting on October 22. Some bait was placed in the trap, and some outside. "After the sheep began utilizing the bait, one to six were observed in the trap practically every day. Since the transplant called for as close to 20 animals as we could get, no effort was made to trap these animals" (Brazda, 1956). The idea was to take a period of ten days or so to move the bait until all of it was inside the trap. When enough animals were taking the bait inside the trap, one blast of the detonator caps would do the job.

> Finally on November 2nd, after several cold nights in a sleeping bag and countless hours of observation, the situation began to develop favorably. Threatening weather developed into intermittent snow, and with no bait remaining outside the trap, the animals were showing considerable activity around the upper gate. Eight sheep, which were in the trap shortly after daybreak, moved out. Then about two hours later, a band of 18 moved to the upper gate and began to filter in one or two at a time. Shortly after 12:00 p. m., all but two wise ewes were placidly feeding inside the trap…. However, about 10 minutes after 12, they too abandoned their cautious ways and entered the trap. Within seconds, the detonator was exploded and the first phase of the operation was complete. (Brazda, 1956)

The following day, November 3, the sheep were maneuvered into a specially prepared truck for their 1,600 mile journey to the Badlands. Forty-two hours later, with one inspection stop at the Customs Bureau at Oroville, Washington, and several for gasoline, the truck ground to a halt at the Grassy Butte enclosure. A waiting Game and Fish crew ear-tagged the sheep, inoculated them against diseases endemic to local livestock populations, and sent them, as it were, into history.

BUILDING THE HERD

Let's move ahead a few years. The last of those original 18 bighorn sheep was found in the South Unit of Theodore Roosevelt National Park on May 16, 1969. The old ram was found dead, tangled in a four-strand barbed wire fence. His tag showed that he was one of the original bunch captured in British Columbia in 1956.

The records on this particular old ram showed that he had been part of several ventures on the part of the Game and Fish Department to manage this nucleus herd of 18 animals and to build new thriving bighorn herds in

229

Releasing the sheep at Magpie Creek, 1956.

other parts of the Badlands. From the beginning the Department's plan had been to use the original 18 sheep from British Columbia as a captive breeding population—the nucleus for new herds. During the first winter, one of the original 18—a lamb—died, and one adult ram disappeared. In the spring of 1957, to the delight of everyone concerned with the transplant, six lambs were born. In the fall of 1957, North Dakota had a thriving herd of 22 bighorns, and in the spring of 1958, four more lambs were born. By the summer of 1958 there were 26 bighorn sheep in the Magpie Creek enclosure and eight mule deer.

It was time for some active management. Department biologists felt that there were too many animals in the enclosure. There was no need for the mule deer to be in there. Also, reproduction in 1958 was not as good as they hoped for. Only four of seven adult ewes bore lambs. The feeling was that too many of the sheep in the enclosure were rams—something we will go into in more detail a bit later. In July of 1958, the Game and Fish Department built a trap similar to the one in British Columbia inside the Magpie Creek enclosure, and in January, 1959, started trapping operations. During 1959, five rams were taken out of the Magpie Creek enclosure and released into the South Unit of Theodore Roosevelt National Park. Obviously, biologists were not trying to establish a new herd with these animals. This first release was mostly to relieve overcrowding, with the extra benefit, perhaps, of being able to watch the animals in the wild. Herd-building releases would come soon, however, in carefully selected sites.

The old ram we were talking about earlier missed out on his first opportunity to be recaptured. He got in on the next round of trapping in February of 1960—the first effort to build a new herd from the British Columbia nucleus. During the previous fall—the fall of 1959—the Game and Fish Department had helped the National Park Service build a sheep enclosure in the South Unit of Theodore Roosevelt National Park. The plan was to stock bighorns into the new enclosure, and as the herd grew in size, to trap the surplus animals out to form more new herds. In February of 1960, the park and the Game and Fish Department signed an agreement (included as Appendix Five) whereby the Department would stock "approximately 10" sheep into the new pasture, with "twice the number placed in the enclosure" to be trapped out over a period of time. The old ram we were talking about was one of four rams and five ewes trapped from the Magpie Creek enclosure and released into the new pasture in the park in February of 1960.

The Department built a third—its last—sheep enclosure in the fall of 1961 near Dutchman's Barn Butte, southwest of Medora. In January of 1962, two rams were trapped out of the enclosure in the South Unit of the Theodore Roosevelt National Park, and three ewes were trapped from the Magpie Creek enclosure. These sheep were released into the new Dutchman's Barn enclosure. The Department's tally of California bighorn sheep at the end of January, 1962, was 15 sheep in the Magpie Creek pasture west of Grassy Butte; 17 in the enclosure in the South Unit of the park; four rams ranging free outside the park enclosure; and five in the new Dutchman's Barn pasture southwest of Medora. With the lambs born in the spring of 1962, there were more than 50 bighorns in North Dakota.

Fifty was a magic number. Department biologists had decided that when the total of all the herds reached 50 animals, some of them would be released into the wild. After six years, and successful reproduction each spring, it was apparent that the animals were doing fine on the range in North Dakota. Twelve sheep, from Theodore Roosevelt National Park and from Magpie Creek, were released in the fall of 1962 in the Devil's Slide area of the Badlands, some 20 miles southwest of Belfield. The animals were watched for a time to see if they would remain together and breed successfully in the wild—the final test of the success of the transplant. By 1966 it was more than apparent that wild bighorns had been established in North Dakota. The last successful attempt to trap sheep out of the original enclosures was in January of 1966, when three ewes were trapped in the park and released into a new area near Moody Plateau in Billings County. After that, the Department opened the gates at Magpie Creek and over the next year took down the fence at both the South Unit of the park and at Magpie Creek. At Dutchman's Barn, flashfloods washed out parts of the fence, and bighorns were roaming free in that area as well.

Sheep trapping and transplanting work. Counterclockwise from left: building the enclosure; trapping sheep; tagging and inoculating.

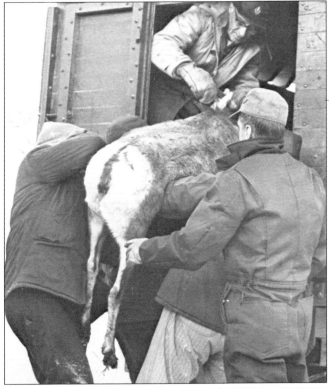

Loading and transporting sheep. Photos courtesy of ND Game and Fish Department.

PROBLEMS IN SHEEP MANAGEMENT

TRAPPING

The sheep restoration project got to be known as "Operation Bighorn" in **North Dakota Outdoors** articles. When Operation Bighorn got started in 1956, the Department knew relatively little about wild sheep. Their confidence in the success of the operation was based to some degree on the fact that a race of wild sheep had lived in the Badlands before. The Department was, however, aware from the beginning that bighorns would not disperse and repopulate the old Audubon range on their own. They would need human intervention. Art Brazda (1956) wrote, "Future plans tentatively call for small transplants to be made from the present nucleus. Past history indicates that sheep do not disperse as readily as do deer and antelope, therefore, attempts may be made to establish several small bands." This failure to disperse has, apparently, helped sheep to succeed in other places—see Chapter Four—but for North Dakota, it meant a labor-intensive management scheme.

Management got more labor-intensive as time went on. The trapping operations in British Columbia were easy compared to later attempts. In British Columbia, the sheep took the bait and walked willingly into the trap. When the Game and Fish Department tried the same method and bait in 1959—trying to trap those first five rams for release into the South Unit of the Theodore Roosevelt National Park—the bighorns ignored the bait. The Department trapped those first five sheep using the drive method, in which a group of men on foot array themselves into the draws and along the ridges within a sheep enclosure and try to work the sheep toward a trap. Over the next several years, the Department continued to use the drive method to catch bighorns, with gradually dwindling success. Ed Bry described such a drive for **North Dakota Outdoors** (Bry, 1966, p. 20-22):

> On the first drive, all six sheep…broke through the drivers and scattered to the far corners of the 200 plus acre pasture. The 17 Department and Park employees quickly reorganized and made another attempt to flush the sheep to the right corner. This time only three ewes were forced into the wing, but they moved well ahead of the drivers down to the trap. After hesitating by the gate, one ewe finally climbed out over a high fence and escaped back into the pasture but the other two were chased into the trap and captured and blindfolded without further trouble.
>
> On the next drive, one ram and the two remaining ewes were driven to the trap wing, but two escaped this time so now we had three ewes corralled, just half the job was done.
>
> …[W]ork was resumed soon after sunrise [next day]. It proved to be a frustrating day for both men and bighorns. The first drive failed completely but the next looked good…The two rams were right down to the gate of the trap where one promptly jumped

the fence and the other put on a display of downfield-running that would light up the eyes of any football scout. The ram turned back on the drivers in the narrow part of the wing and escaped through, among, and between ten men, all who were close enough to make the tackle....

The men were beat, but wouldn't admit it, and another drive was undertaken. This time the sheep were really playing it smart. Snow was falling and visibility was poor. The sheep scattered and hid. Although two were finally found and were again moving toward the wing they never reached it. They had learned to run over a hill and hide in a handy cedar clump, letting the advancing drivers pass by them. The sheep found it easier to hide than to run. Cold and worn out men, fooled by three tired but wiser bighorns, had to give up and leave the pasture to the sheep and the snow.

By the time that the enclosures were taken down in the park and at Magpie Creek in 1967, the sheep were nearly impossible to catch with the drive method. "[T]he sheep remaining in the enclosures became...increasingly difficult to capture. A few more animals were trapped and released, but at the last trapping attempt in January of 1967 at the Magpie Creek enclosure, no animals were taken" (Boldt, et.al., 1973, p. 7).

Today, the Game and Fish Department uses entirely different techniques to catch bighorn sheep. The method-of-choice depends on what's going to be done with the sheep and how many of them it's necessary to catch. The high-tech way to catch sheep is to use a helicopter and either a net gun or dart gun. It works very well, but if you need to catch very many sheep it's an expensive way to go. Most commonly, the Department uses a drop net. A drop net is simply a large net that is suspended on poles above piles of some bait that is likely to attract sheep. The net is rigged so that it can be dropped on the sheep as they feed. Bighorns respond very well to a bait made from apple pulp that has been allowed to ferment for awhile.

LUNGWORM

Most often, sheep have been baited in North Dakota in order to trap them and transplant them to new sites (a summary of trap/transplant activities for bighorn sheep in North Dakota is included in Appendix Six). But the apple-pulp bait that works well for that purpose works well for another of the on-going management efforts for bighorns—the treatment of sheep for a parasite called lungworm. What makes apple-pulp a good bait is that bighorns like to eat it, and if they get used to finding it in a particular spot, you can count on them to come back to that spot to get it. If you lace the bait with lungworm medicine, you can get the sheep to treat themselves.

Lungworm is the major disease threat to bighorn sheep herds throughout the United States. In all probability, lungworm came to North

Dakota from British Columbia along with the first 18 bighorn sheep in 1956. When the Game and Fish Department returned to British Columbia in 1989 for another sheep transplant, all of the new animals carried the parasite. Most of the time, adult sheep carry the parasite without it threatening the population. But the potential for lungworm to wipe out a bighorn herd is always there. It is a difficult problem to control (Fairaizl, 1979a, p. 14):

> Adult lungworms exist in clusters or nodules in the lungs of the sheep. As eggs and immature or larval stages of the lungworm are produced, they are coughed up from the lung, swallowed, and passed out of the bighorn with the fecal material. The larvae will either form a cyst and lie dormant on the ground for a considerable length of time or, when they encounter a land snail, will burrow into it and grow. The bighorn, during normal grazing, will eat and digest the snail thereby liberating the lungworms and reinfecting itself. The problem is further complicated in that some of the larvae will cross the placental barrier and the lambs are born with this parasite.

Certain events or combinations of events can make a potential problem very real. Such was the case in 1978 in North Dakota:

> Intensive studies during spring and summer, 1978, revealed the biggest problem facing the North Dakota bighorn sheep herd is lamb survival. By August, 1978, the bighorn herd in the Moody Plateau study area had 100% reproduction and 50% lamb survival, the Park herd had 37% reproduction and zero lamb survival, and the Magpie Creek herd had 42% reproduction and zero survival....
>
> The problem of lamb survival is not unique to North Dakota and in fact is quite ubiquitous. In most areas across the country the cause has been lungworms and preliminary data indicate this, too, is the problem in the North Dakota herd....
>
> Three hypotheses are proposed to explain the cause of the lungworm outbreak. First the cold wet weather during April and May predisposed the lambs to bacterial pneumonia.
>
> Secondly, stress from overcrowding lowered the resistance of the lambs. It is believed that this over-crowding stress occurred as a result of the high densities within the extremely small home ranges....
>
> Thirdly, the age of the transplants may be causing a deterioration in population quality.... The older herds may have reached carrying capacity and have started to degenerate. (Fairaizl, 1978a, p. 2-3)

We'll come back to the problems that overcrowding causes bighorn sheep in a minute. To deal with the problem of lungworm—and especially the problem of lungworms being passed to the lambs—the Game and Fish Department began to mix a lungworm medicine with the apple pulp that was being used for bait.

> Researchers in Colorado have developed a drug called called fenbendazole which has proven to be about 95 percent effective. Once the sheep move onto the winter range, large piles of apple pulp are placed where the sheep can find and use them. Once the bighorns are using the bait on a daily basis, the drug is mixed with the apple pulp and the sheep treat themselves. The sheep are treated in late winter, which is during the third trimester of pregnancy. The drug will kill both adult and larval stages of the worm, which allows fewer worms to cross the placental barrier and the lambs are born relatively lungworm free. Through this treatment, researchers in Colorado have increased lamb survival by 98 percent. (Fairaizl, 1979a, p. 15)

Most recently, the Department has been mixing the drug Ivermectin with apple pulp to treat sheep. Ivermectin is effective against external parasites like scabies as well as internal ones like lungworm.

STRESS

It was important that biologists come up with some way of treating sheep that did not involve handling them. Bighorn sheep are especially susceptible to "capture myopathy," a disease caused by "shock due to stress from capture and handling" (Fairaizl, 1979b, p. 3). Obviously, the nature of a trap and transplant program to disperse sheep involves handling sheep. Catching and handling them to treat them for disease would be one more risk in an already risky endeavor.

Wild sheep are susceptible to stress from other sources as well, particularly from overcrowding and harassment. They respond to overcrowding and to harassment in similar ways.

Overcrowding simply means that there are too many animals for the range—they exceed its carrying capacity. When white-tailed deer exceed the carrying capacity of their range, they can do considerable damage to it. When bighorns were first brought to North Dakota, the U.S. Forest Service was quite concerned that the sheep herd would grow to the point that the forage and soil would be damaged. In the original agreement with the Forest Service allowing the Department to build the first sheep enclosure it was stipulated that the Department monitor the extent to which forage was being used so that sheep could be removed before they got to be a problem. In August of 1958, the Department began to study the vegetational composition and forage use by bighorns in the Magpie Creek enclosure.

But bighorns are not as likely as deer to destroy their own range. Typically, overcrowded sheep simply stop reproducing. Perhaps it is a

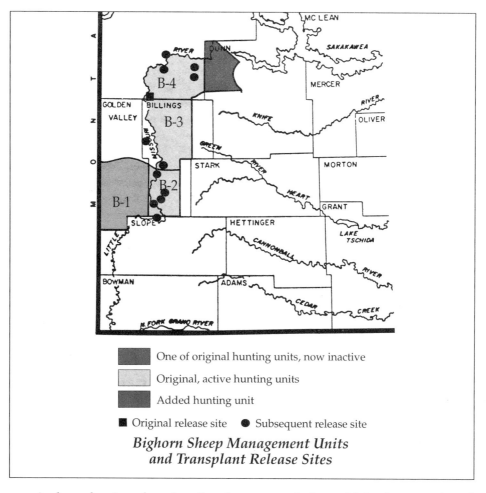

One of original hunting units, now inactive

Original, active hunting units

Added hunting unit

■ Original release site   ● Subsequent release site

Bighorn Sheep Management Units
and Transplant Release Sites

survival mechanism, keeping the sheep population within the capacity of the range to support them. But in North Dakota, that itself is a problem, for two reasons. First, the Department is interested in having a growing, vigorous population. Second, because of lungworm, lamb survival is already low. Anything which further limits reproduction in bighorn sheep is a serious problem.

Since bighorns do not disperse on their own and fill up available range, their ranges remain relatively small. Sheep can become overcrowded very quickly. One way of dealing with the problem is to monitor reproduction in the bighorn herd, and when it begins to show signs of stress from overcrowding—that is, when reproduction drops off—trap some of the animals and transplant them to new range. Trapping and transplanting has been the major focus of sheep management in North Dakota since the beginning, trying to keep reproduction among sheep high, and to increase the number of sheep herds in the state.

This particular aspect of bighorn management is complicated by the fact that sheep respond to harassment in much the same way as they do overcrowding. The first thing to be affected is reproduction. Most often, harassment which causes reproduction to drop off is attributed to too many rams in the population. "[N]umerous studies have suggested that equal sex ratios were indicative of ram surpluses, which may lower the reproductive rate through excessive harassment of ewes" (Fairaizl, 1978b, p. 47). The Game and Fish Department perceived a surplus of rams as causing low reproduction first in 1958 when five rams were trapped out of the Magpie Creek enclosure and released into Theodore Roosevelt National Park.

The limited hunting season on bighorns, instituted by the Game and Fish Department in 1975, was seen as a way to bring the ratio of rams to ewes in the population down, at the same time as it provided recreation to North Dakota's sportsmen. "For example, in the herd just south of Medora there were approximately 32 adult rams and 28 adult ewes with only two lambs; in the area near Tracy Mountain there were approximately 8 adult ewes and 3 rams, but in this herd 7 lambs were observed. Perhaps then by harvesting some of the surplus rams an increase in reproduction may occur" (Fairaizl and McKenna, 1976, p. 9). A ratio of one ram to every four ewes is considered about right for good reproduction. That does not mean, however, that when the ideal ratio is reached that reproduction is guaranteed. This will be discussed in more detail in the section on hunting seasons for bighorns.

Overcrowding and harassment—and the resulting loss of productivity in the bighorn sheep herd—can also result from human activity. "Overcrowding results not only from a lack of migration but also constriction of range due to loss of habitat. Developments such as urbanization, overgrazing, recreation, and surface mining cause losses of habitat and force bighorn sheep to concentrate in small areas. Oil and gas

Oil activity in the Badlands.

239

developments in the North Dakota sheep range have resulted in the loss of much habitat and may ultimately cause abandonment of the range by sheep" (Fairaizl, 1978b, p. 47). Even the roads leading to such projects are limiting factors when it comes to sheep reproduction.

Problems of this sort came to a head in 1988. Early that year, the Enron Oil and Gas Company of Houston, Texas was granted a permit by the North Dakota Industrial Commission to drill for oil near Magpie Creek, west of Grassy Butte. The site was very near the site of the original release of bighorn sheep in 1956, and it was just 1,400 feet from the area that bighorn ewes have used for lambing. The Game and Fish Department protested the decision on the part of the Industrial Commission to grant the permit to drill in this particular spot, and the Department tried to get Enron Oil to consider directional drilling—a more expensive technology, admittedly, but one which would allow the oil company to drill its well but give the sheep more room. The Industrial Commission refused to reconsider its decision. The oil company agreed to put off drilling activities until after the lambing season, but would not consider directional drilling.

It is another situation—like those described in Chapter Seven with regard to water development and white-tailed deer—where the Game and Fish Department has seen its role very clearly as that of an advocate for wildlife values. With regard to that particular well, when it was drilled later that year, it came up dry. But the story, of course, does not, and will not end there. Activity in the Badlands is increasing all the time, and the jury is still out on the long-term effects on the bighorn herd. The past record suggests that since habitat will become more and more constricted, there will be fewer and smaller places into which sheep can be transplanted. Activity in the sheep range will limit the possible size of the sheep herd.

The trap/transplant program has been the major focus of the management program for bighorn sheep, and it will continue to be as long as there is available habitat for sheep. It is the only way to build a larger California bighorn herd in North Dakota. Another aspect of the program goes back to the original transplant in 1956. One of the reasons British Columbia was interested in transplanting some of its bighorns was to increase the number of populations of California bighorns—scatter them around so that no localized disaster could threaten the existence of these animals. For the same reasons, it is important to have as many small populations of bighorns as we can here in North Dakota.

A summary of the trap/transplant program from 1956 to 1990 is included as Appendix Six. In 34 years, 139 animals have been trapped and released onto 12 different sites in North Dakota. It has been a reasonably successful program, considering the risks we have talked about in capturing and handling sheep. It has been successful, but it has not been easy. There have been many years when the Department has not been able to trap and move a single animal. In the 1980s, for example, the trapping effort in the state failed completely in 1980, 81, 82, 84, 85, and 89. 1989 was redeemed by a return trip to British Columbia, where 10 sheep were caught, and nine released. One of these sheep was injured and was given to the Bismarck Zoo.

The effort to distribute sheep throughout the available habitat in the Badlands has been hampered by land use changes in the area. In 1980, the Game and Fish Department began to inventory the Badlands for possible new release sites for bighorns. Eight different possible release sites were picked out, based primarily on their suitability as sheep habitat. "Suitability" was based on a site's similarity to places bighorns were already using. "Topography used by bighorns includes plateaus which range from 2500 feet to 2900 feet and encompass areas of .6 square miles or more. These are surrounded by precipitous cliffs, have a number of juniper pockets which extend from creek bottoms to the top of the plateaus and finger ridges which extend from the sides. Most daily movements of bighorns are on or near these plateaus with a small amount occurring on flat top ridges" (Stotts and Blunt, 1983). The sites were then given a priority number or a rank. The first consideration which went into the ranking—after habitat value—was ownership of the site—federal, state, or private—and if an agreement could be reached for transplanting bighorns. Some other considerations were land use in the area, roads, other wildlife in the area, and the likelihood of development as time went on.

Since the time of that assessment, some of the sites which had a high priority have had to be taken out of consideration as places for transplanting bighorns. In one case, domestic sheep now occupy range too near the intended release site. In other cases, energy development—oil drilling, roads, and constant human presence—has limited a site's usefulness. Good sites are getting hard to come by, and this has some implications for the way bighorns will be managed in the future. We will look at those in the following section.

Hunting Seasons for Bighorns

The first modern-day hunting season on bighorn sheep in North Dakota was held in 1975. In more than one way, the first season marked the culmination of the effort to establish bighorns in the state. The Game and Fish Department felt that two management goals had been achieved. First, bighorns could provide North Dakota hunters with some recreation on a yearly basis, and second, the hunt would become one of the tools for managing the bighorn herd—in this case, removing surplus rams. "The main objective of the bighorn sheep hunting season in North Dakota was to lower the sex ratio by harvesting surplus rams" (Fairaizl, 1979b, p. 3). "Furthermore, hunting opportunities offered by surplus rams are tremendous. This once in a lifetime hunt is coveted by many sportsmen and with a limited season can be continued for many years" (Fairaizl, 1978a, p. 2).

241

Above and right: bighorn sheep hunting. Photos courtesy of ND Game and Fish Department.

243

It took a little doing to get the first season going. The Department had considered a season as early as 1973, but the legislation to handle the kind of season needed for bighorns was not yet in place. Several different considerations had to be accounted for. The season had to accomplish the Department's management goals, so there had to be strict control of how many rams were taken, and of where they were taken. That meant a unit-permit sort of season, where a limited number of permits would be allowed in selected hunting units.

Because of the limited size of bighorn range, and limits to the growth of the population, there would never be very many opportunities to hunt bighorns. To give everyone interested an equal chance at a bighorn permit, the Department wanted permits to be issued by lottery on a once in a lifetime basis. It took legislation to enable the Department to control a season to that extent. Early in 1975, legislation was in place. Twelve hunters were picked by lottery from 2,852 applications, and the first bighorn season in North Dakota opened on November 25, 1975.

Consecutive seasons on bighorn sheep were held from 1975 through 1979. In each of the first three seasons, twelve licenses were issued. Thirty-three out of thirty-six hunters were successful. Success might have been 100 percent except that the winter of 1977-78—as we have seen in the chapter on deer—was one of the most extreme in North Dakota's history. In 1978, ten hunters out of ten got a bighorn ram.

In 1979, only two permits were issued. At that time, it was felt that the season had done its work—that is, the season had brought the ratio of rams to ewes to a good level for reproduction in two of the four bighorn hunting units. However, reproduction had not rebounded in those units. "Ground and aerial surveys indicate the sex ratio in Units B-1 and B-3 have reached the desired level, and ratios in other units are approaching that level. Furthermore, data indicates reproduction has not replaced the rams harvested during the hunting season" (Fairaizl, 1978b, p. 4). One of the "rules" of good game management is that the harvest should not be more than the population can sustain. So two of the bighorn hunting units (B-1 and B-3) were closed in 1979, and the number of available permits in the other units was reduced to one each. In 1980, the season on bighorns was closed, and it remained closed through 1983.

The season on bighorns was reopened on a more conservative basis in 1984. In both 1984 and 1985, six rams were taken by resident North Dakota hunters. In 1986, the bighorn harvest had a new wrinkle, one which has given a tremendous boost to bighorns in North Dakota.

For a number of years, states like Montana and Nevada had been raising money for their bighorn sheep management programs by allowing one of their bighorn sheep permits to be auctioned to the highest bidder. These auctions, which were held by the Foundation for North American Wild Sheep at its annual conventions, were raising surprising amounts of money for these states. Sheep permits were going for as high as 60,000 dollars. These auctioned permits were being bought by wealthy sportsmen who were interested in collecting a bighorn trophy and who were interested in helping sheep.

In 1984, some North Dakota sportsmen approached the Game and Fish Department with the idea of North Dakota offering one of its permits for auction. The Department weighed the pros and cons of the idea. The Department had reservations in two areas. One of them had to do with the sheep itself. North Dakota's bighorns are California bighorns, which are smaller animals than the Rocky Mountain bighorn, and have smaller horns. But in terms of horn measurement for trophy purposes, the California bighorn is put together with the Rocky Mountain sheep. The trophy value of the California bighorn—and thus its value at auction— might not arouse a lot of interest.

The Department also had reservations about who would get the permit. Bighorn permits had never been offered to non-residents, and, since opportunities to hunt bighorns were so limited, it seemed important to keep the permits at home.

On the other hand, a great deal of money might be raised. The Department began to talk with the Foundation for North American Wild Sheep (FNAWS) to see how the auction worked, and how much money the Foundation thought such an auction might raise for North Dakota. There was nothing complicated about the process. The Department simply would give one permit to the Foundation for auction at its annual convention, and the auctioneers would get what they could for it. Their track record was very good. Most of the money would return to the Department, with the stipulation that it be used for sheep programs. The remainder would be held in escrow by the Foundation for grants-in-aid to various sheep programs around the country—for which, by the way, the North Dakota Game and Fish Department was eligible to apply. The Foundation thought that the permit might sell for as much as 25,000 dollars.

The Department decided that the possible benefits outweighed its reservations. Since by law only residents could receive bighorn permits in North Dakota, it took a legislative change for the state to offer a permit for auction to the highest bidder, regardless of residency. The Foundation for North American Wild Sheep was extremely helpful in getting this new law through the legislature, sending a representative to testify before both the State Senate and House on behalf of the bill. The main objection to the auction was, again, allowing one of the few bighorn permits to be sold to a nonresident.

The legislature proved itself to be farsighted, and passed the bill. The first auction of a North Dakota California bighorn permit brought 17,000 dollars from Jim Rockstad, a former North Dakotan living in California. Ninety percent of the money was returned to North Dakota for sheep programs, and 10 percent stayed with FNAWS to be used for grants-in-aid. Since 1986, North Dakota has offered a bighorn permit for auction each year, bringing $21,000 in 1987, $15,000 in 1988, $25,000 in 1989, and $34,000 in 1990. In 1990, the California bighorn permit offered by North Dakota brought more than the Rocky Mountain bighorn permits from some other states.

The amount of money that the auction has brought to the bighorn program is not limited to the sale itself. Every dollar that the state raises with the sale is eligible to be matched by three federal dollars through Pittman-Robertson. And because of its association with FNAWS, North Dakota has been able to receive additional grant money to put toward the sheep program. It is very fair to say that allowing one permit per year to go to a nonresident has increased everyone's opportunities for recreation in the future.

Management of bighorn sheep in North Dakota in the coming years means, in some respects, dealing with old issues that will not go away. Part of the management plan for the next ten years includes locating new areas for transplanting bighorn sheep—areas which will provide the habitat the sheep require, but do not have some kind of development slated. The idea that herds of sheep already occupy a great deal of the habitat that is available leads sheep management down some interesting paths.

There may come a time—there are those who would say we have already reached that time—when we will have to change the way we try to overcome crowding on the bighorn sheep range. The Game and Fish Department has depended to a large degree on new transplant sites to relieve overcrowding and to maintain high levels of reproduction and vigor in the bighorn populations. These days, new sheep habitat is extremely limited. Without new transplant sites, the hunting season will become much more important as a sheep management tool.

With other big game species, the Department has raised the number of permits when it has felt that the herd needed to be trimmed. Those seasons include the harvest of female animals. But the bighorn season has always been a rams-only season—a trophy season. There are problems with the idea of opening up the season on bighorns to include ewes. But in order to increase the harvest to alleviate overcrowding, the season would have to include ewes.

Some of the problems with a ewe season are of the Department's own making. It has always been part of the way the Department has talked about sheep to say that the way to manage them is to remove the surplus rams through the hunting season. The idea that there may come a time when there is no place for the herd to grow into has not entered into the discussion. The Department has educated the public into thinking that harvesting ewes would be detrimental to the population.

There is also a problem with the way the bighorn season is set up. As it is now, the season is a once-in-a-lifetime event. If a hunter has only one chance to take an animal, the tendency is to want to make it memorable, which in the case of bighorn sheep, is to take the best head. Moreover, the Department has traded, to some extent, on the limited nature of the hunt.

Ed Bry

To hunt a bighorn ram in North Dakota is to join a fairly exclusive club of hunters. People have paid a good deal of money for the privilege. In order to bring ewes into the bighorn management scheme, the Department will have to devise some way of protecting that "exclusive" aspect of bighorn hunting in North Dakota.

The rams-only season and trophy hunting for bighorns raise some biological issues. In the late 1970s, the season on bighorns was closed because reproduction was not keeping pace with the harvest—that is to say, the rams taken out of the population were not being replaced by reproduction. It is possible to over-harvest rams, especially when other variables can limit reproduction. When numbers of animals are as limited as they are for bighorns, events such as the outbreak of lungworm can turn what you think is a reasonable harvest into a problem.

With bighorns, there is another controversy which has to do with hunting the animals with the largest horns. The controversy comes from the role that horns play in sheep society.

In Chapter Four, we discussed some of the evolutionary pressures which selected for large horns in sheep, and we talked about the hierarchy of rams based on horn size. What it amounts to is that rams which are the strongest and most vigorous also tend to be the rams with the largest horns. Horn size is a function of nutrition, and so the process of natural selection has made strong, vigorous rams—the ones most capable of commanding access to food supplies—the rams with the largest horns. They are also the rams which do most of the breeding, which is expected. They are the "best" rams, best able to survive and to perpetuate themselves.

There is a school of thought which says that trophy hunting for bighorn rams takes those "best" rams out of the population, working as a kind of artificial selection for less vigorous, smaller horned rams. If this is indeed the case, taking such rams out of a population as small as that in North Dakota would be quite serious.

There is another school of thought which approaches the question from a different direction. Agreeing that rams with the best horn growth are the rams which do most of the breeding, this school of thought does not agree that these are the animals taken as trophies. The reason is this: dominance among rams is determined largely by horn size. But rams with nearly equal horn size settle questions of dominance by fighting—crashing head-on into one another with a crack which can be heard as much as a mile away. The force of these horn-on-horn collisions is tremendous, and the horns themselves suffer accordingly—particularly the tips as the horns curve forward to make the full curl. This tip-breakage—called "brooming"—keeps the horns of these fighting rams from ever reaching their full trophy potential. Based on this scenario, full-curl California bighorns are likely to be subordinate rams, neither fighting for dominance nor doing much breeding. Harvesting these subordinate rams would have little effect on the quality of the population.

Bighorn management for the future in North Dakota depends to some degree on how this controversy gets settled. In the years since the first bighorn permit was auctioned, the trophy potential of the animal has been of tremendous value to the program. At the present time, however, the habitat issue commands greater attention. Trophy questions aside, it is accepted by all sheep managers that when the carrying capacity of the range is reached, the reproduction rate and the quality of a bighorn population begin to decline. Management efforts in the immediate future will emphasize keeping populations well within the limits of habitat.

Sources

Boldt, W., T. Upgren, J. McKenzie, and E. Bry. 1973. The Bighorn Sheep in North Dakota. ND Outdoors 36(6):2-9.

Brazda, A. R. 1956. Saga of the Bighorn. ND Outdoors 19(6):4-9-18.

Bry, E. 1966. Three More Bighorn Sheep Released in the Wild. ND Outdoors 28(9):18-22.

Fairaizl, S. D., and M. G. McKenna. 1976. The Culmination of Operation Bighorn. ND Outdoors 38(8):9-13.

Fairaizl, S. D. 1978a. Bighorn Sheep Population Study. NDGFD Pittman-Robertson Division Project W-67-R-18, Job No. C-III-2, Report No. A-20.

Fairaizl, S. D. 1978b. Bighorn Sheep in North Dakota: Population Estimates, Food Habits, and Their Biogeochemistry (MS Thesis). NDGFD Pittman-Robertson Division Project No. W-67-R-17, Study C-III, Report No. A-013-A.

Fairaizl, S. D. 1979a. The Lungworm Dilemma. ND Outdoors 41(11):14-15.

Fairaizl, S. D. 1979b. Bighorn Population Studies. NDGFD Pittman-Robertson Division Project No. W-67-R-19, Job No. C-III-1, Report No. A-027.

Moxon, M. 1965. Wild Sheep of the World, With Special Emphasis on the North American Bighorns of Western North America. Reprinted as NDGFD Pittman-Robertson Division Report No. 102-A.

Murdy, Ray. 1957. 1956 Bighorn Sheep Transplant. NDGFD Pittman-Robertson Division Project W-42-D-4, Report No. 69.

North Dakota Game and Fish Department (NDGFD). 1956. Letter to the Secretary of the Interior.

Stotts, Bryan R. and W. H. Blunt. 1983. Environmental Assessment Report for Bighorn Sheep Transplanting on the Little Missouri National Grasslands, Custer National Forest, Region 1. NDGFD.

U.S. Fish and Wildlife Service (USFWS). 1956. Letter to the NDGFD.

American Elk (wapiti)

CHAPTER TEN

ELK AND MOOSE

The Game and Fish Department can't claim credit for restoring elk and moose to North Dakota. The credit for the state's modern-day seasons on these animals has to go to other people and to the animals themselves. Accident—if that is the right word—has had something to do with it too. Take, for example, the events which led to today's elk herd in the Badlands near the Killdeer Mountains:

> **McKenzie County Farmer,** Jan. 27, 1977: The Three Tribes Game and Fish Department has made arrangements to stock elk on the Fort Berthold Indian Reservation. Some 50 head of elk arrived last week and will be released this week in the west segment east of Mandaree.
>
> The elk were trucked from southwestern South Dakota and were held at the Tribes roping arena at New Town pending their release.

> **McKenzie County Farmer**, Feb. 3, 1977: The 50 head of elk that were to have been released in the Mandaree area last week escaped from their holding pen before they could be moved to the release site.
>
> The elk...were being held in the Three Tribes enclosed roping arena near the Four Bears Lodge on the west side of Lake Sakakawea. It is not certain how they escaped, they either crashed through a door or one of the doors was left open.
>
> At last reports the elk had broken up into three smaller herds. Some had crossed Lake Sakakawea on the ice and were spotted about seven or eight miles south of New Town.

> **McKenzie County Farmer**, Feb. 10, 1977: McKenzie County can now boast of a number of big game animals, big horn sheep, buffalo, and even a bear or two, not found in many other places in the state.
>
> Now elk may be added to the list as the result of an aborted effort to start a herd on the Fort Berthold Indian Reservation.
>
> The Tribal Council of the Three Affiliated Tribes arranged with the National Park Service and the Bureau of Indian Affairs last month to get free elk from a thinned herd in South Dakota's Wind Cave National Park.
>
> The Council wanted the elk to roam the reservation and reproduce so eventually there might have been elk hunting on the reservation.

Fifty-two animals were tested, vaccinated, given shots for stress and trucked to New Town, arriving January 20th.

Two animals were injured in unloading and another got away and had to be destroyed, said Dale McGrady, tribal planner.

The remaining animals were corraled...for a few days of observation, but they all got away a few days later.

"They were turned loose by vandals, or whatever you want to call it," McGrady said. "We were preparing to transport them to an impoundment in the Mandaree area the next day and they were all turned loose."

The elk scattered over the countryside.

Whether or not this elk release was an accident or a deliberate act of vandalism, the animals were never recaptured. They dispersed over a wide area north of the Killdeers, pushed by their own inclinations and, according to some reports, by snowmobilers, and were impossible to keep track of. At least some of the elk survived that first winter, and over the years they have done quite well in the region.

The restoration of elk and moose to other parts of North Dakota cannot be pinpointed so exactly. Moose and elk populations in the Turtle Mountains and the Pembina Hills regions grew slowly. Moose began to filter into the region in the 1950s and 1960s, coming from expanding herds in northwestern Minnesota and southern Canada. Elk began to show up in the Pembina Hills region later, in the 1970s, apparently wandering down the Pembina River Valley from Canada. The Game and Fish Department took a skeptical look at the emerging situation. Based on what was known about the habitat needs of elk and moose, the area could support only a few animals. Certainly the populations could never grow to manageable proportions. As late as January, 1981 the Department's official view of elk in North Dakota was that "it is doubtful if elk will ever have a manageable surplus in North Dakota" (Samuelson, 1981, p. 11). Nonetheless, the first moose season in North Dakota was held in 1977, and in the fall of 1982, North Dakota hunters were offered their first opportunity to take an elk. The Department had been, perhaps, too cautious in its assessment of the situation. Yet, for both moose and elk, there had been good reasons for skepticism. We will discuss them each in turn.

ELK

In Chapter Five we looked briefly at an attempt to stock elk by the Town Criers—a service club—of Killdeer, North Dakota in the winter of 1942. Twenty-five elk were trapped in Yellowstone National Park, Wyoming, and were trucked to North Dakota. They were released on the 7,000 acre D-C Ranch in the Killdeer Mountains in the spring of 1942. Over time, the animals disappeared and the effort to stock elk in the region had to be

Trapping elk in Yellowstone Park for release in North Dakota, 1942.

judged a failure. In light of the later, "accidental," and quite successful release of elk in much the same region in 1977, the failure of the 1942 effort seems worth exploring.

In fact, the 1942 release seemed quite successful the first few years. The Game and Fish Department's annual big game aerial population survey for 1943 reported six elk in addition to the 25 that were released. The 1944 survey reported 33 elk in the Killdeer Mountains. By 1945, the report noted (Bach, 1945, p. 4), "The elk herd...released a few years ago in the Killdeer Mountain area has increased quite remarkably." The report went on to say, however, "[T]he Department has been receiving complaints from the farmers and ranchers of the vicinity regarding damage by these animals to hay, fences, etc. It is safe to say that the general opinion now is that the animals should not have been originally released in the area. Perhaps a better place for the release would have been one of the Roosevelt National Parks lying not far to the west." After 1945, the elk population in the Killdeer Mountains began to decline. The 1947 population survey noted (Stuart, 1947, p. 4), "This was apparently the peak population, as the farmers and ranchers began sending in complaints of damage to crops and haystacks. They apparently took matters into their own hands and reduced the herd to the point where few reports of damage have been received in late years." A few elk were counted during each yearly survey until 1950. In 1951 and 1952, the census-takers couldn't find any elk in the Killdeer Mountains, and after that, elk were dropped from the survey record.

The 1942 effort to reintroduce elk to North Dakota brought some things about elk and about farmers and ranchers into nice, sharp focus. First, it demonstrated that elk were fully capable of surviving in North Dakota. Second, it showed that elk had a few habits which made them unpopular with farmers and ranchers. And third, it showed that farmers and ranchers were fully capable of taking care—on their own—of what they perceived as a problem.

No one should have been surprised that elk could survive here. Elk, after all, had lived in North Dakota for thousands of years. True, the original elk in North Dakota were Manitoban elk (*Cervus elaphus manitobensis*—see Chapter Five for a discussion of the taxonomy of North American elk), more adapted to a plains environment than the introduced Rocky Mountain elk. But, like all members of the deer family, elk can make adjustments when they have a chance.

Elk's unpopularity with farmers and ranchers in the Killdeers began with their food habits. Unlike whitetails and moose which are mostly browsers, elk are mostly grazers. Studies of elk populations in various states have shown that grass and grasslike plants are an important food source for elk throughout the seasons, becoming most important in early and late summer, and least important in winter (see Boyd, 1978, p. 22). More than other members of the deer family, elk are likely to compete directly with cattle and interfere with agriculture. "Elk often graze on private land and damage haystacks, fences and crops at certain times of the year" (Boyd, 1978, p. 27). In North Dakota, where there is very little public land, and most of that is grazed by livestock, the conflict is worse than in most places where there are elk populations.

But there was more to the elk's unpopularity than just their food habits. Elk tend to stay in herds. There are few times in an elk's life when it is not in the company of other elk. After a calf is born, it takes two or three weeks until it is able to travel. After that "cows and calves begin to congregate, and by mid-July [are herded] on summer home ranges" (Boyd, 1978, p. 16). During summer, young bulls are often mixed with the cows and calves. Adult bulls are the only solitary elk, and even they often congregate in groups of five or six. The herds break apart during the rut— the breeding season—as adult bulls gather cows together into harems. By the middle of October, most of the breeding is done, and, with the onset of winter, the animals begin to congregate on winter ranges. "When early winter snows begin to accumulate, cows, calves and most bulls begin to migrate down to winter ranges where they usually spend December through March" (Boyd, 1978, p. 17). Such behavior may once have helped elk to survive—almost all animal behavior can be traced to successful survival strategies. But times have changed.

Of course, North Dakota is not Wyoming or Colorado, and in the early 1940s we were only talking about 30 or 35 head of elk. Elk are, however, large, conspicuous animals, and they can cause a lot of damage. And there are other things involved as well. In other states, elk have distinct winter and summer ranges. Often the distinctions have to do with altitude, with the herds spending the summer months at higher elevations and moving down with the advancing snow. In North Dakota there is no such choice available to elk, and they tend not to move very far. This loyalty to a range was, apparently, quite unexpected when the Town Criers released their elk into the Killdeer Mountains. "Noting the movements of these animals for several years, as well as the movements of a few others that have been released from the St. John Game Farm in the Turtle Mountain region, has led us to the conclusion that elk have a very strong homing instinct and will invariably return to their usual winter quarters. Indeed, the manager of the St. John Game Farm, Dana Wright, had a difficult time in getting any of the animals to leave the confines of that 800 acre fenced refuge. The animals had to be coaxed out of the area by bait. A few subtle tricks had to be resorted to so that the gate could be shut before the animals would beat the manager to the opening and get back into the refuge. The animals finally released have stayed in the vicinity of the game farm. The same is true of the Killdeer Mountain herd. Each winter they are found in the same small area where they were originally released" (Bach, 1945, p. 4).

Even a small herd of elk can make itself unpopular if it moves into an area with what appears to be every intention of spending the winter. The elk released in 1942 seem to have reached just such nuisance proportions by 1945, and by 1952 they were pretty much gone from the scene. With that kind of reaction from landowners, the Game and Fish Department had no plans to bring any more elk into North Dakota.

When elk began to appear in the Pembina Hills in the 1970s, and when they were accidentally released into the Badlands west of the Killdeers in 1977, it posed something of a dilemma for the Game and Fish Department. Unquestionably there was an opportunity here to restore another game species to the state. If the Department took a "wait and see" attitude to the new elk herds, the prospects for their survival—based on past experience—weren't very good. On the other hand, if the Department took on responsibility for the animals, it was going to mean taking on all the problems that these animals were likely to cause.

When it finally came to choosing, the Department came down on the side of having the elk. It was better to have an elk herd and some problems than not to have an elk herd. In the east—in the Pembina Hills— where there were very few elk and local residents seemed to welcome them, the Department kept tabs on them at the same time as the annual surveys for moose. In the west, where elk had such a bad reputation, the Department held public meetings with residents and ranchers to get public input on how the situation should be handled and to let them know that the Department was going to keep track of the animals, was going to listen to the needs of landowners, and, if elk populations got to the point where the animals were causing problems, the Department would use an elk season and other techniques to take the burden off the landowners.

The herd which resulted from the accidental release of elk on the Fort Berthold Reservation has prospered where the elk released in 1942 did not. It's difficult to say how much of that success has come from a more active cooperation between landowners in the area and the Game and Fish Department, and how much is part of a growing sense of the value of wildlife since 1945. A feeling of how the attitude of the public has changed regarding elk in North Dakota can be gotten from public opposition to the first hunting season for elk in 1982. The public was not convinced that the herds had grown to the point where the population would not be hurt by a hunting season.

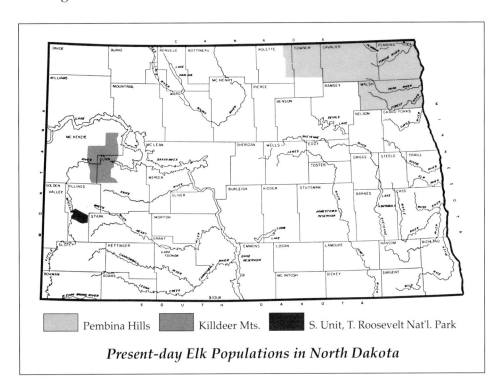

Pembina Hills	Killdeer Mts.		S. Unit, T. Roosevelt Nat'l. Park

Present-day Elk Populations in North Dakota

PRESENT-DAY ELK HERDS

Today there are three elk populations in North Dakota. Two of them we have talked about—the populations in the Pembina Hills and the population which grew out of the herd which escaped from the Fort Berthold Reservation. These "escapees" have grown into the largest herd in the state, ranging today in the northern Badlands between Watford City and Killdeer. The third elk population is in the South Unit of Theodore Roosevelt National Park. This herd came from a group of 47 Rocky Mountain elk which were trapped in 1985 in Wind Cave National Park in South Dakota—the same area that produced the elk now in the northern Badlands. It is interesting to note that the herd in Wind Cave National Park is the result of a transplant made from the Yellowstone Park herd, which produced the animals which were released by the Town Criers in the Killdeer Mountains in 1942.

The Pembina Hills elk population probably came down the Pembina River Valley from Canada. The first sightings of these animals caused some local excitement, but no one really expected them to find a home in North

North Dakota. Occasionally in the past an elk had found its way into the state, was seen a few times, and then disappeared, either harassed back in the direction from which it came, or poached. Given the intensiveness of land use in the area surrounding the Pembina Hills and the relatively large areas that elk need to provide themselves with enough forage, the region would not support very many elk under the best of circumstances. But in the late seventies, people in the area seemed to want the animals to stay, and elk got a foothold in the Pembina Hills. To the extent that they could,

David Jensen

Tab Johnson with North Dakota's first modern-day elk.

elk have done well. The elk which have been harvested in this area are the largest elk taken in North Dakota, animals from the Pembina Hills weighing as much as 900 pounds, with those from the Badlands about 100 pounds lighter. Whether that statistic reflects better forage in the Pembina Hills, or simply a different genetic make-up is unstudied.

The first limited season on elk in North Dakota was held in 1982 on the Pembina Hills herd. Moose hunters in the Pembina Hills were offered the opportunity to take either a moose or a bull elk. The harvest goal was five bull elk, but none of the hunters took an elk. There was, as we have said, a certain amount of opposition to the season on the part of the public, especially sportsmen, who thought that the population could not sustain a harvest at that time. It was not until 1983 that the first elk was taken in the Pembina Hills, and public opposition seemed to have fallen away. Perhaps elk were reaching nuisance levels, and local residents were seeing the wisdom of a season. This second season was handled differently than the first. Five permits for bull elk were issued by lottery for a once in a lifetime opportunity to hunt an elk.

North Dakota's first successful elk hunter was Tab Johnson of Osnabrock, North Dakota. His elk caused something of a local stir (Jensen, 1984, p. 10):

> It didn't take long before the word spread that the first elk had been taken…. When the pickup with Tab's bull elk pulled into the town of Walhalla, cars stopped and turned around to take a look at the huge elk. Trucks loaded with townspeople headed for the elevator where the bull was being weighed. Traffic jams occurred wherever the bull elk went.
>
> The small Forest Service shop being used as a checking station was so crowded that there wasn't room for everyone to get inside. Game and Fish biologists worked in a crowd of curious onlookers as they weighed and dressed the animal…. The area near the shop became so congested that the highway patrol had to be called to direct traffic and get vehicles blocking the highway moving again.

The public in the Pembina Hills region hasn't lost its enthusiasm for elk. In the few years since the first elk season, people in the area have let the Game and Fish Department know their views about how the elk herd there should be managed. In 1987 and 1988, the season on elk in the Pembina Hills was closed, largely due to public pressure. Population survey figures from the Game and Fish Department showed a stable population in the area, with no downward trend because of the annual harvest of a couple of bull elk. But area landowners felt that the herd could be helped by closing the season, and, indeed, the annual survey following the closed seasons showed a slowly growing population. The season was reopened in 1989.

We have already talked about the progress of the elk herd in the Badlands. From an undetermined number of animals which made it through the first winter after their escape from the Ft. Berthold Reservation, the herd now numbers some 200 animals. The first season on this herd was held in 1984. Twenty-five permittees were drawn by lottery for a once in a lifetime hunt. The difference between the hunts in the Pembina Hills and the hunt in the Badlands was that the permits in the Badlands were for any elk rather than bull elk.

The elk season in the Badlands has helped to keep depredation problems down. The number of permits has grown each year—a chart of elk permits and harvests is contained in Appendix Seven—in order to help curb population growth. And to some extent the hunting season has distributed the animals more evenly throughout the region. In the last couple of years, Badlands elk have been using the Killdeer Mountains, something they hadn't done in the past, and something they probably wouldn't have done without hunting pressure. If elk are finding everything they need—food, water, cover, and so on—in one area, they don't have much motivation for moving to new habitat. Back in the 1940s, this loyalty to an area made elk fairly unpopular. Hunting pressure gets them moving into new areas, and if they find all they need in a new area, it's likely they will stay.

The newest elk herd—the herd in the South Unit of Theodore Roosevelt National Park—is also the most-studied herd of elk in North Dakota. "Following the introduction of elk into the South Unit, the National Park Service contracted personnel at Montana State University to begin a two year (later changed to a four year) study of elk in the Park. The objective of this study was to determine the optimum carrying capacity of elk in Theodore Roosevelt National Park" (Sullivan, et. al., 1989, p. 16).

The herd in the park is unique in North Dakota. Other elk contend with private ownership of land, compete with domestic livestock, and have been known to supplement their diets with crops and other cultivated food supplies. Despite the differences between park elk and other herds, the Montana State University study of elk in Theodore Roosevelt National Park is a valuable tool. Because elk are so recent an addition to the big game picture in North Dakota, very little is known about their relationship to this environment. "This study is…scientifically significant due to the lack of information on elk ecology in the Northern Great Plains" (Sullivan, et. al.., p. 16). Of particular interest to researchers were the food habits of elk, their daily and seasonal movements and habitat use, and their population growth. Researchers also wanted to learn about elk in relationship to other herbivores in the park—buffalo, antelope, white-tailed and mule deer, and feral horses, which are the offspring of domestic horses which run wild in the park.

Between 1985 and 1988, the park herd grew from 47 animals to 148. "Judging from the rapid growth of the Theodore Roosevelt National Park herd, habitat and forage in the park are very suitable for elk" (Sullivan, et. al., 1989, p. 16). In terms of an effect on other herbivores in the park, it appeared that a growing elk population might have the greatest effect on the mule deer in the park:

Among large herbivores, the following order of dominance was observed in Theodore Roosevelt National Park: bison>horses>elk>mule deer. Bison graze wherever they please while mule deer are displaced when approached by a herd of bison, horses, or elk....

The rapidly growing elk population will probably not have much of an impact on bison or feral horses, but similarities in habitat use and diet between elk and mule deer could result in a decreased mule deer population. Mule deer feed heavily on browse (woody or shrubby plants) throughout the year. Elk are mostly grazers, but feed on browse also. Because of their greater diet adaptability, elk would probably not be as affected as mule deer if browse became limiting. (Sullivan, et. al., p. 17)

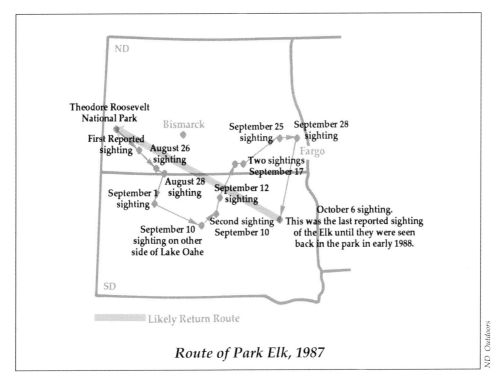

Route of Park Elk, 1987

Elk within the park have expanded their range slowly, remaining concentrated in the eastern third of the park. But at least two bull elk have taken a fairly remarkable journey. In August of 1987, two young bulls apparently leaped the six-foot fence which surrounds the park, and set off for parts unknown:

No one is sure exactly when they left the park, but two bull elk were spotted southeast of New England in Hettinger County August 21, 50 miles from the park. One of the bulls, a five-pointer, was wearing a light-colored collar, according to the observer. This identified the bulls with the park, as the collar

261

carried a radio transmitter and one of the park elk fitted with
collars was missing. The light collar was an identifying trademark
in each of the reported sightings. (Bihrle, 1988, p. 15)

The elk took a meandering tour of the southern half of North Dakota
and the northern part of South Dakota. "[O]n August 26, they were seen
70 miles to the southeast, north of Morristown, S.D., a few miles north of
the N.D.-S.D. border" (Bihrle, p. 15). The animals then headed southwest,
and were spotted again (September 1) near Glad Valley, S.D. From there
they seemed to have gone southeast again, crossing Lake Oahe somewhere
near the U.S. Highway 212 bridge on September 10th.

Over the next two weeks, the elk were seen three times, heading
generally northeast. On September 28th, they were reported in the Red
River Valley along the Sheyenne River southwest of West Fargo. From
there they headed southwest in the general direction of Aberdeen, and
were spotted October 6th near Conde, South Dakota. A map of all these
turns and sightings is on page 261. After the sighting on October 6th,
having wandered some 640 miles, the two elk disappeared.

> Consensus among National Park Service and Game and Fish
> personnel was that the elk probably wound up in someone's
> freezer. To some, in fact, it was surprising the elk's journey had
> not ended sooner.
> That was the train of thought, until January at least, when Jerry
> Westfall, a graduate student working at Theodore Roosevelt
> National Park, began taking inventory of radio-collared park elk.
> Lo and behold, the missing collar, and the animal it was attached
> to, were back. (Bihrle, 1988, p. 15)

Researchers are not sure exactly what this goes to show. The two
animals left the park at the beginning of the rut, so perhaps the journey
was associated with an urge to gather a harem of receptive females. But
cow elk have also been known to travel long distances. "In one instance, a
neck-banded cow was observed in early June in the Rio Grande River
drainage of Colorado. Two and one-half months later the cow and its calf
were observed 177 kilometers (110 miles) to the northwest" (Boyd, 1978, p.
18). In any event, the wanderings of the animals does not seem to be the
sort of colonizing movement that can be seen in moose (see the next
section of this chapter). The two wandering bull elk returned to the park,
showing a loyalty to the park range and a sophisticated sense of direction.

At the present time, the future of elk in North Dakota seems secure. The
three populations of elk in the state are stable, and in the Badlands and
Theodore Roosevelt National Park they are growing. The huntable
populations in the Badlands and in the Pembina Hills will continue to
provide a limited amount of seasonal recreation for North Dakota hunters,
and all of the populations get year-round attention of a non-consumptive
variety. In terms of management goals, the Game and Fish Department

would like to achieve a better distribution of animals, especially in the Badlands, where there are some areas which look good for elk, but which the animals have not managed to find. The Department has been putting hunting pressure into the places where elk tend to concentrate. The pressure gets them moving, but no one can predict where they will go. If the animals move into areas of good habitat, they'll probably stay.

Spreading out the concentrations of animals also keeps the pressure off individual landowners. Conflicts with agricultural and livestock producers will continue to be the major limit to population growth for elk in North Dakota. Since seasons on elk have been held in North Dakota, elk hunters and landowners have enjoyed a good relationship, something which has gone a long way toward keeping elk depredation problems at a minimum. That relationship is also vital to the purposes of the Game and Fish Department, which are to provide recreation and maintain a harvestable surplus of animals each hunting season.

North Dakota moose.

MOOSE

Moose are unique in North Dakota. In spite of the fact that hardly any of North Dakota looks like the sort of place a moose might want to live, moose came back. And they did it without the benefit of the kind of the trapping programs and transplanting efforts that have helped restore

263

pronghorns, bighorns, and elk. A game manager in the early days of Pittman-Robertson would have given very long odds for moose ever needing management in North Dakota. Moose had been so rare since the turn of the century (see Chapter Five) that in June of 1951, **North Dakota Outdoors** listed them as "extinct" in North Dakota, and left its readers with the impression that there was no hope for their return.

The **Outdoors** should have been more cautious. On August 1, 1951, Dick Korfhage of Grand Forks took a picture of a cow and a bull moose five miles southwest of Grafton. Longtime **Outdoors** editor Ed Bry, then a game warden in that district, wrote (Bry, 1984, p. 3), "Moose had been extinct in North Dakota for many years and the sighting of a cow and a bull near Grafton in 1951 was totally unexpected. I looked for the two moose, but found only tracks..." Moose sightings became more frequent in the late 1950s and early 1960s, creating a good bit of local excitement. There were instances, as there were when elk wandered into the state, when the excitement got out of hand, and moose were literally run to death.

By the late 1960s, North Dakota had a small resident population of moose in the Pembina Hills, and moose were being seen in other parts of the state, mostly along the Canadian border and the Red River. In 1971, the Game and Fish Department began a project to keep track of these moose sightings. In 1972, the Department reported (Karpen, 1972, p. 2) that "the sighting of moose in North Dakota is still quite rare except in the Pembina Hills area...[where they] are becoming so common that records regarding these sightings are not maintained." Local residents were excited about the animals, and district wardens were concerned that if the Department published too much information about the moose, people would go sightseeing, and a few might go poaching.

Moose spotted by Dick Korfhage, 1951.

The first question that everyone asked when they saw moose was, "What are moose doing in a place like North Dakota?" It seemed an especially good question in areas outside the Pembina Hills. The Pembina Hills at least looked like moose habitat. But moose, alone or sometimes in pairs, were turning up a long way from the Pembina Hills. The following moose sightings were compiled by the Game and Fish Department in 1972 (Karpen, 1973).

> July 6, 1971. Paul Wacek of Makoti reported a cow moose with calf 8 miles north and 1 mile east of Ryder.

> Oct. 7, 1971. Personnel of the N.D. Truck Regulatory Dept. reported a cow moose observed on I-94 at the next exchange east of Crystal Springs.

> July 26, 1972. Ardmore Quamme of Regent reported observing two bull moose in Sec. 5-134-95 on the Cannonball River.

> Aug. 10, 1972. Ed Bry NDGFD observed and photographed 2 cow moose about 7 miles east of Bismarck.

> Nov. 7, 1972. Joe Miller of Mandan reported a large moose just off I-94 at Crown Butte Dam. Animal apparently moving west.

To find moose doing well in the Pembina Hills should not be surprising. Like elk, moose survived there for centuries before people's activities eliminated them from the scene. What seems puzzling is why moose began to move back into the area in the 1950s and 1960s, and why they seem to go exploring so much more than other animals—bighorns, for example. To disperse bighorns into new habitat, the Game and Fish Department had to capture them and transport them. Bighorns would not do it themselves. But moose are different.

In Chapters Four and Nine we saw how, historically, bighorns got a survival advantage out of staying on the same range, generation after generation. The sort of habitat that sheep live in is climax habitat—"long-lasting, climax grass communities" (Geist, 1971). New sheep habitat is not created quickly, and in a historical period when all sheep habitat was filled to capacity with sheep, there was no advantage to a young sheep striking out on its own. Sheep behavior reflects this situation. They do not disperse into new habitat.

But moose have evolved in a different set of ecological circumstances. "Throughout much of its range in America, the moose is associated with short-lived subclimax communities that follow in the wake of forest fires. Once the climax coniferous forest is burned, herbs, shrubs, and deciduous trees usually flourish on the burn for a number of years and provide moose with an abundant food supply. Moose invade 'burns' a few years after the fire, and rapidly build up large populations" (Geist, 1971, p. 122). Behavior

Pembina Hills aspen forest, 1950s.

Ed Bry

266

on the part of moose which pushed them out into new regions would be as advantageous for moose as it was disadvantageous for bighorns. "[M]oose as a species can depend of the appearance of new habitat although they cannot know where and when it will appear" (Geist, 1971, p. 123). Given all of that, it is not too surprising to find lone moose and small groups of moose striking out in different directions.

Why the Pembina Hills in the 1950s and 1960s? The answer may lie in events in moose range in Minnesota as much as anything that was happening in North Dakota. Moose in Minnesota had come onto very hard times after the turn of the century, just as they had in North Dakota. Between 1900 and 1945, moose range in the state of Minnesota dwindled until it was limited to the northernmost counties (Peterson, 1955, p. 26). Moose were protected in Minnesota beginning in 1922, when the entire state population was estimated at 2,500 (Krefting, 1973, p. 85). Populations fluctuated over the next two decades, reaching a high in 1939 of just over 5,000 animals, and a low in 1948 of 1,100 (Peterson, 1955, p. 27). After that, the moose population in Minnesota seems to have stabilized, and moose began to expand their range. Krefting (1974, p. 85) reports that in 1922, moose in Minnesota were concentrated into a range of only 432 square miles. By 1973, "the major moose range along the Ontario border occupie[d] 20,700 km (8,000 sq mi) and the southerly peripheral range about 23,300 sq km (9,000 sq mi).... The present [1973] population has been estimated at 7 to 8 thousand."

North Dakota apparently reaped some of the benefit of range expansion by Minnesota moose. But that is only part of the story. Moose have evolved a behavioral system which pushes them to disperse in all directions, but for them to take up residence in new places, they have particular habitat requirements. As we discussed earlier, those requirements are usually fulfilled by the vegetation which fills in forested areas following a fire or logging. Typically, a burned-over section of coniferous forest in these northern climates will be filled in with shrubs and aspen trees which, before the fire, were shaded out by the dense cover of the conifers. North Dakota is short on both coniferous forest and forest fires, but in the valley of the Pembina River, the Pembina Gorge, and in the Pembina Hills, aspen and aspen-type forest abounds. When moose made their way back into North Dakota in the 1950s and 1960s, they followed the highway formed by the aspen forest along the Pembina River Valley.

The forest, which seems ideal for an expanding population of moose, has been there for a long time. Why moose have done well there the past thirty years but not before is still a question. Roger Johnson, a big game biologist with the North Dakota Game and Fish Department speculates (Johnson, personal communication) that moose have always filtered into North Dakota along the Pembina River, but it is only since the 1950s that there has been very many of them and that circumstances have allowed them to proliferate. The economics of the region have changed. Where once there were a lot of small farms, each of which grazed a few cattle, now there are fewer farms, larger farms, which are strictly grain operations. The people who continue to live in rural areas do not depend on wild meat for food or on wood for fuel. Moose wandering into the region have, perhaps, found better habitat, less competition, and a smaller chance of being harassed or ending up in someone's freezer. In any event, it is certainly true that as populations grew in northwestern Minnesota and southern Canada, more and more moose found their way into North Dakota.

Until the mid-1970s, moose were rare enough to be curiosities, and for a time people were willing to put up with them in order to have them around. But moose are the largest member of the deer family, and it takes a lot of forage to feed them. Studies have shown that moose can eat up to 60 pounds of green forage every day (Peterson, 1955, p. 114). Like white-tailed deer, moose are mostly browsers. They do not compete directly with cattle for food; nor, given the choice, will they choose croplands to feed in. But, like whitetails, they are adaptable, and they can learn to use crops if that is what is available to them. They can also wreak hovoc in a tree-planting, browsing it down and trampling it. Moreover, they are such large animals that there is very little that can stand between them and where they want to go. "Moose seldom attempt to jump obstacles. Normally they merely step over or go around. When forced to jump they rear up on their hind feet, place their front feet over the obstacle, and spring or dive over" (Peterson, 1955, p. 109). The net result is often a torn-down wire fence.

The typical moose areas of North Dakota are not very large, and by the mid-1970s, even the small resident moose population was beginning to seem like too many moose. The following letter (reprinted from Karpen, 1975) is typical of the kind of complaints the Game and Fish Department began to receive:

> Dear Sir:
>
> This is to inform you that there are moose in this area causing extensive damage to fences and crops. This is not the first year that this has occurred—I've had trouble with moose ever since they first came into the area, just like a lot of farmers in the community.
>
> These animals have fed on my crops all summer, and have torn down fences allowing my cattle to get out. I have been kept busy repairing fence where moose have smashed it down. My cattle have been out causing damage to the neighbor's grain, hay, and gardens. Needless to say, this has been an expense and a great annoyance to me....

The Game and Fish Department began to talk about a moose season as a means of controlling the population as early as 1974. "Though moose numbers generally are still very low in North Dakota, it appears that... landowner resistance is developing.... It appears that the time is approaching when the Department will have to examine the options open to it to more intensively manage these animals" (Karpen, 1975, p. 3).

Lloyd Gardner – one of North Dakota's first modern day moose hunters, 1977.

ND Game and Fish Department

MOOSE SEASONS

In 1975, the Game and Fish Department recommended the harvest of five moose. But moose in North Dakota had been protected by closed seasons since 1901 and it took an act of the legislature to get it opened again. The legal machinery for a limited moose season was passed by the Forty-fifth North Dakota Legislative Assembly, and the first moose season in North Dakota opened for 9 ½ days starting December 2, 1977. Ten permits for bull moose were issued by lottery to 10 resident hunters for a once in a lifetime opportunity. Nine out of the 10 hunters bagged their bull moose.

Since that first season, moose have continued to increase in numbers, and the number of moose permits has grown right along with them (a chart of moose seasons, moose permits, and hunter success for moose is included in Appendix Seven). In 1987 and 1988, 131 "any moose" permits were issued. The season is growing more popular among North Dakota hunters, too. In 1987, the Department received 9,254 applications for the 131 licenses.

The first moose seasons were held after deer gun season was over, usually starting in early December. In 1986, the Department recommended that the season be held before deer season opened. The reason for such an early season was to give North Dakota moose and elk hunters the opportunity to take advantage of the growing sport of calling. Calling has been a popular way to hunt wild turkeys since the Indians made turkey-calls out of the wing bones of hen turkeys, and it has gotten to be a very popular way to hunt predators in North Dakota. But calling moose—that is, imitating the various noises that moose make during the rut to get each other's attention—had never been possible in North Dakota because the season was held after the rut was over. In 1986, the Department set the season to take place during the rut, starting October 10, and closing before the start of deer gun season.

The new time did not work out very well. Landowners in the moose country of North Dakota objected to the early season because they were still out in the fields trying to get crops like sunflowers harvested. Hunters objected because the weather was still pretty warm and there wasn't any snow on the ground to assist those interested in tracking. In 1987, the Department tried a compromise, holding moose season at the same time as deer season. The crops would be in, and the weather more appropriate for a traditional hunt, but calling would still be effective. Again there were objections, mostly on the basis of too many hunters in the field, with too much harassment of the animals. In 1988 and 1989, moose season was moved back so that it once again followed deer season.

This brings up an interesting sidenote to the way that seasons are set in North Dakota. Traditionally, moose and elk seasons in North Dakota have been set at roughly the same time. When moose season was set earlier, so was elk season. Biologically speaking, it doesn't matter whether the season comes early or late. And in terms of the harvest—that is, in terms of the number of moose or elk that the Department sets as a harvest goal—the late season has been just as effective as the early season. The only reason that the Department had for moving the opening date was to provide a different kind of recreational opportunity. In 1990, the Department was satisfied with having the opening date for the moose and elk seasons come after deer season, and that is what it recommended. But when the final dates were set, the elk season was set to open early, on November 2nd. The recommedation for this date came from the Game and Fish Advisory Board.

The Game and Fish Advisory Board is an eight-member board appointed by the governor to represent the public on game and fish issues and operations. By law, no fewer than four members of the board must be farmers or ranchers. Each of the board members is required to hold public meetings in his or her district twice a year, and twice a year all the members meet to give the commissioner whatever recommendations they have about game regulations and Department operations. These recommendations are forwarded to the governor, and occasionally the recommendations of the board are given priority over the recommendations of the Department. Such was the case when it came to setting the moose and elk seasons for 1990. At this writing, public reaction to the new opening date for elk season has not made itself felt. The Department is hoping for a favorable reaction.

North Dakota's wandering moose – taken six miles east of Bismarck, 1973.

THE FUTURE OF MOOSE IN NORTH DAKOTA

The Game and Fish Department began a population survey effort specifically for moose in 1974. At that time, the greatest concentrations of moose were in the "triangle" area of the Pembina Hills—an 85 square mile tract of land bounded on the north by the Great Northern Railroad tracks running between Walhalla and Cavalier, on the south by State Highway 5, and on the west by State Highway 32. The triangle area was designated the Department's first moose study area.

By the time of the first moose season in 1977, moose observations in the triangle survey area had increased 40 percent. The 1978 population survey, which followed the first season, showed that the moose population was still growing, and that moose were spreading out into other areas of the state. In 1978, another moose study area was established in the Turtle Mountains.

The pattern of increasing moose populations in widening areas of the state has continued. The 1981 annual report of the Game and Fish Department (Johnson, 1982) stated, "From local sighting, the moose population appears to be increasing as well as spreading to the south and west. The 1981 hunting season saw an extension of the hunting unit...and the number of sightings in northern Towner County indicate[s] that moose are becoming permanent residents in this area also." By 1983, the moose hunting area included Pembina, Cavalier, Walsh, and Grand Forks counties

Craig Bihrle

Pembina Hills moose.

and the northern portion of Towner County. In 1985, the number of moose permits hit 100, and the number of hunting units increased to seven, extending all the way to the South Dakota line along the Red River Valley. A map comparing the growth in hunting units for moose—and, incidentally, the spread of moose over North Dakota—follows.

Moose populations are doing well in North Dakota. One of the most interesting phenomena of the spread of moose across the state is that they have begun to fill in areas which in no way can be considered traditional moose habitat. "In North Dakota and northwestern Minnesota, moose populations have expanded into prairies and prairie fringing forest and shrublands, and have adapted to and increased in unoccupied habitat that was not previously considered to be moose range" (Kelsall, 1987, p. 7). To date, no one is offering an explanation of the phenomenon other than to say that moose are obviously more adaptable than we had given them credit for being, and that this spread bears watching because of possible conflicts with other land use practices. It still seems unlikely that moose will spread very far away from the cover of trees. Although cold does not seem to be much of a limiting factor for moose (see Chapter Five), they

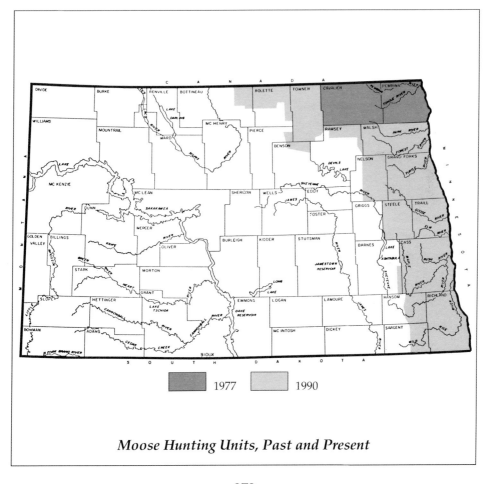

Moose Hunting Units, Past and Present

273

need trees to get out of the wind in winter and to provide them with some shade in summer.

With proper management, and without large unforeseen land use changes in the major moose ranges of the Pembina Hills and Turtle Mountains, moose have a secure future in North Dakota. How much moose can grow will depend to some degree on the phenomenon of "prairie moose," and the tolerance of landowners in the area to the damage caused by moose. As it is with elk, the relationship between hunters and landowners is extremely important in moose management. The primary tool of moose management is the hunting season, and a poor relationship between hunters and landowners can render it completely ineffective. The relationship between moose hunters and landowners in the moose range in North Dakota has always been marked by the highest degree of friendliness and cooperation. Moose and recreation surrounding moose populations has a bright future in North Dakota.

Sources

Bach, R. N. 1945. 1945 Aerial Census of North Dakota's Big Game. NDGFD Division of Federal Aid Project 7R, Report No. 7.

Bihrle, Craig. 1988. Walkabout Elk. ND Outdoors 50(10):14-15.

Boyd, R. J. 1978. American Elk. pps. 11-29 of Big Game of North America: Ecology and Management. Wildlife Management Institute. Stackpole Books, Harrisburg, PA.

Bry, Ed. 1984. Dakota Moose. ND Outdoors 47(3):3-5.

Geist, Valerius. 1971. Mountain Sheep: A Study in Behavior and Evolution. University of Chicago Press.

Jensen, David. 1984. North Dakota's First Elk. ND Outdoors 46(8):10-11.

Johnson, Roger. 1982. Annual Report, Moose. ND Outdoors 44(7):13.

Karpen, George. 1972. Moose and Elk Population Study. NDGFD Pittman-Robertson Division Project No. W-67-R-12, Phase C, Study No. C-IV, Report No. 181.

Karpen, George. 1973. Moose and Elk Population Study. NDGFD Pittman-Robertson Division Project No. W-67-R-13, Phase C, Study No. C-IV, Report No. 187.

Karpen, George. 1975. Moose and Elk Population Study. NDGFD Pittman-Robertson Division Project No. W-67-R-15, Phase C, Study C-IV, Report No. A-002.

Kelsall, J. P. 1987. The Distribution and Status of Moose (*Alces alces*) in North America. Swedish Wildlife Research Suppl. 1, 1987:1-10.

Krefting, L. W. 1974. Moose Distribution and Habitat Selection in North Central North America. Naturaliste Can., 101:81-100.

McKenzie County Farmer. 1977. Watford City, North Dakota. 69(21-23).

Peterson, Randolph L. 1955. North American Moose. University of Toronto Press.

Samuelson, Jack. 1981. Moose and Elk. ND Outdoors 43(7):11.

Stuart, R. W. 1947. 1947 Aerial Survey of North Dakota's Big Game. NDGFD Division of Federal Aid Project 7R, Report No. 9.

Sullivan, Mark G., Jerry A. Westfall, and Lynn Irby. 1989. Buglers of the Badlands. ND Outdoors 52(4):15-17.

Moose

CHAPTER ELEVEN

FINAL THOUGHTS

This short history of big game in North Dakota began as it should have—with the development of North Dakota as a grassland. Grasslands are among the most productive environments on earth; and large, hardy mammals, culled by the rigors of the ice age, found in them almost limitless opportunity. But by the beginning of the twentieth century—about in the middle of this story—the grasslands of North Dakota had been transformed. The climate and rainfall which had favored grasses over trees were still there, but the grasses themselves were almost gone. And so, unsurprisingly, were buffalo, antelope, bighorns, elk, and moose. The only huntable animals left were white-tailed deer, living in North Dakota's riparian forests, the trees in the bottomlands and ancient floodplains of the rivers.

By the end of the 1930s it was apparent that the stability of the grasslands had ended. A grassland ecosystem is a beautiful and complex community of life, which, over time in the Great Plains, had been resilient enough to withstand the effects of fire, drought, wind, and the trampling and grazing of millions of animals. The grasses had held the system together, so to speak, protecting the soil from the huge forces of the wind, the sun, and the rain; building the soil with centuries of decaying leaves; and feeding animals like the buffalo. But by the end of the 1930s, erosion had stripped the topsoil in the Great Plains, and it was clear that if anything was going to be left, we were going to have to manage things better. It was as true for wildlife populations as it was for agriculture. If we were going to have any wildlife populations, we were going to have to give back to them what they needed.

Not that any fledgling game manager thought that human endeavor could replace what the grasslands had lost, even if the losses could somehow be grasped. Any large-scale habitat improvement ambitions that anyone might have had were discouraged by events like the Garrison and Oahe dams. North Dakota's Game and Fish Department struggled to replace even one percent of the habitat lost to Lake Sakakawea (see Chapter Seven). Game management ambitions were on a very modest scale. Game managers wanted to acquire what areas they could of good habitat, and manage them in such a way that the areas would yield a huntable surplus of animals every year. Whenever possible, game managers and habitat specialists would increase the size of the area, and improve it in ways which would encourage a healthy and growing wildlife population. In places like North Dakota, where nearly all of the land is privately owned, game managers tried to foster good relationships with farmers and ranchers, and encourage them to leave room for some deer in their thinking.

Wildlife managers compared their methods to ranching. "Managing wildlife resources has much in common with farm and ranch management" (NDGFD, 1944, p. 17). The reason for managing game was to produce more animals than were needed to perpetuate the herd. "Today the game manager is endeavoring to produce a shootable surplus of game for an ever increasing number of hunters.... Good game management provides for the harvest of surplus game. What is the surplus? It is all the game which is not needed as breeding stock to perpetuate the species and produce future surpluses" (NDGFD, 1952, p. 6-7). There was more to it than that: if that "shootable surplus" wasn't removed, the animals would outgrow their limited habitat. Hunting was thus both the means and end of game management. Game was being managed for the recreational hunter, and the hunter was the primary tool for game management.

Hunting remains today a primary focus of game management, and the first of its tools. We have seen in earlier chapters how the annual season has been used to change the structure—the number of rams compared to ewes—of bighorn sheep populations, and used to shift the distribution of whitetails and elk. We have also seen how, over the past five decades, game managers have become responsible to a wider range of recreation interests. We have seen good game management come to mean making sure that wildlife values are a prominent part of all land use decisions. There are at least two reasons for these changes. The first is an increased interest and awareness on the part of the public in the outdoors. Recreation is recognized as one of the largest industries in North Dakota, and there is every sign that its role will continue to grow. At least some of the growth in outdoor recreation can be traced to the shift, in North Dakota and in the country as a whole, to an increasingly urban and more affluent population (for an exploration of this growth and some of its implications for North Dakota, see **Of Time and the Prairie**, the North Dakota Game and Fish Department's Centennial book).

The second reason for the changes to game management is perhaps more basic. In the 1940s and 1950s, there was good deal of confidence that science and technology were going to be able to provide what nature failed to do. In the past thirty years, confidence in technology has eroded. Protecting "the environment" has reemerged as the best insurance for perpetuating life on the planet. As we have tried to show throughout this book, the relationship between big game in North Dakota and the grasslands environment is extremely complex, influencing not only the food and shelter requirements of big game populations but even the social systems around which the populations are organized. Game managers acknowledge that there is much they do not know about the environmental needs of big game animals. Thus they have to work within the system—the grasslands ecosystem—and so it is vital that as much of it as possible remains intact.

279

In these last few pages we want to discuss two things. The first is the on-going effort to study epizootic hemorrhagic disease (EHD) in white-tailed deer in North Dakota, and the second is the "value" of big game in the state—its contribution to North Dakota. EHD is interesting because the effort to study the disease has raised all kinds of questions about the interplay of environmental forces and their effects on white-tailed deer. The value of big game has a number of different faces, but one is abundantly clear. Outdoor recreation, much of which is connected with big game, is big business in North Dakota. As an economic opportunity, outdoor recreation will be a force in North Dakota's future. And as that future goes, so will go game management in North Dakota.

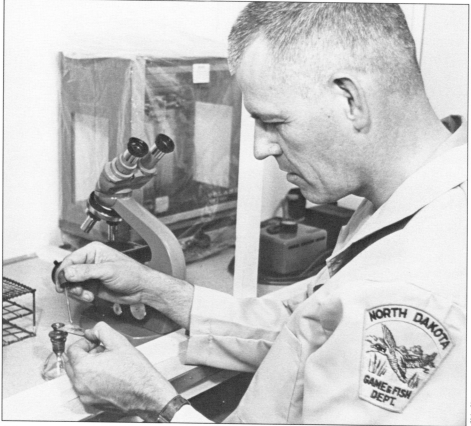

Disease research.

EHD

For a long time, wildlife disease studies in North Dakota did not have much to do with big game. Disease research began in 1953 with a study of rabies. Among the various goals of the research were to find out which animals were the most likely carriers of rabies, and to test the likelihood of the disease being transferred back and forth between wild animals and domestic livestock and pets. The Game and Fish Department also had a public information goal: movies were taken and a booklet was produced which described the behavior and symptoms of animals at different stages of rabies so that a diseased animal could be recognized on sight.

In the late 1950s and early 1960s, the Game and Fish Department did some work with parasites in deer and antelope, and tested big game animals for various diseases—brucellosis, for example—which might affect cattle which used the same ranges. The issue of serious disease problems in big game animals did not attract much attention until August and September of 1962 when an outbreak of disease hit the white-tailed deer herd along the Little Missouri River. Two hundred deer died from what was identified as epizootic hemorrhagic disease (EHD), which until that time had been extremely rare in North Dakota.

EHD is a disease which causes extensive hemorrhaging of the tissues and organs of animals—the "HD" part of its name. The disease is epizootic in nature, an epizootic being to animals what an epidemic is to

ND Game and Fish Department

Taking a sample from a deer during the 1962 EHD outbreak.

281

humans. The disease "attacks and destroys the red blood cells and sets up areas of inflammation. The destruction of the red blood cells, which carry oxygen to the cells in all parts of the body, puts increasing pressure on the heart... Death often results from an overworked heart that is damaged by over exertion and the destruction of its muscle tissue due to lack of oxygen" (Richards, 1976, p. 17). The epizootic in 1962 caused some concern, but there was nothing in the history of the white-tailed deer herd in North Dakota to suggest that it was anything more than an isolated event.

But it was not an isolated event. The disease recurred in epizootic proportions in 1970, and at five or six year intervals since—in 1976, 1981, and 1987. All of the outbreaks have occurred in the Badlands, and they have affected primarily white-tailed deer. Very few mule deer or antelope have died from EHD. Studies of the disease in other places had shown it to be caused by a virus which was carried to deer by a species of biting gnat, known technically as *Culicoides variipennis*. In 1970, after the second epizootic, the Game and Fish Department began studies to find out more about the disease in North Dakota. "In 1970, following the second EHD epizootic, studies were initiated to determine the incidence of immunity to EHD in white-tailed deer herds and small mammal populations. This was a start in determining some of the factors that operate, lead to, and eventually produce a deer die-off" (Richards, 1982, p. 12). The Department began, in 1970, to give out vials to hunters and ask them to collect a sample of blood from harvested deer to be tested for EHD antibodies. Although only a few hunters returned the vials in the first years of the effort, it seemed that there was indeed a five year cycle operating. "The data from these collections indicate[d] that the greatest number of deer have EHD antibodies...in the year of the epizootic and that this incidence decreases yearly until the fifth year when few deer have any antibodies" (Richards, 1982, p. 13). The data confirmed what was already indicated by the five-year intervals between outbreaks of the disease, but it left much unknown. Was the insect carrier in North Dakota the same as in other places? During intervals between epizootics, what animal or animals played host to the virus? Why did the disease attack whitetails so much more than mule deer or antelope? Why were outbreaks limited to the Badlands? What environmental circumstances precipitated an epizootic? The answers to these and other questions might help prevent further outbreaks in the Badlands. If enough were known about why, until now, the disease had been limited to particular areas, perhaps it could be controlled. If nothing else, perhaps some predictability would allow hunters to take the animals before disease took them.

In 1983, the Game and Fish Department and the University of Wisconsin began a joint project to expand the study of EHD in North Dakota. The project, which was slated to continue for three years, began with possible insect carriers—"vectors"—which spread the disease, and the animal hosts which harbored the virus between outbreaks. "The investigation of

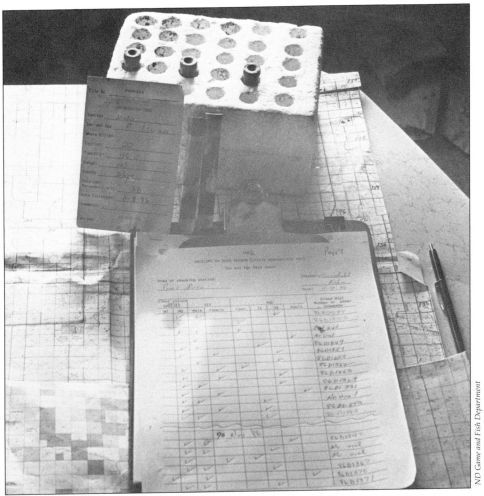

Blood vials collected by hunters plus maps and charts for record-keeping.

ND Game and Fish Department

possible insect vectors began in August, 1983, with trapping of insects at various locations in southwest North Dakota where previous deer die-offs had occurred.... The search for vertebrate species that may serve as reservoirs of the disease requires an extensive survey of blood samples of various species for antibodies to the disease" (Sohn, 1984, p. 11). Blood samples were collected from deer and antelope during the hunting seasons, and from wild turkeys, pheasants, sharp-tailed grouse, partridges, cottontails, jackrabbits, coyotes, deer mice, moose, and elk. Blood samples were also taken from cattle, sheep, and bison. If antibodies to EHD were found in the blood of any of these animals, it would mean that the animal had been exposed to the disease and that it might be a possible reservoir host of the virus. The greater the number of animals of a species which carried antibodies, the greater the likelihood that the species was a reservoir host.

Symptoms like the ones we have described for EHD are caused by bluetongue (BT) virus and two EHD viruses, identified as EHD-1 and EHD-2. In North Dakota, high levels of antibodies to EHD-2 were found in antelope, mule deer, cattle, and bison. All of them are possible reservoir hosts. The insect vector has been shown to be *Culicoides variipennis*, the same as in other areas of the United States, and concentrations of the insect were "greatest in the extreme southwest [part of North Dakota] and were lower in non-disease areas" (Sohn, 1987, p. 20).

There was another outbreak of EHD in 1987. The outbreak pointed to the need for continued monitoring of possible host animals to gain some predictability for the disease. "Our research to date suggests that prediction of impending hemorrhagic disease outbreaks may be feasible by consistently monitoring virus activity, ruminant immunity levels, and insect vector populations. Understanding of the cyclical nature of the various factors involved in virus maintenance and transmission will allow reasonable assessment of the probability of disease occurrence at epizootic levels" (Sohn, 1989, p. 2). The animals which seem the most important to monitor are antelope and cattle:

> The unique role of antelope as the one native, wild ruminant apparently displaying some degree of migration between southwest North Dakota and surrounding states with greater and more persistent hemorrhagic disease problems and the curious correlation of antelope range with historic areas of hemorrhagic disease in North Dakota strongly argues for continued study of this species.
>
> ...[C]attle populations far exceed other ruminant species in the region. A substantial proportion of animals in the population become infected with EHD virus, but no overt disease has ever been established. It has been demonstrated with bluetongue virus that cattle can produce long term high levels of virus in the blood where it is available to biting arthropods. The longevity of many animals in the poulation exceed the interepizootic period for hemorrhagic disease...which is not the case for the wild ruminants. Large numbers of cattle are imported into North Dakota from regions of the country where EHD virus is endemic at high levels in ruminants. The collection of cattle samples has the additional advantages that unlike wildlife sampling the return is directly proportional to the effort invested and cattle can be retested year after year. (Sohn, 1989, p. 1)

Control of the disease may lie with a better understanding—and control of—the biting gnat which spreads the disease. In 1989, a graduate student from the biology department at the University of North Dakota began a three year effort to study the geographic distribution and population dynamics of *C. variipennis*. "The geographic distribution of the vector will determine the potential for HD outbreaks in regions of North Dakota not previously impacted by HD outbreaks. Knowledge of the population dynamics of *C. variipennis* will address the potential for predicting impending HD outbreaks by monitoring vector populations and the potential of someday controlling HD outbreaks by vector control" (Sohn, 1990, p. 4).

Wildlife disease studies are extremely important, but they are difficult, time consuming, and expensive. The bulk of knowledge that has been gained from the study of EHD has been due to the cooperation of sportsmen in providing blood samples. In this regard as well as others, hunters have been an integral part of game management. Many questions regarding the disease are still unanswered. Some will never be answered. One of these is the question of how the virus came to North Dakota in the first place. Wild animals move; other animals can harbor the virus without becoming ill themselves. The long term effort needed to study EHD—and still not control it—points to the serious threat that disease poses to all wildlife populations. It is entirely possible that a new disease could be brought to North Dakota without being detected, simply because no one would know to look for it. It could move through wildlife populations, decimating them because they would have no resistance to a disease which was new to the ecosystem. And there would be very little that anyone could do about it. This danger exists every time an animal is brought into a new area.

The study of wildlife diseases leads one to think in terms of ecosystems. The difficulty in studying diseases—much less treating them or controlling the means by which they are spread—argues for prevention by means of leaving the system intact. There are simply too many environmental variables for a game manager to think that he can control the situation. Worse yet, the trend has been for less good habitat rather than more. Our big game populations—bighorns are a good case in point—have fewer and smaller areas of good habitat. To protect our big game populations from disease we should be increasing habitat, and scattering populations, but the trend has been the other way.

THE ECONOMICS OF BIG GAME

One of the things that game managers and planners have tried to do over the years is find ways of describing and measuring the "value" of wildlife. Most often, the value of big game has been expressed in terms of how much money people have spent on recreation connected with it. Thus, the economic value of the 1956 deer season in North Dakota was expressed as follows (Murdy, 1956, p. 11):

> Based on 38,000 hunters expending an average of $25.78 each, it is estimated that the 1956 deer season resulted in a total expenditure by hunters of about $980,000. This estimate may well

285

be low because it is believed that hunters would tend to over-look some of the costs of hunting.... The $980,000 expenditure to harvest 29,200 deer represents an average cost of $35.56 per deer.

Similar estimates during the past three years (1954-1956) have averaged $934,000 per year. Capitalizing this average expenditure at 5% results in an estimate that the North Dakota deer herd of recent years has an economic value, resulting from rifle hunting alone, of at least 19 million dollars.

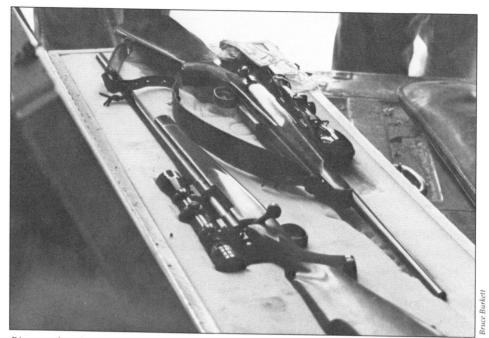

Big game hunting adds to the income of sporting goods stores and other businesses.

The Game and Fish Department still tries to keep track of what hunters spend on their sport. Unfortunately, today's numbers can't be compared to 1956 numbers. There's no way to know what those hunters in 1956 included when they added up their expenses. They may have included such things as ammunition, clothing, and motel rooms, but they may well have left out what they spent on meat processing or taxidermy. When the Game and Fish Department surveys today's hunters, expenses are listed in two categories. First there are fixed expenses—money spent on camping equipment, guns, binoculars, clothing, and so on. These are things that a hunter uses over and over again. The other category is variable expenses such as food, motel rooms, ammunition, meat processing, film—things that vary according to the time spent hunting, the distance a hunter travels from home, or the individual tastes of the hunter. The average North Dakota hunter during the 1986 deer gun season spent around $122 on variable expenses and spent an additional $475 on fixed expenses. A comparative table of fixed and variable expenses for deer and other big game species in 1986 is included as Appendix Nine. In 1986, 73,388 residents bought licenses and hunted in North Dakota (there were others who bought licenses but didn't hunt, and still others who had gratis licenses). If each of the hunters who bought a license and hunted spent nearly $600, then resident deer gun hunters spent more than $44,000,000 on their sport in 1986. One thing is abundantly clear. Deer hunting adds significantly to North Dakota's economy. It has been estimated (Baltezore and Leitch, 1988) that resident big game hunters taken as a whole—deer, antelope, elk, moose, and bighorn sheep hunters—spent $56,500,000 dollars in 1986.

The numbers we have been using so far represent simply the total dollars that big game hunters have spent in North Dakota. It is one measure of the value of big game in the state—that is, how much people have been willing to spend on this kind of recreation. According to economists, though, the impact of this money on the state's economy is far larger. To an economist, each dollar spent by a sportsman—we are talking about both hunters and fisherman here—multiplies to nearly three and a third dollars in terms of the business volume it generates.

It works like this. Let's suppose that a big game hunter travels from his home town in North Dakota to another small town in North Dakota to do his hunting. When he arrives, he goes to the local cafe to buy himself something to eat—let's say a hamburger and some french fries and a cup of coffee. Let's also say that the meal costs him four dollars. By going to that small town and buying a meal, that big game hunter has generated four dollars worth of business activity at that cafe.

Now to the multiplier part. The thing you have to remember is that it takes more than the cafe to put that meal on the table. To put the hamburger, fries, and coffee on the table you have the activity of the cafe, plus you have the activity of a bunch of other businesses. There are the meat processors, the livestock growers, the cattle feed producers. There are potato growers, potato truckers, and potato processors. To cook all this someone has to supply electricity. You need lights. You need tables and chairs. To put a hamburger and fries on the table takes activity—at least a little—from all these sources and quite a few more. To see the total business activity that a hamburger, fries, and coffee represents, you need to add the value of all these little activities to the four dollars of business activity in the cafe.

The difficulty is in figuring out what the value of these little activities is. The way economists have done that is to figure out how much one business needs other businesses. Let's go back to the hamburger. Let's suppose that to make that meal, the cafe only needed four other businesses—the meat producers, the potato producers, the coffee producers, and the electricity producers. Let's suppose that it took 25 cents worth of meat, 25 cents worth of potatoes, and 25 cents worth of coffee to make the meal, and 25 cents worth of electricity to cook them. The total business activity in the four other businesses is one dollar—25 cents worth of activity in four businesses. The total business activity of the meal is now five dollars worth—four dollars at the cafe plus one from the other businesses. To conduct his business, the cafe owner needs other businesses to the tune of one dollar for every four. One dollar at the cafe means one and one-fourth dollars worth of activity in the economy, so the multiplier effect for our hypothetical situation is 1.25.

In the real world there are more businesses involved in the kind of transaction we are talking about, and the multiplier has more levels than our hypothetical one. In the real world, the second level of businesses needs a third level, and so on. In the real world, the multiplier for the money spent by resident sportsmen in North Dakota is 3.31. Every dollar spent by a resident sportsman in North Dakota represents another $2.31 in business activity for other businesses (Coon et. al., 1990, p. 15).

The concept of the multiplier effect on business activity is important for measuring the total value of any economic activity, including big game. It is also important if you are trying to plan for the future. Not all business activities have the same multiplier. Some business activities stimulate more activity than others, and if you want an economy to grow, you want to encourage the businesses which stimulate the most activity. Big game hunting has a higher multiplier for small rural North Dakota towns than many other businesses. Very often, other businesses buy what they need from outside the local economy, and sell their goods elsewhere too.

The multiplier concept is useful. It makes it possible to compare the economic effects of a hunting season to those of businesses like energy development. Moreover, the business activity generated by the big game season in 1986 can be compared to the activity generated in 1988. But not everyone is convinced that money spent really measures the value of wildlife to the state. Another way to measure the value of big game hunting to people is to measure participation in the sport. The way that participation is measured is with the rather awkward concept of "man-days of recreation."

A man-day of recreation is, basically, a day spent by one hunter in the field. Let's go back to the 1986 deer season. In 1986 there were 82,697 hunters (73,388 non-gratis licenses and 9,309 gratis licenses). All told, the 82,697 hunters spent 324,263 days in the field, so the average number of man-days of recreation per hunter for that season was 4.1. There are several things you can do with that number. One of the things you can do is divide it into the average amount of money that each hunter spent over a season and get a figure for what a man-day of recreation for a deer hunter is worth. Then you can compare that to what a man-day of recreation in some other sport—fishing, let's say—is worth, and from that, do some planning. Another thing you might do is take the numbers from a period of years and see whether the amount of effort deer hunters are giving to their sport is rising or falling. If the average number of man-days is rising, it may indicate that deer numbers are down—hunters are taking more time to find an animal. That, along with other indicators, will help form a management plan.

Neither of these uses of the concept of man-days of recreation really measures the value of that kind of recreation to people in North Dakota. Like the figure for dollars spent by hunters, it doesn't really get at what big game and big game hunting means to North Dakotans—the real "value" of the animals. It's not so much what people are willing to spend for the animals as it is what people get back from the recreation. That value may be impossible to measure. But we can show that the value is there.

We can use the three "special" big game animals in North Dakota— moose, elk, and bighorn sheep—for a couple of examples. The three species are special because of the way their licenses are issued. Every big game license in North Dakota is issued by lottery, but the winners of the moose, elk, and bighorn lotteries have a once in a lifetime opportunity. Only residents can apply.

One of the measures of the "value" that people place on these animals is the number of people who apply for the permits. In 1982, for example, there were 25 moose permits available. Eleven thousand people applied for those permits. In spite of the long odds in 1982, 9,379 people applied for 30 permits in 1983. The odds against getting any of these permits are high. But people keep trying. The fact that people—so many people—try to beat such long odds is one indication of how much such a hunt gives back.

Another example. Hunters who beat the odds get a few fine days of recreation. But the recreational value of these special seasons doesn't stop with the hunter. Since 1977, the Game and Fish Department has kept tabs on the days of recreation these seasons have given to people besides the hunter—guides, drivers, family, friends, and, often, hunters from previous seasons. The 1989 elk season, for example, meant 244 days of recreation to 39 hunters, and another 547 days for others. The number of days of recreation these special seasons offer to people who will not take home an animal is some indication that the recreation offered by the hunt is at least as important as taking an animal. A table which summarizes these special seasons—the number of licenses offered, the number of applicants, days of recreation, and the harvest—is included as Appendix Seven.

In 1940, deer were the only huntable big game animals in North Dakota. Pronghorn season opened in 1951, for the first time in over fifty years. In 1954, a statewide bow season for deer was added. In 1956, a bow season was added for pronghorns. The first bighorn season was held in 1975, followed by moose in 1977, and elk in 1982. Bows were legal weapons for these animals since the seasons first opened. In 1987, a deer muzzleloader season was added. Every time a new season has opened in North Dakota, there have been hunters ready to take advantage of the opportunity. In almost every case there have been more hunters than there were licenses available. Only the last three deer seasons (1987, 1988, and 1989), has it been necessary to allow some hunters to take two deer in order to meet management goals.

Recreation involving big game is big business in North Dakota, and North Dakotans hold it in very high regard. There is more hunting opportunity now in North Dakota, and more variety in seasons and choice of weapons than there has been since the state was settled. Good management will see to it that those opportunities do not diminish. But not all of the interest in big game revolves around hunting and recreation connected with hunting. There is absolutely no question that people simply want to have the animals around. Even farmers and ranchers, for whom big game animals are sometimes a nuisance, sometimes a problem, and sometimes an economic liability, like having the animals around. There are plenty of examples, some of which we have looked at in other chapters. In the winter of 1978, when snow and ice pushed a portion of North Dakota's deer herd into farmers' haystacks and to the edge of starvation, the people of North Dakota dug into their own pockets to Save the Deer. Many times in hard winters, North Dakota's landowners have quietly and anonymously fed wildlife. In 1987 and 1988, the annual season on elk in the Pembina Hills area was closed because of public concern that the elk herd in that area was being over-hunted.

There are many other examples of public concern for the welfare of big game animals. In 1984, the North Dakota Wildlife Federation started the Report All Poachers (RAP) program in North Dakota, a program which

Big game hunting provides recreation for more than hunters.

invites the public to get involved in making sure that game laws are followed:

> In a nutshell, RAP works like this. Anyone who sees or hears of a wildlife violation can call 1-800-472-2121, toll-free, 24 hours a day. This is the state radio number. State radio can then contact the state game warden in a matter of minutes. Violators can also be reported to a county sheriff's office, or directly to a game warden....
>
> If the information leads to a conviction, the caller is eligible for a reward....
>
> Through August of 1988, RAP calls have resulted in 122 cases with convictions. Nearly 200 wildlife law violators...have been convicted... (Bihrle, 1988, p. 7)

Less direct, but nonetheless significant are the millions of acres of trees and other vegetation which have been planted by landowners, by themselves and with the cooperation of the Game and Fish Department, for the benefit of wildlife.

There is no sign that the importance of big game to the state of North Dakota and its people is going to diminish any time soon. It is true that as go the fortunes of agriculture in the state, so go the fortunes of wildlife. North Dakota remains dependent on agriculture for the bulk of its economy, and so big game and other wildlife species depend largely on the goodwill of the farmers and ranchers of the state for their survival. History has shown that a booming farm economy tends to work against wildlife interests because land use for agriculture and livestock gets more intense.

But the trend in North Dakota is for more and more people to work in urban settings, and fewer and fewer people to live on the farm. This trend seems to be having an effect on outdoor recreation. People seem to go outdoors more and more for the variety they can find rather than for one particular activity. When people go outdoors they seem to want to know more about the places they go to. They want to know the natural and cultural history of a place, its plants, animals, and maybe something about why the place looks the way it does—how nature made it, and what people have done to it. North Dakotans go hunting mule deer in the Badlands, but they also go there in the springtime and summer and winter. The more they know about mule deer, mule deer habitats, and the natural history of the Badlands, the more likely they are to find the animals, and, it would seem, the richer their experience.

It puts a new light on the value of big game. It spreads the recreation associated with the animals over a much longer period of time. The longest hunting season, the bow season on deer, still only lasts four months. Hunting remains the primary recreation centered around big game and the primary tool for keeping wildlife within the carrying capacity of habitat. Without hunting, game management would be extremely difficult. But bighorns in the Badlands and moose in the Pembina Hills add much to camping and hiking in those places in every season of the year.

As values shift to include other forms of recreation, there needs to be innovations in the ways that the restoration and management of wildlife populations are funded. To date, the funding for big game management comes, directly or indirectly, from sportsmen. Sportsmen pay license fees. Pittman-Robertson monies—which fund nearly all of the research and management programs of game and fish departments around the country—come from excise taxes on arms and ammunition. Sportsmen, banding together to form organizations like the Foundation for North American Wild Sheep, assist programs for propagating and managing different species of wild animals. But non-consumptive use of big game— enjoyment of the animals without harvesting them—is hard to measure. The recreation which is associated with the animals can't be separated from the scenery, the climate, the history and the rest of what makes the experience complete. Yet most of those who gain from the recreation want to give something back. There needs to be a mechanism for it.

In 1955, the goal of the Game and Fish Department was expressed as "the efficient and practical application of management to the state's wildlife resources for the maximum development of game species produced in competition with agriculture and water use without unduly influencing man's ability to produce his direct needs" (NDGFD, 1955, p. 6). Today, the goal of game management is expressed differently. "The principal goal of wildlife management is to maintain wildlife populations at levels which are in the best interests of the animals themselves and at the same time consistent with the social, economic, and cultural needs of the people" (Poole and Trefethan, 1978, p. 339). Both statements recognize that conflicts may arise between development and wildlife. But the first statement seems to picture the relationship between man and wildife as essentially antagonistic. The second allows for a wider range of possibilties. It allows for wildlife to become part of the social and cultural needs of people, and part of the economic fabric. As time passes, big game may take on a larger and more integral role in the lives of North Dakotans.

Sources

Baltezore, James F. and Jay A. Leitch. 1988. Economic Impact of Resident Hunters and Anglers in North Dakota in 1986. North Dakota Farm Research 46(1):22-24.

Bihrle, Craig. 1988. RAP 1-800-472-2121. ND Outdoors 51(4):6-8.

Coon, Randal C., Theresa K. Golz, and Jay A. Leitch. 1990. Expanding the North Dakota Input-Output Model to Include Recreation and Tourism. Agicultural Economics Report No. 255. Dept of Ag Economics, North Dakota State University, Fargo, ND.

Murdy, Ray. 1956. The 1956 Deer Harvest. NDGFD Pittman-Robertson Division Project No. W-37-R-4, Job No. 10, Report No. 65.

North Dakota Game and Fish Department (NDGFD). 1944. Annual Report, July 1, 1943-June 30, 1944.

NDGFD. 1952. Annual Report, July 1, 1951-June 30, 1952.

NDGFD. 1955. Annual Report, July 1, 1954-June 30, 1955.

Poole, Daniel A. and James B. Trefethan. 1978. The Maintenance of Wildlife Populations. pps 339-349 of Wildlife in America. U.S. Dept of Interior Fish and Wildlife Service and National Oceanic and Atmospheric Administration, Council on Environmental Quality.

Richards, S. H. 1976. Epizootic Hemorrhagic Disease of White-tailed Deer. ND Outdoors 39(4):16-17.

Richards, S. H. 1982. EHD...What It Is and Where We Are Going With It. ND Outdoors 45(4):11-13.

Sohn, Rex. 1984. Hemorrhagic Disease Study. ND Outdoors 46(7):11.

Sohn, Rex. 1987. Hemorrhagic Disease Study. ND Outdoors 49(7):19-20.

Sohn, Rex. 1989. EHD Research in North Dakota Antelope. Unpublished Special Report to the Game and Fish Commissioner. NDGFD.

Sohn, Rex. 1990. Wildlife Disease Research. Unpublished NDGFD Annual Report.

APPENDICES

SUMMARY OF DEER RIFLE SEASONS AND REGULATIONS, 1881-1989

Prior to 1881 records do not reveal regulations (if any) governing the hunting, killing or taking of large game animals (including deer).

1881 – The territorial laws prohibited the killing and leaving remains of buffalo, deer, antelope and other large animals on the prairie. This was apparently the initial law relative to big game in, what is now, North Dakota.

1887 – The territorial legislative session laws state, in part, that, "it shall be unlawful for any person, persons, company or corporation to ship for any purpose whatsoever from the Territory of the Dakota the carcass of any buffalo, elk, deer, antelope or mountain sheep."

1891 – The first effort to regulate the period for taking deer was enacted during this session of the North Dakota legislature. The period for killing, trapping or taking in any manner any buffalo, elk, deer, antelope or mountain sheep was limited to the period from September 1 through December 31; dogs were not permitted in the hunt; and trapping was not allowed.

1897 – It became illegal to kill buffalo, moose, elk, deer, antelope, caribou or mountain sheep except during the two month period from October 15 through December 15 of each year. This was the first year that a license was required and the daily bag and the possession limit was set at five animals per person.

1899 – The daily bag and possession limit continued at five deer per person. (The season on all other big game animals was closed for the first time.) The deer season extended from November 10 through December 10.

1901 – The five deer limit continued for deer; however, the season length was reduced to twenty days (November 10 through November 30) and only daylight hunting was permitted.

1909 – The daily and seasonal bag limit was reduced to two deer (any age, sex or species); the season continued during the period from November 10 through November 30; and parties were limited to four hunters.

1913 – The season was closed for the first time on deer. It remained closed during the years 1914, 1915, 1916, 1917, 1918, 1919, and 1920.

1921 and 1922 – A season on "horned" bucks was the rule each year. The season length was reduced to the period from November 21 through November 30 and shooting hours were from ½ hour before sunrise to actual sunset. Black or blue coats and caps were required while hunting deer and one antlered deer per season was the season limit for the first time.

1923 – The deer season was again closed. This closure continued for the years 1924, 1925, 1926, 1927, 1928, 1929, and 1930.

1931 – Antlered bucks were legal during the five day period (sunrise to actual sunset) from November 16 through November 20 in those counties bordering the Missouri River. Although records are incomplete prior to this time, this apparently was the first attempt at regionalizing deer hunting in North Dakota. The legislature limited the deer season framework to the period from November 16 through November 25, 1931, with subsequent season dates being proclaimed by executive order of the governor of North Dakota upon the recommendations of the game and fish commissioner. This authority was vested in the governor to meet situations not foreseen by the 1931 legislature.

1932 – No open season. The policy of proclaiming an open season for deer on an every other year basis apparently had its start in 1932.

1933 – The 1933 season was proclaimed on a county or partial county basis between sunrise and sunset from November 19 through November 22 (4 days).

The season limit was one antlered buck per person and the open area included those counties or parts of counties bordering the Missouri River, those parts of counties including the Turtle Mountains, and Cavalier and Pembina counties in the extreme northeastern corner of North Dakota. Red caps were to be worn by all deer hunters.

1934 – No open season.

1935 – The 1935 deer gun season was proclaimed in the same counties or parts of counties that were open in 1933 and one antlered buck per licensee was the season limit. The season dates extended from November 22 to November 25 with hunting allowed from sunrise to sunset each day.

1936 – No open season.

1937 – With minor changes, the same counties or parts of counties as in 1933 and 1935 were opened to the taking of one adult deer (male or female). Season dates included the four days from November 16 through November 19 and shooting hours were established from 7:00 AM to 5:00 PM each day. Two rest areas totaling 176 square miles were established, one in McLean County and the other in Burleigh and Morton counties adjacent to the cities of Bismarck and Mandan.

1938 – No open season.

1939 – The 1939 season was identical to that held in 1937 with the exception that only antlered bucks were legal and that the season was extended to six days from November 10 through November 15.

1940 – Sportsmen petitioned the North Dakota Game and Fish Department to open Bottineau County east of Range 77 and all of Rolette County to deer hunting. The season was proclaimed from sunrise to sunset each day of a five day period between November 21 through November 25 with one adult deer (male or female) being the season limit.

1941 – Any deer was legal game, regardless of age, sex or species, during a five day period between November 22 and November 26, 1941. The area opened to deer hunting included all of McKenzie and Billings counties which comprised a portion of the Badlands mule deer range that had been closed since 1922; also, Mercer, Oliver, McHenry, and Rolette counties and portions of Mountrail, McLean, Morton, Burleigh, Bottineau, Cavalier, Pembina and Walsh counties were opened for the 1941 deer season. The deer season on the Lower Souris Refuge was to extend to December 19 or until 400 deer had been harvested.

1942 – No open season.

1943 – The 1943 deer season represented the first attempt at regulating the harvest in an area by limiting the number of permits available and by limiting the legal bag on a unitized (counties or parts of counties) basis. Ransom County and a portion of Richland County were opened on a permit basis until 500 deer had been harvested. This same harvest method was applied on the Upper Souris and on the Lower Souris Refuges until 200 and 500 deer, respectively, had been removed. Rolette County and part of Bottineau County were open to the taking of any deer on an unrestricted basis, while in those counties or parts of counties bordering the Missouri River and declared open in 1943, hunters were limited to male deer having two or more prongs per antler as a season bag. Sunrise to sunset hunting was allowed in all areas during the five day period from November 26 through November 30, 1943.

1944 – No open season.

1945 – All of North Dakota lying west of U.S. Highway 81 was opened to deer hunting for a five day period from November 26 through November 30, 1945. The narrow fringe of North Dakota between U.S. Highway 81 and the Red River remained closed. The season limit was one male deer with 2 or more prongs per antler in all areas except in Bottineau and Rolette counties where adults of either sex were legal and on the Upper and Lower Souris Refuges where 200 and 400 deer, respectively, regardless of age or sex, were to be harvested. Sunrise to sunset hunting prevailed during the season.

1946 – No open season.

1947 – Burleigh, McLean, Ward, Renville, McHenry, Bottineau, Rolette and Ramsey counties were opened to the taking of one adult deer (male or female) per licensee during the five day period from November 21 through November 25, 1947. The areas of the state lying west and south of N.D. Highways #6, #25 (present day #200) and south of the McKenzie County line in southwestern North Dakota, plus McIntosh County, Logan County, that portion of Emmons county lying east of U.S. Highway #83 and Kidder County south of U.S. Highway #10 in south central North Dakota were closed to deer hunting in 1947. The remainder of North Dakota was opened to the taking of antlered males (2 or more prongs per antler) during the five-day season.

1948 – The areas of North Dakota between U.S. Highway #81 in the east and N.D. Highways #6, #25 (present day #200) and #8 in the west were open to the taking of one deer regardless of age, sex or species during a three-day season beginning on November 27 and closing November 29, 1948. This was the first year that county lines (at least in part) were not used as hunting unit boundaries. Sunrise to sunset hours were again the rule for the entire season. The northwest prairie-marsh deer range (Coteau Hills), the upper Missouri Slope deer ranges were closed to hunting in 1948.

1949 – No open season.

1950 – The unitized system of deer harvest in North Dakota continued during this year. Fundamentally, the 1950 season involved different season lengths and legal game by area. The boundaries of the areas open to deer hunting were again designated by easily recognized features such as highways and rivers.

For the first time, the season had to open at 12:00 noon on a Friday in November (legislative action). The season opened at noon on Friday, November 10, 1950, and ran for five and one-half days along the Missouri River and for three and one-half days over the remaining open area.

Any one deer was the season limit on the Missouri River hunting unit and antlered bucks (two or more prongs per antler) were legal on the remaining open area.

The extreme northwest prairie-marsh habitat, the Missouri Slope, part of the lower Missouri River and approximately 14,440 square miles in southeastern North Dakota were closed to deer hunting.

1951 – No open season.

1952 – For the first time since, presumably, 1922, the deer season was opened throughout North Dakota. The unitized system of deer harvest prevailed with the season length varying from two and one-half (November 7 through November 9) to four and one-half (November 7 through November 11) days and the season limit varying from antlered buck to any deer by area. The unit boundaries followed state or federal highways.

1953 – No open season.

1954 – About two-thirds (65.9%) of North Dakota was opened for deer hunting in 1954. The open area involved seven hunting units with regulations pertaining to season length and season limit varying by unit; in addition, an effort to regulate the mule deer harvest was initiated. The season limit varied from antlered bucks to any deer by hunting unit. The season involving mule deer harvest regulations in one area was a "split" season with any white-tailed deer being legal game for the length of the season (8½ days) and mule deer being legal the last two days (November 13 and 14). Shooting hours were from one-half hour before sunrise to sunset after the opening day. Unit boundaries were designated by following state and federal highways. The closed portions of North Dakota included four large areas: one area in the prairie-butte deer range of the Missouri Slope totaling 1400 square miles; a second area involving 3780 square miles of the northwestern prairie-marsh deer range; a third area located in the central prairie-marsh range totaling 1500 square miles; and a final area totaling 17,425 square miles in the southern and eastern part of the state.

1955 – Eighty-eight percent (62,225 square miles) of North Dakota was open to deer hunting for two and one-half days between November 11 and November 13, 1955. The season limit varied by unit from bucks only through a split season (bucks the first one and one-half days and any deer the last day) to any deer regardless of age, sex or species. Shooting hours were from one-half hour before sunrise to sunset each day after the opening day.

The closed areas included 4,390 square miles adjacent to the Souris and Des Lacs rivers in north central North Dakota; 1,670 square miles in the Devils Lake and upper Sheyenne River drainage; three areas totaling 1,335 square miles on the prairie-marsh deer range; one area totaling 1,040 square miles on the prairie-butte deer range; and 100 square miles included in 21 small rest areas scattered throughout the state.

1956 – Twenty large "rest areas" (closed to deer hunting), totaling 6,015 square miles, were established during the 1956 deer season. Two rest areas, totaling 50 square miles, were established in the Badlands; four rest areas, totaling 1,470 square miles, were established on the prairie-butte deer range; nine rest areas, totaling 2,885 square miles, were established in the prairie-marsh habitat; three rest areas, totaling 965 square miles, were established on the James and Sheyenne River drainages; and two rest areas, totaling 645 square miles, were established in the Red River Valley.

The remaining 64,645 (91.5%) square miles in North Dakota were opened in six hunting units for either a two and one-half (November 9 through November 11, 1956) or a three and one-half day period (November 9 through November 12, 1956). The season limit ranged from any deer in two units through a split season (white-tailed male deer for the first one and one-half days and any white-tailed deer the last day) in one large unit to any white-tailed deer in three other units. The shooting hours were from one-half hour before sunrise to sunset each day after the opening day.

1957 – The 1957 deer season was proclaimed statewide with eight hunting units. These units were open for varying lengths of time and the season limit varied by unit.

Fundamentally, the season extended for three and one-half days from November 8 through November 11, 1957 in all units; however, an earlier season was held in one unit from November 1 through 3, 1957 (2½ days). This early season was in conjunction with the regulation of the harvest by species.

The legal bag or season limit for each open area varied from any antlered buck to white-tailed buck deer only, through split seasons of any white-tailed deer with mule deer bucks, white-tailed buck deer for two and one-half days with any white-tailed deer the last day and white-tailed or mule deer bucks for two and one-half days with any deer being legal the last day, to any white-tailed deer for the entire season. The season limit for the one unit open during the early season mentioned previously was any white-tailed deer. Any white-tailed deer and mule deer bucks (the last two days) were legal during the three and one-half day regular season. The shooting hours were from one-half hour before sunrise to sunset each day after the opening day(s).

The eight hunting units included 60,025 square miles (85%) of the land area of North Dakota. The remaining 10,635 square miles (15%) were classified as rest areas. They included 15 large areas bounded by highways and were located as follows: Badlands, two rest areas totaling 1,375 square miles; prairie-butte (Missouri Slope), three areas totaling 700 square miles; Missouri River, one area totaling 1,710 square miles; prairie-marsh (Coteau Hills), five areas totaling 1,565 square miles; Souris-Des Lacs River drainages, two areas totaling 1,045 square miles; Sheyenne-James River drainages, one area totaling 250 square miles; and the final rest area totaling 3,990 square miles, including the Pembina Hills and the northern portion of the Red River Valley.

1958 – The 1958 deer season was a statewide situation with U.S. Highway #83 forming the boundary between two hunting units. The area east of this line was opened for antlered bucks from November 7 through 9, 1958 (2½ days); to the west, antlered bucks were legal for four and one-half days until November 11, 1958. The legal shooting hours regulation was changed to from sunrise to sunset each day after the opening day.

The area open to hunting encompassed 64,425 square miles (91%) and the remaining 6,235 square miles (9%) included large rest areas situated as follows: prairie-butte (Slope) deer range, one huge rest area totaling 3,015 square miles, prairie - marsh (Coteau Hills) range, three rest areas totaling 1,230 square miles, Souris-Des Lacs River drainages, one rest area totaling 640 square miles; Sheyenne River drainage, one rest area totaling 525 square miles; and one rest area including portions of the Pembina Hills and the Red River Valley and totaling 825 square miles.

1959 – Permit hunting of both mule deer and white-tailed deer was initiated in North Dakota during the 1959 deer season. The entire state was open and no rest areas were established during that year. State and federal highways provided the boundaries between hunting sub-units and hunting units.

The season limit varied in the six hunting units from any deer by permit in the eastern one-third of the state through a split season on white-tailed deer (antlered bucks during the first one and one-half days and any white-tailed deer the last day), and a split season on both white-tailed deer and mule deer by permit (antlered bucks during the first one and one-half days and any deer the last day) to any white-tailed deer and any mule deer by permit in the remaining units.

The season extended from November 13 through November 15 (2½ days) in three hunting units and extended from November 13 through November 22 (9½ days) in the remaining three units. Shooting hours were from sunrise to sunset after the opening day.

1960 – The 1960 season limit varied by hunting unit (6 units) as was the rule in 1959. Legal game and season length ranged from any white-tailed deer for two and one-half days through any white-tailed deer or any mule deer by permit for five and one-half days to any white-tailed deer by permit, any white-tailed deer or any mule deer by permit and any white-tailed deer for nine and one-half days depending upon the unit involved. The season opened on November 11 and ran through November 16 or November 20, 1960, depending upon the unit in question. Sunrise to sunset hunting was the rule after the opening day.

All but 1300 square miles (about 2%) of North Dakota was opened to deer hunting. The closed areas involved a 750 square mile rest area for mule deer bordering Montana on the upper Missouri River drainage and a 550 square mile rest area for white-tailed deer bordering both Minnesota and Canada in the northeast corner of North Dakota.

1961 – The 1961 deer season involved all of North Dakota in five hunting units with no rest areas.

The season varied from four and one-half to nine and one-half days between November 10 and November 19, 1961, depending upon the unit involved. Sunrise to sunset hunting was permissible after the opening day.

The season limit ranged from any white-tailed deer through white-tailed deer by permit and mule deer by permit to a split season situation where two-pronged white-tailed male deer were legal the first 1½ days and any white-tailed deer being legal for the remainder of the season (3 days).

1962 – All of North Dakota except a token eight square mile rest area along the Sheyenne River was open to deer hunting in 1962.

The season extended for either five and one-half days or eight and one-half days between Tuesday, November 20 through Wednesday, November 28, depending upon which of the five hunting units was referred to. Shooting hours were from sunrise to sunset after the opening day. The 1961-1962 legislature authorized an opening in November (deleting the Friday opening). The 1962 deer season utilized a mid-week opening (Tuesday) to better distribute the hunting pressure.

The season limit in the eastern one-third of the state was any deer by permit. The remainder of the state was open to any white-tailed deer and in the Badlands, the upper Missouri River, a portion of the northwest prairie-marsh deer range and most of the Cannonball River drainage on the prairie-butte range, to any mule deer by permit.

1963 – The 1963 deer hunting season extended for nine and one-half days from November 8 through November 17, 1963. The entire state was open to the hunting of antlered bucks (either species); however, mule deer bucks were legal only by permit. Shooting hours continued from sunrise to sunset after the opening day. The Friday opening (noon) was again implemented by legislative action.

1964 – All of North Dakota was open to deer hunting for either five and one-half days or nine and one-half days between November 6 and November 15, 1964, in four hunting units. No rest areas were established and shooting hours remained at sunrise to sunset after the opening day.

Legal game ranged from antlered bucks in the Red River Valley through any deer by permit with a supplemental buck provision in the central part of the state and through mule deer by permit with a supplemental any white-tailed deer in the western ranges to any deer in the Turtle Mountains.

1965 – The deer season in 1965 was identical to that held in 1964 with two exceptions: first, the season in three hunting units extended for either nine and one-half days or sixteen and one-half days between November 12 and November 28, 1965 (the week extension was in the Turtle Mountains); and second, the any deer permit hunting with the supplemental antlered buck provision was again extended to the Red River Valley.

1966 – The 1966 deer season was on a statewide basis and no rest areas were established.

The season length varied from nine and one-half to sixteen and one-half days between November 11 and November 27, 1966. Shooting hours remained the same.

The season limit for the three separate hunting units was any deer by permit with a supplemental antlered buck provision; any mule deer by permit with a supplemental any white-tailed deer provision; and any deer regardless of age, sex or species.

1967 – All regulations and provisions relative to the 1967 deer season were identical to those implemented in 1966. The season dates were from November 10 through November 19 and extended through November 26, 1967, in the Turtle Mountains.

1968 – The 1968 deer hunting season was on a statewide basis with no rest areas. The season opened at noon on Friday, November 8 and ran for nine and one-half days until sunset November 17. Sunrise to sunset shooting after the opening day continued in 1968.

One antlered buck was the season limit through the state; however, permits were required to harvest an antlered mule deer.

1969 – The nine and one-half day deer season in 1969 ran from November 7 through November 16 throughout North Dakota. No rest areas were established and shooting hours continued from sunrise to sunset after the opening day.

The season limit varied in each of the four hunting units from antlered bucks through any deer by permit; through any white-tailed deer and antlered mule deer bucks by permit; and through any mule deer by permit with a supplementary provision for any white-tailed deer to any deer regardless of age, sex or species.

1970 – The 1970 deer hunting season opened statewide on November 7 in all four hunting units in North Dakota. The season extended through November 15 throughout most of the state, and extended until November 22, 1970 in the one remaining unit in the Turtle Mountains. This allowed for either nine and one-half or sixteen and one-half days of hunting depending upon the unit involved. Legal shooting hours remained the same.

The season limit by hunting unit, as in 1969, varied from antlered bucks through both white-tailed deer by permit and mule deer by permit to any deer regardless of age, sex or species.

1971 – A permit type of any deer season with a supplemental antlered buck provision were the deer season regulations over most of the state in 1971. The remainder of the state (Badlands, Turtle Mountains and the upper Missouri River range adjacent to the Badlands) was open to any white-tailed deer. Mule deer were legal game by permit in the Badlands and antlered mule deer bucks were legal game by white-tailed deer permittees in the western-most white-tailed deer permit area. Four hunting units, involving all of North Dakota, were utilized in 1971 and shooting hours remained the same as in the recent past.

The season length was again either nine and one-half days or sixteen and one-half days (Turtle Mountains). It opened at noon on Friday, November 12 and closed either on November 21 or November 28, 1971, depending upon the hunting unit in question.

1972 – A permit type of any deer season with a supplemental buck only regulation for general licensees continued over most of North Dakota in 1972. Any white-tailed deer was legal game in Unit IV (the Badlands and on the Missouri River range adjacent to the Badlands) and any deer was legal in the Turtle Mountains (Unit I). Any mule deer was legal by permit in Unit IV and for permittees in hunting Unit II; finally, antlered mule deer were legal for white-tailed deer permittees on the western most white-tailed deer permit area in Unit III. These four hunting units involved all of North Dakota in 1972; and, as in recent years, no rest areas were established.

302

The shooting hours remained the same as in the recent past and the season length returned to strictly a nine and one-half day season statewide. It opened at noon on Friday, November 10 and continued through November 19, 1977.

1973 – A permit type of any white-tailed deer season with a buck only supplement for general licensees was initiated for all areas of North Dakota in 1973. In addition, any mule deer could legally be taken by Unit I and II permittees and antlered mule deer could legally be taken by Unit III and IV permittees.

The shooting hours remained the same and no rest areas were established as in the recent past. The nine and one-half day season extended from noon November 9 through sunset November 18, 1973.

1974 – The regulations governing the 1974 deer season included a permit type of any white-tailed deer season with a supplemental antlered white-tailed deer regulation for general licensees throughout North Dakota. In addition, mule deer were legal game for those white-tailed deer permittees and general licensees in Units I and II; antlered mule deer were legal for white-tailed deer permittees in Unit III; and antlered mule deer were legal for mule deer permittees only in Unit IV.

The shooting hours remained the same and no rest areas were proclaimed during the nine and one-half day season that opened at noon on November 8 and ran until sunset on November 17, 1974.

1975 – A unitized permit regulation for specific types of deer (antlered and antlerless white-tailed deer and antlered and antlerless mule deer) was initiated for the 1975 deer season. Gratis licenses fundamentally remained any deer permits depending upon what area of the state an individual owned or operated land.

The season length (9½ days), shooting hours and the rest area policy remained the same as in the recent past. The season extended from noon, November 14 to sunset November 23, 1975.

1976 – The unitized permit season for specific deer continued throughout North Dakota in 1976; also, gratis licenses continued as any deer permits for those areas where an individual owned or operated land.

The shooting hours, rest area policy and season length remained the same as in recent years. The season opened at noon, November 12 and closed at sunset on November 21, 1976.

1977 – The unitized permit season for specific deer continued throughout North Dakota in 1977; also gratis licenses continued as any deer permits for those areas where individuals owned or operated the land.

The shooting hours, rest area policy and season length remained the same as in recent years. The season opened at noon, November 11 and closed at sunset on November 20, 1977.

1978 – The unitized permit season for specific deer continued throughout North Dakota in 1978; also gratis licenses continued as any deer permits for those areas where individuals owned or operated the land.

The shooting hours, rest area policy and season length remained the same as in recent years. The season opened at noon, November 17 and closed at sunset on November 26, 1978.

1979 – The unitized permit season for specific deer continued throughout North Dakota in 1979; gratis licenses continued as any deer permits for those areas where individuals owned or operated the land.

The shooting hours, rest area policy and season length remained the same as in recent years. The season opened at noon, November 9 and closed at sunset on November 18, 1979.

1980 – The unitized permit season for specific deer continued throughout North Dakota in 1980, and gratis licenses continued as any deer permits for those areas where an individual owned or operated the land.

During the 1980 season, the split season concept was initiated in three hunting units (IIA, IID, and IIIC). In these three units, the season was divided into an early and a late season. General permit holders could hunt only in one portion of the season. Gratis license holders could hunt during both portions of the season.

The shooting hours, rest area policy and season length remained the same as in recent years except for the split season units. The season opened at noon November 7 and closed at sunset November 16 for all except the split season units. In the split season units, the early season started at noon November 7 and closed at sunset November 10, the late season opened at noon November 11 and closed at sunset November 16, 1980.

1981 – The unitized permit season for specific deer continued throughout North Dakota in 1981 and gratis licenses continued as any deer permits for those areas where an individual owned or operated the land.

During the 1981 season, the split season was again used in five hunting units (IIA, IIB, IIC, IID, IIIC). In these five hunting units, the split season was carried out the same as in 1980. General permit holders for these units could hunt only one portion of the season. Gratis license holders could hunt during both portions of the season. The shooting hours, rest area policy and season length remained the same as in recent years except for the split season units. The season opened at noon November 6 and closed at sunset November 15, 1981. In the split season units, the early season started at noon November 6 and closed at sunset November 9, the late season opened at noon November 10 and closed at sunset November 16, 1981.

1982 – Regulations for the 1982 firearms deer season were established for all 41 management subunits. All deer hunting licenses were issued through a lottery drawing except for landowner permits. The unitized permits were issued for specific deer types (antlered or antlerless white-tailed deer, antlered or antlerless mule deer and antlered or antlerless deer).

A total of 55,542 deer licenses were issued; 49,129 through the lottery drawing and 6,413 to landowners. The nine and one-half day season started at noon on November 12 and continued until sunset November 21.

The split season concept was used in eleven management subunits.

1983 – Regulations for the 1983 firearms deer season were established for all 41 management subunits. All deer hunting licenses were issued through a lottery drawing except for landowner permits. The unitized permits were issued for specific deer types (antlered or antlerless white-tailed deer, antlered or antlerless mule deer and antlered or antlerless deer). A total of 57,550 deer gun licenses were issued, 49,808 through the lottery drawing and 7,742 to landowners.

A variety of season lengths were offered to deer gun hunters this year with a new 16½ day season in some units. The deer gun season in management subunits 3-3, 3-4, 3-5, 3-6, 3-7, 5-1, 6-1, 7-1, 7-2, 7-3, 7-4, and 7-5 (the eastern portion of the state) started at noon CST November 4th and continued for 16½ days. The season in management subunits 0-1, 0-2, 0-3, 0-4, 1-1, 1-2, 1-3, 1-4, 1-5, 1-6, 2-1, 2-2, 2-3, 2-4, 2-5, 2-6, 3-1, 3-2, 4-1, and 4-2 (the western portion of the state) started at noon CST November 11th and continued for nine and one-half days. The deer gun season in management subunits 2-7, 2-8, 2-9, 2-10, 8-1, 9-1, 9-2, and 9-3 was a split season. The early season started at noon CST November 4th and continued for nine and one-half days.

1984 – Regulations for the 1984 firearms deer season were established for all 41 management subunits. A record number of licenses were sold in 1984. A total of 62,175 deer gun licenses were issued, 53,087 through the lottery drawing and 9,088 to landowners.

A variety of season types were again offered to deer gun hunters in 1984. The 16½ day season started in 1983 was well accepted by the public. This type of season was extended into the northwest corner of the state as well (management subunits 2-1, 2-2, 3-1, 3-2, 3-3, 3-4, 3-5, 3-6, 3-7, 4-1, 4-2, 5-1, 6-1, 7-1, 7-2, 7-3, 7-4, and 7-5). The deer gun season in these areas started at noon CST November 9th and continued for 16½ days. The deer gun season in the rest of the state (management subunits 0-1, 0-2, 0-3, 0-4, 1-1, 1-2, 1-3, 1-4, 1-5, 1-6, 2-3, 2-4, 2-5, and 2-6) also started at noon CST November 9th, but continued for only nine and one-half days. A split season (early and late) was also offered in 1984 near the population center along the extreme eastern edge of the state and the Missouri River south of Bismarck (management subunits 2-7, 2-8, 2-9, 2-10, 8-1, 9-1, 9-2, and 9-3). The early season started at noon CST November 9th and continued for six and one-half days. The late season started at noon CST November 16 and continued for nine and one-half days. This type of split allowed for both the early and late season to be held within the 16½ day season.

1985 – Regulations for the 1985 firearms deer season were established for all 41 management subunits. All deer hunting licenses were issued through a lottery drawing except for landowner permits. The unitized permits were issued for specific deer types (antlered or antlerless white-tailed deer, antlered or antlerless mule deer and antlered or antlerless deer). A record number of licenses were sold in 1985. A total of 70,625 deer gun licenses were issued, 60,703 through the lottery drawing and 9,922 to landowners.

A variety of season types were again offered to deer gun hunters in 1985. The 16½ day season started in 1983 was well accepted by the public. This type of season was again expanded to the state except the Badlands (0-1, 0-2, 0-3, and 0-4). The deer gun season started at noon CST November 8th and continued for 16½ days. The deer gun season in the Badlands also started at noon CST November 8th but continued for only nine and one-half days. A split season (early and late) was also offered in 1985 near the population center along the extreme eastern edge of the state and the Missouri River south of Bismarck (management subunits 2-7, 2-8, 2-9, 2-10, 8-1, 9-1, 9-2, and 9-3). The early season started at noon CST November 8th and continued for six and one-half days. The late season started at noon CST November 15 and continued for nine and one-half days. This type of split allowed for both the early and late seasons to be held within the 16½ day season framework.

1986 – A record number of licenses were again sold in 1986. A total of 86,000 deer gun licenses were issued, 75,829 through the lottery drawing and 10,671 to landowners.

A variety of season types were again offered to deer gun hunters in 1986. The season was extended from 16½ days in 1985 to 23½ days in 1986. The long season was in effect for the whole state. The deer gun season started at noon CST November 7 and continued through November 30, 1986. A split season (early and late) was also offered in 1986 near the population centers of the state along the extreme eastern edge of the state and the Missouri River south of Bismarck (management subunits 2-7, 2-8, 2-9, 2-10, 8-1, 9-1, 9-2, and 9-3). The early season started at noon CST November 7th and continued for 7½ days. The late season started one-half hour before sunrise November 15 and continued through

November 30, thus allowing both early and late seasons to be held within the 23½ day season framework. Because of a blizzard the opening weekend of the deer gun season, the early season hunters were allowed to hunt the last week of the season (November 22-30, 1986). A total of 88,935 permits were allocated for the 1986 season. This was an increase of 18,310 permits from the 70,625 permits allocated in 1985. All of the licenses were not sold through the lottery for the season (76,653 of 88,935) so a second season was proclaimed from December 1 – December 14, 1986. The licenses available for this season were for only antlerless white-tailed deer. This resulted in the sale of 9,847 additional licenses in 35 of the 41 management subunits of the state. The licenses for the second season were sold on a first come first serve basis, allowing deer gun hunters to harvest two deer for the first time in the recent history of North Dakota.

1987 – In 1987, the regular deer gun season was divided into three lengths, a 23½ days, a 16½ days and a split season. The split was 7½ days for the early portion and 16 days for the late portion. The three types were run concurrently in different areas of the state from November 6, 1987 through November 29, 1987. A second season was also proclaimed to run concurrently with the regular season. The second season was only for antlerless deer permits left over from the regular season lottery drawing. The licenses were sold on a first come, first served basis to anyone who wanted a license. For the second time in recent history, North Dakota hunters could obtain two deer gun licenses in one year.

1988 – In 1988, there were two types of deer gun seasons; the regular 16½ day season and the split season. The split was 6½ days for the early portion and 10 days for the late portion. The two types were run concurrently in different areas of the state from November 4, 1988 through November 20, 1988.

1989 – In 1989, there were two types of deer gun seasons; the regular 16½ day season and the split season. The split was 6½ days for the early portion and 10 days for the late portion. The two types were run concurrently in different areas of the state from November 10, 1989 through November 26, 1989.

A second deer season was also proclaimed to run concurrently with the regular season. The second season was only for antlerless deer permits left over from the regular season lottery drawing. The licenses were sold on a first come, first serve basis to anyone who wanted a license. For the third time in recent history, North Dakota hunters could obtain two deer gun licenses in one year.

APPENDIX TWO

TABLE ONE

PROFILE: DEER RIFLE SEASONS 1931-1989

YEAR	SEASON LENGTH	PUBLIC* LICENSES	GRATIS LICENSES	TOTAL LICENSES	TOTAL HUNTERS	MAN DAYS	AVERAGE SUCCESS	TOTAL HARVEST	TOTAL WHITETAILS	M : Fm : F	TOTAL MULE DEER	M : Fm : F
1931	5	2061		2061	NA	NA	57.0	1174	NA	NA	NA	NA
1932	NOS**											
1933	4	3112		3112	NA	NA	38.6	1200	NA	NA	NA	NA
1934	NOS											
1935	4	3144		3144	NA	NA	49.0	1540	NA	NA	NA	NA
1936	NOS											
1937	4	2182		2182	NA	NA	NA	NA	NA	NA	NA	NA
1938	NOS											
1939	6	2958		2958	NA	NA	NA	NA	NA	NA	NA	NA
1940	5	1000E***		1000E***	NA	NA	47.5	475E***	NA	NA	NA	NA
1941	5	5181		5181	NA	NA	55.8	2890	2665	NA	225	NA
1942	NOS											
1943	5	7042		7042	NA	NA	41.5	2925	2765	NA	160	NA
1944	NOS											
1945	5	14760	480	15240	NA	NA	32.8	5000	NA	NA	NA	NA
1946	NOS											
1947	5	27549	600	28149	NA	NA	60.8	17108	NA	NA	NA	NA
1948	3	33710	678	34388	NA	NA	58.6	20151	NA	NA	NA	NA
1949	NOS											
1950	3½	25275	328	25603	25263	NA	60.6	15515	13933	1.3 : 1 : .9	1582	6.2 : 1 : .8
1951	NOS											
1952	2½ + 4½	41208	1663	42871	42090	NA	75.0	32155	27024	1.5 : 1 : .3	5131	1.7 : 1 : .4
1953	NOS											
1954	2½ + 4½	40311	805	41116	40458	NA	71.4	29373	22705	1.6 : 1 : .4	6668	2.0 : 1 : .4
1955	2½	34907	781	35688	35046	NA	61.3	21869	17123	NA	4746	NA
1956	2½ + 3½	38280	656	38936	38702	NA	76.0	29607	21790	1.7 : 1 : .5	7817	1.3 : 1 : .3
1957	2½ + 3½	33606	618	34224	33638	NA	66.4	22739	19714	2.6 : 1 : .4	3025	15.3 : 1 : .3
1958	2½ + 4½	30263	506	30769	30019	NA	44.5	13688	9828	ALL MALE	3860	ALL MALE
1959	2½ + 9½	32935	1546	34481	33771	80375	86.2	29729	23812	1.9 : 1 : .5	5917	1.7 : 1 : .3
1960	2½, 5½, 9½	38379	1557	39936	38884	108486	79.1	31578	25262	1.3 : 1 : .6	6316	1.3 : 1 : .4
1961	4½, 9½	40763	1513	42276	41794	117441	77.1	32590	26324	1.7 : 1 : .4	6266	1.3 : 1 : .2
1962	5½, 8½	39221	1252	40473	39487	131492	69.3	28055	23429	1.4 : 1 : .4	4626	1.7 : 1 : .2
1963	9½	29328	811	30039	29753	121987	41.7	12537	9929	ALL MALE	2608	ALL MALE
1964	5½, 9½	38441	840	39281	38656	123699	71.4	28056	24311	2.5 : 1 : 1.0	3745	1.7 : 1 : .6
1965	9½, 16½	43991	856	44847	43910	144025	68.0	30491	25837	2.4 : 1 : 1.2	4654	1.7 : 1 : .7
1966	9½, 16½	45792	752	46544	45706	151754	67.1	31236	26469	2.0 : 1 : 1.2	4767	1.3 : 1 : .6
1967	9½, 16½	48212	843	49055	48308	171010	63.3	31028	26524	2.0 : 1 : 1.2	4504	1.3 : 1 : .5
1968	9½	34738	652	35390	34677	135240	34.9	12366	10761	ALL MALE	1605	ALL MALE
1969	9½	40245	697	40942	40051	148589	54.8	22442	18367	3.1 : 1 : 1.0	4075	2.6 : 1 : .6
1970	9½, 16½	45869	776	46645	45103	158312	57.4	26783	22882	3.4 : 1 : 1.2	3901	2.4 : 1 : .7
1971	9½, 16½	53309	772	54081	52687	183878	61.2	33121	28673	3.9 : 1 : 1.2	4448	2.8 : 1 : .5
1972	9½	56056	920	56976	55403	204437	52.2	29713	25424	3.6 : 1 : 1.2	4289	3.3 : 1 : .9

*Public Licenses Includes Non-Residents

**NOS = No Open Season

****E = Estimated

TABLE ONE (CONT.)

PROFILE: DEER RIFLE SEASONS 1931-1989

YEAR	SEASON LENGTH	PUBLIC* LICENSES	GRATIS LICENSES	TOTAL LICENSES	TOTAL HUNTERS	MAN DAYS	AVERAGE SUCCESS	TOTAL HARVEST	TOTAL WHITETAILS	M	Fm	F	TOTAL MULE DEER	M	Fm	F
1973	9½	58038	978	59016	57412	217017	50.8	30002	27780	4.6	1	1.0	2222	85.7	1	1.3
1974	9½	58946	1149	60095	58523	224728	43.2	25969	23445	4.6	1	.9	2524	224.7	1	3.7
1975	9½	40010	3761	43771	42379	148744	56.3	24627	20666	2.1	1	.9	3961	2.1	1	.7
1976	9½	39026	3509	42535	40998	150367	55.0	23408	19969	2.2	1	1.0	3439	1.7	1	.4
1977	9½	NA	NA	36884	34960	122843	58.0	20074	17201	2.53	1	.86	2873	1.83	1	.46
1978	9½	NA	NA	41620	34214	128260	56.0	19330	17120	1.94	1	.91	2210	2.48	1	1.00
1979	9½	38997	4201	43198	40722	147613	51.0	20743	18118	1.99	1	1.10	2625	1.89	1	.62
1980	9½	38649	4835	43484	42025	145077	64.0	26819	24179	2.78	1	1.03	2640	3.07	1	.56
1981	9½	43257	5801	49058	47375	165975	63.0	29923	27006	3.01	1	1.01	2917	3.18	1	.61
1982	9½	49435	6413	55542	53831	179373	64.9	34950	31234	2.45	1	.95	3716	2.80	1	.64
1983	16½	50144	7742	57550	55948	205091	71.4	39947	35709	2.41	1	.97	4238	2.71	1	.61
1984	16½	53509	9088	62175	60273	209178	77.8	46881	41592	2.35	1	.84	5289	1.94	1	.45
1985	16½	61264	9922	70625	68341	238293	79.0	54007	48074	1.80	1	.89	5933	1.45	1	.52
1986	37½	75829	10671	86500	82697	324263	78.5	64939	60122	1.20	1	.97	4817	1.86	1	.54
1987	23½	73136	10738	83874	81113	355050	71.8	58217	53025	1.14	1	.65	5192	1.68	1	.54
1988	16½	53687	10442	64129	61742	252387	74.2	45829	41190	1.62	1	.84	4639	2.16	1	.50
1989	16½	62065	10683	72748	69259	266472	75.2	52108	46739	1.62	1	.89	5369	2.22	1	.65

*PUBLIC LICENSES INCLUDES NONRESIDENTS

TABLE TWO

PROFILE: DEER ARCHERY SEASONS 1984-89*

YEAR	TOTAL LICENSES	TOTAL HUNTERS	MAN DAYS	AVERAGE SUCCESS	TOTAL HARVEST	TOTAL WHITETAILS	M	Fm	F	TOTAL MULE DEER	M	Fm	F
1984	9977	9687	111250	29.6	2863	2253	1.92	1	1.04	610	2.07	1	.59
1985	10776	10249	131039	28.0	2874	2533	2.22	1	1.35	341	2.01	1	.70
1986	10735	9904	129160	33.9	3355	3061	2.12	1	1.04	294	8.62	1	
1987	9629	9333	113344	29.3	2739	2411	1.98	1	.62	328	1.10	1	.20
1988	9565	9207	113009	33.6	3096	2868	2.13	1	.62	228	1.21	1	
1989	10099	9948	121502	33.0	3281	2934	2.30	1	.66	347	2.01	1	.60

*THESE ARE THE ONLY YEARS FOR WHICH SURVEY INFORMATION IS AVAILABLE.

PRONGHORN SEASONS AND REGULATIONS
SUMMARY OF CHANGES IN REGULATIONS: 1881-1989

1881 – The territorial laws prohibited killing and leaving the remains of buffalo, deer, antelope, and other large animals on the prairie. This was apparently the initial law relative to big game in what is now North Dakota.

1887 – The territorial legislative sessions laws state that "it shall be unlawful for any person, persons, company or corporation to ship for any purpose whatsoever from the Territory of the Dakota the carcass of any buffalo, elk, deer, antelope or mountain sheep."

1891 – The first attempt to regulate the season for taking big game was enacted. The period for killing, trapping, or taking in any manner any buffalo, elk, deer, antelope, or mountain sheep was limited to the period from September 1 through December 31. Dogs were not permitted in the hunt, and trapping was not allowed.

1897 – First hunting licenses required.

1899 – Season on all big game animals except deer was closed.

1901 – Season on pronghorn antelope closed until 1911.

1909 – Closed season on pronghorns extended until 1920.

1915 – Hunting of pronghorn antelope, moose, and elk banned completely in North Dakota. Season would remain closed until 1951.

1951 – Antelope season opened at noon on September 22, 1951, and closed at sunset on September 24. The season was open on a permit basis to the taking of 1,000 antelope of either sex and any age in a 2,482 square mile area comprising parts of Bowman, Slope, Golden Valley and McKenzie counties. Permits were issued by lottery. Agricultural operators were given preference by being able to enter a separate drawing held prior to a statewide drawing. To be eligible for the separate drawing, a landowner had to be residing upon and operating lands within the open antelope units. Landowners could apply for the special drawing every year, successful or not. Successful applicants in the statewide drawing could apply again after a four year waiting period.

1953 – No season.

1958 – The first archery season for antelope was held for 8½ days from September 6, 1958 to September 14. An unlimited number of bow licenses were made available (246 issued) for any antelope regardless of age or sex. The season was held in eight western counties. Other regulations required a successful bow hunter to report the kill and show the animal to a department official within 24 hours of the kill and before the animal was skinned. Antelope gun season opened at noon on September 18, and closed at sunset on September 21. Regulations were the same as 1957 except that the season opened on Thursday instead of Friday to spread the hunting pressure. Please refer to the maps for open areas. It was legal for a hunter to buy both a bow and a gun license and to kill an antelope in each of the two seasons.

1961 – The landowner preference law and the waiting period law were changed. The landowners' right to apply for a special drawing was changed to give landowners the right to purchase an antelope license. The requirements that landowners live within the boundaries of the hunting unit remained the same. This law took away the Department's ability to control the number of permits which could be issued in a hunting unit, making it impossible to limit the harvest. In addition, in some units no permits were available to the general public.

The new waiting period law gave applicants who had been unsuccessful in the lottery for four successive years the right to receive a license without going through the lottery.

1963 – The provision which guaranteed a license to applicants who had been unsuccessful in the lottery for four consecutive years was removed. The waiting period for hunters who received a permit through the lottery was increased to five years.

1964 – An experimental "buck-only" season was held on a small portion of the antelope range open to hunting. The purpose of the experimental season was to test whether or not this management tool could be used effectively in North Dakota. Investigation during and after the season revealed a high percentage of illegal antelope – buck kids and horned does – killed and left lying in the field.

1975 – The landowner preference law was changed to a gratis permit law. Landowners, upon filing an affidavit describing a minimum of a quarter section of land which they owned or leased within an open hunting unit, could receive a free license to hunt antelope on that land. The Department had no power to limit the number of gratis permits.

1978-1981 – Season closed due to severe winter kill of pronghorns during the winters of 1977-78 and 1978-79. The season might have been opened in 1981, but due to the inability of the Department to limit the harvest because of the gratis permit law, the season remained closed.

1983 – The gratis permit law was changed to give the Department the ability to limit the antelope harvest and to give the general public more opportunities to hunt antelope. Gratis permits were limited to the number of permits that were available for a given hunting unit. In units where the number of available permits exceeded fifty, half of the number exceeding fifty were made available to the general public by lottery.

PRONGHORN RIFLE SEASON HUNTING UNITS 1951-1986

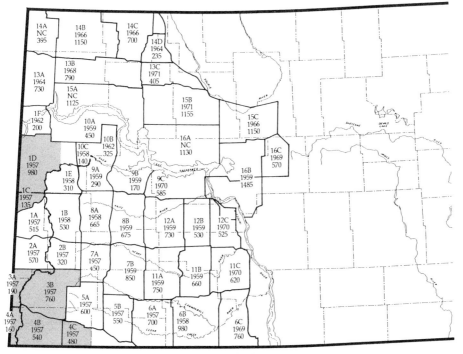

PRONGHORN ANTELOPE RIFLE SEASON HUNTING UNITS – 1951

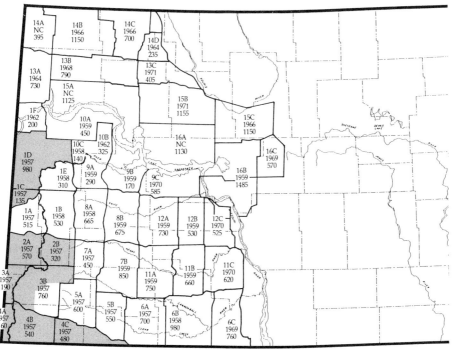

PRONGHORN ANTELOPE RIFLE SEASON HUNTING UNITS – 1956

311

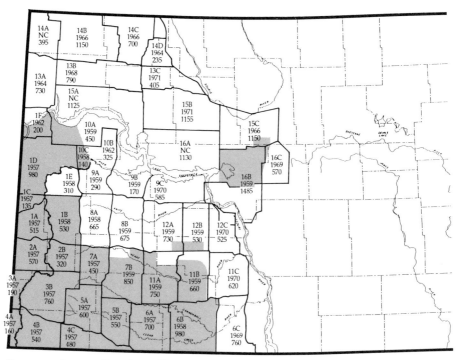

PRONGHORN ANTELOPE RIFLE SEASON HUNTING UNITS – 1961

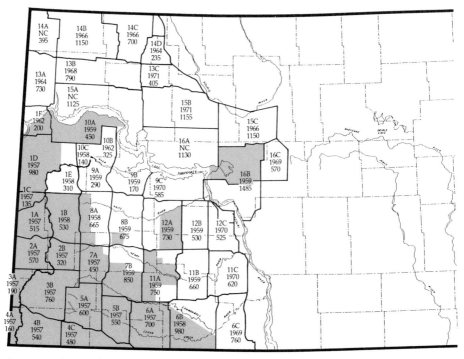

PRONGHORN ANTELOPE RIFLE SEASON HUNTING UNITS – 1963

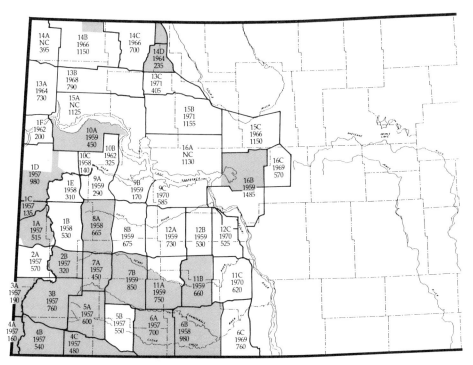

PRONGHORN ANTELOPE RIFLE SEASON HUNTING UNITS – 1966

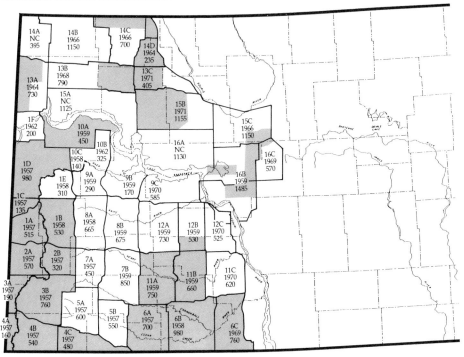

PRONGHORN ANTELOPE RIFLE SEASON HUNTING UNITS – 1971

313

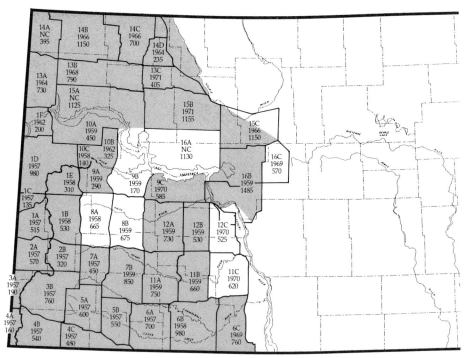

PRONGHORN ANTELOPE RIFLE SEASON HUNTING UNITS – 1976

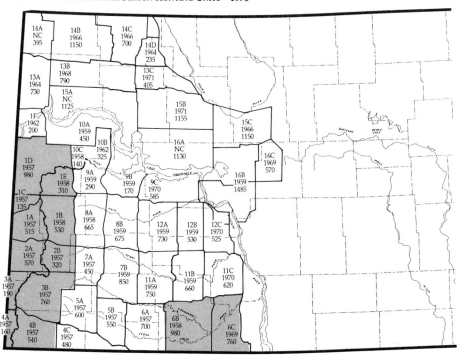

PRONGHORN ANTELOPE RIFLE SEASON HUNTING UNITS – 1982

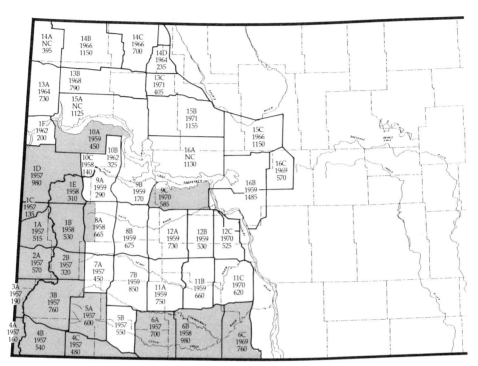

PRONGHORN ANTELOPE RIFLE SEASON HUNTING UNITS – 1984

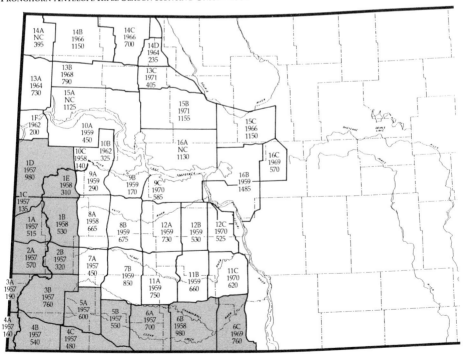

PRONGHORN ANTELOPE RIFLE SEASON HUNTING UNITS – 1986

315

TABLE TWO

PROFILE: PRONGHORN
ARCHERY SEASONS 1985-1989

YEAR	TOTAL LICENSES	TOTAL HUNTERS	MAN DAYS	SUCCESS	TOTAL HARVEST	M : Fm : F
1985	760	688	5071	16.9	116	4.78 : 1 : 1.35
1986	732	666	4901	20.9	139	3.20 : 1 : 2.46
1987						
1988						
1989						

TABLE ONE

PROFILE: PRONGHORN RIFLE SEASONS 1951-1989

YEAR	AVAILABLE LICENSES	APPLI-CATIONS	LANDOWNER LICENSES	PUBLIC LICENSES	TOTAL LICENSES	TOTAL HUNTERS	MAN DAYS	SUCCESS	HARVEST	M : Fm : F
1951	1000	NA		1004*	1004*	955	NA	96.0	913	2.0 : 1 : 1.2
1952	1100	7000		1077*	1077*	1050	NA	91.5	986	1.39 : 1 : .47
1953	NOS									
1954	2000	6024		1977*	1977*	1852	NA	96.9	1794	1.63 : 1 : .54
1955	1600		485	1106	1591	1561	NA	95.7	1494	1.57 : 1 : .50
1956	NA		349	880	1229	1217	NA	94.6	1151	1.66 : 1 : .53
1957	NA		401	1028	1429	1423	NA	97.0	1381	2.0 : 1 : .57
1958			617	1206	1823**	1823E	NA	97.0E	1771E	1.6 : 1 : .45
1959			867	1308	2226***	2226E	NA	94.4	2101E	1.6 : 1 : .50
1960	NA		738	1434	2172	2160	NA	96.5	2085	1.74 : 1 : .45
1961	NA		1183	1881	3064	3049	NA	96.8	2948	1.63 : 1 : .44
1962	NA		765	2234	2999	2865	NA	91.9	2634	1.56 : 1 : .49
1963	NA		591	2119	2710	2588	NA	91.9	2378	NA
1964	NA		627	3373	4000	3817	NA	91.9	3502	NA
1965	NA		294	1183	1477	1415	2146	85.6	1211	1.60 : 1 : .80
1966	NA		624	745	1369	1316	2222	87.6	1153	2.27 : 1 : .88
1967	NA		819	1082	1901	1844	2906	90.3	1631	2.42 : 1 : .76
1968	NA		966	1419	2385	2256	3805	90.0	2030	1.97 : 1 : .78
1969	NA		218	993	1211	1192	2260	83.9	1000	1.89 : 1 : .77
1970	NA		848	1277	2125	2040	3589	88.6	1807	2.29 : 1 : .76
1971	NA		832	898	1730	1668	2866	89.2	1486	2.66 : 1 : .63
1972	NA		662	626	1288	1239	2169	91.4	1132	2.57 : 1 : .64
1973	NA		977	578	1555	1487	2339	92.7	1378	2.71 : 1 : .59
1974	NA		1307	800	2107	2014	2866	90.2	1816	2.46 : 1 : .54
1975	NA		923	1255	2178	2004	4010	84.0	1683	2.62 : 1 : .47
1976	NA		1072	828	1900	1647	3376	74.4	1225	2.77 : 1 : .53
1977	NA		962	784	1746	1527	3301	78.0	1194	3.91 : 1 : .75
1978	NOS									
1979	NOS									
1980	NOS									
1981	NOS									
1982	725	4067	200	532	732	698	1470	88.0	617	8.8 : 1 : 1.7
1983	1390	4570	263	1102	1365	1303	2260	91.1	1187	4.62 : 1 : .93
1984	1375	4523	275	1100	1375	1297	2389	89.9	1166	4.58 : 1 : 1.16
1985	1025	4374	310	715	1025	966	1790	89.8	867	4.35 : 1 : .89
1986	630	3199	305	325	630	574	1033	84.1	483	5.75 : 1 : 1.16
1987	910	3857	356	554	910	846	1441	87.6	741	9.95 : 1 : 1.40
1988	1530	5216	500	968	1468	1349	2806	89.6	1209	2.36 : 1 : .66
1989	2280	5863	632	1519	2151	2019	3809	90.1	1819	3.18 : 1 : .71

*LANDOWNER AND PUBLIC LICENSES NOT SEPARATED.
**FIGURES ASSUME THAT EVERY LICENSEE HUNTED (E = ESTIMATED).

MUTUAL AGREEMENT BETWEEN THEODORE ROOSEVELT NATIONAL MEMORIAL PARK AND NORTH DAKOTA GAME AND FISH DEPARTMENT

WHEREAS, It is desired to establish nucleus breeding herds of California Bighorn Sheep within the area which was the historical range of the Audubon Sheep and which includes that portion of the Badlands that lies within Theodore Roosevelt National Memorial Park;
  NOW THEREFORE, It is agreed and understood by and between the parties hereto signing:

That the North Dakota Game and Fish Department will:
1.   Live trap from the enclosure on Magpie Creek approximately ten (10) California Bighorn Sheep. These animals are to be of age and sex composition to accomplish objective of producing animals for release.

2.   Immunize the animals against (1) Brucellosis, (2) Shipping fever, and/or any other disease, as deemed necessary.

3.   Transport the sheep to an enclosure inside the Park at no expense to the Theodore Roosevelt National Memorial Park. Delivery will be made no later than March 1, 1960.

4.   Lend technical assistance to aid in establishing the nucleus herd within the Park enclosure and to gain the greatest possible increase of sheep consistent with good management of the range in the enclosure.

5. Vaccinate all reproduction in the Park enclosure at the time of future trapping operations.

That the Theodore Roosevelt National Memorial Park will:
1.   Erect a fenced enclosure of approximately 160-200 acres within the South Unit of the Park. The enclosure will be of such construction to hold bighorn sheep.

2.   Permit introduction in the enclosure of approximately 10 bighorn sheep from the Magpie Creek enclosure.

3.   Maintain as vigorous a breeding stock as possible within the Park enclosure until such time as a satisfactory herd has been established in the Park and the enclosure has been removed, but not to continue after 1970.

4.   Allow the North Dakota Game and Fish Department to trap and remove from the enclosure the surplus bighorn sheep until twice the number placed in the enclosure by the State is obtained. The number of lambs removed by the State each year will be determined by mutual agreement between the two agencies. After fulfillment of this commitment, the surplus sheep will be released to the National Park Service. The number and sex composition of all animals removed shall be such as to enhance sustained productivity within the enclosure insofar as possible.

5.   Permit a monthly check of the area by North Dakota Game and Fish Department biologists for the purpose of collecting biological data and permit ecological studies in connection with this project.

Conditional Revision of Mutual Agreement:
This agreement is not binding in the event of conditions brought about by natural causes which make fulfillment impractical and is amendable in writing by mutual consent of the participating parties.

Date_____2-16-60_____   Signed_s/ I. G. Bue_____
                                                                                  Title___Commissioner_____
                                                                                  North Dakota Game & Fish Department

Date_____Feb. 15, 1960_____   Signed_s/ John W. Jay, Jr._____
                                                                                  Title_____Superintendent_____
                                                                                  Theodore Roosevelt National Memorial Park

BIGHORN SHEEP TRANSLOCATION RECORD IN NORTH DAKOTA

Year	# Animals	Source	Release Location
1956	18	Williams Lake, BC	Magpie Creek, ND
1959	5	Magpie Creek, ND	Theo. Roosevelt Park
1960	9	Magpie Creek, ND	Theo. Roosevelt Park
1962	5	Magpie Creek, ND	Dutchman's Barn, ND
1962	2	Magpie Creek, ND	North Park Unit, ND
1962	10	Magpie Creek, ND	Devils Slide, ND
1962	2	Theo. Roosevelt Park, ND	Dutchman's Barn, ND
1962	2	Theo. Roosevelt Park, ND	Devils Slide, ND
1966	3	Theo. Roosevelt Park, ND	Moody Plateau, ND
1983	9	Highline Plateau, ND	Lone Butte, ND
1986	2	Dutchman's Barn, ND	Theo. Roosevelt Park
1986	4	Dutchman's Barn, ND	Moody Plateau, ND
1987	10	Moody Plateau, ND	Sheep Creek, ND
1987	3	Moody Plateau, ND	Dutchman's Barn, ND
1988	2	Lone Butte, ND	1) Dutchman's Barn, ND 1) Hettinger Exp. Sta.
1988	10	Dutchman's Barn, ND	Wannagan Creek, ND
1989	9	Williams Lake, BC	N. Bullion Butte, ND
1990	1	Theo. Roosevelt Park, ND	Dutchman's Barn, ND
1990	3	Theo. Roosevelt Park, ND	Lone Butte, ND
1990	2	Sully Creek, ND	Theo. Roosevelt Park
1990	6	Sully Creek, ND	Dutchman's Barn, ND
1990	2	Moody Plateau, ND	Theo. Roosevelt Park
1990	9	Moody Plateau, ND	Lone Butte, ND
1990	11	Magpie Creek, ND	Bullion Butte, ND

TOTAL   139 animals translocated during 24 operations

APPENDIX SEVEN

TABLE ONE   PROFILE: ELK SEASONS 1983-1989

YEAR	LICENSES AVAILABLE	APPLICATIONS	LICENSES ISSUED	HUNTERS	HUNTING DAYS	AVERAGE PER HUNTER	OTHER RECREATION DAYS	TOTAL DAYS/ELK	HARVEST	HUNTER SUCCESS	BULL/COW/ CALF RATIO
1983	5	865	5	5	27	5.4	107	67.0	2	40.0	2 / /
1984	30	3069	30	28	92	3.3	206	11.9	25	89.3	19 / 5 / 1
1985	30	2950	30	28	87	3.1	254	14.8	23	82.1	14 / 8 / 1
1986	40	5732	40	40	204	5.1	419	23.1	27	67.5	19 / 7 / 1
1987	70	6059	70	69	342	5.0	699	22.6	46	66.7	15 / 24 / 7
1988	50	5344	50	48	246	5.1	475	20.0	36	75.0	12 / 19 / 5
1989	40	6858	40	39	244	6.3	547	30.4	26	66.7	9 / 15 / 2

TABLE TWO   PROFILE: MOOSE SEASONS 1977-1989

YEAR	LICENSES AVAILABLE	APPLICATIONS	LICENSES ISSUED	HUNTERS	HUNTING DAYS	AVERAGE PER HUNTER	OTHER RECREATION DAYS	TOTAL DAYS/MOOSE	HARVEST	HUNTER SUCCESS	BULL/COW/ CALF RATIO
1977	10	4982	10	9	22	2.4	68	10.0	9	100.0	9 / /
1978	15	4075	15	15	61	4.1	219	18.7	15	100.0	11 / 4 /
1979	15	4441	15	15					15	100.0	5 / 9 / 1
1980	15	6159	15	15	73	4.9	238	22.2	14	93.3	11 / 3 /
1981	15	8196	15	15	54	3.6	206	18.6	14	93.3	12 / 2 /
1982	25	11124	25	25	103	4.1	440	23.6	23	92.0	15 / 7 / 1
1983	30	9379	30	30	79	2.6	406	16.2	30	100.0	28 / 2 /
1984	50	8673	50	50	149	3.0	670	16.4	50	100.0	39 / 8 / 3
1985	100	10235	100	100	336	3.4	942	13.7	93	93.0	42 / 38 / 13
1986	105	8780	105	105	359	3.4	697	11.0	96	91.4	63 / 31 / 2
1987	131	9254	131	131	438	3.3	1284	13.7	126	96.2	67 / 46 / 13
1988	131	9160	131	130	421	3.2	1307	13.7	126	96.9	76 / 41 / 9
1989	119	9990	119	119	459	3.9	1191	14.1	117	98.3	61 / 50 / 6

TABLE THREE   PROFILE: BIGHORN SEASONS 1975-1979 – 1984-1989

YEAR	LICENSES AVAILABLE	APPLICATIONS	LICENSES ISSUED	HUNTERS	HUNTING DAYS	AVERAGE PER HUNTER	OTHER RECREATION DAYS	TOTAL DAYS/BIGHORN	HARVEST	HUNTER SUCCESS	BULL/COW/ CALF RATIO
1975	12		12	12					12	100.0	12 / /
1976	12		12	12					12	100.0	12 / /
1977	12	3596	12	12	61	5.1	100	17.9	9	75.0	9 / /
1978	10	2836	10	10	34	3.4	41	7.5	10	100.0	10 / /
1979	2	2176	2	2					1	50.0	1 / /
1984	6	1154	6	6	28	4.7	49	12.8	6	100.0	6 / /
1985	6	1027	6	6	17	2.8	41	9.7	6	100.0	6 / /
1986	7	3143	7	7	13	1.9	25	6.3	6	85.7	6 / /
1987	8	3657	8	8	33	4.1	27	7.5	8	100.0	8 / /
1988	8	3467	8	8	20	2.5	35	6.9	8	100.0	8 / /
1989	8	4197	8	8	33	4.1	38	8.9	8	100.0	8 / /

APPENDIX EIGHT

BOONE AND CROCKETT OFFICIAL SCORING SYSTEM

Reprinted with permission from the Boone and Crockett Club, Dumfries, VA

TYPICAL WHITETAIL AND COUES' DEER

OFFICIAL SCORING SYSTEM FOR NORTH AMERICAN BIG GAME TROPHIES

Records of North American
Big Game

BOONE AND CROCKETT CLUB

P.O. Box 547
Dumfries, VA 22026

Minimum Score:	Awards	All-time
whitetail	160	170
Coues'	100	110

TYPICAL
WHITETAIL AND COUES' DEER

Kind of Deer _____

DETAIL OF POINT MEASUREMENT

	Abnormal Points	
	Right Antler	Left Antler

E. Total of Lengths of Abnormal Points

SEE OTHER SIDE FOR INSTRUCTIONS			Column 1	Column 2	Column 3	Column 4
			Spread Credit	Right Antler	Left Antler	Difference
A. No. Points on Right Antler		No. Points on Left Antler				
B. Tip to Tip Spread		C. Greatest Spread				
D. Inside Spread of Main Beams		(Credit May Equal But Not Exceed Longer Antler)				
F. Length of Main Beam						
G-1. Length of First Point, If Present						
G-2. Length of Second Point						
G-3. Length of Third Point						
G-4. Length of Fourth Point, If Present						
G-5. Length of Fifth Point, If Present						
G-6. Length of Sixth Point, If Present						
G-7. Length of Seventh Point, If Present						
H-1. Circumference at Smallest Place Between Burr and First Point						
H-2. Circumference at Smallest Place Between First and Second Points						
H-3. Circumference at Smallest Place Between Second and Third Points						
H-4. Circumference at Smallest Place Between Third and Fourth Points						
TOTALS						

Enter Total of Columns 1, 2, and 3		Exact Locality Where Killed:	
Subtract Column 4		Date Killed:	By Whom Killed:
Subtotal		Present Owner:	
Subtract (E) Total of Lengths of Abn. Points		Guide Name and Address:	
FINAL SCORE		Remarks:	

320

I certify that I have measured the above trophy on _____ 19 _____

at (address) _____ City _____ State _____
and that these measurements and data are, to the best of my knowledge and belief, made in accordance with the
instructions given.

Witness: _____ Signature: _____

B&C OFFICIAL MEASURER

I.D. Number

INSTRUCTIONS FOR MEASURING TYPICAL WHITETAIL AND COUES' DEER

All measurements must be made with a 1/4-inch flexible steel tape to the nearest one-eighth of an inch. Wherever it is necessary to change direction of measurement, mark a control point and swing tape at this point. (Note: a flexible steel cable can be used to measure points and main beams only.) Enter fractional figures in eighths, without reduction. Official measurements cannot be taken until antlers have dried for at least 60 days after the animal was killed.

A. Number of Points on Each Antler: to be counted a point, the projection must be at least one inch long, with the length exceeding width at one inch or more of length. All points are measured from tip of point to nearest edge of beam as illustrated. Beam tip is counted as a point but not measured as a point.

B. Tip to Tip Spread is measured between tips of main beams.

C. Greatest Spread is measured between perpendiculars at a right angle to the center line of the skull at widest part, whether across main beams or points.

D. Inside Spread of Main Beams is measured at a right angle to the center line of the skull at widest point between main beams. Enter this measurement again as the Spread Credit if it is less than or equal to the length of longer antler; if longer, enter longer antler length for Spread Credit.

E. Total of Lengths of all Abnormal Points: Abnormal Points are those non-typical in location (such as points originating from a point or from bottom or sides of main beam) or extra points beyond the normal pattern of points. Measure in usual manner and enter in appropriate blanks.

F. Length of Main Beam is measured from lowest outside edge of burr over outer curve to the most distant point of what is, or appears to be, the main beam. The point of beginning is that point on the burr where the center line along the outer curve of the beam intersects the burr, then following generally the line of the illustration.

G. 1-2-3-4-5-6-7 Length of Normal Points: Normal points project from the top of the main beam. They are measured from nearest edge of main beam over outer curve to tip. Lay the tape along the outer curve of the beam so that the top edge of the tape coincides with the top edge of the beam on both sides of the point to determine the baseline for point measurements. Record point lengths in appropriate blanks.

H. 1-2-3-4 Circumferences are taken as detailed for each measurement. If brow point is missing, take H-1 and H-2 at smallest place between burr and G-2. If G-4 is missing, take H-4 halfway between G-3 and tip of main beam.

* * * * * * * * * * * * * * * * * *

FAIR CHASE STATEMENT FOR ALL HUNTER-TAKEN TROPHIES

To make use of the following methods shall be deemed as UNFAIR CHASE and unsportsmanlike, and any trophy obtained by use of such means is disqualified from entry.

   I. Spotting or herding game from the air, followed by landing in its vicinity for pursuit;

  II. Herding or pursuing game with motor-powered vehicles;

 III. Use of electronic communications for attracting, locating or observing game, or guiding the hunter to such game;

 IV. Hunting game confined by artificial barriers, including escape-proof fencing; or hunting game transplanted solely for the purpose of commercial shooting.

* * * * * * * * * * * * * * * * * *

I certify that the trophy scored on this chart was not taken in UNFAIR CHASE as defined above by the Boone and Crockett Club. I further certify that it was taken in full compliance with local game laws of the state, province, or territory.

Date: _____ Signature of Hunter: _____

(Have signature notarized by a Notary Public)

NON-TYPICAL WHITETAIL AND COUES' DEER

Records of North American
Big Game

BOONE AND CROCKETT CLUB

P.O. Box 547
Dumfries, VA 22026

Minimum Score: Awards All-time
whitetail   185   195
Coues'   105   120

NON-TYPICAL
WHITETAIL AND COUES' DEER

Kind of Deer _____

DETAIL OF POINT MEASUREMENT

	Abnormal Points	
	Right Antler	Left Antler
E. Total of Lengths of Abnormal Points		

SEE OTHER SIDE FOR INSTRUCTIONS			Column 1	Column 2	Column 3	Column 4
A. No. Points on Right Antler		No. Points on Left Antler	Spread Credit	Right Antler	Left Antler	Difference
B. Tip to Tip Spread		C. Greatest Spread				
D. Inside Spread of Main Beams		(Credit May Equal But Not Exceed Longer Antler)				
F. Length of Main Beam						
G-1. Length of First Point, If Present						
G-2. Length of Second Point						
G-3. Length of Third Point						
G-4. Length of Fourth Point, If Present						
G-5. Length of Fifth Point, If Present						
G-6. Length of Sixth Point, If Present						
G-7. Length of Seventh Point, If Present						
H-1. Circumference at Smallest Place Between Burr and First Point						
H-2. Circumference at Smallest Place Between First and Second Points						
H-3. Circumference at Smallest Place Between Second and Third Points						
H-4. Circumference at Smallest Place Between Third and Fourth Points						
TOTALS						

Enter Total of Columns 1, 2, and 3		Exact Locality Where Killed:	
Subtract Column 4		Date Killed:	By Whom Killed:
Subtotal		Present Owner:	
Add (E) Total of Lengths of Abnormal Points		Guide Name and Address:	
FINAL SCORE		Remarks:	

I certify that I have measured the above trophy on _____ 19 _____

at (address) _____ City _____ State _____
and that these measurements and data are, to the best of my knowledge and belief, made in accordance with the
instructions given.

Witness: _____ Signature: _____

B&C OFFICIAL MEASURER

I.D. Number

<u>INSTRUCTIONS FOR MEASURING NON-TYPICAL WHITETAIL AND COUES' DEER</u>

All measurements must be made with a 1/4-inch flexible steel tape to the nearest one-eighth of an inch. Wherever it is necessary to change direction of measurement, mark a control point and swing tape at this point. (Note: a flexible steel cable can be used to measure points and main beams only.) Enter fractional figures in eighths, without reduction. Official measurements cannot be taken until antlers have dried for at least 60 days after the animal was killed.

A. Number of Points on Each Antler: to be counted a point, the projection must be at least one inch long, with the length exceeding width at one inch or more of length. All points are measured from tip of point to nearest edge of beam as illustrated. Beam tip is counted as a point but not measured as a point.

B. Tip to Tip Spread is measured between tips of main beams.

C. Greatest Spread is measured between perpendiculars at a right angle to the center line of the skull at widest part, whether across main beams or points.

D. Inside Spread of Main Beams is measured at a right angle to the center line of the skull at widest point between main beams. Enter this measurement again as the Spread Credit if it is less than or equal to the length of longer antler; if longer, enter longer antler length for Spread Credit.

E. Total of Lengths of all Abnormal Points: Abnormal Points are those non-typical in location (such as points originating from a point or from bottom or sides of main beam) or extra points beyond the normal pattern of points. Measure in usual manner and enter in appropriate blanks.

F. Length of Main Beam is measured from lowest outside edge of burr over outer curve to the most distant point of what is, or appears to be, the main beam. The point of beginning is that point on the burr where the center line along the outer curve of the beam intersects the burr, then following generally the line of the illustration.

G. 1-2-3-4-5-6-7 Length of Normal Points: Normal points project from the top of the main beam. They are measured from nearest edge of main beam over outer curve to tip. Lay the tape along the outer curve of the beam so that the top edge of the tape coincides with the top edge of the beam on both sides of the point to determine the baseline for point measurement. Record point lengths in appropriate blanks.

H. 1-2-3-4 Circumferences are taken as detailed for each measurement. If brow point is missing, take H-1 and H-2 at smallest place between burr and G-2. If G-4 is missing, take H-4 halfway between G-3 and tip of main beam.

* * * * * * * * * * * * * * * * * * *

FAIR CHASE STATEMENT FOR ALL HUNTER-TAKEN TROPHIES

To make use of the following methods shall be deemed as UNFAIR CHASE and unsportsmanlike, and any trophy obtained by use of such means is disqualified from entry.

    I.   Spotting or herding game from the air, followed by landing in its vicinity for pursuit;

    II. Herding or pursuing game with motor-powered vehicles;

    III. Use of electronic communications for attracting, locating or observing game, or guiding the
         hunter to such game;

    IV. Hunting game confined by artificial barriers, including escape-proof fencing; or hunting game
         transplanted solely for the purpose of commercial shooting.

* * * * * * * * * * * * * * * * * * *

I certify that the trophy scored on this chart was not taken in UNFAIR CHASE as defined above by the Boone and Crockett Club. I further certify that it was taken in full compliance with local game laws of the state, province, or territory.

Date: _____ Signature of Hunter: _____

(Have signature notarized by a Notary Public)

TYPICAL MULE AND BLACKTAIL DEER

OFFICIAL SCORING SYSTEM FOR NORTH AMERICAN BIG GAME TROPHIES

Records of North American
Big Game

BOONE AND CROCKETT CLUB

P.Q. Box 547
Dumfries, VA 22026

Minimum Score:	Awards	All-time
mule	185	195
Columbia	120	130
Sitka	100	108

TYPICAL
MULE AND BLACKTAIL DEER

Kind of Deer _____

DETAIL OF POINT MEASUREMENT

Abnormal Points	
Right Antler	Left Antler

E. Total of Lengths of Abnormal Points

SEE OTHER SIDE FOR INSTRUCTIONS				Column 1	Column 2	Column 3	Column 4
A. No. Points on Right Antler		No. Points on Left Antler		Spread Credit	Right Antler	Left Antler	Difference
B. Tip to Tip Spread		C. Greatest Spread					
D. Inside Spread of Main Beams		(Credit May Equal But Not Exceed Longer Antler)					
F. Length of Main Beam							
G-1. Length of First Point, If Present							
G-2. Length of Second Point							
G-3. Length of Third Point, If Present							
G-4. Length of Fourth Point, If Present							
H-1. Circumference at Smallest Place Between Burr and First Point							
H-2. Circumference at Smallest Place Between First and Second Points							
H-3. Circumference at Smallest Place Between Main Beam and Third Point							
H-4. Circumference at Smallest Place Between Second and Fourth Points							
TOTALS							

Enter Total of Columns 1, 2, and 3		Exact Locality Where Killed:	
Subtract Column 4		Date Killed:	By Whom Killed:
Subtotal		Present Owner:	
Subtract (E) Total of Lengths of Abn. Points		Guide Name and Address:	
FINAL SCORE		Remarks:	

I certify that I have measured the above trophy on _____ _____ 19 _____

at (address) _____ City _____ State _____
and that these measurements and data are, to the best of my knowledge and belief, made in accordance with the
instructions given.

Witness: _____ Signature: _____

B&C OFFICIAL MEASURER [| | | |]

I.D. Number

All measurements must be made with a 1/4-inch flexible steel tape to the nearest one-eighth of an inch. Wherever
it is necessary to change direction of measurement, mark a control point and swing tape at this point. (Note: a
flexible steel cable can be used to take point and beam length measurements only.) Enter fractional figures in
eighths, without reduction. Official measurements cannot be taken until antlers have dried for at least 60 days
after the animal was killed.

A. Number of Points on Each Antler: to be counted a point, the projection must be at least one inch long, with
length exceeding width at one inch or more of length. All points are measured from tip of point to nearest edge
of beam as illustrated. Beam tip is counted as a point but not measured as a point.

B. Tip to Tip Spread is measured between tips of main beams.

C. Greatest Spread is measured between perpendiculars at a right angle to the center line of the skull at widest
part, whether across main beams or points.

D. Inside Spread of Main Beams is measured at a right angle to the center line of the skull at widest point
between main beams. Enter this measurement again as Spread Credit if it is less than or equal to the length of
longer antler; if longer, enter longer antler length for Spread Credit.

E. Total of Lengths of all Abnormal Points: Abnormal Points are those non-typical in location such as points
originating from a point (exception: G-3 originates from G-2 in perfectly normal fashion) or from bottom or sides
of main beam, or any points beyond the normal pattern of five (including beam tip) per antler. Measure each
abnormal point in usual manner and enter in appropriate blanks.

F. Length of Main Beam is measured from lowest outside edge of burr over outer curve to the most distant point of
what is, or appears to be, the Main Beam. The point of beginning is that point on the burr where the center line
along the outer curve of the beam intersects the burr, then following generally the line of the illustration.

G. 1-2-3-4 Length of Normal Points: Normal points are the brow and the upper and lower forks as shown in the
illustration. They are measured from nearest edge of beam over outer curve to tip. Lay the tape along the outer
curve of the beam so that the top edge of the tape coincides with the top edge of the beam on both sides of point
to determine the baseline for point measurement. Record point lengths in appropriate blanks.

H. 1-2-3-4 Circumferences are taken as detailed for each measurement. If brow point is missing, take H-1 and H-
2 at smallest place between burr and G-2. If G-3 is missing, take H-3 halfway between the base and tip of second
point. If G-4 is missing, take H-4 halfway between second point and tip of main beam.

* * * * * * * * * * * * * * * * * *

FAIR CHASE STATEMENT FOR ALL HUNTER-TAKEN TROPHIES

To make use of the following methods shall be deemed as UNFAIR CHASE and unsportsmanlike, and any trophy obtained
by use of such means is disqualified from entry.

   I. Spotting or herding game from the air, followed by landing in its vicinity for pursuit;

  II. Herding or pursuing game with motor-powered vehicles;

 III. Use of electronic communications for attracting, locating or observing game, or guiding the
     hunter to such game;

 IV. Hunting game confined by artificial barriers, including escape-proof fencing; or hunting game
     transplanted solely for the purpose of commercial shooting.

* * * * * * * * * * * * * * * * * *

I certify that the trophy scored on this chart was not taken in UNFAIR CHASE as defined above by the Boone and
Crockett Club. I further certify that it was taken in full compliance with local game laws of the state,
province, or territory.

Date: _____ Signature of Hunter: _____

(Have signature notarized by a Notary Public)

NON-TYPICAL MULE DEER

OFFICIAL SCORING SYSTEM FOR NORTH AMERICAN BIG GAME TROPHIES

Records of North American
Big Game

BOONE AND CROCKETT CLUB

P.Q. Box 547
Dumfries, VA 22026

Minimum Score: Awards All-time
225   240

NON-TYPICAL
MULE DEER

Abnormal Points	
Right Antler	Left Antler

DETAIL OF POINT
MEASUREMENT

E. Total of Lengths
of Abnormal Points

SEE OTHER SIDE FOR INSTRUCTIONS				Column 1	Column 2	Column 3	Column 4
A. No. Points on Right Antler		No. Points on Left Antler		Spread Credit	Right Antler	Left Antler	Difference
B. Tip to Tip Spread		C. Greatest Spread					
D. Inside Spread of Main Beams		(Credit May Equal But Not Exceed Longer Antler)					
F. Length of Main Beam							
G-1. Length of First Point, If Present							
G-2. Length of Second Point							
G-3. Length of Third Point, If Present							
G-4. Length of Fourth Point, If Present							
H-1. Circumference at Smallest Place Between Burr and First Point							
H-2. Circumference at Smallest Place Between First and Second Points							
H-3. Circumference at Smallest Place Between Main Beam and Third Point							
H-4. Circumference at Smallest Place Between Second and Fourth Points							
		TOTALS					

Enter Total of Columns 1, 2, and 3		Exact Locality Where Killed:	
Subtract Column 4		Date Killed:	By Whom Killed:
Subtotal		Present Owner:	
Add (E) Total of Lengths of Abnormal Points		Guide Name and Address:	
FINAL SCORE		Remarks:	

326

I certify that I have measured the above trophy on _____ 19 _____

at (address) _____ City _____ State _____
and that these measurements and data are, to the best of my knowledge and belief, made in accordance with the
instructions given.

Witness: _____ Signature: _____

B&C OFFICIAL MEASURER   [ ][ ][ ][ ]

<u>INSTRUCTIONS FOR MEASURING NON-TYPICAL MULE DEER</u>   I.D. Number

All measurements must be made with a 1/4-inch flexible steel tape to the nearest one-eighth of an inch. Wherever
it is necessary to change direction of measurement, mark a control point and swing tape at this point. (Note: a
flexible steel cable can be used to measure points and main beams only.) Enter fractional figures in eighths,
without reduction. Official measurements cannot be taken until antlers have dried for at least 60 days after the
animal was killed.

A. Number of Points on Each Antler: to be counted a point, the projection must be at least one inch long, with
the length exceeding width at one inch or more of length. All points are measured from tip of point to nearest
edge of beam as illustrated. Beam tip is counted as a point but is not measured as a point.

B. Tip to Tip Spread is measured between tips of main beams.

C. Greatest Spread is measured between perpendiculars at a right angle to the center line of the skull at widest
part, whether across main beams or points.

D. Inside Spread of Main Beams is measured at a right angle to the center line of the skull at widest point
between main beams. Enter this measurement again as the Spread Credit if it is less than or equal to the length
of longer antler; if longer, enter longer antler length for Spread Credit.

E. Total of Lengths of all Abnormal Points: Abnormal Points are those non-typical in location such as points
originating from a point (exception: G-3 originates from G-2 in perfectly normal fashion) or from bottom or sides
of main beam, or any points beyond the normal pattern of five (including beam tip) per antler. Measure each
abnormal point in usual manner and enter in appropriate blanks.

F. Length of Main Beam is measured from lowest outside edge of burr over outer curve to the most distant point of
what is, or appears to be, the main beam. The point of beginning is that point on the burr where the center line
along the outer curve of the beam intersects the burr, then following generally the line of the illustration.

G. 1-2-3-4 Length of Normal Points: Normal points are the brow and the upper and lower forks, as shown in the
illustration. They are measured from nearest edge of main beam over outer curve to tip. Lay the tape along the
outer curve of the beam so that the top edge of the tape coincides with the top edge of the beam on both sides of
point to determine the baseline for point measurement. Record point lengths in appropriate blanks.

H. 1-2-3-4 Circumferences are taken as detailed for each measurement. If brow point is missing, take H-1 and
H-2 at smallest place between burr and G-2. If G-3 is missing, take H-3 halfway between the base and tip of
second point. If G-4 is missing, take H-4 halfway between second point and tip of main beam.

* * * * * * * * * * * * * * * * * *

FAIR CHASE STATEMENT FOR ALL HUNTER-TAKEN TROPHIES

To make use of the following methods shall be deemed as UNFAIR CHASE and unsportsmanlike, and any trophy obtained
by use of such means is disqualified from entry.

    I. Spotting or herding game from the air, followed by landing in its vicinity for pursuit;

   II. Herding or pursuing game with motor-powered vehicles;

  III. Use of electronic communications for attracting, locating or observing game, or guiding the
      hunter to such game;

  IV. Hunting game confined by artificial barriers, including escape-proof fencing; or hunting game
      transplanted solely for the purpose of commercial shooting.

* * * * * * * * * * * * * * * * * *

I certify that the trophy scored on this chart was not taken in UNFAIR CHASE as defined above by the Boone and
Crockett Club. I further certify that it was taken in full compliance with local game laws of the state,
province, or territory.

Date: _____ Signature of Hunter: _____

(Have signature notarized by a Notary Public)

TYPICAL AMERICAN ELK (WAPITI)

TYPICAL
AMERICAN ELK (WAPITI)

OFFICIAL SCORING SYSTEM FOR NORTH AMERICAN BIG GAME TROPHIES

Records of North American
Big Game

BOONE AND CROCKETT CLUB

P.O. Box 547
Dumfries, VA 22026

Minimum Score: Awards All-time
                360   375

DETAIL OF POINT MEASUREMENT

	Abnormal Points	
	Right Antler	Left Antler
E. Total of Lengths of Abnormal Points		

SEE OTHER SIDE FOR INSTRUCTIONS				Column 1	Column 2	Column 3	Column 4
A. No. Points on Right Antler		No. Points on Left Antler		Spread Credit	Right Antler	Left Antler	Difference
B. Tip to Tip Spread		C. Greatest Spread					
D. Inside Spread of Main Beams		(Credit May Equal But Not Exceed Longer Antler)					
F. Length of Main Beam							
G-1. Length of First Point							
G-2. Length of Second Point							
G-3. Length of Third Point							
G-4. Length of Fourth (Royal) Point							
G-5. Length of Fifth Point							
G-6. Length of Sixth Point, If Present							
G-7. Length of Seventh Point, If Present							
H-1. Circumference at Smallest Place Between First and Second Points							
H-2. Circumference at Smallest Place Between Second and Third Points							
H-3. Circumference at Smallest Place Between Third and Fourth Points							
H-4. Circumference at Smallest Place Between Fourth and Fifth Points							
TOTALS							

Enter Total of Columns 1, 2, and 3		Exact Locality Where Killed:	
Subtract Column 4		Date Killed:	By Whom Killed:
Subtotal		Present Owner:	
Subtract (E) Total of Lengths of Abn. Points		Guide Name and Address:	
FINAL SCORE		Remarks:	

328

I certify that I have measured the above trophy on _____ 19 _____

at (address) _____ City _____ State _____
and that these measurements and data are, to the best of my knowledge and belief, made in accordance with the
instructions given.

Witness: _____ Signature _____

B&C OFFICIAL MEASURER

I.D. Number

INSTRUCTIONS FOR MEASURING TYPICAL AMERICAN ELK (WAPITI)

All measurements must be made with a 1/4-inch flexible steel tape to the nearest one-eighth of an inch. Wherever
it is necessary to change direction of measurement, mark a control point and swing tape at this point. (Note: a
flexible steel cable can be used to measure points and main beams only.) Enter fractional figures in eighths,
without reduction. Official measurements cannot be taken until the antlers have dried for at least 60 days after
the animal was killed.

A. Number of Points on Each Antler: to be counted a point, the projection must be at least one inch long, with
length exceeding width at one inch or more of length. All points are measured from tip of point to nearest edge
of beam as illustrated. Beam tip is counted as a point but not measured as a point.

B. Tip to Tip Spread is measured between tips of main beams.

C. Greatest Spread is measured between perpendiculars at a right angle to the center line of the skull at widest
part, whether across main beams or points.

D. Inside Spread of Main Beams is measured at a right angle to the center line of the skull at widest point
between main beams. Enter this measurement again as Spread Credit if it is less than or equal to the length of
longer antler; if longer, enter longer antler length for Spread Credit.

E. Total of Lengths of all Abnormal Points: Abnormal Points are those non-typical in location (such as points
originating from a point or from bottom or sides of main beam) or pattern (extra points, not generally paired).
Measure in usual manner and record in appropriate blanks.

F. Length of Main Beam is measured from lowest outside edge of burr over outer curve to the most distant point of
what is, or appears to be, the main beam. The point of beginning is that point on the burr where the center line
along the outer curve of the beam intersects the burr, then following generally the line of the illustration.

G. 1-2-3-4-5-6-7 Length of Normal Points: Normal points project from the top or front of the main beam in the
general pattern illustrated. They are measured from nearest edge of main beam over outer curve to tip. Lay the
tape along the outer curve of the beam so that the top edge of the tape coincides with the top edge of the beam
on both sides of point to determine the baseline for point measurement. Record point length in appropriate
blanks.

H. 1-2-3-4 Circumferences are taken as detailed for each measurement.

* * * * * * * * * * * * * * * * * *

FAIR CHASE STATEMENT FOR ALL HUNTER-TAKEN TROPHIES

To make use of the following methods shall be deemed as UNFAIR CHASE and unsportsmanlike, and any trophy
obtained by use of such means is disqualified from entry.

   I. Spotting or herding game from the air, followed by landing in its vicinity for pursuit;

   II. Herding or pursuing game with motor-powered vehicles;

   III. Use of electronic communications for attracting, locating or observing game, or guiding the
      hunter to such game;

   IV. Hunting game confined by artificial barriers, including escape-proof fencing; or hunting game
      transplanted solely for the purpose of commercial shooting.

* * * * * * * * * * * * * * * * * *

I certify that the trophy scored on this chart was not taken in UNFAIR CHASE as defined above by the Boone
and Crockett Club. I further certify that it was taken in full compliance with local game laws of the
state, province, or territory.

Date _____ Signature of Hunter _____

(Have signature notarized by a Notary Public)

NON-TYPICAL AMERICAN ELK (WAPITI)

Records of North American
Big Game

BOONE AND CROCKETT CLUB

P.O. Box 547
Dumfries, VA 22026

Minimum Score: Awards All-time
385   385

NON-TYPICAL
AMERICAN ELK (WAPITI)

Abnormal Points	
Right Antler	Left Antler

DETAIL OF POINT MEASUREMENT

E. Total of Lengths of Abnormal Points

SEE OTHER SIDE FOR INSTRUCTIONS			Column 1	Column 2	Column 3	Column 4
A. No. Points on Right Antler		No. Points on Left Antler	Spread Credit	Right Antler	Left Antler	Difference
B. Tip to Tip Spread		C. Greatest Spread				
D. Inside Spread of Main Beams		(Credit May Equal But Not Exceed Longer Antler)				
F. Length of Main Beam						
G-1. Length of First Point						
G-2. Length of Second Point						
G-3. Length of Third Point						
G-4. Length of Fourth (Royal) Point						
G-5. Length of Fifth Point						
G-6. Length of Sixth Point, If Present						
G-7. Length of Seventh Point, If Present						
H-1. Circumference at Smallest Place Between First and Second Points						
H-2. Circumference at Smallest Place Between Second and Third Points						
H-3. Circumference at Smallest Place Between Third and Fourth Points						
H-4. Circumference at Smallest Place Between Fourth and Fifth Points						
TOTALS						

Enter Total of Columns 1, 2, and 3		Exact Locality Where Killed:	
Subtract Column 4		Date Killed:	By Whom Killed:
Subtotal		Present Owner:	
Add (E) Total of Lengths of Abnormal Points		Guide Name and Address:	
FINAL SCORE		Remarks:	

I certify that I have measured the above trophy on _____ 19 _____

at (address) _____ City _____ State _____
and that these measurements and data are, to the best of my knowledge and belief, made in accordance with the
instructions given.

Witness: _____ Signature _____

B&C OFFICIAL MEASURER

I.D. Number

INSTRUCTIONS FOR MEASURING NON-TYPICAL AMERICAN ELK (WAPITI)

All measurements must be with a 1/4-inch flexible steel tape to the nearest one-eighth of an inch. Wherever
it is necessary to change direction of measurement, mark a control point and swing tape at this point. (Note: a
flexible steel cable can be used to measure points and main beams only.) Enter fractional figures in eighths,
without reduction. Official measurements cannot be taken until the antlers have dried for at least 60 days after
the animal was killed.

A. Number of Points on Each Antler: to be counted a point, the projection must be at least one inch long, with
length exceeding width at one inch or more of length. All points are measured from tip of point to nearest edge
of beam as illustrated. Beam tip is counted as a point but not measured as a point.

B. Tip to Tip Spread is measured between tips of main beams.

C. Greatest Spread is measured between perpendiculars at a right angle to the center line of the skull at widest
part, whether across main beams or points.

D. Inside Spread of Main Beams is measured at a right angle to the center line of the skull at widest point
between main beams. Enter this measurement again as the Spread Credit if it is less than or equal to the length
of longer antler; if longer, enter longer antler length for Spread Credit.

E. Total of Lengths of all Abnormal Points: Abnormal Points are those non-typical in location (such as points
originating from a point or from bottom or sides of main beam) or pattern (extra points, not generally paired).
Measure in usual manner and record in appropriate blanks.

F. Length of Main Beam is measured from lowest outside edge of burr over outer curve to the most distant point of
what is, or appears to be, the main beam. The point of beginning is that point on the burr where the center line
along the outer curve of the beam intersects the burr, then following generally the line of the illustration.

G. 1-2-3-4-5-6-7 Length of Normal Points: Normal points project from the top or front of the main beam in the
general pattern illustrated. They are measured from nearest edge of main beam over outer curve to tip. Lay the
tape along the outer curve of the beam so that the top edge of the tape coincides with the top edge of the beam
on both sides of point to determine the baseline for point measurement. Record point length in appropriate
blanks.

H. 1-2-3-4 Circumferences are taken as detailed for each measurement.

* * * * * * * * * * * * * * * * * *

FAIR CHASE STATEMENT FOR ALL HUNTER-TAKEN TROPHIES

To make use of the following methods shall be deemed as UNFAIR CHASE and unsportsmanlike, and any trophy
obtained by use of such means is disqualified from entry.

  I. Spotting or herding game from the air, followed by landing in its vicinity for pursuit;
  II. Herding or pursuing game with motor-powered vehicles;
  III. Use of electronic communications for attracting, locating or observing game, or guiding the
       hunter to such game;
  IV. Hunting game confined by artificial barriers, including escape-proof fencing; or hunting game
      transplanted solely for the purpose of commercial shooting.

* * * * * * * * * * * * * * * * * *

I certify that the trophy scored on this chart was not taken in UNFAIR CHASE as defined above by the Boone
and Crockett Club. I further certify that it was taken in full compliance with local game laws of the
state, province, or territory.

Date _____._____ Signature of Hunter _____

(Have signature notarized by a Notary Public)

PRONGHORN

OFFICIAL SCORING SYSTEM FOR NORTH AMERICAN BIG GAME TROPHIES

Records of North American
Big Game

BOONE AND CROCKETT CLUB

P.O. Box 547
Dumfries, VA 22026

Minimum Score: Awards All-time
80   82

PRONGHORN

SEE OTHER SIDE FOR INSTRUCTIONS		Column 1	Column 2	Column 3
A. Tip to Tip Spread		Right Horn	Left Horn	Difference
B. Inside Spread of Main Beams				
IF Inside Spread Exceeds Longer Horn, Enter Difference				
C. Length of Horn				
D-1. Circumference of Base				
D-2. Circumference at First Quarter				
D-3. Circumference at Second Quarter				
D-4. Circumference at Third Quarter				
E. Length of Prong				
TOTALS				

Enter Total of Columns 1 and 2		Exact Locality Where Killed:
Subtract Column 3		Date Killed: / By Whom Killed:
FINAL SCORE		Present Owner:
		Guide Name and Address:
		Remarks:

I certify that I have measured the above trophy on _____ 19 _____

at (Address) _____ (City) _____ (State) _____

and that these measurements and data are, to the best of my knowledge and belief, made in accordance with the

instructions given.

Witness: _____ Signature: _____

B&C OFFICIAL MEASURER

I.D. Number

All measurements must be made with a 1/4-inch, flexible steel tape to the nearest one-eighth of an inch. Wherever it is necessary to change direction of measurement, mark a control point and swing tape at this point. Enter fractional figures in eighths, without reduction. Official measurement cannot be taken until horns have dried for at least sixty days after the animal was killed.

A. Tip to Tip Spread is measured between tips of horns.

B. Inside Spread of Main Beams is measured at a right angle to the center line of the skull, at widest point between main beams.

C. Length of Horn is measured on the outside curve on the general line illustrated. The line taken will vary with different heads, depending on the direction of their curvature. Measure along the center of the outer curve from tip of horn to a point in line with the lowest edge of the base, using a straight edge to establish the line end.

D-1 Measure around base of horn at a right angle to long axis. Tape must be in contact with the lowest circumference of the horn in which there are no serrations.

D. 2-3-4 Divide measurement C of longer horn by four. Starting at base, mark both horns at these quarters (even though the other horn is shorter) and measure circumferences at these marks. If the prong interferes with D-2, move the measurement down to just below the swelling of the prong. If the prong interferes with D-3, move the measurement up to just above the swelling of the prong.

E. Length of Prong: Measure from the tip of the prong along the upper edge of the outer curve to the horn; then continue around the horn to a point at the rear of the horn where a straight edge across the back of both horns touches the horn, with the latter part being at a right angle to the long axis of horn.

* * * * * * * * * * * * * * * * * *

FAIR CHASE STATEMENT FOR ALL HUNTER-TAKEN TROPHIES

To make use of the following methods shall be deemed as UNFAIR CHASE and unsportsmanlike, and any trophy obtained by use of such means is disqualified from entry.

    I. Spotting or herding game from the air, followed by landing in its vicinity for pursuit;

    II. Herding or pursuing game with motor-powered vehicles;

    III. Use of electronic communications for attracting, locating or observing game, or guiding the hunter to such game;

    IV. Hunting game confined by artificial barriers, including escape-proof fencing; or hunting game transplanted solely for the purpose of commercial shooting.

* * * * * * * * * * * * * * * * * *

I certify that the trophy scored on this chart was not taken in UNFAIR CHASE as defined above by the Boone and Crockett Club. I further certify that it was taken in full compliance with local game laws of the state, province, or territory.

Date: _____ Signature of Hunter: _____

(Have Signature Notarized by a Notary Public)

SHEEP

OFFICIAL SCORING SYSTEM FOR NORTH AMERICAN BIG GAME TROPHIES

Records of North American
Big Game

BOONE AND CROCKETT CLUB

P.O. Box 547
Dumfries, VA 22026

Minimum Score:	Awards	All-time
bighorn	175	180
desert	165	168
Dall's	165	170
Stone's	165	170

SHEEP

Kind of Sheep _____

MEASURE TO
A POINT IN
LINE WITH
HORN TIP

SEE OTHER SIDE FOR INSTRUCTIONS		Column 1	Column 2	Column 3
A. Greatest Spread (Is Often Tip to Tip Spread)		Right Horn	Left Horn	Difference
B. Tip to Tip Spread				
C. Length of Horn				
D-1. Circumference of Base				
D-2. Circumference at First Quarter				
D-3. Circumference at Second Quarter				
D-4. Circumference at Third Quarter				
TOTALS				

Enter Total of Columns 1 and 2		Exact Locality Where Killed:
Subtract Column 3		Date Killed: / By Whom Killed:
FINAL SCORE		Present Owner:
		Guide Name and Address:
		Remarks:

I certify that I have measured the above trophy on _____ 19 _____

at (Address) _____ (City) _____ (State) _____

and that these measurements and data are, to the best of my knowledge and belief, made in accordance with the

instructions given.

Witness: _____ Signature: _____

B&C OFFICIAL MEASURER

I.D. Number

334

INSTRUCTIONS FOR MEASURING SHEEP

All measurements must be made with a 1/4-inch, flexible steel tape to the nearest one-eighth of an inch. Wherever it is necessary to change direction of measurement, mark a control point and swing tape at this point. Enter fractional figures in eighths, without reduction. Official measurement cannot be taken until horns have dried for at least sixty days after the animal was killed.

A. Greatest Spread is measured between perpendiculars at a right angle to the center line of the skull.

B. Tip to Tip Spread is measured between tips of horns.

C. Length of Horn is measured from the lowest point in front on outer curve to a point in line with tip. Do not press tape into depressions. The low point of the outer curve of the horn is considered to be the low point of the frontal portion of the horn, situated above and slightly medial to the eye socket (not the outside edge). Use a straight edge, perpendicular to horn axis, to end measurement on "broomed" horns.

D-1 Circumference of Base is measured at a right angle to axis of horn. Do not follow irregular edge of horn; the line of measurement must be entirely on horn material, not the jagged edge often noted.

D. 2-3-4 Divide measurement C of longer horn by four. Starting at base, mark both horns at these quarters (even though the other horn is shorter) and measure circumferences at these marks, with measurements taken at right angles to horn axis.

* * * * * * * * * * * * * * * * * * *

FAIR CHASE STATEMENT FOR ALL HUNTER-TAKEN TROPHIES

To make use of the following methods shall be deemed as UNFAIR CHASE and unsportsmanlike, and any trophy obtained by use of such means is disqualified from entry.

   I. Spotting or herding game from the air, followed by landing in its vicinity for pursuit;

   II. Herding or pursuing game with motor-powered vehicles;

   III. Use of electronic communications for attracting, locating or observing game, or guiding the hunter to such game;

   IV. Hunting game confined by artificial barriers, including escape-proof fencing; or hunting game transplanted solely for the purpose of commercial shooting.

* * * * * * * * * * * * * * * * * * *

I certify that the trophy scored on this chart was not taken in UNFAIR CHASE as defined above by the Boone and Crockett Club. I further certify that it was taken in full compliance with local game laws of the state, province, or territory.

Date: _____   Signature of Hunter: _____

(Have Signature Notarized by a Notary Public)

MOOSE

OFFICIAL SCORING SYSTEM FOR NORTH AMERICAN BIG GAME TROPHIES

Records of North American
Big Game

BOONE AND CROCKETT CLUB

P.O. Box 547
Dumfries, VA 22026

Minimum Score:	Awards	All-time		Kind of Moose _____
Alaska-Yukon	210	224	MOOSE	
Canada	185	195		
Wyoming	140	155		

DETAIL OF POINT MEASUREMENT

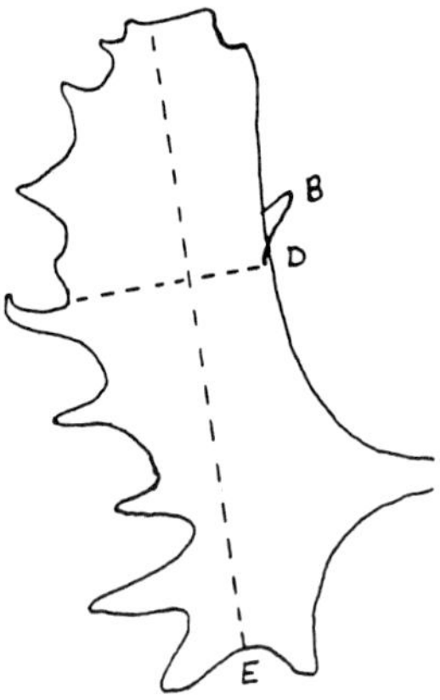

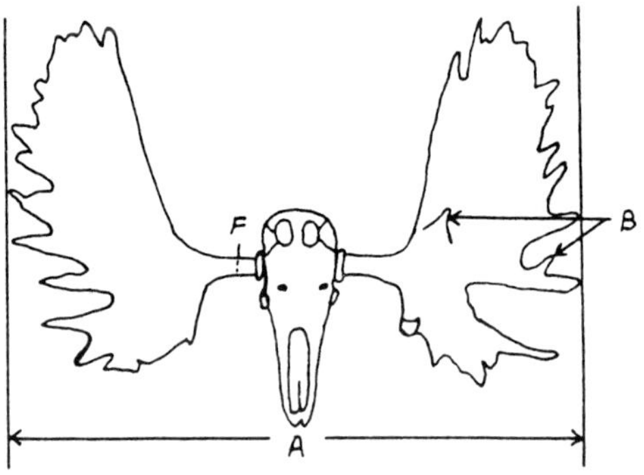

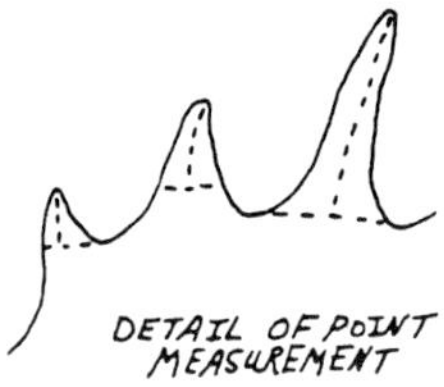

SEE OTHER SIDE FOR INSTRUCTIONS	Column 1	Column 2	Column 3	Column 4
A. Greatest Spread		Right Antler	Left Antler	Difference
B. Number of Abnormal Points on Both Antlers				
C. Number of Normal Points				
D. Width of Palm				
E. Length of Palm Including Brow Palm				
F. Circumference of Beam at Smallest Place				
TOTALS				

Enter Total of Columns 1, 2, and 3		Exact Locality Where Killed:
Subtract Column 4		Date Killed: By Whom Killed:
FINAL SCORE		Present Owner:
		Guide Name and Address:
		Remarks:

I certify that I have measured the above trophy on _____ 19 _____

at (Address) _____ (City) _____ (State) _____

and that these measurements and data are, to the best of my knowledge and belief, made in accordance with the

instructions given.

Witness: _____ Signature: _____

B&C OFFICIAL MEASURER

I.D. Number

All measurements must be made with a 1/4-inch flexible steel tape to the nearest one-eighth of an inch. Enter fractional figures in eighths, without reduction. Official measurements cannot be taken until antlers have dried for at least sixty days after animal was killed.

A. Greatest Spread is measured between perpendiculars in a straight line at a right angle to the center line of the skull.

B. Number of Abnormal Points on Both Antlers: Abnormal points are those projections originating from normal points or from the upper or lower palm surface, or from the inner edge of palm (see illustration). Abnormal points must be at least one inch long, with length exceeding width at one inch or more of length.

C. Number of Normal Points: Normal points originate from the outer edge of palm. To be counted a point, a projection must be at least one inch long, with the length exceeding width at one inch or more of length.

D. Width of Palm is taken in contact with the under surface of palm, at a right angle to the length of palm measurement line. The line of measurement should begin and end at the midpoint of the palm edge, which gives credit for the desirable character of palm thickness.

E. Length of Palm Including Brow Palm is taken in contact with the surface along the underside of the palm, parallel to the inner edge, from dips between points at the top to dips between points (if present) at the bottom. If a bay is present, measure across the open bay if the proper line of measurement, parallel to inner edge, follows this path. The line of measurement should begin and end at the midpoint of the palm edge, which gives credit for the desirable character of palm thickness.

F. Circumference of Beam at Smallest Place is taken as illustrated.

* * * * * * * * * * * * * * * * * *

FAIR CHASE STATEMENT FOR ALL HUNTER-TAKEN TROPHIES

To make use of the following methods shall be deemed as UNFAIR CHASE and unsportsmanlike, and any trophy obtained by use of such means is disqualified from entry.

I. Spotting or herding game from the air, followed by landing in its vicinity for pursuit;

II. Herding or pursuing game with motor-powered vehicles;

III. Use of electronic communications for attracting, locating or observing game, or guiding the hunter to such game;

IV. Hunting game confined by artificial barriers, including escape-proof fencing; or hunting game transplanted solely for the purpose of commercial shooting.

* * * * * * * * * * * * * * * * * *

I certify that the trophy scored on this chart was not taken in UNFAIR CHASE as defined above by the Boone and Crockett Club. I further certify that it was taken in full compliance with local game laws of the state, province, or territory.

Date: _____ Signature of Hunter: _____

(Have Signature Notarized by a Notary Public)

COMPARISON OF HUNTER EXPENDITURES – 1986 BIG GAME SEASONS

	1986 DEER GUN	1986 PRONGHORN GUN	1986 BIGHORN	1986 ELK	1986 MOOSE
Licenses Sold	75848	630	7	40	105
Variable Expenses					
Food and Beverages	23.97	22.78	73.00	106.23	52.24
Lodging	5.47	9.18	36.40	64.43	23.99
Transportation	44.90	35.17	57.00	103.52	66.79
Ammunition	11.92	9.50	36.00	30.60	16.48
Access Fees	0.28	0.47	0.00	1.79	2.93
Meat Processing	28.34	10.08	40.00	73.19	86.19
Film	1.00	1.92	16.40	11.15	10.89
Taxidermy	0.00	34.03	307.00	148.75	83.80
Other	6.18	1.72	10.00	6.25	3.82
Total Variable Expenses	122.05	124.85	575.80	545.91	347.14
Daily Variable Expenses	38.92	89.86	473.40	201.96	150.75
Fixed Expenses					
Arrows	0.00	0.00	0.00	0.00	2.17
Bows and Guns	42.43	23.62	216.67	95.30	115.86
Camping Equipment	9.74	1.56	66.67	40.50	5.32
Clothing	15.45	7.93	56.67	47.27	14.52
Vehicles, Campers	386.69	434.45	5,400.00	76.00	955.52
Other	4.19	13.09	33.33	19.00	18.42
Total Fixed Expenses	474.27	480.67	5,773.33	278.07	1,111.80
Daily Fixed Expenses	171.95	409.60	5,694.67	136.46	584.92
Total Seasonal Expenses	597.18	605.52	6,425.33	804.11	1,492.10
Daily Total	211.16	499.46	6,716.00	370.47	738.33
Average Man Days	4.47	1.79	1.80	5.10	3.42

ALL FIGURES ARE ACTUAL DOLLARS.

LOCATIONS AND DESCRIPTIONS OF WILDLIFE MANAGEMENT AREAS

Following is a list of State Wildlife Management Areas. Each area is numbered to match the approximate location of the number on the map. The name of each area, acreage, location, most common game species, and if fishing is available is listed for each area. Unless otherwise specified, the areas are open to hunting and fishing. Check the current hunting and fishing proclamations for details. Many of the areas also provide hunting or trapping for nongame species and furbearers. Most of the areas are ideal for nature study, hiking, and primitive camping. Areas marked with an asterisk are leased to the Game and Fish Department by other agencies for management.

1. *Trenton WMA - 2,647 acres; adjacent to Trenton. Along Missouri River and Lake Sakakawea and provides fishing, waterfowl, deer, and pheasants.
2. *Lewis and Clark WMA - 7,835 acres; 6 miles southwest of Williston. Along Missouri River and Lake Sakakawea and provides fishing, waterfowl, deer, and pheasants.
3. Overlook WMA - 32 acres; 6½ miles north of Cartwright. Deer.
4. *Tobacco Garden WMA - 399 acres; 25 miles northeast of Watford City. Fronts on Lake Sakakawea and provides fishing, waterfowl, deer, sharptails, pheasants, Huns.
5. *Hofflund WMA - 1,558 acres; 15 miles southeast of Ray. Fronts on Lake Sakakawea and provides fishing, waterfowl, deer, sharptails, pheasants, Huns.
6. *Sand Creek WMA - 661 acres; 8 miles west and 4 miles north of Charlson. Fronts on Lake Sakakawea and provides fishing, sharptails, deer, pheasants.
7. *Antelope Creek WMA - 963 acres; 12 miles northwest of New Town. Fronts on Lake Sakakawea and provides fishing, waterfowl, deer, sharptails, pheasants, Huns.
8. *Van Hook WMA - 4,512 acres; 5 miles east and 2 miles south of New Town. Fronts on Lake Sakakawea and provides fishing, waterfowl, deer, pheasants, sharptails, Huns.
9. *Deep Water Creek WMA - 2,447 acres; 15 miles south of Parshall. Fronts on Lake Sakakawea and provides fishing, waterfowl, deer, sharptails, pheasants, Huns.
10. *Beaver Creek WMA - 298 acres; 12 miles north of Zap. Fronts on Lake Sakakawea and provides fishing, waterfowl, deer, pheasants, sharptails, Huns.
11. *Hille WMA - 2,989 acres; 14 miles north of Beulah. Fronts on Lake Sakakawea and provides fishing, waterfowl, deer, sharptails, pheasants, Huns.
12. *Douglas Creek WMA - 1,980 acres; two units, 2½ miles south and 6 miles east of Emmet. Fronts on Lake Sakakawea and provides fishing, waterfowl, deer, sharptails, pheasants, Huns.
13. *deTrobriand WMA - 2,020 acres; 4 miles south of Garrison. Fronts on Lake Sakakawea and provides fishing, waterfowl, sharptails, pheasants, deer, Huns.
14. *Custer Mine WMA - 694 acres; 5 miles east and 1 mile south of Garrison. Deer, pheasants, Huns, sharptails.
15. *Audubon WMA - 11,285 acres; 8 miles east of Garrison. Fronts on Lake Audubon and provides fishing, waterfowl, deer, sharptails, pheasants, Huns.
16. *Wolf Creek WMA - 4,772 acres; 2 miles west of Coleharbor. Fronts on Lake Sakakawea and provides fishing, waterfowl, pheasants, sharptails, deer, Huns.
17. *Riverdale WMA - 2,198 acres; 2 miles southwest of Riverdale. Missouri River bottoms provides fishing, pheasants, squirrels, rabbits, sharptails, deer (shotgun slug, muzzleloader, handguns, and archery for deer only).
18. Lewis and Clark WMA - 121 acres; 1 mile west of Washburn. Deer, squirrels, turkeys, fishing.

19. Smith Grove WMA - 24 acres; 1½ miles south of Sanger. River bottom woodland study area, no camping, no hunting.
20. Square Butte WMA - 38 acres; 2 miles south and 2 miles east of Price. River bottom woodland study area. Closed to hunting.
21. *Oahe WMA - 23,491 acres; along Missouri River and Oahe Reservoir about 8 miles south of Bismarck and Mandan. Deer, pheasants, cottontails, turkeys, sharptails, squirrels, fishing.
22. Morton County WMA - 642 acres; 11 miles south and ½ mile east of Mandan. Sharptails, pheasants, Huns, cottontails, deer.
23. Lake Patricia WMA - 631 acres; 2 miles east of Flasher. Pheasants, sharptails, Huns, deer (shotgun slug, muzzleloader, and archery for deer only). Closed to waterfowl hunting.
24. Froelich Dam WMA - 299 acres; 9 miles north and 2 miles west of Selfridge. Fishing, waterfowl, sharptails.
25. Otter Creek WMA - 320 acres; 6 miles north and 4 miles east of Lark. Deer, sharptails.
26. N. Lemmon Lake WMA - 110 acres; 4½ miles north of Lemmon, S.Dak. Fishing, waterfowl.
27. Dog Town WMA - 37 acres; 13 miles north and 5 miles east of Haynes. Prairie dogs.
28. Indian Creek WMA - 1,174 acres; 3 miles west and 5 miles south of Regent. Fishing, waterfowl, pheasants, Huns.
29. Cedar Lake WMA - 818 acres; 16 miles south and 5 miles west of New England. Waterfowl, deer, pheasants (parts closed to hunting).
30. Speck Davis Pond WMA - 160 acres; 10 miles west, 1 mile south, 6 miles west, and 4 miles north of Amidon. Fishing, sharptails.
31. Camel Hump Lake WMA - 112 acres; ½ mile east of Sentinel Butte on Interstate 94. Fishing, waterfowl.
32. Killdeer Mountains WMA - 6,731 acres; 10 miles west and 5 miles north of Killdeer. Sharptails, deer, turkeys, pheasants.
33. *N. Beulah Mine WMA - 2,018 acres; 2 miles north and 1½ miles east of Beulah. Sharptails, pheasants, Huns, deer (part closed to hunting).
34. Golden Valley WMA - 160 acres; 8 miles north and 1 mile east of Golden Valley. Sharptails, deer.
35. Arroda Lake WMA - 384 acres; 1 mile east of Fort Clark. Fishing, deer, pheasants, sharptails, waterfowl.
36. Crown Butte Lake WMA - 84 acres; 4 miles west of I-94 Exit 30 on north frontage road. Fishing.
37. Sweet Briar Lake WMA - 888 acres; 18 miles west of Mandan on I-94. Fishing, waterfowl, Huns.
38. Fish Creek WMA - 190 acres; 8 miles south, 2 miles east, and 1 mile south of I-94 Exit 28. Fishing, sharptails.
39. Storm Creek WMA - 480 acres; 2 miles north, 1 mile west, ½ mile north of I-94 Exit 25. Fishing, waterfowl, sharptails, Huns.
40. Heart Butte Reservoir WMA - 5,500 acres; 16 miles south of Glen Ullin. Fishing, waterfowl, deer, sharptails, pheasants, Huns.
41. Blacktail Dam WMA - 46 acres; 17 miles north, 5 miles west, ½ mile north of Williston. Fishing.
42. Blue Ridge WMA - 240 acres; 1½ miles east and 4 miles north of Appam. Waterfowl.
43. McGregor Dam WMA - 191 acres; 1 mile southwest of McGregor. Fishing, waterfowl.
44. Short Creek WMA - 132 acres; 5 miles north of Columbus. Fishing, waterfowl.
45. Leaf Mountain WMA - 160 acres; 11 miles north and 1½ miles east of Battleview. Deer, sharptails, waterfowl.
46. Smishek Lake WMA - 174 acres; 4 miles north of Powers Lake. Fishing, waterfowl.
47. White Earth Valley WMA - 280 acres; two units; 7½ miles

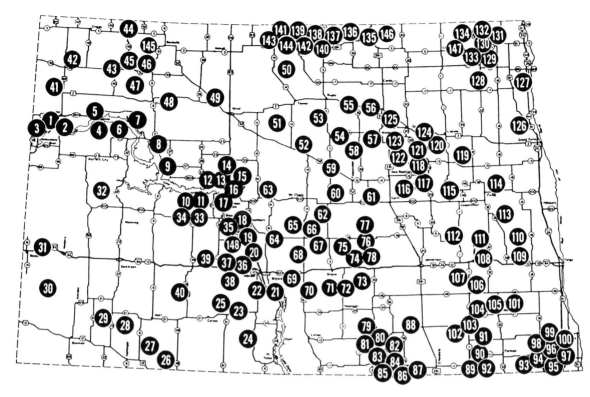

north of White Earth and 2 miles south of White Earth. Deer, cottontails, pheasants, fishing.

48. Palermo WMA - 40 acres; 1½ miles southwest of Palermo. Waterfowl.

49. Foxholm WMA - 40 acres; 2 miles northwest of Foxholm. Deer, sharptails.

50. Upham WMA - 78 acres; 7 miles east of Upham. Goose pass, deer.

51. Heffner Lake WMA - 277 acres; 11 miles east and 4 miles north of Verendrye. Waterfowl.

52. Round Lake Township WMA - 160 acres; 11 miles north and 3½ miles east of Drake. Deer, sharptails.

53. Balta WMA - 105 acres; ½ mile south of Balta. Fishing, waterfowl.

54. Buffalo Lake WMA - 855 acres; 5 miles west of Esmond. Waterfowl, fishing (part closed to hunting).

55. Knox Slough WMA - 518 acres; 1 mile west of Knox. Waterfowl, Huns.

56. Nesvig WMA - 162 acres; 1½ miles southeast of Leeds. Waterfowl, Huns.

57. Minnewaukan WMA - 160 acres; 6 miles west and 4 miles south of Minnewaukan. Waterfowl.

58. Lake Legreid WMA - 200 acres; 1 mile south, 5 miles west, ½ mile south of Maddock. Waterfowl, Huns.

59. Harvey Dam WMA - 425 acres; ½ mile southeast of Harvey. Fishing, waterfowl.

60. Wells County WMA - 637 acres; 7 miles north of Hurdsfield. Deer, Huns, sharptails, pheasants.

61. Sykeston Dam WMA - 54 acres; 1 mile north of Sykeston. Fishing, waterfowl.

62. Karl T. Frederick WMA - 400 acres; 2 miles west, 7 miles south, and ½ mile west of Hurdsfield. Watefowl, deer, sharptails, Huns, pheasants.

63. Blue Lake WMA - 13 acres; 5 miles north, 2½ miles west, and ½ mile south of Mercer. Waterfowl.

64. Wilton Mine WMA - 302 acres; 1 mile east of Wilton.

Sharptails, pheasants, deer, Huns, cottontails.

65. Bunker Lake WMA - 161 acres; 3 miles west, 6 miles north, and ½ mile west of Wing. Waterfowl.

66. Phoenix Township WMA - 80 acres; 5 miles north and 4½ miles east of Wing. Waterfowl.

67. Arena Lake WMA - 800 acres; 1 mile south and ½ mile east of Arena. Waterfowl.

68. *Rice Lake WMA - 976 acres; 10 miles north of Sterling. Waterfowl, deer.

69. McKenzie Slough WMA - 682 acres; ½ mile south of McKenzie. Waterfowl, Huns, pheasants.

70. Moffit WMA - 160 acres; 3 miles south and ½ mile east of Moffit. Sharptails, Huns, pheasants, deer.

71. Long Lake WMA - 320 acres; 5 miles south of Steele. Huns.

72. Dawson WMA - 2,951 acres; 6 miles south of Dawson. Deer, sharptails, pheasants.

73. Alkaline Lake WMA - 47 acres; 11 miles south and 1 mile east of Tappen. Waterfowl.

74. McPhail WMA - 171 acres; 5 miles north, 1 mile west, 2 miles north, and ½ mile west of Tappen. Waterfowl.

75. Horsehead Lake WMA - 437 acres; 1 mile west and 6 miles south of Robinson. Waterfowl, Huns, sharptails, sandhill cranes.

76. Lake Williams WMA - 44 acres; ½ mile south of Lake Williams. Fishing.

77. Frettim Township WMA - 80 acres; 6 miles north of Lake Williams. Waterfowl.

78. Chase Lake WMA - 116 acres; 7 miles south, 7 miles west, and 1 mile south of Woodworth. Waterfowl.

79. Logan County WMA - 598 acres; 5 miles west and 6 miles north of Lehr. Waterfowl, deer.

80. Lehr WMA - 611 acres; 2 miles east and 1 mile south of Lehr. Waterfowl, deer, Huns.

81. Green Lake WMA - 101 acres; 5 miles east and 3½ miles south of Wishek. Fishing, waterfowl.

82. McIntosh County WMA - 80 acres; 9 miles east and

8½ miles south of Lehr. Waterfowl.

83. Ashley WMA - 80 acres; 8 miles northeast of Ashley. Waterfowl.

84. Kisselberry WMA - 120 acres; 2½ miles east and 1 mile north of Ashley. Waterfowl.

85. Camp Lake WMA - 799 acres; 12 miles east and 5 miles south of Ashley. Waterfowl, deer, pheasants.

86. Coldwater Lake WMA - 331 acres; 14 miles east, 2 miles south, and ½ mile east of Ashley. Waterfowl, fishing.

87. Johnson's Gulch WMA - 1,402 acres; ½ mile east of Junction Hwys. 11 & 56, 2 miles south, 1 mile east. Deer, squirrels, sharptails, cottontails, waterfowl.

88. Kulm Dam WMA - 39 acres; 7 miles east and 2 miles north of Kulm. Fishing, waterfowl.

89. Hyatt Slough WMA - 1,354 acres; 1 mile west and 4 miles south of Ludden. Waterfowl, pheasants, deer.

90. Taayer Lake WMA - 80 acres; 8 miles east of Oakes. Waterfowl.

91. Crete Slough WMA - 151 acres; 1 mile north and 3½ miles east of Crete. Waterfowl.

92. Meszaros Slough WMA - 598 acres; 3 miles south and 3 miles west of Cogswell. Waterfowl, pheasants.

93. Tewaukon WMA - 1,284 acres; 3 miles south of Cayuga. Waterfowl, deer, pheasants, fishing.

94. Park Lake WMA - 160 acres; 6 miles south and 3 miles west of Lidgerwood. Pheasants.

95. Grant Township WMA - 160 acres; 4 miles west and 1 mile south of Lidgerwood. Waterfowl, pheasants.

96. Stack Slough WMA - 597 acres; 1 mile north and 4 miles west of Hankinson. Waterfowl, pheasants.

97. Mud Lake WMA - 351 acres; 2 miles southwest of Hankinson. Waterfowl, pheasants.

98. Swan Lake WMA - 289 acres; ½ mile east of Lidgerwood. Waterfowl, pheasants.

99. Wild Rice WMA - 2,089 acres; 1 mile west and 1 mile north of Lidgerwood. Waterfowl, pheasants.

100. Mooreton Pond WMA - 57 acres; 1 mile east of Mooreton. Fishing.

101. Mirror Pool WMA - 547 acres; 5 miles east, 4½ miles south, and 2 miles east of Sheldon. Deer, fishing, squirrels, turkeys.

102. Cottonwood Creek (includes Cottonwood Creek Recreation Area and Cottonwood Creek) WMA - 1,774 acres; 3 miles south of LaMoure. Fishing, waterfowl (portion of area waterfowl rest area).

103. Seth Gordon WMA - 482 acres; 7 miles east and 1 mile south of LaMoure. Waterfowl, deer.

104. Englevale Slough WMA - 160 acres; 3 miles north and 2½ miles west of Englevale. Waterfowl rest area.

105. Fort Ransom WMA - 230 acres; 1 mile southwest of Fort Ransom. Deer, squirrels.

106. Clausen Springs WMA - 540 acres; 2½ miles east of Hastings. Fishing, waterfowl.

107. Moon Lake Fishing Access - 16 acres; 2 miles west, 5½ miles south, 4 miles west, and 2 miles north of Valley City. Fishing.

108. Koldok WMA - 214 acres; 2½ miles east of Oriska. Waterfowl.

109. Magnolia WMA - 103 acres; 5 miles east of Buffalo. Waterfowl, Huns.

110. Erie Dam and Recreation Area - 1,031 acres; 1 mile south and 1 mile west of Erie. Fishing, waterfowl, deer, pheasants, Huns (part closed to hunting).

111. Valley City WMA - 799 acres; 6 miles north, 2 miles east, and ½ mile south of Valley City. Waterfowl, Huns.

112. Ray Holland Marsh WMA - 201 acres; 1 mile north, 3 miles west, and 2 miles north of Rogers. Waterfowl, Huns.

113. Fuller's Lake WMA - 720 acres; 6 miles east and 1 mile south of Hope. Waterfowl, deer, Huns, pheasants.

114. Golden Lake WMA - 579 acres; 10 miles east and 3 miles north of Finley. Fishing, waterfowl.

115. Sibley Lake WMA - 103 acres; 1 mile north, 4 miles south, and 1 mile west of Binford. Waterfowl, deer, Huns.

116. Rusten Slough WMA - 160 acres; 3½ miles southwest of Grace City. Waterfowl, deer.

117. Howard Stone Memorial WMA - 400 acres; 4 miles north and 1 mile west of McHenry. Waterfowl, deer.

118. Lake Washington WMA - 910 acres; 6 miles south of Warwick. Waterfowl, Huns, deer, sharptails.

119. McVille WMA - 244 acres; 5 miles north of McVille. Waterfowl.

120. Black Swan WMA - 855 acres; 6 miles south of Bartlett. Waterfowl, Huns.

121. Warwick Springs WMA - 17 acres; 3 miles south of Warwick. Nature study area, closed to hunting.

122. Sheyenne WMA - 40 acres; 2 miles east and 2 miles south of Sheyenne. Deer, sharptails.

123. Warsing Dam WMA - 86 acres; 1 mile northeast of Sheyenne. Fishing, waterfowl.

124. Crary WMA - 315 acres; 7 miles east, 3 miles south, and 1 mile east of Devils Lake. Waterfowl, Huns

125. Pelican Township WMA - 60 acres; 6 miles south and 2½ miles west of Penn. Waterfowl.

126. Prairie Chicken WMA - 3,150 acres; several tracts located about 7 miles west and 3 miles north of Manvel, 2 miles north of Mekinock. Deer, sharptails.

127. North Salt Lake WMA - 95 acres; 3 miles north and 1 mile west of Cashel. Waterfowl, Huns.

128. Charles C. Cook WMA - 324 acres; 2 miles west of Edinburg. Waterfowl.

129. Eyolfson WMA - 24 acres; 1 mile west and 1½ miles north of Hensel. Ruffed grouse, nature study area.

130. Jay V. Wessels WMA - 3,343 acres; 7 miles south and 3 miles east of Walhalla. Deer, ruffed grouse, snowshoe rabbits, moose.

131. Clifford WMA - 80 acres; ½ mile east, 2 miles south, and ½ mile east of Leyden. Deer, ruffed grouse, snowshoe rabbits.

132. Martineau WMA - 120 acres; ½ mile east of LeRoy. Woodland nature study, closed to hunting.

133. Cavalier County WMA - 1,433 acres; several tracts located about 2 miles southwest of Concrete. Deer, snowshoe rabbits, ruffed grouse, moose.

134. Pembina Hills WMA - 3,819 acres; several tracts located about 4 miles north and 13 miles west of Walhalla and 1½ miles north, 1 mile west and 1½ miles north of Olga. Deer, ruffed grouse, snowshoe rabbits, moose.

135. Armourdale Lake WMA - 23 acres; 9 miles east and 1½ miles north of Rolla. Fishing.

136. Wakopa WMA - 6,739 acres; 8 miles west of St. John. Deer, ruffed grouse, snowshoe rabbits, waterfowl, fishing.

137. School Section Lake WMA - 300 acres; 8 miles north and 2 miles east of Dunseith. Fishing. Closed to hunting, Federal easement refuge.

138. Rab Lake WMA - 22 acres; 13 miles north and 4½ miles west of Dunseith. Waterfowl.

139. Turtle Mountain Forest WMA - 160 acres; 6½ miles west and 8 miles north of Dunseith. Deer, ruffed grouse.

140. Thompson Lake WMA - 892 acres; 4 miles north and 6 miles east of Bottineau. Waterfowl, deer, ruffed grouse, snowshoe rabbits.

141. Nickelson WMA - 160 acres; 7 miles north and 9 miles east of Bottineau. Deer, ruffed grouse, snowshoe rabbits.

142. Turtle Mountain WMA - 440 acres; 10 miles north and 1 mile west of Bottineau. Deer, ruffed grouse, snowshoe rabbits.

143. V.V. Bull WMA - 200 acres; 5½ miles north and 1 mile west of Bottineau. Deer, ruffed grouse, snowshoe rabbits.

144. Black Lake WMA - 180 acres; 7 miles north and 2 miles west of Bottineau. Deer, ruffed grouse, snowshoe rabbits.

145. Harris M. Baukol WMA - 1,418 acres; 1½ miles southeast of Noonan. Fishing, upland game, waterfowl, deer.

146. C.C. Underwood WMA - 320 acres; 2 miles west of Hansboro. Huns, waterfowl.

147. Wilbur Allen WMA - 520 acres; 13 miles north and 9½ miles east of Langdon. Deer, moose, ruffed grouse, snowshoe rabbits.

148. Wilbur J. Boldt WMA - 160 acres; 6 miles east and 2 miles south of Center. Sharptails, Huns, deer, pheasants.

Public Use Regulations for State Wildlife Management Areas

NORTH DAKOTA GAME AND FISH DEPARTMENT

The following rules are authorized by Chapter 20.1-11 of the North Dakota Century Code and established in Chapter 30-04-02 4th North Dakota Administrative Code.

1. **Public Access and Use.** All state wildlife management areas are open for public hunting, fishing and trapping, except as provided under this chapter, governor's proclamation, other valid rules and regulations or laws, or as posted at public road entry points.

2. **Motor Vehicles.** Mallard and Matthews Islands are closed to the use of all motorized vehicles and aircraft. On all other state wildlife management areas, the use of all motorized vehicles is restricted to those constructed roads, well worn trails, and parking areas normally used by passenger cars. Established roads and trails do not include temporary trails across cultivated land used for agricultural purposes. Motor vehicles may be used on the ice of lakes for access for fishing unless otherwise prohibited by posting or by proclamation. Persons operating any motor vehicle on the ice of any lake or other water area on a state wildlife management area do so at their own risk. All motorized vehicles which produce a noise level of 85 decibels or greater, measured on scale A at a distance of 50 feet, [15.2 meters] are prohibited.

3. **Watercraft.** Watercraft shall not be left unattended for more than 24 hours, except in mooring areas designated by the Department.

4. **Firearms.** Use of firearms is prohibited for such periods of time as are posted at public road and trail entry points, except that firearms are permitted on target ranges designated by the Department. Promiscuous shooting is prohibited on all state wildlife management areas.

5. **Littering and Abandonment of Property.** The disposal of refuse, rubbish, bottles, cans, or other waste materials is prohibited except in garbage containers where provided. Abandonment of vehicles or other personal property is prohibited. Holding tanks of campers shall not be dumped within a state wildlife management area.

6. **Removal and Destruction of Property.** Trees, shrubs, vines, plants, gravel, fill, sod, water, crops, firewood, posts, poles or other property may not be removed without a permit issued by the Department, except that firewood may be removed under certain stated conditions from Department designated firewood cutting plots. Commercial cutting of firewood is prohibited on designated firewood cutting plots. Removal of property from a state wildlife management area by permit shall be only in a manner, limit, and/or conditions specified by the permit. Berries and fruit may be picked, for non-commercial use - unless posting prohibits same. Property may not be destroyed or defaced.

7. **Private Property and Structures.** No person shall construct or maintain any building, cabin, dock, fence, beehive, billboard, sign, or other structure except by permit issued by the Department. Fish houses may be used during the ice fishing season in accordance with the governor's proclamation. Duck, goose, crane and other type decoys may not be left unattended in the field on any state wildlife management area.

8. **Tree Stands.** No person shall construct or use a permanent tree stand or permanent steps to a tree stand on any state wildlife management area except as provided by a permit issued by the Department.

    Permanent tree stands and steps are defined as those which are (1) fastened to the tree with nails, spikes, bolts or other metal fasteners driven or screwed into the tree or are (2) themselves fixtures driven or screwed into the tree.

    Portable tree stands and natural tree stands may be used without a permit. Portable tree stands and steps to the tree stand are defined as those which are held to the tree with ropes, straps, cables or bars which do not penetrate the bark of the tree. The ladder type stands which lean against the tree are portable stands. The notched board placed in a tree crotch is a portable stand. Natural stands are those crotches, trunks, down trees, etc. where no platform is used. Tree stands do not preempt hunting rights in the vicinity of the tree stand. Tree stands, both permanent and portable, may not be put up prior to August 20 of the year, and they shall be taken down by January 10th of the following year. Stands not removed by the 10th of January are considered abandoned property and are subject to removal and confiscation by the Department.

9. **Cropping, Haying and Commercial Enterprises.** No person shall conduct any cropping, haying, or other commercial enterprises, except by permit issued by the Department.

10. **Animal Trespass.** Livestock shall not be permitted on any state wildlife management area except as provided for by a grazing permit issued by the Department. Pets shall not be permitted to run unattended.

11. **Dogs.** Field trials for dogs are prohibited without a permit issued by the Department. Training of bird and gun dogs is prohibited April 1st through August 15th on all state wildlife management areas. Training of dogs on any state wildlife management areas by a professional trainer is prohibited at all times.

12. **Camping.** Camping for longer than 10 consecutive days on any state wildlife management area is prohibited. Trailers, campers, motor homes, or tents may not be left unattended for more than 24 hours on any state wildlife management area. Camping is prohibited on those state wildlife management areas where posted at public road entry points.

13. **Organized Group Activities.** Organized group activities attended by more than 25 persons are prohibited without a permit issued by the Department.

14. **Noise.** Excessive noise, which unreasonably disturbs other persons, is prohibited on state wildlife management areas.

15. **Department Work.** These rules shall not apply to activities by Department personnel and other persons designated by the Department which are necessary for law enforcement or for development, management, or maintenance of any state wildlife management area.

Bruce Wendt

About the Author:

Joseph Knue was born in Denver, Colorado. When he was still very young his family moved to Asia, an experience after which no one is ever entirely the same. Since then, Mr. Knue has graduated from Colorado State University with a degree in English; has been a proofreader, a cabinetmaker, and a teacher of English in times when writing has been lean; and has, in fat times, written books, articles and film scripts, often from his hilltop and seasonal home on the outskirts of tiny Judson, North Dakota. **Big Game in North Dakota** is the third book that Mr. Knue has contributed to North Dakota's outdoors library. The others are **Of Time and the Prairie**, a 100-year history of North Dakota and the outdoors, and **Feathers From the Prairie**, a revision of Morris Johnson's 1964 history of upland game birds in the state. Mr. Knue also wrote the scripts for the Game and Fish Department's multi-image productions **New Days** and **Celebration 100**. These days, Knue makes his home in Kittredge, Colorado and Judson, working as a free-lance writer and editor.

...and the Illustrator:

Deb Jaeger was born in Bismarck, North Dakota. She has spent her life in North Dakota. Deb makes commercial art her career and owns Graphic Communications – an award-winning graphic design studio in Bismarck. She produces the North Dakota OUTOORS magazine, and enjoys pen and ink wildlife illustration as a hobby. The illustrations included in this book have also been featured on January covers of the OUTDOORS magazine.